GATHER

SECOND EDITION

GIA PUBLICATIONS, INC.

CHICAGO

Special Note: With the current printing of this hymnal, twelve texts edited for inclusive language in the first printing have been returned to their original versions at the request of the authors. The permission request originally sent to the publisher of these texts included a declaration and actual copy of our editing, which was inadvertently overlooked by that publisher who did not then clear our alterations with the respective authors. Although GIA believes that it acted properly, pursuing the matter according to procedures commonly practiced in the publishing industry, it does not wish to contest the matter out of deference to the right of authors to control their intellectual property. GIA deeply regrets and apologizes for any inconvenience this causes parishes in the course of celebrating their community worship.

Copyright © 1994 by GIA Publications, Inc.
7404 South Mason Avenue, Chicago, Illinois 60638.
International copyright secured. All rights reserved.
Printed in the United States of America.

The English translation of the psalm responses, gospel
verses, and Lenten gospel acclamations from the
Lectionary for Mass © 1969, 1981, International
Committee on English in the Liturgy, Inc. (ICEL);
excerpts from the English translation of *Rite of Holy
Week* © 1970, ICEL; excerpts from the English translation of *The Roman Missal* © 1973, ICEL; excerpts from
the English translation of *Liturgy of the Hours* © 1974,
ICEL; excerpts from the English translation of the *Order
of Christian Funerals* © 1985, ICEL. All rights reserved.

Book design is based upon *Worship—Third Edition* by
Michael Tapia. Cover design by John Buscemi.

Published with ecclesiastical approval, Archdiocese of
Chicago, June 2, 1994.

ISBN 0-941050-57-2
      8 9 10 11 12 13 14 15 16 17 18 19

PREFACE

As the name implies, this is the second generation of a hymnal originally published in 1988. This second edition is truly a new hymnal in that it is almost double the size of the original *Gather* and over one-half of the content is new to this volume. Nonetheless, for the most part, the principles which guided the creation of the original edition still apply today.

When GIA's acclaimed classical hymnal, *Worship—Third Edition,* was published in 1986, followed in 1988 by the original *Gather,* it was stated that the two were carefully designed to be used in combination—one complementing the other. The classical hymnody of *Worship* and the contemporary "folk" hymnody of *Gather* were isolated into two volumes, however, precisely for the reason which now becomes apparent with the publication of *Gather Second Edition.* Music of the genre generally included in *Gather* (almost exclusively the work of living composers) tends to be generated at a quicker rate than the classical hymnody of *Worship* (which includes an extensive offering of hymnody from past centuries along with that of contemporary writers); therefore, *Gather* calls for revision more frequently than does the more classical hymnal.

The increased size of *Gather—Second Edition* is due to three main factors. First, the well-known composers whose work was found in the original edition have continued to write and have in this volume been joined by others. Second, this edition paves new territory, untouched in the 1988 collection. The second edition includes a representative offering of music from the Hispanic and African-American churches, as well as songs from the repertoire of the world church. Third, the psalm section has been significantly expanded to cover the entire church year.

It should be kept in mind that *Gather* is a hymnal, and it is therefore inherently a book for the assembly. Many of the selections contained herein have been edited from the familiar recorded octavo versions into versions which can essentially be sung by an assembly with basic keyboard accompaniment. Those wishing fuller arrangements of selections need only revert to the choral editions where they exist. When the choir and instruments are using a more complex version, however, the assembly can still sing their part by simply using the hymnal.

The combined *Gather—Second Edition* and *Worship—Third Edition* contain over 1,500 musical selections: hymns, psalms, inspired songs, rituals, and settings of ritual texts. This is clearly the fullest repertoire available to the American parish today, developed for those parishes who desire the greatest degree of option.

Acknowledgment is given to Diana Kodner, project director and editor; to staff engraver Marc Southard, assisted by Arne Eigenfeldt and Clarence Reiels; to Robert M. Sacha, book layout; to Alec Harris, technical coordinator; to Neil Borgstrom, Kelly Dobbs Mickus, Jeffry Mickus, and Edwina Schaufler, proofreaders; to Deborah L. Schmitz, permissions editor; and to David Blaszak, production.

Further acknowledgment is given to Mary Beth Kunde-Anderson, Rory Cooney, David Haas, and Marty Haugen for their invaluable study of and detailed comments on the draft version of this collection.

Finally, a distinguishing quality of this and all GIA hymnals published in the past twenty years is the extensive scriptural, liturgical, and topical indexes carefully prepared by Robert H. Oldershaw.

That God may be glorified.

Edward Harris
  Publisher
Robert J. Batastini
Michael A. Cymbala
  General Editors

Contents

Indexes

Morning Praise

The Church's sense for how to pray in the morning comes from our Jewish heritage. Whatever the day, whatever the difficulties, the tradition has been to begin the day with praise for the creator. The sign of the cross, first traced on the Christian at baptism, is again made to begin the new day and its prayer. In the hymn and the psalms, in the scripture and intercessions, each one who prays and the community together finds what it is to stand at the beginning of a new day as a Christian. The morning's prayer gives the day its meaning when, through the years, these prayers become one's own.

OPENING DIALOG 1

Stand

Ho-ly God! Fill us this day with new breath! And we shall be liv-ing words of praise!

Text: J. Tasch Jordan, adapt.
Music: David Haas
© 1986, GIA Publications, Inc.

2 MORNING HYMN

1. Sing your joy, pro - claim God's glo - ry!
2. All the earth is filled with re - joic - ing,
3. May we learn to be - come your King - dom.
4. Light our way, O God of the liv - ing,

Rise and sing, the morn - ing has come!
Light and life the won - der of God!
May we be your kind - ness and truth!
May we learn to see with new eyes!

Bless our God and praise all cre - a - tion;
Christ has tri - umphed! Ris - en for ev - er!
Love is our call - ing, gift of your pres - ence;
Je - sus the Lord, our pow - er and prom - ise;

Song of the earth, and light from heav - en:
Joy of our hearts, and hope of our dream - ing:
Chil - dren of God, and spir - it of Je - sus:
Light for the blind, and food for the hun - gry:

God is a - live! Al - le - lu - ia!
God is a - live! Al - le - lu - ia!
God is a - live! Al - le - lu - ia!
God is a - live! Al - le - lu - ia!

Text: David Haas, b.1957
Tune: SUMMIT HILL, Irregular; David Haas, b.1957
© 1987, GIA Publications, Inc.

PSALMODY

The singing of one or more psalms is a central part of Morning Praise. Psalm 63, given below, is one of the premier morning psalms. Psalm 51 is commonly substituted for Psalm 63 on Wednesday and Friday, as well as during Lent. Other appropriate psalms for morning are Psalms 5, 8, 33, 42, 47, 66, 72, 80, 85, 93, 95, 98, 100, 118, 148, 149, and 150.

PSALM 63

3

Sit

Refrain

As morn-ing breaks I look to you; I look to you, O Lord, to be my strength this day, as morn-ing breaks, as morn - ing breaks.

Verses

1. O God, you are my God, for you I long; for you my soul is thirsting.
   My body pines for you like a dry, weary land without water.
   So I gaze on you in your holy place to see your strength and your glory.

2. For your love is better than life, my lips will speak your praise.
   So I will bless you all my life, in your name I will lift up my hands.
   My soul shall be filled as with a banquet, my mouth shall praise you with joy.

3. On my bed I remember you. On you I muse through the night
   for you have been my help; in the shadow of your wings I rejoice.
   My soul clings to you; your right hand holds me fast.

Text: Psalm 63:2-3, 4-6, 7-9; © 1963, 1986, The Grail, GIA Publications, Inc. agent; refrain trans. © 1974, ICEL
Music: Michael Joncas, © 1985, New Dawn Music

PSALM PRAYER

Stand
All respond: Amen.

WORD OF GOD

4

Sit
Reader concludes: The word of the Lord.
      Assembly: Thanks be to God.

5 GOSPEL CANTICLE

Stand. All make the sign of the cross as the canticle begins.

1. Now bless the God of Is - ra - el, Who comes in love and pow'r, Who rais - es from the roy - al house De - liv - 'rance in this hour. Through ho - ly proph - ets God has sworn To free us from a - larm, To save us from the heav - y hand Of all who wish us harm.

2. Re - mem - ber - ing the cov - e - nant, God res - cues us from fear, That we might serve in hol - i - ness And peace from year to year. And you, my child, shall go be - fore To preach, to proph - e - sy, That all may know the ten - der love, The grace of God most high.

3. In ten - der mer - cy, God will send The day - spring from on high, Our ris - ing sun, the light of life For those who sit and sigh. And God comes to guide our way to peace, That death shall reign no more. Sing prais - es to the Ho - ly One! O wor - ship and a - dore!

Text: *Benedictus*, Luke 1:68-79; Ruth Duck, b.1947, © 1992, GIA Publications, Inc.
Tune: MELBOURNE, 8 6 8 6 D; Marty Haugen, b.1950, © 1994, GIA Publications, Inc.

MORNING PRAYERS

6

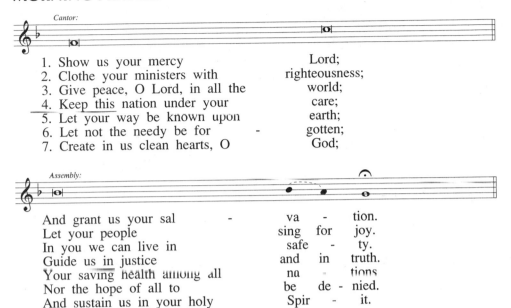

Cantor:

1. Show us your mercy   Lord;
2. Clothe your ministers with   righteousness;
3. Give peace, O Lord, in all the   world;
4. Keep this nation under your   care;
5. Let your way be known upon   earth;
6. Let not the needy be for - gotten;
7. Create in us clean hearts, O   God;

Assembly:

And grant us your sal - va - tion.
Let your people   sing for joy.
In you we can live in   safe - ty.
Guide us in justice   and in truth.
Your saving health among all   na - tions
Nor the hope of all to   be de - nied.
And sustain us in your holy   Spir - it.

Text: *The Book of Common Prayer*
Music: David Haas, © 1986, GIA Publications, Inc.

CONCLUDING PRAYER

All respond: Amen.

7 LORD'S PRAYER

Our Fa-ther in heav-en, hal-low-ed be your name, your king-dom come, your will be done on earth as in heav-en. Give us to-day our dai-ly bread. For-give us our sins as we for-give those who sin a-gainst us. Save us from the time of trial and de-liv-er us from e-vil, for the king-dom, the pow'r and the glo-ry are yours, now and for ev-er.

Music: David Haas, © 1986, GIA Publications, Inc.

8 FINAL BLESSING

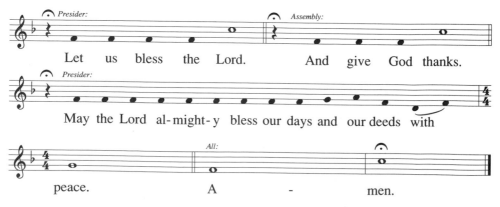

Presider: Let us bless the Lord. Assembly: And give God thanks.

Presider: May the Lord al-might-y bless our days and our deeds with peace. All: A-men.

Evensong

The church gathers in the evening to give thanks for the day that is ending. In the earliest tradition, this began with the lighting of the lamps as darkness fell and the hymn of praise of Christ who is "radiant Light . . . of God the Father's deathless face." The evening psalms and the Magnificat bring the day just past to focus for the Christian: "God has cast down the mighty from their thrones, and has lifted up the lowly"; "God has remembered the promise of mercy, the promise made to our ancestors." Prayers of intercession are almost always part of the church's liturgy, but those which conclude evening prayer are especially important. As day ends, the church again and again lifts up to God the needs and sorrows and failures of all the world. Such intercession is the daily task and joy of the baptized.

LIGHT PROCLAMATION   9

Stand

Light and peace in Je-sus Christ our Lord. Thanks be to God.

Music: Michael Joncas, © 1979, GIA Publications, Inc.

10 EVENING HYMN

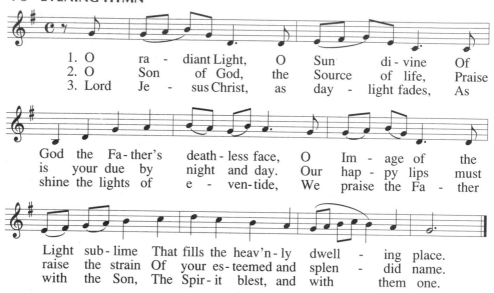

1. O ra - diant Light, O Sun di - vine Of
2. O Son of God, the Source of life, Praise
3. Lord Je - sus Christ, as day - light fades, As

God the Fa - ther's death - less face, O Im - age of the
is your due by night and day. Our hap - py lips must
shine the lights of e - ven-tide, We praise the Fa - ther

Light sub - lime That fills the heav'n - ly dwell - ing place.
raise the strain Of your es - teemed and splen - did name.
with the Son, The Spir - it blest, and with them one.

Text: *Phos Hilaron;* tr. by William G. Storey, ©
Tune: RADIANT LIGHT, LM; Michael Joncas, b. 1951, © 1979, GIA Publications, Inc.

11 EVENING THANKSGIVING

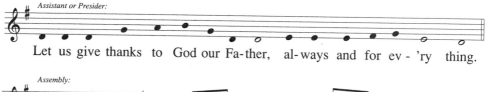

Assistant or Presider:

Let us give thanks to God our Fa-ther, al-ways and for ev - 'ry thing.

Assembly:

In the name of our Lord Je - sus Christ.

The assistant sings the Thanksgiving to which all respond:

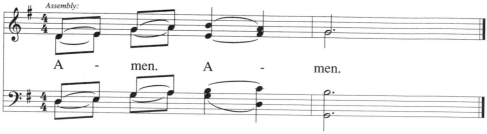

Assembly:

A - men. A - men.

Music: Michael Joncas, © 1979, GIA Publications, Inc.

PSALMODY

The singing of one or more psalms is a central part of Evensong. Psalm 141, given below, is one of the premier evening psalms. It is customary to use incense as it is sung. Other appropriate psalms for evening are Psalms 4, 19, 23, 27, 84, 91, 104, 110, 111, 112, 114, 115, 117, 118, 121, 122, 130, 136, 139, and 145.

PSALM 141/INCENSE PSALM 12

Refrain

Like burn-ing in-cense, O Lord, let my prayer rise up to you.

Verses

1. I have called to you, Lord; hasten to help me! Hear my voice when I cry to you.
   Let my prayer arise before you like incense,
   the raising of my hands like an evening oblation.

2. Set, O Lord, a guard over my mouth; Keep watch, O Lord, at the door of my lips!
   Do not turn my heart to things that are wrong,
   to evil deeds with those who are sinners.

3. Never allow me to share in their feasting.
   If the upright strike or reprove me it is kindness;
   but let the oil of the wicked not anoint my head.
   Let my prayer be ever against their malice.

4. To you, Lord God, my eyes are turned: in you I take refuge, spare my soul!
   From the trap they have laid for me keep me safe:
   Keep me from the snares of those who do evil.

5. Glory to the Father, and to the Son, and to the Holy Spirit:
   as it was in the beginning, is now, and will be for ever. Amen.

PSALM PRAYER
All respond: Amen.

13 WORD OF GOD

Sit
Reader concludes: The Word of the Lord.
        Assembly: Thanks be to God.

14 GOSPEL CANTICLE

Stand. All make the sign of the cross as the canticle begins.

1. My soul gives glo - ry to the Lord, In
2. His mer - cy goes to all who fear, From
3. He raised his ser - vant Is - ra - el, Re -

God my Sav - ior I re - joice. My low - li -
age to age and to all parts. His arm of
mem - b'ring his e - ter - nal grace, As from of

ness he did re - gard, Ex - alt - ing me by
strength to all is near; He scat - ters those who
old he did fore - tell To A - bra - ham and

his own choice. From this day all shall call me
have proud hearts. He casts the might- y from their
all his race. O Fa - ther, Son and Spir - it

blest, For he has done great things for me, Of
throne And rais - es those of low de - gree; He
blest, In three - fold Name are you a - dored, To

all great names his is the best, For
feeds the hun - gry as his own, The
you be ev - 'ry prayer ad - dressed, From

it   is   ho - ly;   strong   is   he.
rich   de - part   in   pov - er - ty.
age   to   age   the   on - ly   Lord.

Text: Luke 1:46-55; J.T. Mueller, 1885-1967, alt.
Tune: MAGNIFICAT, LMD; Michael Joncas, b.1951, © 1979, 1988, GIA Publications, Inc.

PETITIONS

15

Invitation

Let us com - plete our eve - ning prayer to the Lord.

Refrain

Lord,   have mer - cy.   Lord,   have mer - cy.

D.S.

let   us   pray   to   the   Lord:

Text: Michael Joncas
Music: Michael Joncas
© 1988, GIA Publications, Inc.

CONCLUDING PRAYER

All respond: Amen.

16 LORD'S PRAYER

Our Fa-ther in heav-en, hal-lowed be your name, your
king - dom come, your will be done on earth as in heav-en.
Give us to - day our dai - ly bread; give us to -
day our dai - ly bread. For-give us our sins as we for-give
those who sin a - gainst us. Save us from the time of trial
and de - liv - er us from e - vil. For the king-dom, the
pow-er, and the glo-ry are yours, now and for ev - er.

Music: Michael Joncas, © 1988, GIA Publications, Inc.

FINAL BLESSING

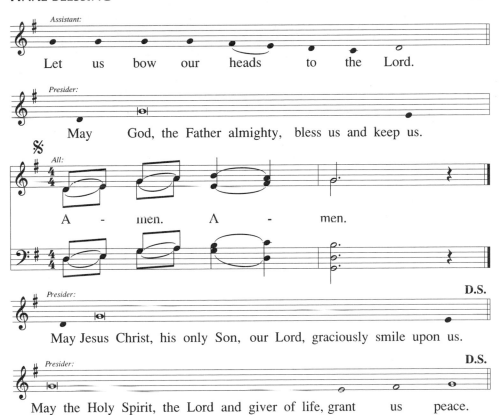

Assistant:

Let us bow our heads to the Lord.

Presider:

May God, the Father almighty, bless us and keep us.

All:

A - men. A - men.

Presider: D.S.

May Jesus Christ, his only Son, our Lord, graciously smile upon us.

Presider: D.S.

May the Holy Spirit, the Lord and giver of life, grant us peace.

18 Psalm 1: Happy Are They

Refrain

Hap - py are they who hope in God.

Verses

1. Happy are they who do not seek to walk the way of those who sin,
   but delight in the law of the Lord. Happy, happy are they.

2. Like a tree planted near water, there it blooms, like our God,
   whose leaves will not fade, but remain. Happy, happy are they.

3. The wicked, the lawless, who, like the chaff, our God, like wind, will drive away.
   God will keep watch for the just. Happy, happy are they.

Text: Psalm 1:1-2, 3-4, 6; David Haas, © 1989, GIA Publications, Inc.; refrain trans. © 1969, ICEL
Music: David Haas, © 1989, GIA Publications, Inc.

19 Psalm 4: Let Your Face Shine upon Us

Refrain

Lord, let your face shine up - on us, shine up - on us, shine up - on us.

Verses

1. Listen to my song, hear me when I call, Oh Lord, my God, be gracious,
   hear my prayer.

2. You have called my name, set your seal upon my heart,
   you hear me when I call.

3. Fill me with your joy, grant to me your peaceful rest,
   to dwell in safety with my Lord.

Text: Psalm 4:2, 4, 9; Marty Haugen
Music: Marty Haugen
© 1980, GIA Publications, Inc.

Psalm 8: How Glorious Is Your Name   20

Refrain

O Lord, our God, how glo-ri-ous is your name! How glo-ri-ous is your name o - ver all the earth!

Verses

1. When I see the heavens, the work of your hands,
   the moon and the stars which you arranged,
   What are we that you keep us in mind? Your children that you remember them at all?

2. Yet you have made us little less than gods, with glory and honor you crowned us,
   Gave us pow'r over the work of your hands, dominion over all that you have made.

3. All sheep and oxen, birds of the air, all things that swim in the sea.
   Beasts without number, life without names, you have placed under our feet.

Text: Psalm 8:4-5, 6-7, 8-9; Rory Cooney
Music: Rory Cooney
© 1990, GIA Publications, Inc.

21 Psalm 15: They Who Do Justice

Refrain

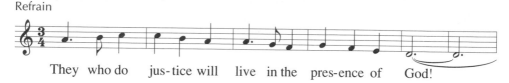

They who do   jus-tice will   live in the   pres-ence of   God!

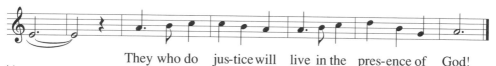

They who do   jus-tice will   live in the   pres-ence of   God!

Verses

1. Those who walk blamelessly and live their lives doing justice,
   who keep the truth in their heart, and slander not with their tongue!

2. Who harm not another, nor take up reproach to their neighbor,
   who hate the sight of the wicked, but honor the people of God!

3. Who show no condition in sharing the gifts of their treasure,
   who live not off the poor: They will stand firm forever!

Text: Psalm 15: 2-5; David Haas, © 1989, GIA Publications, Inc.; refrain trans. © 1969, ICEL
Music: David Haas, ©1989, GIA Publications, Inc.

22 Psalm 16: Keep Me Safe, O God

Refrain

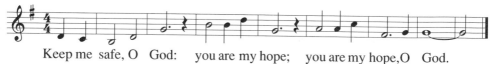

Keep me safe, O   God: you are my hope;   you are my hope,O   God.

Verses

1. I say to God, "you are my only God, I have no good except in you."

2. I find in God always my cup of joy; and God will keep my life secure.

3. I bless my God: God who has counseled me. At night my heart gives counsel too.

4. I keep my God always before my eyes; with God beside me I'm secure.

5. And so my heart always is glad in God; my body too shall dwell secure.

6. For you will not ever abandon me, or let your servant lose the path.

7. The path of life you have revealed to me, and in your presence is my joy.

Psalm 16: You Will Show Me the Path of Life   23

Refrain I

You will show me the path of life, you, my hope and my shel-ter;

In your pres-ence is end-less joy, at your side is my home for - ev - er.

Refrain II

Keep me safe, O God, I take ref - uge in you.

Refrain III

You are my in - her - i - tance, O Lord.

Verses

1. Faithful God, I look to you, you alone my life and fortune,
   never shall I look to other gods, you shall be my one hope.

2. From of old you are my heritage, you my wisdom and my safety,
   through the night you speak within my heart, silently you teach me.

3. So my heart shall sing for joy, in your arms I rest securely,
   you will not abandon me to death, you shall not desert me.

24 Psalm 17: Lord, When Your Glory Appears

Refrain

Lord, when your glo - ry ap - pears, my joy, my joy will be full, my joy, my joy will be full.

Verses

1. Hear, O Lord, a just suit, attend to my outcry. Hear the pray'r of my lips;
   lips without deceit.

2. My steps are fast in your path, my feet have faltered not.
   I call and you answer me; incline your ear to me.

3. Keep me in your gentle care. Hide me under your wings.
   In justice shall I see your face, on waking shall I be content.

Text: Psalm 17:1, 5-6, 8-9, 15; Roy James Stewart, © 1993, GIA Publications, Inc.; refrain trans. © 1969, ICEL
Music: Roy James Stewart, © 1993, GIA Publications, Inc.

25 Psalm 18: I Love You Lord, My Strength

Refrain

I love you, Lord, my strength, my strength.

Verses

1. I love you, Lord, my strength, my rock, my fortress, my savior.
   God, you are the rock where I take refuge;
   my shield, my mighty help, my stronghold.
   Lord, you are worthy of all praise, when I call I am saved from my foes.

2. Long life to you, Lord, my rock! Praise to you, God, who saves me,
   You have given great victories to your king and shown your love for your anointed.

Text: Psalm 18:2-3, 3-4, 47, 51; © 1963, 1993, The Grail, GIA Publications, Inc., agent; refrain trans. © 1969, ICEL
Music: Michel Guimont, © 1994, GIA Publications, Inc.

Psalm 19: Lord, You Have the Words   26

Refrain

Lord, you have the words of ev-er-last-ing life.

Verses

1. The law of the Lord is perfect, refreshing the soul;
   the Lord's rule is to be trusted, the simple find wisdom.

2. The fear of the Lord is holy, abiding for ever;
   the decrees of the Lord are true, all of them just.

3. The precepts of the Lord are right, they gladden the heart,
   the command of the Lord is clear, giving light to the eye.

4. They are worth more than gold, than the finest gold,
   sweeter than honey, than honey from the comb.

Psalm 22: I Will Praise You, Lord   27

Refrain

I will praise you, Lord, in the as-sem-bly of your peo - ple.

Verses

1. My vows I will pay before those who fear God.
   The poor shall eat and shall have their fill.
   Those who seek the Lord shall praise the Lord.
   May their hearts live for ever and ever!

2. All the earth shall remember and return to the Lord,
   all families of the nations shall bow down in awe.
   They shall bow down in awe, all the mighty of the earth,
   all who must die and go down to the dust.

3. My soul shall live for God and my children too shall serve.
   They shall tell of the Lord to generations yet to come;
   declare to those unborn, the faithfulness of God. These things the Lord has done.

28 Psalm 22: My God, My God

Refrain

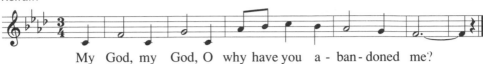

My God, my God, O why have you a - ban - doned me?

Verses

1. All who see me laugh at me, they mock me and they shake their heads:
   "He relied on the Lord, let the Lord be his refuge."

2. As dogs around me, they circle me about.
   Wounded me and pierced me, I can number all my bones.

3. My clothing they divided, for my garments casting lots,
   O Lord, do not desert me, but hasten to my aid.

4. I will praise you to my people, and proclaim you in their midst,
   O fear the Lord, my people, give glory to God's name.

Text: Psalm 22:8-9; 17-18; 19-20; 23-24; Marty Haugen, © 1983, GIA Publications, Inc.; refrain trans. © 1969, ICEL
Music: Marty Haugen, © 1983, GIA Publications, Inc.

29 Psalm 23: Shepherd Me, O God

Refrain

Shep - herd me, O God, be - yond my wants, be -

yond my fears, from death in - to life.

Verses

1. God is my shepherd, so nothing shall I want,
   I rest in the meadows of faithfulness and love,
   I walk by the quiet waters of peace.

2. Gently you raise me and heal my weary soul,
   you lead me by pathways of righteousness and truth,
   my spirit shall sing the music of your name.

3. Though I should wander the valley of death,
   I fear no evil, for you are at my side, your rod and your staff,
   my comfort and my hope.

4. You have set me a banquet of love in the face of hatred,
   crowning me with love beyond my pow'r to hold.

5. Surely your kindness and mercy follow me all the days of my life;
   I will dwell in the house of my God for evermore.

Text: Psalm 23; Marty Haugen
Music: Marty Haugen
© 1986, GIA Publications, Inc.

Psalm 23: The Lord Is My Shepherd   30

Refrain

The Lord is my shep-herd, I shall not want. The

Lord is my shep - herd, I shall not want.

Verses

1. The pastures are fresh where you give me rest; Calm waters lift up my soul.
   You lead me on paths that are righteous and good; Your name is hallowed by all.

2. Though I am brought down to the valley deep, No evil great will I fear;
   The strength of your rod and the pow'r of your staff Will give me comfort and cheer.

3. A feast you have held in the sight of foes; Oil has anointed my head;
   My cup overflows with your mercy and love: With blessings great am I fed.

4. Today and for all of my days to come Goodness and love follow me,
   And now I will dwell in the house of the Lord As long as life there shall be.

Text: Psalm 23; Randall Sensmeier
Music: Randall Sensmeier
© 1994, GIA Publications, Inc.

31 Psalm 23: Nada Me Falta

Refrain

El Se - ñor es mi pas - tor, na - da me fal - ta. El Se -

ñor es mi pas - tor, na-da me fal - ta - rá.

Verses

1. El Señor es mi pastor, nada me falta: En verdes praderas me hace recostar;
   Me conduce hacia fuentes tranquilas y repara mis fuerzas.

2. Me guía por el sendero justo en gracia de su nombre.
   Aunque camine por cañadas oscuras, nada temo porque tú vas conmigo:
   tu vara y tu cayado me sosiegan.

3. Preparas una mesa ante mí, enfrente de mis enemigos;
   me unges la cabeza con perfume, y mi copa rebosa.

4. Tu bondad y tu engencia me acompañan. Todos los días de mi vida,
   y habitaré en la casa del Señor por siempre.

Text: Psalm 23, Spanish Lectionary; Donna Peña
Music: Donna Peña; acc. by Diana Kodner
© 1988, 1993 GIA Publications, Inc.

32 Psalm 24: We Long to See Your Face

Refrain I

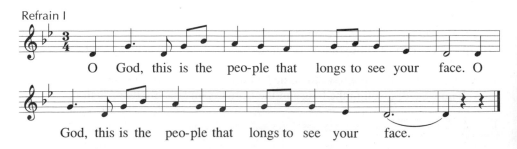

O God, this is the peo-ple that longs to see your face. O

God, this is the peo-ple that longs to see your face.

Refrain II

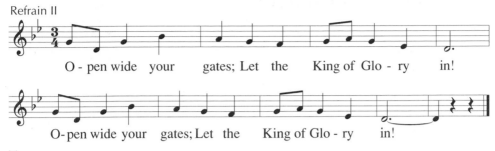

O - pen wide your gates; Let the King of Glo - ry in!

O-pen wide your gates; Let the King of Glo - ry in!

Verses

1. All the earth is yours, O God, the world and those who dwell on it.
   You have founded it upon the seas and established it upon the rivers.

2. Who can ascend your mountain, God? Or who may stand in this holy place?
   Those whose hands are sinless, hearts are clean, and desire not the vanity of earth.

3. They shall receive your blessing, God, their Savior shall reward them.
   Such is the face that seeks for you, that seeks your face, O God of Jacob.

Text: Psalm 24; Kevin Keil, © 1993, GIA Publications, Inc.; refrain I trans. © 1969, ICEL
Music: Kevin Keil, © 1993 GIA Publications, Inc.

Psalm 25: Remember Your Mercies   33

Refrain I

Re - mem - ber your mer-cies, O Lord.

Refrain II

Teach me your ways, O Lord.

Verses

1. Your ways, O Lord, make known to me, teach me your paths.
   Guide me, teach me, for you are my Savior.

2. Remember your compassion, Lord, and your kindness of old.
   Remember this, and not my sins, in your goodness, O Lord.

3. Good and just is the Lord, the sinners know the way.
   God guides the meek to justice, and teaches the humble.

Text: Psalm 25:4-5, 6-7, 8-9; David Haas, © 1985, GIA Publications, Inc.; refrain trans. © 1969, ICEL
Music: David Haas, © 1985, GIA Publications, Inc.

34 Psalm 25: To You, O Lord

Refrain

To you, O Lord, I lift my soul, to you, I lift my soul.

Verses

1. Lord, make me know your ways, teach me your paths
   and keep me in the way of your truth, for you are God, my Savior.

2. For the Lord is good and righteous, revealing the way to those who wander,
   gently leading the poor and the humble.

3. To the ones who seek the Lord, who look to God's word, who live God's love,
   God will always be near, and will show them mercy.

Text: Psalm 25:4-5, 8-9, 12-14; Marty Haugen, © 1982, GIA Publications, Inc.; refrain trans. © 1969, ICEL
Music: Marty Haugen, © 1982, GIA Publications, Inc.

35 Psalm 25: Levanto Mi Alma

Refrain

Oh Dios mí-o, le-van-to mi al - ma,

le-van-to a ti Se-ñor, mi sal-va-ción.

Verses

1. Sólo en ti confio, estaré sin vergüenza. Y no triunfaran mis enemigos.
   No hay dudas.

2. Muestrame tus caminos. Enséñame tus sendas.
   Guíame Señor en tu verdad y a mi salvación.

3. Todo el día espero en ti, espero por tu bondad.
   No recuerdes Señor los pecados de mi juventud, sino, dame tu amor.

4. Mis ojos estan en Yahveh. Mirame y ten compasión,
   porque estoy solo y estoy desdichado.

Text: Psalm 25; Donna Peña
Music: Donna Peña; acc. by Diana Kodner
© 1988, 1993, GIA Publications, Inc.

Psalm 27: In the Land of the Living   36

Refrain

I be - lieve I shall see the good things of the Lord in the land of the liv - ing.

Verses

1. The Lord is my light, the Lord is my help, of whom should I be afraid?
   The Lord is the stronghold of my life, before whom should I shrink?

2. When I cry out, O Lord, hear my voice! Have mercy on me and answer.
   My heart has told me, "seek his face!" It is your face, Lord, I seek.

3. There is only one thing I ask of the Lord: to live in God's house forever,
   to savor the sweetness of the Lord, to behold his temple.

Text: Psalm 27; *The Jerusalem Bible,* © 1966, Darton, Longman and Todd, Ltd. and Doubleday, a division of Bantam Doubleday Dell
   Publishing Group, Inc.
Music: Carl Johengen, © 1993, GIA Publications, Inc.

37   Psalm 27: The Lord Is My Light

Refrain

The Lord is my light and my sal - va - tion, of
whom should I be a - fraid, of whom should I be a - fraid?

Verses

1. The Lord is my light and my help; whom should I fear?
   The Lord is the stronghold of my life; before whom should I shrink?

2. There is one thing I ask of the Lord; for this I long:
   to live in the house of the Lord all the days of my life.

3. I believe I shall see the goodness of the Lord in the land of the living;
   hope in God, and take heart. Hope in the Lord!

Text: Psalm 27:1-2, 4, 13-14; David Haas
Music: David Haas
© 1983, GIA Publications, Inc.

38   Psalm 29: The Lord Will Bless His People

Refrain

The Lord will bless his peo- ple with peace.

Verses

1. O give the Lord, you children of God, give the Lord glory and power;
   give the Lord the glory of his name. Adore the Lord, resplendent and holy.

2. The Lord's voice resounding on the waters; the Lord on the immensity of waters;
   the voice of the Lord, full of power, the voice of the Lord, full of splendor.

3. The God of glory thunders. In his temple they all cry:
   "Glory!" the Lord sat enthroned over the flood; the Lord sits as king for ever.

Text: Psalm 29:1-2, 3-4, 3, 9-10; © 1963, 1993, The Grail, GIA Publications, Inc., agent; refrain trans. © 1969, ICEL
Music: Michel Guimont, © 1994, GIA Publications, Inc.

Psalm 30: I Will Praise You, Lord   39

Refrain

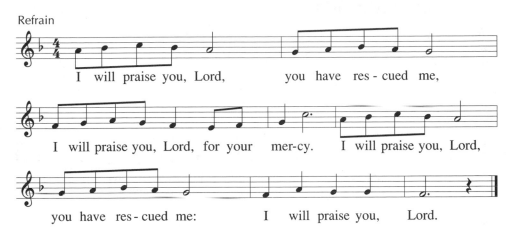

I will praise you, Lord, you have res - cued me,

I will praise you, Lord, for your mer-cy. I will praise you, Lord,

you have res - cued me: I will praise you, Lord.

Verses

1. I will praise you, Lord, you have rescued me
   and have not let my enemies rejoice over me.
   O Lord, you have raised my soul from the dead,
   restored me to life from those who sink into the grave.

2. Sing psalms to the Lord, you who love him, give thanks to his holy name.
   His anger lasts but a moment; his favor through life.
   At night there are tears, but joy comes with dawn.

3. The Lord listened and had pity. The Lord came to my help.
   For me you have changed my mourning into dancing;
   O Lord my God, I will thank you for ever.

Text: Psalm 30:2, 4, 5-6, 11-13; © 1963, The Grail, GIA Publications, Inc., agent; refrain, Paul Inwood, © 1985
Music: Paul Inwood, © 1985
Published by OCP Publications

40 Psalm 31: I Put My Life in Your Hands / Pongo Mi Vida

Refrain

Ab - ba,   Ab - ba,   I   put   my   life   in   your   hands.
Ab - ba,   Ab - ba,   pon - go   mi   vi - da   en   tus   ma - nos.

Ab - ba,   Ab - ba,   I   put   my   life   in   your   hands.
Ab - ba,   Ab - ba,   pon - go   mi   vi - da   en   tus   ma - nos.

Verses

1. In you, O Lord I take refuge; let me never be put to shame.
   In your justice rescue me, in your hands I commend my spirit.

2. For all my foes reproach me; all my friends are now put to flight.
   I am forgotten, like the dead, like a dish that now is broken.

3. I place my trust in you; in your hands is my destiny.
   Let your face shine upon your servant, in your hands I will place my life.

1. *En ti busco protección. No me defraudes nunca jamás.*
   Ponme a salvo pues tú eres justo. En tus manos encomiendo mi espíritu.

2. *En ti pongo toda mi fe hablaré de tu bondad,*
   por favor está siempre conmigo. Tú haces la luz del caos.

3. *Tú eres mi esperanza; sólo tú mi salvación.*
   Con tu misericordia, ven. Escucha mi oración.

Text: Psalm 31; David Haas; Spanish trans. by Jeffrey Judge
Music: David Haas
© 1993, GIA Publications, Inc.

Psalm 31: I Put My Life in Your Hands   41

Refrain I

Fa - ther, I put my life in your hands.

Refrain II

O Lord, be my rock of safe - ty.

Verses

1. In you, O Lord I take refuge; let me never be put to shame.
   In your justice rescue me, oh my faithful Lord, in your hands I commend my spirit.

2. For all my foes reproach me; all my friends are now put to flight.
   I am forgotten, like the unremembered dead, like a dish that now is broken.

3. I place my trust in you, Lord; in your hands is my destiny.
   Let your face shine upon your servant, Lord, in your hands I will place my life.

Text: Psalm 31: 2, 6, 12-13, 15-16, 17; Marty Haugen, © 1983, GIA Publications, Inc., refrains trans. © 1969, ICEL
Music: Marty Haugen; refrain II adapt. by Diana Kodner, © 1983, 1994 GIA Publications, Inc.

42 Psalm 32: I Turn to You

Refrain

I turn to you in time of trou - ble,

and you fill me with the joy of sal - va - tion.

Verses

1. Happy is he whose sin is forgiven, whose fault is taken away.
   Happy is she whom God shall find of an innocent heart,
   in whose soul there is no guile.

2. I kept my sin held deep in my soul, and my frame was wasted away.
   Night and day was your hand a weight upon my heart:
   I was weak, wracked with fever and alone.

3. Then I acknowledged the pain of my sin, and my guilt I covered not.
   I said I confess my fault unto you, and you took away the guilt of my sin.

4. O be glad in our God; exult, you just; rejoice, all you upright of heart.

Text: Psalm 32:1-2, 3-4, 5, 11; Rory Cooney, © 1991, GIA Publications, Inc.; refrain trans. © 1969, ICEL
Music: Rory Cooney, © 1991, GIA Publications, Inc.

Psalm 33: Let Your Mercy Be on Us   43

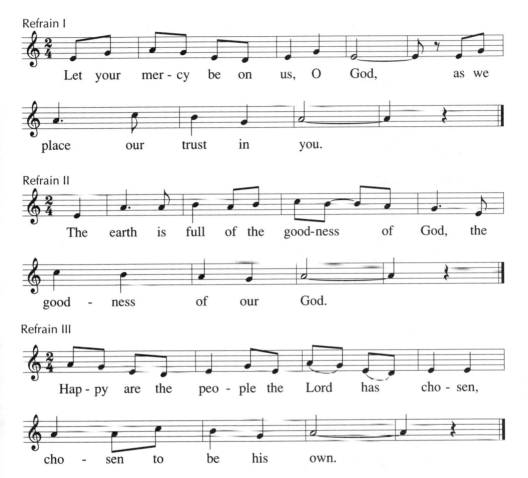

Refrain I

Let your mer - cy be on us, O God, as we place our trust in you.

Refrain II

The earth is full of the good-ness of God, the good - ness of our God.

Refrain III

Hap - py are the peo - ple the Lord has cho - sen, cho - sen to be his own.

Verses

1. Your words, O God, are truth indeed, and all your works are ever faithful;
   you love justice and right, your compassion fills all creation.

2. See how the eye of God is watching, ever guarding all who wait in hope,
   to deliver them from death and sustain them in time of famine.

3. Exult, you just, in the Lord, for praise is the song of the righteous!
   How happy the people of God, the ones whom God has chosen!

4. Our soul is waiting for God, for God is our help and our shield.
   May your kindness, O God, be upon us who place our hope in you.

Text: Psalm 33:1, 4-5, 12, 18-19, 20, 22; Marty Haugen; refrain I trans. © 1969, ICEL; refrains II, III, and verses © 1987, 1994 GIA Publications, Inc.
Music: Marty Haugen; refrain III adapt. by Diana Kodner, © 1987, 1994, GIA Publications, Inc.

44 Psalm 34: I Will Bless the Lord

Refrain

I will bless the Lord; God's praise shall be ev-er on my lips.

Verses

1. Let my soul glory in the Lord. Let the lowly hear me and be glad.
   Glorify the Lord with me! Let us all praise God's holy name.

2. I looked to God and my prayer was answered; God delivered me from all my fear.
   Look to God that you may be radiant with joy;
   that your faces may not blush with shame.

3. Taste and see the goodness of God; happy those who take shelter in the Lord.
   Fear the Lord, all you holy ones, for nothing is lacking to those who fear the Lord.

Text: Psalm 34; Normand Gouin
Music: Normand Gouin
© 1993, GIA Publications, Inc.

45 Psalm 34: Taste and See

Refrain

Taste and see the good-ness of the Lord, the good - ness of the Lord.

Verses

1. I will bless the Lord at all times, God's praise ever in my mouth.
   Glory in the Lord for ever, and the lowly will hear and be glad.

2. Glory in the Lord with me, let us together extol God's name.
   I sought the Lord, who answered me and delivered me from all my fears.

3. Look to God that you might be radiant with joy,
   and your faces free from all shame.
   The Lord hears the suffering souls, and saves them from all distress.

Text: Psalm 34:2-3, 4-5, 6-7; Marty Haugen, © 1980, GIA Publications, Inc.; refrain trans. © 1969, ICEL
Music: Marty Haugen, © 1980, GIA Publications, Inc.

Psalm 34: The Cry of the Poor   46

Refrain

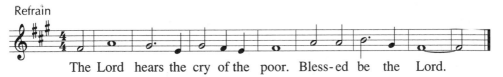

The Lord hears the cry of the poor. Bless-ed be the Lord.

Verses

1. I will bless the Lord at all times, with praise ever in my mouth.
   Let my soul glory in the Lord, who will hear the cry of the poor.

2. Let the lowly hear and be glad: the Lord listens to their pleas;
   and to hearts broken God is near, who will hear the cry of the poor.

3. Ev'ry spirit crushed God will save; will be ransom for their lives;
   will be safe shelter for their fears, and will hear the cry of the poor.

4. We proclaim your greatness, O God, your praise ever in our mouth;
   ev'ry face brightened in your light, for you hear the cry of the poor.

Text: Psalm 34:2-3, 6-7, 18-19, 23; John Foley, SJ
Music: John Foley, SJ
© 1978, 1990, John B. Foley, SJ, and New Dawn Music

47 Psalm 40: Here I Am

Refrain

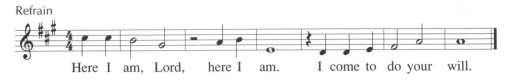

Here I am, Lord, here I am. I come to do your will.

Verses

1. Long was I waiting for God, and then he heard my cry.
   It was he who taught this song to me, a song of praise to God.

2. You asked me not for sacrifice, for slaughtered goats or lambs.
   No, my heart, you gave me ears to hear you, then I said, "Here I am."

3. You wrote it in the scrolls of law what you would have me do.
   Doing that is what has made me happy, your law is in my heart.

4. I spoke before your holy people, the good news that you save.
   Now you know that I will not be silent. I'll always sing your praise.

Text: Psalm 40; Rory Cooney
Music: Rory Cooney
© 1971, 1991, NALR

48 Psalm 41: Lord, Heal My Soul

Refrain

Lord, heal my soul, for I have sinned a - gainst you.

Verses

1. Happy those who consider the poor and the weak.
   The Lord will save them in the evil day,
   will guard them, give them life, make them happy in the land
   and will not give them up to the will of their foes.

2. The Lord will give them strength in their pain,
   will bring them back from sickness to health.
   As for me, I said: Lord, have mercy on me,
   heal my soul for I have sinned against you.

3. If you uphold me I shall be unharmed and set in your presence for evermore.
   Blessed be the Lord, the God of Israel from age to age. Amen. Amen.

Text: Psalm 41:2-3, 4-5, 13-14; © 1963, 1993, The Grail, GIA Publications, Inc., agent; refrain trans. © 1969, ICEL
Music: Michel Guimont, © 1994, GIA Publications, Inc.

Psalm 41-42: Song of Longing   49

Refrain

Like a deer that longs for the run-ning wa-ter,

so my soul longs for you, O God, my God.

Verses

1. My soul is longing for God, When shall I look on the face of God?
   The God who gives me my life. When shall I look on the face of God?
   Like a land rainless and barren, So do I long for my God.
   Like a man far from his homeland, So do I long for my God.
   O your love is better than living, and my lips shall sing your praise.
   In your name I lift my hands, I will bless you all my days.

2. My God is gladness and joy, When shall I look on the face of God?
   My rock and shelter is God, When shall I look on the face of God?
   As the sky gladdens the sparrow, So do I long for my God.
   As the dawn gladdens the watchman, So do I long for my God.
   To my eyes your light is a vision, to my heart your truth you give.
   These, O God, shall lead me on to the mountain where you live.

3. Why are you so downcast, my soul? Why do you sigh within me?
   Hope in God! O I will praise him still.

Text: Psalm 41, 42; Rory Cooney
Music: Rory Cooney
© 1974, 1991, NALR

50 Psalm 45: The Queen Stands at Your Right Hand

Refrain

The queen stands at your right hand, ar - rayed in gold.

Verses

1. Listen, O Daughter, give ear to my words:
   Forget your people and your father's house.
   So will the king desire your beauty; He is your lord, pay homage to him.

2. They are escorted with gladness and joy; they pass within the palace of the king,
   He is our God, pay homage to him.

Text: Psalm 45:10, 11, 12, 16; verses trans. © 1970, Confraternity of Christian Doctrine, Washington, D.C., alt.; refrain trans. © 1969, 1981, ICEL
Music: Diana Kodner, © 1994, GIA Publications, Inc.

51 Psalm 47: God Mounts His Throne

Ostinato Refrain*

God mounts his throne to shouts of joy, O

sing your prais - es to the Lord!

Verses

1. All you peoples, clap your hands, shout to God in gladness,
   the Lord we must fear, king of all the earth.

2. God goes up to shouts of joy, sound the trumpet blast.
   Sing praise to our God, praise unto our king!

3. God is king of all the earth, sing with all your skill
   to the king of all nations, God enthroned on high!

May be sung in canon.

Text: Psalm 47:2-3, 6-7, 8-9; Marty Haugen, © 1983, GIA Publications, Inc.; refrain trans. © 1969, ICEL
Music: Marty Haugen, © 1983, GIA Publications, Inc.

Psalm 50: To the Upright 52

Refrain

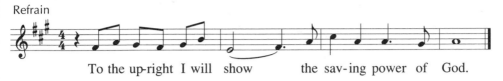

To the up-right I will show   the sav-ing power of God.

Verses

1. The God of gods, the Lord, has spoken and summoned the earth,
   from the rising of the sun to its setting,
   "I find no fault with your sacrifices, your offerings are always before me.

2. Were I hungry, I would not tell you, for I own the world and all it holds.
   Do you think I eat the flesh of bulls, or drink the blood of goats?

3. Offer to God your sacrifice; to the Most High pay your vows.
   Call on me in the day of distress. I will free you and you shall honor me."

Text: Psalm 50:1, 8, 12-13, 14-15; © 1963, 1993, The Grail, GIA Publications, Inc., agent; refrain trans. © 1969, ICEL
Music: Michel Guimont, © 1994, GIA Publications, Inc.

53   Psalm 51: Be Merciful, O Lord

Refrain

Be mer-ci-ful, O Lord, for we have sinned; be

mer-ci-ful, O Lord, for we have sinned.

Verses

1. Have mercy on me, God, in your kindness, in your compassion,
   blot out my offense.
   O wash me more and more from my guilt and my sorrow,
   and cleanse me from all of my sin.

2. My offenses, truly I know them, and my sins are always before me;
   against you alone have I sinned, O Lord, what is evil in your sight I have done.

3. Create in me a clean heart, O God, put your steadfast spirit in my soul.
   Cast me not away from your presence, O Lord, and take not your spirit from me.

4. Give back to me the joy of your salvation, let your willing spirit bear me up
   and I shall teach your way to the ones who have wandered,
   and bring them all home to your side.

Text: Psalm 51:3-4, 5-6, 12-13, 14-15; Marty Haugen, © 1983, GIA Publications, Inc.; refrain trans. © 1969, ICEL
Music: Marty Haugen, © 1983, GIA Publications, Inc.

Psalm 51: Create in Me   54

Refrains

I Cre - ate in me a clean heart, O God.
II I will a - rise and go to my God.

Verses

1. Have mercy on me, O God. In the greatness of your love,
   cleanse me from my sin. Wash me.

2. Stay close to me, O God. In your presence keep me safe.
   Fill me with your spirit. Renew me.

3. Your salvation is joy to me. In your wisdom show the way. Lead me back to you.
   Teach me.

Text: Psalm 51:3-4, 12-13, 14-15; David Haas
Music: David Haas
© 1987, GIA Publications, Inc.

Psalm 54: The Lord Upholds My Life   55

Refrain

The Lord up - holds my life.

Verses

1. O God, save me by your name; by your power, uphold my cause.
   O God, hear my prayer; listen to the words of my mouth.

2. For the proud have risen against me, ruthless foes seek my life.
   They have no regard for God. (They have no regard for God).

3. But I have God for my help. The Lord upholds my life.
   I will sacrifice to you with willing heart and praise your name,
   O Lord, for it is good.

Text: Psalm 54:3-4, 6-8, © 1963, 1986, The Grail, GIA Publications, Inc., agent; refrain trans. © 1969, ICEL
Music: Michel Guimont, © 1994, GIA Publications, Inc.

56   Psalm 62: In God Alone

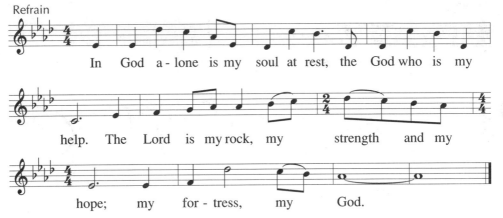

Refrain

In God a-lone is my soul at rest, the God who is my help. The Lord is my rock, my strength and my hope; my for-tress, my God.

Verses

1. Only in God is my soul at rest, from my God comes my salvation.
   God is my rock, the salvation of my life.
   I shall not be shaken, for the Lord is my strength!

2. Only in God is my soul at rest, from my God comes my hope.
   God is my rock, my salvation and my hope.
   I will rest in the Lord. I will not be afraid!

3. Glory and safety, God is my joy, God is my rock and my strength.
   God is my refuge, I trust with all my strength.
   Pour out your hearts, before the Lord!

Text: Psalm 62: 2-3, 6-7, 8-9; David Haas
Music: David Haas

Psalm 63: My Soul Is Thirsting   57

Refrain

My soul is thirst - ing, my soul is thirst - ing,

my soul is thirst- ing for you, O Lord my God.

Verses

1. O God, you are my God whom I seek;
   O God, you are my God whom I seek;
   for you my flesh pines, my soul thirsts like the earth, parched, lifeless,
   without water.

2. Thus have I gazed toward you in your holy place to see your power
   and your glory.
   Your kindness is a greater good than life itself; my lips will glorify you.

3. Thus will I bless you while I live;
   Lifting up my hands I will call upon your name.
   As with a banquet shall my soul be satisfied;
   with exultant lips my mouth shall praise you.

4. For you have been my help, you have been my help;
   in the shadow of your wings I shout for joy.
   My soul clings fast to you; your right hand holds me firm;
   in the shadow of your wings I sing for joy.

Text: Psalm 63:2, 3-4, 5-6, 8-9; verses trans. © 1970, Confraternity of Christian Doctrine, Washington, D.C.; refrain by Michael Joncas, © 1987,
   GIA Publications, Inc.
Music: Michael Joncas, © 1987, GIA Publications, Inc.

58　Psalm 63: Your Love Is Finer Than Life

Refrain

O God, I seek you, my soul thirsts for you, your love is fin-er than life.

Verses

1. As a dry and weary desert land, so my soul is thirsting for my God,
   and my flesh is faint for the God I seek, for your love is more to me than life.

2. I think of you when at night I rest, I reflect upon your steadfast love,
   I will cling to you, O Lord my God, in the shadow of your wings I sing.

3. I will bless your name all the days I live, I will raise my hands and call on you,
   my joyful lips shall sing your praise, you alone have filled my hungry soul.

Text: Psalm 63; Marty Haugen
Music: Marty Haugen
© 1982, GIA Publications, Inc.

59　Psalm 63: I Long for You

Refrain

I long for you, O Lord. With all my soul I thirst for you.

Verses

1. God, my God, it is you I seek; for you my soul is thirsting.
   Like a dry and weary land my spirit longs for you.

2. I have sought your presence, Lord; to see your pow'r and glory.
   Lord, your love means more than life; I shall sing your praise.

3. Thus will I bless you while I live, and I will call your name, Lord.
   As with the riches of a feast, my soul is filled by you.

4. Through the night I remember you for you have been my savior.
   In the shadow of your wings I will shout for joy.

Psalm 65: The Seed That Falls on Good Ground 60

Refrain

The seed that falls on good ground will yield a fruit-ful har-vest.

Verses

1. You care for the earth, give it water; you fill it with riches.
   Your river in heaven brims over to provide its grain.

2. And thus you provide for the earth; you drench its furrows;
   you level it, soften it with showers; you bless its growth.

3. You crown the year with your goodness. Abundance flows in your steps;
   in the pastures of the wilderness it flows.

4. The hills are girded with joy, the meadows covered with flocks,
   the valleys are decked with wheat. They shout for joy, yes they sing.

61 Psalm 66: Let All the Earth

Refrain

Let all the earth cry out in joy to the Lord;

Let all the earth cry out in joy to the

1.-3. *To verses* | *Last time*

Lord! Lord! to the Lord!

Verses

1. Cry out in joy to the Lord, all peoples on earth,
   sing to the praise of God's name, proclaiming for ever,
   "tremendous your deeds for us."

2. Leading your people safe through fire and water,
   bringing their souls to life, we sing of your glory, your love is eternal.

3. Hearken to me as I sing my love of the Lord,
   who answers the prayer of my heart. God leads me in safety, from death unto life.

Text: Psalm 66:1-3, 12, 16; Marty Haugen
Music: Marty Haugen
© 1982, GIA Publications, Inc.

Psalm 67: May God Bless Us in His Mercy   62

Refrain I

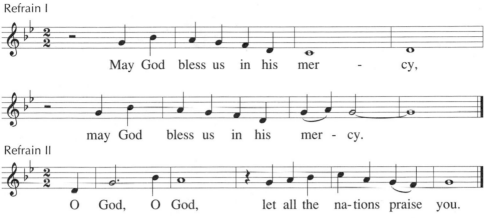

May God bless us in his mer - cy,

may God bless us in his mer - cy.

Refrain II

O God, O God, let all the na-tions praise you.

Verses

1. O God, be gracious and bless us and let your face shed its light upon us.
   So will your ways be known upon earth and all nations learn your saving help.

2. Let the nations be glad and exult for you rule the world with justice.
   With fairness you rule the peoples, you guide the nations on earth.

3. Let the peoples praise you, O God; let all the peoples praise you.
   May God still give us blessing till the ends of the earth stand in awe.

Text: Psalm 67:2-3, 5, 6, 6-8; © 1963, 1993, The Grail, GIA Publications, Inc., agent; refrain trans. © 1969, ICEL
Music: Michel Guimont, © 1994, GIA Publications, Inc.

63   Psalm 68: You Have Made a Home for the Poor

Refrain

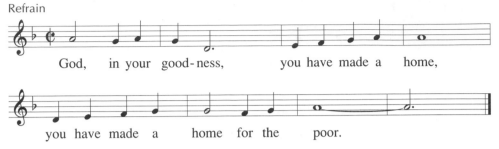

God,   in your   good-ness,   you have made a   home,
you have made   a   home   for   the   poor.

Verses

1. Your presence all around them, the just proclaim your glory;
   Laughing, dancing, singing, they revel in your story.
   O let us sing our praises! God's name inspire our song,
   For God is ever near us, let our praise be loud and long.

2. A parent to the orphan, the widow's strong defender,
   This is how our God is, both terrible and tender.
   With mercy for the lowly, God builds for them a home,
   To lead them into freedom in a land to call their own.

3. Upon a thirsty nation, you rained refreshing rain,
   And when your own were starving, you gave them life again.
   So where there once was nothing, a nation formed and grew;
   A home at last, a country vast the poor received from you.

Text: Psalm 68:4-5, 6-7, 10-11; Rory Cooney, © 1991, GIA Publications, Inc.; refrain trans. © 1969, ICEL
Music: Rory Cooney, © 1991, GIA Publications, Inc.

64   Psalm 69: Lord, in Your Great Love

Refrain

Lord,   in   your   great   love,   an - swer   me.

Verses

1. It is for you that I suffer taunts, that shame covers my face,
   that I have become a stranger to my family, an alien to my brothers and sisters.
   I burn with zeal for your house and taunts against you fall on me.

2. This is my prayer to you, my prayer for your favor.
   In your great love, answer me, O God, with your help that never fails;
   Lord, answer, for your love is kind; in your compassion, turn towards me.

3. The poor when they see it will be glad and God-seeking hearts will revive;
   for the Lord listens to the needy and does not spurn captives in their chains.
   Let the heavens and the earth give God praise, the sea and all its living creatures.

Text: Psalm 69:8-10, 14, 17, 33-35; © 1963, 1993, The Grail, GIA Publications, Inc., agent; refrain trans. © 1969, ICEL
Music: Michel Guimont, © 1994, GIA Publications, Inc.

Psalm 69: Turn to the Lord in Your Need   65

Refrain

Turn to the Lord in your need and you will live.

Verses

1. This is my prayer to you, my prayer for your favor.
   In your great love, answer me, O God, with your help that never fails;
   Lord, answer, for your love is kind; in your compassion turn towards me.

2. As for me in my poverty and pain, let your help, O God, lift me up.
   I will praise God's name with a song; I will glorify God with thanksgiving.

3. The poor when they see it will be glad and God-seeking hearts will revive;
   for the Lord listens to the needy and does not spurn captives in their chains.

4. For God will bring help to Zion and rebuild the cities of Judah.
   The children of God's servants shall inherit it; those who love God's name shall dwell there.

Text: Psalm 69:14, 17, 30-31, 33-34, 36, 37; © 1963, 1993, The Grail, GIA Publications, Inc., agent; refrain trans. © 1969, ICEL
Music: Michel Guimont, © 1994, GIA Publications, Inc.

66 Psalm 71: I Will Sing

Refrain

I will sing, I will sing of your sal - va - tion.

Verses

1. In you, O God, I place my fears, protect me from all shame.
   Save me from my guilt, listen to me, Lord.

2. In you, O God, my hope returns, the trust of my youth.
   To you I pray, for you are my strength.

3. My mouth shall proclaim your name, your praises day by day.
   O God, you are my song; forever I will sing.

Text: Psalm 71:1, 5, 15; David Haas, © 1989, GIA Publications, Inc.; refrain trans. © 1969, ICEL
Music: David Haas, © 1989, GIA Publications, Inc.

Psalm 72: Every Nation on Earth   67

Refrain I

Ev - 'ry na - tion on earth will a - dore you, Lord;

ev - 'ry na - tion on earth will a - dore you, Lord.

Refrain II

In his days jus - tice will flou - rish;

in his days full - ness of peace for - ev - er - more.

Verses

1. O God, with your judgment endow the king;
   with your justice endow the king's son.
   With justice he will govern your people,
   your afflicted ones with right judgment.

2. Justice shall flow'r in his days,
   lasting peace 'til the moon be no more.
   May he rule from sea to sea,
   from the river to the ends of the earth.

3. The kings of Tarsish and the Isles offer gifts,
   those from Seba and Arabia bring tribute.
   All kings shall pay him their homage,
   all nations shall serve him.

4. He rescues the poor when they cry out,
   the afflicted with no one to help.
   The lowly and poor he shall pity,
   the lives of the poor he will save.

Text: Psalm 72:1-2, 7-8, 10-11, 12-13; Michael Joncas
Music: Michael Joncas

68   Psalm 78: The Lord Gave Them Bread

Refrain

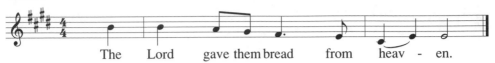

The Lord gave them bread from heav - en.

Verses

1. The things we have heard and understood,
   the things our ancestors have told us,
   these we will not hide from their children
   but will tell them to the next generation:

2. The glories and might of the Lord
   and the marvelous deeds God has done.

3. Yet God commanded the clouds above
   and opened the gates of heaven;
   God rained down manna for their food,
   and gave them bread from heaven.

4. Mere mortals ate the bread of angels.
   The Lord sent them meat in abundance.
   So God brought them to that holy land,
   to the mountain that was won by his hand.

Text: Psalm 78:3-4, 23-24, 25, 57; © 1963, 1993, The Grail, GIA Publications, Inc., agent; refrain trans. © 1969, ICEL
Music: Michel Guimont, © 1994, GIA Publications, Inc.

Psalm 80: The Vineyard of the Lord   69

Refrain

The vine-yard of the Lord is the house of Is - ra - el.

Verses

1. You brought a vine out of Egypt; to plant it you drove out the nations.
   It stretched out its branches to the sea,
   to the Great River it stretched out its shoots.

2. Then why have you broken down its walls?
   It is plucked by all who pass by.
   It is ravaged by the boar of the forest, devoured by the beasts of the field.

3. God of hosts, turn again, we implore look down from heaven and see.
   Visit the vine and protect it, the vine your right hand has planted.

4. And we shall never forsake you again;
   give us life that we may call upon your name.
   God of hosts, bring us back;
   let your face shine on us and we shall be saved.

Text: Psalm 80:9, 12-14, 15-16, 19-20; © 1963, 1993, The Grail, GIA Publications, Inc., agent; refrain trans. © 1969, ICEL
Music: Michel Guimont, © 1994, GIA Publications, Inc.

70 Psalm 80/85/Luke 1: Lord, Make Us Turn to You

Refrain

Lord, make us turn to you, show us your face, and

we shall be saved.

Verses

1. Shepherd of Israel, hearken from your throne and shine forth,
   O rouse your power, and come to save us.

2. We are your chosen vine, only by your care do we live,
   reach out your hand, O Lord, unto your people.

3. If you will dwell with us, we shall live anew in your love,
   O shine upon us, great Lord of life.

4. Lord, we are present here, show us your kindness and love,
   O speak your word of peace unto your people.

5. Lord, let salvation rain, shower down your justice and peace,
   the earth shall bring forth truth, the skies your love.

6. See, Lord, we look to you, you alone can bring us to life,
   O walk before us to light our pathways.

7. You have done wondrous things, holy is your name for all time,
   your mercy and your love are with your people.

8. You are my joy and song, I would have my life speak your praise,
   on me your love has shown, your blessings given.

9. You fill all hungry hearts, sending the rich empty forth,
   and holding up in love the meek and lowly.

Text: Psalm 80:2-3, 15-16, 18-20; Psalm 85:9-14; Luke 1:46-55; Marty Haugen
Music: Marty Haugen
© 1982, GIA Publications, Inc.

Psalm 81: Sing with Joy to God   71

Refrain

Sing with joy to God!   Sing to God our help!

Verses

1. Raise a song and sound the timbrel, the sweet-sounding harp and the lute;
   blow the trumpet at the new moon, when the moon is full, on our feast.

2. For this is Israel's law, a command of the God of Jacob.
   Imposed as a law on Joseph's people,
   when they went out against the land of Egypt.

3. A voice I did not know said to me:
   "I freed your shoulder from the burden;
   your hands were freed from the load.
   You called in distress and I saved you.

4. Let there be no foreign god among you, no worship of an alien god.
   I am the Lord your God, who brought you from the land of Egypt."

Text: Psalm 81:3-4, 5-6, 6-8, 10 11; © 1963, 1993, The Grail, GIA Publications, Inc., agent; refrain trans. © 1969, ICEL
Music: Michel Guimont, © 1994, GIA Publications, Inc.

72 Psalm 84: Happy Are They

Refrain

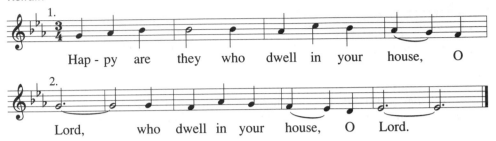

Hap-py are they who dwell in your house, O Lord, who dwell in your house, O Lord.

Verses

1. My soul yearns and pines for the courts of the Lord.
   My heart and my flesh cry to the living God.

2. The sparrow finds a home and the swallow a nest;
   Your altars, O Lord, my King and my God.

3. Happy are they who abide in your house.
   You are their strength, your praises they will sing.

Text: Psalm 84:2, 3, 4, 5-6; Thomas J. Porter
Music: Thomas J. Porter
© 1987, GIA Publications, Inc.

73 Psalm 85: Lord, Let Us See Your Kindness

Refrain

Lord, let us see your kind-ness; Lord, let us see your kind-ness.

Verses

1. Let us hear what our God proclaims: Peace to the people of God,
   salvation is near to the ones who fear God.

75 Psalm 86: Lord, You Are Good and Forgiving

Refrain

Lord, you are good and for-giv-ing.

Verses

1. O Lord, you are good and forgiving, full of love to all who call.
   Give heed, O Lord, to my prayer and attend to the sound of my voice.

2. All the nations shall come to adore you and glorify your name, O Lord,
   for you are great and do marvelous deeds, you who alone are God.

3. But you, God of mercy and compassion,
   slow to anger, O Lord, abounding in love and truth,
   turn and take pity on me. O give your strength to your servant.

76 Psalm 89: For Ever I Will Sing

Refrain

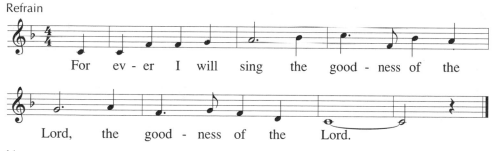

For ev-er I will sing the good-ness of the

Lord, the good-ness of the Lord.

Verses

1. "With my chosen one I have made a covenant; I have sworn to David my servant:
   I will establish your dynasty forever and set up your throne through all ages."

2. Happy the people who acclaim such a God,
   who walk, O Lord, in the light of your face,
   who find their joy ev'ry day in your name,
   who make your justice the source of their bliss.

3. He will say to me: "You are my father, my God, the rock who saves me!"
   I will keep my love for him always; with him my covenant shall last.

2. Kindness and truth, justice and peace;
    truth shall spring up as the water from the earth,
    justice shall rain from the heavens.

3. The Lord will come and you shall know his love,
    justice shall walk in his pathways, salvation the gift that he brings.

Text: Psalm 85:9-10, 11-12, 13-14; Marty Haugen, © 1983, GIA Publications, Inc.; refrain trans. © 1969, ICEL
Music: Marty Haugen, © 1983, GIA Publications, Inc.

Psalm 85: Come, O Lord, and Set Us Free   74

Refrain I

Come, O Lord, and set us free. Come, and set us free.

Refrain II

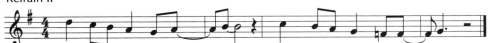

Lord, let us see your kind - ness; Lord, grant us your sal-va - tion.

Verses

1. Now I will hear what God proclaims, the Lord who speaks of peace.
    Near to us now, God's saving love for those who believe.

2. Mercy and faithfulness shall meet, in justice and peace, embrace.
    Truth shall blossom from the earth as the heavens rejoice.

3. Our God shall grant abundant gifts, the earth shall yield its fruit.
    Justice shall march before our God and guide us to peace.

Text: Psalm 85; refrains I and II, © 1969, ICEL; verses by Mike Balhoff, Gary Daigle, Darryl Ducote, © 1978, 1993, Damean Music.
    Distributed by GIA Publications, Inc.
Music: Mike Balhoff, Gary Daigle, Darryl Ducote, © 1978, 1993, Damean Music. Distributed by GIA Publications, Inc.

Alternate Verses

1. I have found David my servant,
   with my holy oil I have anointed him,
   that my hand may ever be with him
   and my arm make him strong.

2. My faithfulness and love shall be with you,
   in my Name your name will be exalted.

3. He shall cry to me, "My God, my rock of salvation, my salvation."

Text: Psalm 89: 4-5, 16-17, 27-29, © 1963, 1993, The Grail, GIA Publications, Inc., agent; alt. verses 21-22, 25, 27, Marty Haugen, © 1988, 1994,
    GIA Publications, Inc.; refrain trans. © 1969, ICEL
Music: Marty Haugen, © 1988, 1994, GIA Publications, Inc.

Psalm 90: In Ev'ry Age 77

Refrain

In ev-'ry age, O Lord, you have been our ref - uge.

Verses

1. You turn us back into dust and say: "Go back, children of the earth."
   To your eyes a thousand years are like yesterday, come and gone,
   no more than a watch in the night.

2. You sweep us away like a dream,
   like grass which springs up in the morning.
   In the morning it springs up and flowers; by evening it withers and fades.

3. Make us know the shortness of our life that we may gain wisdom of heart.
   Lord, relent! Is your anger for ever? Show pity to your servants.

4. In the morning, fill us with love; we shall exult and rejoice all our days.
   Let the favor of the Lord be upon us: give success to the work of our hands.

Text: Psalm 90:3-4, 5-6, 12-13, 14, 17; © 1963, 1993, The Grail, GIA Publications, Inc., agent; refrain trans. © 1969, ICEL
Music: Michel Guimont, © 1994, GIA Publications, Inc.

78 Psalm 90: Fill Us with Your Love, O Lord

Refrain

Fill us with your love, O Lord, and we will sing for joy!

Verses

1. Teach us to number our days, that we may gain wisdom of heart.
   Return, O Lord our God, have pity on your servants.

2. Fill us at dawn with your kindness,
   that we may shout for joy and gladness.
   Make us glad for the days when you afflicted us,
   for the years when we saw evil.

3. Let your work be seen by your servants, and your glory by their children.
   May your gracious care be ours. Prosper the work of our hands.

79 Psalm 91: Be with Me

Refrain

Be with me, Lord, when I am in trou-ble, be with me, Lord, I pray.

Verses

1. You who dwell in the shelter of the Lord, Most High,
   who abide in the shadow of our God,
   say to the Lord: "My refuge and fortress, the God in whom I trust."

2. No evil shall befall you, no pain come near,
   for the angels stand close by your side,
   guarding you always and bearing you gently, watching over your life.

3. Those who cling to the Lord live secure in God's love,
   lifted high, those who trust in God's name,
   call on the Lord, who will never forsake you.
   God will bring you salvation and joy.

Psalm 92: Lord, It Is Good   80

Refrain

Lord, it is good to give thanks to you.

Verses

1. It is good to give thanks to the Lord,
   to make music to your name, O Most High,
   to proclaim your love in the morning
   and your truth in the watches of the night.

2. The just will flourish like the palm tree and grow like a Lebanon cedar.
   Planted in the house of the Lord they will flourish in the courts of our God.

3. Still bearing fruit when they are old, still full of sap, still green,
   to proclaim that the Lord is just. My rock, in whom there is no wrong.

Psalm 93: The Lord Is King   81

Refrain

The Lord is king; he is robed in maj-es-ty.

Verses

1. The Lord is king, with majesty enrobed;
   the Lord is robed with might, and girded round with power.

2. The world you made firm, not to be moved;
   your throne has stood firm from of old. From all eternity, O Lord, you are.

3. Truly your decrees are to be trusted.
   Holiness is fitting to your house, O Lord, until the end of time.

82 Psalm 95: If Today You Hear God's Voice

Refrain

If to - day you hear God's voice, hard- en not your hearts.

If to - day you hear God's voice, hard- en not your hearts.

Verses

1. Come, ring out our joy to the Lord, hail the rock who saves us,
   let us come now before our God, with songs let us hail the Lord.

2. Come, let us bow and bend low, let us kneel before God who made us,
   for here is our God; we the people, the flock that is led by God's hand.

3. O that today you would hear God's voice, "Harden not your hearts,
   as on that day in the desert, when your parents put me to the test."

Text: Psalm 95:1-2, 6-7, 8-9; David Haas
Music: David Haas
© 1983, 1994, GIA Publications, Inc.

Psalm 96: Proclaim to All the Nations   83

Refrain I

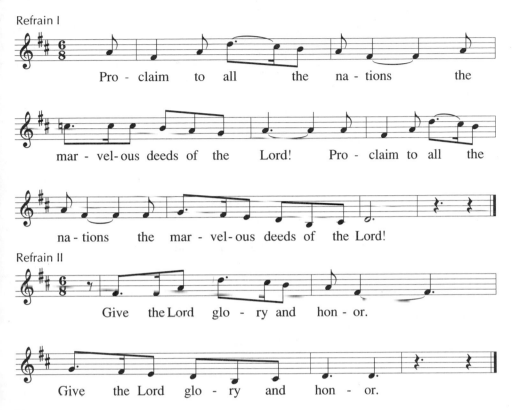

Pro - claim to all the na - tions the
mar - vel-ous deeds of the Lord! Pro - claim to all the
na - tions the mar - vel-ous deeds of the Lord!

Refrain II

Give the Lord glo - ry and hon - or.

Give the Lord glo - ry and hon - or.

Verses

1. Sing to the Lord a new song. Sing to the Lord all you lands!
   Sing to the Lord with all your heart, and bless God's name!

2. Announce salvation day by day, God's glory throughout the earth!
   Among all the people in ev'ry land, God's wondrous deeds!

3. Give to the Lord, you nations, praise to the Lord of all!
   Sing glory and praise and sing to the name, above all names!

4. Worship the Lord, and tremble, proclaim the one who reigns!
   Say to the nations: "The Lord is King;" who rules with justice!

Text: Psalm 96:1-2, 3, 7-8, 9; David Haas, © 1989, GIA Publications, Inc.; refrains trans. © 1969, ICEL
Music: Marty Haugen; refrain I, David Haas; refrain II adapt. by Diana Kodner; © 1989, 1994, GIA Publications, Inc.

84 Psalm 96: Today Is Born Our Savior

Refrain

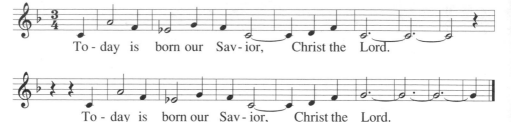

To - day is born our Sav-ior, Christ the Lord.

To - day is born our Sav-ior, Christ the Lord.

Verses

1. Sing out to God a new song, Sing out to God all you lands;
   Sing out in joy, sing out in love to our God!

2. Announce God's salvation forever, and glory proclaim to the earth;
   tell all the peoples the wondrous deeds of our God.

3. Let us rejoice in our Savior, who has come now to rule the earth;
   rule it in justice, rule it in mercy forever!

4. Let the heavens be glad and the earth rejoice,
   let the seas now resound in your praise!
   Let the plains be joyful, and the forests exult!

Text: Psalm 96:1-2, 2-3, 11-12, 13; Marty Haugen, © 1988, GIA Publications, Inc.; refrain trans. © 1969, ICEL
Music: Marty Haugen, © 1988, GIA Publications, Inc.

Psalm 97: The Lord Is King   85

Refrain

The Lord is king, the Lord most high o-ver all the earth.

Verses

1. The Lord is king, let earth rejoice, let all the coastlands be glad.
   Justice and right, God's throne.

2. The skies proclaim God's justice; all peoples see God's glory.
   All you spirits worship the Lord.

3. For you indeed are the Lord most high above all the earth,
   exalted far above all spirits.

Text: Psalm 97:1-2, 6-7, 9; © 1963, 1993, The Grail, GIA Publications, Inc., agent; refrain trans. © 1969, ICEL
Music: Michel Guimont, © 1994, GIA Publications, Inc.

86   Psalm 98: All the Ends of the Earth

Refrain I

All the ends of the earth have seen the pow-er of God; all the ends of the earth have seen the pow - er of God.

Refrain II

Sing to the Lord a new song, for God has done won - der-ful deeds. Sing to the Lord a new song, for God has done won - der - ful deeds.

Refrain III

The Lord comes to the earth to rule the earth with jus - tice. The Lord comes to the earth to rule the earth with jus - tice.

Verses

1. Sing to the Lord a new song, for God has done wondrous deeds;
   whose right hand has won the vict'ry for us, God's holy arm.

2. The Lord has made salvation known, and justice revealed to all,
   remembering kindness and faithfulness to Israel.

3. All of the ends of earth have seen salvation by our God.
   Joyfully sing out all you lands, break forth in song.

4. Sing to the Lord with harp and song, with trumpet and with horn.
   Sing in your joy before the king, the king, our Lord.

Text: Psalm 98:1, 2-3, 3-4, 5-6; David Haas, Marty Haugen
Music: David Haas, Marty Haugen; refrain II, III adapt. by Diana Kodner
© 1983, 1994, GIA Publications, Inc.

Psalm 100: We Are God's People   87

Ostinato Refrain

We are God's peo - ple, the flock of the Lord.

Verses

1. Cry out with joy to the Lord, all you lands, all you lands.
   Serve the Lord now with gladness, come before God singing for joy!

2. Know that the Lord is God! Know that the Lord is God,
   who made us, to God we belong, God's people, the sheep of the flock!

3. Go, now within the gates giving thanks, giving thanks.
   Enter the courts singing praise, give thanks and bless God's name!

4. Indeed, how good is the Lord, whose mercy endures for ever,
   for the Lord is faithful, is faithful from age to age!

Text: Psalm 100:1-2, 3, 4, 5; David Haas
Music: David Haas
© 1983, GIA Publications, Inc.

88 Psalm 103: The Lord Is Kind and Merciful

Refrain

The Lord is kind and mer - ci-ful; the Lord is kind and mer - ci - ful. Slow to an - ger, rich in kind-ness, the Lord is kind and mer - ci - ful.

Verses

1. Bless the Lord, O my soul; all my being bless God's name.
   Bless the Lord, O my soul; forget not all God's blessings.

2. The Lord is gracious and merciful, slow to anger, full of kindness.
   God is good to all creation, full of compassion.

3. The goodness of God is from age to age,
   blessing those who choose to love.
   And justice toward God's children; on all who keep the covenant.

Text: Psalm 103; Jeanne Cotter
Music: Jeanne Cotter
© 1993, GIA Publications, Inc.

89 Psalm 103: The Lord Is Kind and Merciful

Refrain

The Lord is kind and mer-ci - ful, the Lord is kind and mer - ci - ful.

Verses

1. Bless the Lord, O my soul, and all my being bless God's name;
   bless the Lord, and forget not God's benefits.

2. God pardons all your iniquities, and comforts your sorrows,
   redeems your life from destruction and crowns you with kindness.

3. Merciful, merciful, and gracious is our God;
   slow to anger, abounding in kindness.

Text: Psalm 103:1-2, 3-4, 8; para. by Marty Haugen, © 1983, GIA Publications, Inc.; refrain trans. © 1969, ICEL
Music: Marty Haugen, © 1983, GIA Publications, Inc.

Psalm 104: Lord, Send Out Your Spirit   90

Lord, send out your Spir-it, and re-new the face of the earth!

Verses

1. Bless the Lord, O my soul; O Lord, my God, you are great indeed!
   How manifold are your works, O Lord! The earth is full of your creatures!

2. If you take away their breath, they die and they return to their dust.
   When you send forth your Spirit of life, they are created in your sight!

3. May his glory last for all time; may the Lord be glad in his works.
   Pleasing to him will be my theme; I will be glad in the Lord!

Text: Psalm 104:1, 24, 29-30, 31, 34; Paul Lisicky, © 1985, GIA Publications, Inc.; refrain trans. © 1969, ICEL
Music: Paul Lisicky, © 1985, GIA Publications, Inc.

91   Psalm 107: Give Thanks to the Lord

Refrain

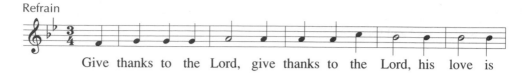

Give thanks to the Lord, give thanks to the Lord, his love is

To verses || *Last time*

ev - er - last - ing.   last - ing.

Verses

1. Those who sailed the sea in ships trading on the deep waters;
   they saw the works of the Lord and his wonders in the abyss.

2. God's command raised up a storm wind which tossed its waves on high.
   They sank down to the depths; their hearts melted away.

3. They cried to the Lord in distress. From their straits he rescued them.
   God hushed the storm to a breeze and the waves of the sea were stilled.

Psalm 107: 23-24, 25-26, 28-29; Roy James Stewart, © 1993, GIA Publications, Inc.; refrain trans. © 1969, ICEL
Music: Roy James Stewart, © 1993, GIA Publications, Inc.

92   Psalm 110: You Are a Priest for Ever

Refrain

You are a priest for ev-er   in the line of Mel - chi - ze - dek.

Verses

1. The Lord's revelation to my Master: "Sit on my right;
   your foes I will put beneath your feet."

2. The Lord will wield from Zion your scepter of power;
   rule in the midst of all your foes.

3. A prince from the day of your birth on the holy mountains;
   from the womb before the dawn I begot you.

4. The Lord has sworn an oath and will not change.
   "You are a priest for ever, a priest like Melchizedek of old."

Text: Psalm 110:1, 2, 3, 4, © 1963, 1993, The Grail, GIA Publications, Inc., agent; refrain trans. © 1969, ICEL
Music: Michel Guimont, © 1994, GIA Publications, Inc.

Psalm 112: A Light Rises in the Darkness 93

Refrain

A light ris-es in the dark-ness; a light for the up-right.

Verses

1. They are lights in the darkness for the upright;
   they are generous, merciful and just.
   Good people take pity and lend, they conduct their affairs with honor.

2. The just will never waver, they will be remembered for ever.
   They have no fear of evil news; with firm hearts they trust in the Lord.

3. With steadfast hearts they will not fear. Openhanded, they give to the poor;
   their justice stands firm for ever. Their heads will be raised in glory.

Text: Psalm 112:4-5, 6-7, 8-9; © 1963, 1993, The Grail, GIA Publications, Inc., agent; refrain trans. © 1969, ICEL
Music: Michel Guimont, © 1994, GIA Publications, Inc.

94 Psalm 113: Praise His Name

Refrain

Al - le - lu - ia! Al-le-lu-ia! Al - le - lu - ia!

Verses

1. You servants of the Lord, bless the Lord: Blessed be the name for ever!
From east to west, praised be the name of the Lord our God!

2. High above the nations the Lord is God;
high above the heavens God's glory!
Who is like God, enthroned on the stars above earth and sky?

3. Raising up the lowly and the poor from the dust,
God gives them a home among rulers:
blessing the barren, giving them children singing for joy!

4. Glory to the Father and glory to the Son; glory to the Holy Spirit:
glory and honor, wisdom and power for evermore!

Text: Psalm 113; Michael Joncas, alt.
Music: Michael Joncas
© 1979, New Dawn Music

95 Psalm 113: Praise the Lord

Refrain

Praise the Lord, praise the Lord who lifts up the poor.

Verses

1. Praise, O servants of the Lord; praise the name of the Lord!
May the name of the Lord be blessed both now and for evermore!

2. High above all nations is the Lord, above the heavens God's glory.
Who is like the Lord, our God, the one enthroned on high,
who stoops from the heights to look down,
to look down upon heaven and earth?

3. From the dust God lifts up the lowly,
   from the dungheap God raises the poor
   to set them in the company of rulers, yes, with the rulers of the people.

Psalm 116: Our Blessing-Cup   96

Refrain

Our bless-ing-cup is a com-mun-ion with the blood of the Lord.

Verses

1. How can I make a return to the Lord for all God has done for me?
   The cup of salvation I will take up, I will call on the name of the Lord.

2. Precious, indeed, in the sight of the Lord is the death of his faithful ones;
   and I am your servant, your chosen one, for you have set me free.

3. Unto your name I will offer my thanks for the debt that I owe to you.
   In the presence of all who have called on your name,
   in the courts of the house of the Lord.

97 Psalm 116: I Will Walk in the Presence of God

Refrain

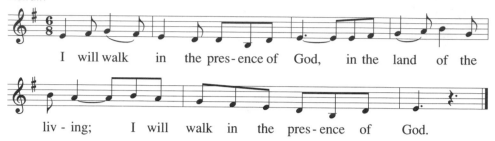

I will walk in the pres-ence of God, in the land of the liv-ing; I will walk in the pres-ence of God.

Verses

1. In my hour of despair, bereft and betrayed,
   I prayed, "Save me! Be my breath!"
   The death of a servant cuts close to your heart,
   For God of the living you are.

2. Your servant am I like my mother before me.
   You restore me, loosing my bonds.
   My hands in thanksgiving to God I will raise.
   O join me in glorious praise!

3. My vows I will make, and may ev'ryone hear me!
   Draw near me, O servants of God.
   I stand here in the midst of them:
   Your house, your heart, Jerusalem.

Text: Psalm 116 adapt. by Rory Cooney, © 1990, GIA Publications, Inc.; refrain trans. © 1969, ICEL
Music: Gary Daigle and Rory Cooney, © 1990, GIA Publications, Inc.

98 Psalm 116: The Name of God

Refrain I

I will take the cup of life, I will call God's name all my days.

Refrain II

Our bless-ing cup is a com-mun-ion with the blood of Christ.

Refrain III

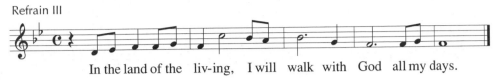

In the land of the liv-ing, I will walk with God all my days.

Verses

1. How can I make a return for the goodness of God?
   This saving cup I will bless and sing, and call the name of God!

2. The dying of those who keep faith is precious to our God.
   I am your servant called from your hands, you have set me free!

3. To you I will offer my thanks and call upon your name.
   You are my promise for all to see. I love your name, O God!

Text: Psalm 116; David Haas, © 1987, GIA Publications, Inc.; refrain II trans. © 1969, ICEL
Music: David Haas, © 1987, GIA Publications, Inc.

Psalm 117: Holy Is God, Holy and Strong   99

Refrain

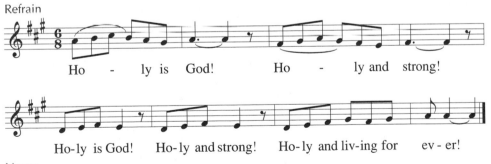

Ho - ly is God!   Ho - ly and strong!

Ho-ly is God!   Ho-ly and strong!   Ho-ly and liv-ing for   ev - er!

Verses

1. O praise the Lord, all you nations, acclaim God, all you peoples!
   Strong is God's love for us, the Lord is faithful for ever!

2. Give glory to the Father Almighty, to his Son Jesus Christ the Lord,
   to the Spirit who dwells in our hearts, both now and for ever. Amen!

Text: Psalm 117; The Grail, © 1963, 1993, GIA Publications, Inc., agent; refrain trans. © 1969, ICEL
Music: Michael Joncas, © 1979, GIA Publications, Inc.

100 Psalm 117: Go Out to All the World

Refrain

Go out to all the world, and tell the good news!

Go out to all the world, and sing: "Al - le - lu - ia!"

Verses

1. Praise the Lord, all you nations! Glorify God, all you peoples!

2. Steadfast is God's love to all people!
   And the promise of God endures for ever!

Text: Psalm 117; David Haas, © 1991, GIA Publications, Inc.; refrain trans. © 1969, ICEL
Music: David Haas; © 1991, GIA Publications, Inc.

101 Psalm 118: Alleluia, Alleluia

Refrain

Cantors:

Al - le - lu - ia! Al - le - lu - ia! All: Al - le - lu - ia!

Al - le - lu - ia! Cantors: Al - le - lu - ia! Al - le - lu - ia!

All: Al - le - lu - ia! Al - le - lu - ia!

Verses

1. This is the day the Lord has made, let us rejoice, be glad, and sing!
   Thanks and praise be to our God, for his mercy endures for evermore!

2. The right hand of God has come with power,
   the Lord, our God, is lifted high!
   I shall not die, but I shall live and rejoice in the works of the Lord!

3. The stone which the builders once denied now has become the cornerstone.
   By the Lord has this been done; it has brought wonder to our eyes!

Text: Psalm 118:24, 1, 16-17, 22-23; David Haas
Music: David Haas
© 1986, GIA Publications, Inc.

Psalm 118: Let Us Rejoice   102

Refrain

This is the day the Lord has made, let us re-
Or: Al - le - lu - ia, al - le - lu - ia! Al - le -

joice and be glad; this is the day the Lord has
lu - ia! Al - le - lu - ia, al - le - lu -

made, let us re - joice and be glad!
ia! Al - le - lu - ia!

Verses

1. Give thanks to the Lord, for God is good; God's mercy endures for ever;
   Let the house of Israel say: "God's mercy endures for ever."

2. The hand of the Lord has struck with power, God's right hand is exalted,
   I shall not die, but live anew, declaring the works of the Lord.

3. The stone which the builders rejected has become the cornerstone,
   the Lord of love and mercy has brought wonder to our eyes!

Text: Psalm 118:1-2, 16-17, 22-23; Marty Haugen, © 1983, GIA Publications, Inc.; refrain trans. © 1969, ICEL
Music: Marty Haugen, © 1983, GIA Publications, Inc.

103 Psalm 119: Happy Are Those Who Follow

Refrain

Hap-py are those who fol-low in the law of the Lord.

Hap-py are those who fol-low in the law of the Lord.

Verses

1. Happy are they whose way is blameless, who walk in the law of the Lord.
   Happy are they who observe God's decrees, who seek God with all their heart.
   Happy are they who walk in the law of the Lord.

2. You have commanded that all your precepts be kept with diligence.
   Oh, that I might be strong in the ways of keeping to your law.
   Happy are they who walk in the law of the Lord.

3. Be good to your servant that I may live, may live to keep your word.
   Open my heart that I may consider the wonders of your law.
   Happy are they who walk in the law of the Lord.

4. Instruct me, O God, in the way of your statutes,
   that I may exactly observe them.
   Give me discernment, that I may observe your law.
   Give me discernment to keep it with all my heart.
   Happy are they who walk in the law of the Lord.

Text: Psalm 119:1-2, 5-6, 17-18, 33-34; Rory Cooney
Music: Rory Cooney
© 1991, GIA Publications, Inc.

104 Psalm 119: Lord, I Love Your Commands

Refrain

Lord, I love your com - mands.

Verses

1. My part, I have resolved, O Lord, is to obey your word.
   The law from your mouth means more to me than silver and gold.

2. Let your love be ready to console me by your promise to your servant.
   Let your love come and I shall live for your law is my delight.

3. That is why I love your commands more than finest gold,
   why I rule my life by your precepts, and hate false ways.

4. Your will is wonderful indeed; therefore I obey it.
   The unfolding of your word gives light and teaches the simple.

Psalm 121: I Lift Up My Eyes   105

Refrain

To you, O Lord, I have lift-ed up my eyes. To you, O Lord, I have lift-ed up my soul.

Verses

1. I lift up my eyes to the mountains; from where shall come my help?
   My help shall come from the Lord who made the heavens and the earth.

2. The Lord is your guard and your shade, for ever by your side.
   By day the sun shall not smite you nor the moon in the night.

3. The Lord ever watches over you, the guardian of your soul.
   The Lord will guard your coming and your going now and for ever.

106 Psalm 121: Our Help Comes from the Lord

Refrain

Our help comes from the Lord, the
mak - er of heav - en and earth.

Verses

1. I lift up my eyes to the mountains: from where shall come my help?
   My help shall come from the Lord who made heaven and earth.

2. May God never allow you to stumble! Let God sleep not, your guard.
   Neither sleeping nor slumbering, God, Israel's guard.

3. The Lord is your guard and your shade: and at your right side stands,
   By day the sun shall not smite you nor the moon in the night.

4. The Lord will guard you from evil: God will guard your soul.
   The Lord will guard your going and coming both now and for ever.

5. Glory to the Father, and to the Son, and to the Holy Spirit:
   as it was in the beginning, is now, and will be for ever. Amen.

Text: Psalm 121; © 1963, 1993, The Grail, GIA Publications, Inc., agent; refrain by Michael Joncas, © 1979, GIA Publications, Inc.
Music: Michael Joncas, © 1979, GIA Publications, Inc.

Psalm 122: Let Us Go Rejoicing   107

Refrain

Let   us   go   re - joic- ing   to   the   house   of   the   Lord;

Let   us   go,   re - joic- ing   to   the   house   of   the   Lord.

Verses

1. I rejoiced when I heard them say: "Let us go to the house of the Lord,"
   and now our feet are standing within your gates, O Jerusalem.

2. Jerusalem is a city built with unity and strength.
   It is there, it is there that the tribes go up, the tribes of the Lord.

3. For Israel's law is to praise God's name and there to give God thanks.
   There are set the judgment thrones for all of David's house.

4. Pray for the peace of Jerusalem! "May those who love you prosper;
   May peace ever reign within your walls, and wealth within your buildings!"

5. For love of my fam'ly and love of my friends, I pray that peace be yours.
   For love of the house of the Lord our God I pray for your good.

Text: Psalm 122; Michael Joncas, © 1987, GIA Publications, Inc.; refrain trans.© 1969, ICEL
Music: Michael Joncas, 1987, GIA Publications, Inc.

108 Psalm 122: I Was Glad

Refrain

I was glad when they said to me,

"Come with us to the house of the Lord!"

Verses

1. I was glad when they said to me: "Come with us to the house of the Lord."
   Now our feet are standing firm, within your gates, O Jerusalem!

2. Jerusalem— strongly built, walled around with unity.
   It is there that the tribes of God are lifted high, to the mountain of God!

3. Israel, this is your law to praise the name of the Lord.
   Here are placed the judgment seats, for the just, here the house of David!

4. For the love of my fam'ly and friends, "may the peace of God be with you!"
   For the love of the house of God I will pray, I will pray for your good!"

Text: Psalm 122; David Haas
Music: David Haas
© 1994, GIA Publications, Inc.

109 Psalm 123: Our Eyes Are Fixed on the Lord

Refrain

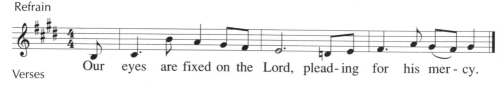

Verses

Our eyes are fixed on the Lord, plead-ing for his mer-cy.

1. To you I have lifted up my eyes, you who dwell in the heavens;
   my eyes, like the eyes of slaves on the hand of their lords.

2. Like the eyes of a servant on the hand of her mistress,
   so our eyes are on the Lord our God till we are shown mercy.

3. Have mercy on us Lord, have mercy. We are filled with contempt.
   Indeed all too full is our soul with the scorn of the rich,
   (the disdain of the proud).

Text: Psalm 123:1-2, 3-4; © 1963, 1993, The Grail, GIA Publications, Inc., agent; refrain trans. © 1969, ICEL
Music: Michel Guimont, © 1994, GIA Publications, Inc.

Psalm 126: God Has Done Great Things for Us   110

Refrain

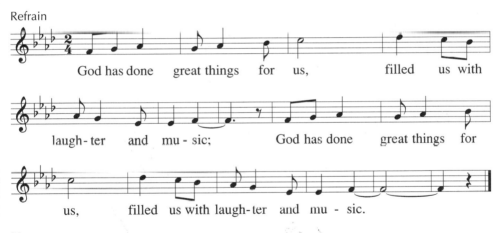

God has done   great things   for   us,   filled   us with
laugh-ter   and   mu - sic;   God has done   great things   for
us,   filled   us with laugh-ter   and   mu - sic.

Verses

1. When our God led us back to freedom,
   like dreamers we beheld the promised land again;
   our mouths were filled with laughter and rejoicing.

2. We proclaimed to the nations what you had done for us;
   your mighty deeds of love, restoring us to life,
   you lead your people home to you rejoicing.

3. Come restore our fortune, renew us in your love,
   as rivers through the sand, as springs within the desert;
   those who sow in tears shall reap rejoicing.

Text: Psalm 126:1-6; Marty Haugen
Music: Marty Haugen
© 1988, GIA Publications, Inc.

111 Psalm 128: Blest Are Those Who Love You

Refrain I

Blest are those who love you, hap-py those who fol-low you, blest are those who seek you, O God.

Refrain II

May the Lord bless us, May the Lord pro-tect us, all the days, all the days of our life.

Verses

1. Happy all those who fear the Lord, and walk in God's pathway;
   you will find what you long for: the riches of our God.

2. Your spouse shall be like a fruitful vine in the midst of your home,
   your children flourish like olive plants rejoicing at your table.

3. May the blessings of God be yours all the days of your life,
   may the peace and the love of God live always in your heart.

Text: Psalm 128:1-2, 3, 5; Marty Haugen
Music: Marty Haugen; refrain II adapt. by Diana Kodner
© 1987, 1993, GIA Publications, Inc.

112 Psalm 130: If You, O God, Laid Bare Our Guilt

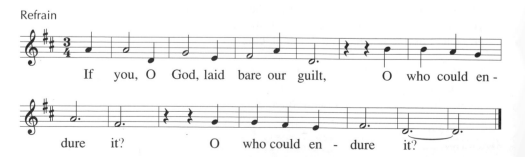

Refrain

If you, O God, laid bare our guilt, O who could en-dure it? O who could en - dure it?

Verses

1. Out of the depths I cry to you. Lord, hear my plea.
   Let your ear be attentive to the sound of my call.

2. If you, O God, lay bare our sin, Lord, who can stand?
   But with you is forgiveness, so your name is revered.

3. Waiting for you, our souls await, hoping in God.
   Like the sent'nel for daybreak, so our souls wait for you.

4. For with the Lord is steadfast love: pow'r to redeem.
   God will save us from sorrows, bring us back from our sin.

Text: Psalm 130; John Foley, SJ
Music: John Foley, SJ
© 1994, GIA Publications, Inc.

Psalm 130: With the Lord There Is Mercy   113

Refrain

With the Lord there is mer-cy, and full-ness of re-demp-tion.

Verses

1. From out of the depths, I cry unto you,
   Lord, hear my voice, come hear my prayer;
   O let your ear be open to my pleading.

2. If you, O Lord, should mark our guilt,
   then who could stand within your sight?
   But in you is found forgiveness for our failings.

3. Just as those who wait for the morning light,
   even more I long for the Lord, my God,
   whose word to me shall ever be my comfort.

Text: Psalm 130:1-2, 3-4, 5-6; Marty Haugen, © 1983, GIA Publications, Inc.; refrain trans. © 1969, ICEL
Music: Marty Haugen, © 1983, GIA Publications, Inc.

114 Psalm 131: My Soul Is Still

Refrain

In you, O Lord, I have found my peace, I have found my peace.

Verses

1. My heart is not proud, my eyes not above you;
   You fill my soul. I am not filled with great things,
   nor with thoughts beyond me.

2. My soul is still, my soul stays quiet,
   longing for you like a weaned child
   in its mother's arms; so is my soul a child with you.

Text: Psalm 131; verses, David Haas, © 1985, GIA Publications, Inc.; refrain trans. © 1969, ICEL
Music: David Haas, © 1985, GIA Publications, Inc.

Psalm 136: Love Is Never Ending   115

Cantor:

1. We give thanks un - to you, O God of might:
2. In your wis - dom and love you shaped the skies:
3. You have filled all the skies with glo - ry and light:
4. From of old you have led your peo - ple in faith:
5. You de - liv - ered the ones who called un - to you:
6. You have o - pened the sea and brought your peo - ple through:
7. You re - mem - ber your prom - ise age to age:
8. You give food and life to all liv - ing things:

All:

for your love is nev - er end - ing,

Cantor:

We give thanks un - to you, the God of gods:
You spread out the earth up - on the sea:
The sun for the day and moon for night:
You have shown your com - pas - sion, strength and love:
From bond - age to free - dom, you brought them forth:
Brought them in - to a land that flows with life:
You show mer - cy on those of low de - gree:
We give thanks un - to you, the God of all:

All:

for your love is nev - er end - ing.

Text: Psalm 136; Marty Haugen
Music: Marty Haugen
© 1987, GIA Publications, Inc.

116   Psalm 137: Let My Tongue Be Silent

Refrain

Let my tongue be si - lent, if ev - er I for - get you!

Verses

1. By Babylonian rivers, we sat and wept, rememb'ring Zion.
   There on the poplars we retired our harps.

2. For there our captors demanded songs of joy:
   "Sing to us one of the songs of Zion!"

3. How can we sing the songs of the Lord while in a foreign land?
   How can we sing the songs of the Lord while in a foreign land?

4. If I should fail to remember you, O Zion, Let my tongue be silenced,
   let my right hand be forgotten,
   If I do not consider Jerusalem to be my highest joy.

Text: Psalm 137:1-6; Carl Johengen, © 1992, GIA Publications, Inc.; refrain trans. © 1969, ICEL
Music: Carl Johengen, © 1992, GIA Publications, Inc.

117   Psalm 138: Lord, Your Love Is Eternal

Refrain

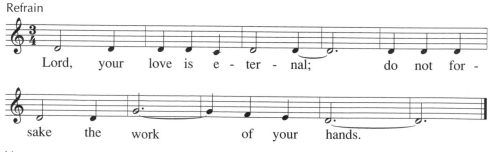

Lord, your love is e - ter - nal; do not for -

sake the work of your hands.

Verses

1. I give thanks to you, O Lord, with all my heart, with all my soul.
   I will sing your praise with the angels. I will worship in your temple.

2. I give thanks to your holy name, for all your kindness and your truth.
   When I called, you answered me, and you built up strength within me.

3. The Lord God is exalted, yet he sees you, he sees me.
   And his kindness endures for ever, O forsake not the work of your hands.

Text: Psalm 138:1-2, 3, 7; Roy James Stewart, © 1993, GIA Publications, Inc.; refrain trans. © 1969, ICEL
Music: Roy James Stewart, © 1993, GIA Publications, Inc.

Psalm 138: The Fragrance of Christ   118

Refrains I-III

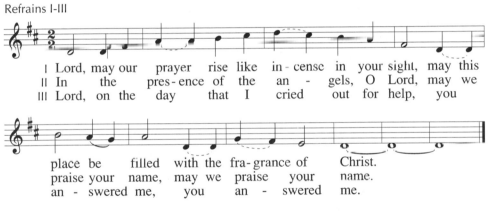

```
I   Lord, may our    prayer   rise like  in-cense  in  your sight,  may this
II  In       the    pres-ence of  the    an  -  gels, O  Lord,  may we
III Lord, on the     day      that  I    cried     out for help,    you

    place be       filled  with the fra-grance of    Christ.
    praise your   name,   may we  praise    your    name.
    an - swered me,       you     an -  swered  me.
```

Verses

1. I will thank you, Lord, with all of my heart,
   you have heard the words of my mouth.
   In the presence of the angels I will bless you,
   I will adore before your holy temple.

2. I will thank you, Lord, for your faithfulness and love,
   beyond all my hopes and dreams.
   On the day that I called you answered;
   you gave life to the strength of my soul.

3. All who live on earth shall give you thanks when they hear
   the words of your voice.
   And all shall sing of your ways: "How great is the glory of God!"

Text: Psalm 138:1-5; David Haas
Music: David Haas
© 1989, GIA Publications, Inc.

119 Psalm 139: Filling Me with Joy

Refrain

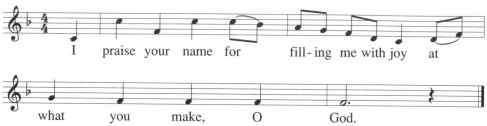

I praise your name for fill-ing me with joy at what you make, O God.

Verses

1. O God, you search me and you know me.
   You know when I sit and when I stand.
   You understand my thoughts from afar.
   With all my ways you are familiar.

2. God, you have formed my inmost being.
   You knit me in my mother's womb.
   I give you thanks for you have made me.
   How wondrous, wondrous are your works.

3. You knew my soul completely.
   Nor was my frame unknown to you
   when I was formed in the depths,
   when I was fashioned in secret.

Text: Psalm 139; Paul Lisicky
Music: Paul Lisicky
© 1992, GIA Publications, Inc.

Psalm 141: Evening Offering 120

Refrain

Let my prayer rise be-fore you like in-cense, O Lord,

and my hands like an eve - ning of - f'ring.

Verses

1. To you, O Lord, I call out for help.
   O hear my voice when I cry out to you.
   Let my prayer rise up before you like incense,
   my hands lifted up at the end of the day.

2. May my words, O Lord, speak only your truth;
   my heart be filled with a longing for you.
   Keep my hands, O Lord, from all wicked deeds;
   let me not rejoice with those set against you.

3. Let your holy ones confront me in kindness;
   their words I hear as your wisdom for me.
   But the wicked ones shall never mislead me;
   I will pray for strength to conquer their evil.

4. I look to you, O Lord, for my hope.
   For you, my God, are the strength of my soul.
   Keep me safe from those who tempt me to sin,
   and free my heart to rest in your peace.

Text: Psalm 141; Darryl Ducote
Music: Darryl Ducote; arr. by Gary Daigle
© 1985, 1993, Damean Music. Distributed by GIA Publications, Inc.

121 Psalm 145: I Will Praise Your Name

Refrain

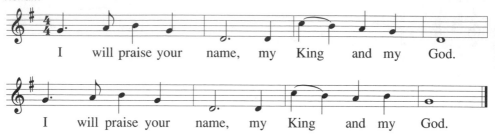

I will praise your name, my King and my God.

I will praise your name, my King and my God.

Verses

1. I will give you glory, my God above, and I will bless your name for ever.
Ev'ry day I will bless and praise your name for ever.

2. The Lord is full of grace and mercy, who is kind and slow to anger.
God is good in ev'ry way, and full of compassion.

3. Let all your works give you thanks, O Lord,
and let all the faithful bless you.
Let them speak of your might, O Lord, the glory of your kingdom.

4. The Lord is faithful in word and deed,
and always near, his name is holy.
Lifting up all those who fall, God raises up the lowly.

Text: Psalm 145:1-2, 8-9, 10-11, 13b-14; David Haas
Music: David Haas
© 1983, GIA Publications, Inc.

Psalm 145: Our God Is Compassion 122

Refrain

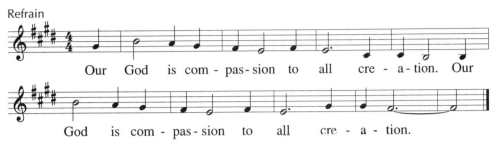

Our God is com - pas - sion to all cre - a - tion. Our
God is com - pas - sion to all cre - a - tion.

Verses

1. The Lord is grace and mercy, slow to anger, full of love.
   God is good to all creation; full of compassion.

2. Let all your works give thanks, O God. Let the faithful bless you.
   The eyes of all are filled with hope; you give them all they need.

3. The Lord is just in ev'ry way, full of love for all.
   God is near to those in need; who call out from their hearts

Text: Psalm 145; Jeanne Cotter
Music: Jeanne Cotter
© 1993, GIA Publications, Inc.

Psalm 146: Happy the Poor in Spirit 123

Refrain

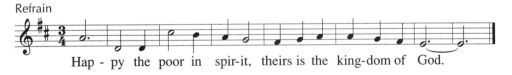

Hap - py the poor in spir-it, theirs is the king-dom of God.

Verses

1. Lord, you keep faith for ever, secure justice for the oppressed.
   You give food to all who are hungry. O Lord, you set captives free.

2. Lord, you open up blind eyes, and you raise up all those bowed down.
   The alien people are welcomed. The just, secure in your love.

3. Orphans, widows find comfort, but the wicked you take to their ruin.
   Your reign lasts for all generations, both now and for evermore.

Text: Psalm 146:7, 8-9, 8c-10; Thomas J. Porter
Music: Thomas J. Porter
© 1990, GIA Publications, Inc.

124　Psalm 146: Lord, Come and Save Us

Refrain

Lord, come and save us. Lord, come and
save us. Lord, come and save us.

Verses

1. For all my life I will sing to you, O ever faithful God.
   You fill the heavens with wondrous lights, the earth sings out your glory.

2. Put not your trust in those who rule, the mighty of this earth.
   Their breath shall fail, their power die, their plans shall fade and vanish.

3. You give your sight to all the blind, you raise up those bent low.
   Your heart is near to the broken ones, you welcome in the stranger.

4. Happy those who keep faith with you, securing justice for the oppressed,
   who give your food to each hungry heart, your freedom to each captive.

5. The weak and poor you sustain in love,
   the wicked ones you bring to destruction;
   for ever more shall your reign endure, to ev'ry generation.

Text: Psalm 146:3-4, 8-9, 6b-7, 8c-10; Marty Haugen, © 1987, GIA Publications, Inc.; refrain trans. © 1969, ICEL
Music: Marty Haugen, © 1987, GIA Publications, Inc.

125　Psalm 147: Bless the Lord, My Soul

Refrain

Bless the Lord, my soul, who heals the bro-ken-heart-ed.

Verses

1. Praise the Lord, O Jerusalem, chant praises to your God.
   The strength of God is your fortress sure, and blessed are your children.

2. All praise to you, O gracious God, your goodness fills the earth.
   You raise anew Jerusalem, and gather all your lost ones.

3. You heal the hurt and broken heart, you bind up ev'ry wound,
   you number all the stars of night and call each one by name.

4. The peace of God shall be your hope, God's finest wheat, your food,
   the word of God fills all the earth, as rapid as the whirlwind.

Text: Psalm 147:12-13, 1-2, 3-4, 14-15; Marty Haugen
Music: Marty Haugen
© 1987, GIA Publications, Inc.

Song at the Sea / Exodus 15   126

Refrain

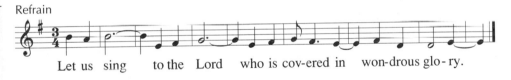

Let us sing   to the Lord   who is cov-ered in   won-drous glo-ry.

Verses

1. I will sing to the Lord, in glory triumphant;
   horse and rider are thrown to the sea.
   God of strength, of song, of salvation, God of mine, hear these praises.

2. My God is a warrior whose name is "The Lord."
   Pharoah's army is thrown to the sea.
   Your right hand is magnificent in pow'r,
   your right hand has crushed the enemy.

3. In your mercy you led the people you redeemed.
   You brought them to your sacred home.
   There you will plant them on the mountain that is yours.
   The Lord shall reign for ever!

Text: Exodus 15; Niamh O'Kelly-Fischer
Music: Niamh O'Kelly-Fischer
© 1992, GIA Publications, Inc.

127 Magnificat / Luke 1:46-55

Refrain

Pro - claim the great-ness of God; re - joice in God, my Sav - ior! Re - joice in God, my Sav-ior!

Verses

1. For he has favored his lowly one, and all shall call me blessed.
   The almighty has done great things for me, and holy is his name.

2. He favors those who fear his name, in ev'ry generation.
   He has shown the might and strength of his arm,
   and scattered the proud of heart.

3. He has cast the mighty from their thrones, and lifted up the lowly.
   He has filled the hungry with all good gifts, and sent the rich away.

4. He has helped his servant Israel, remembering his mercy.
   He promised his mercy to Abraham and his children for evermore.

Text: Luke 1:46-55; James J. Chepponis
Music: James J. Chepponis
© 1980, GIA Publications, Inc.

Holy Is Your Name / Luke 1:46-55   128

Refrain

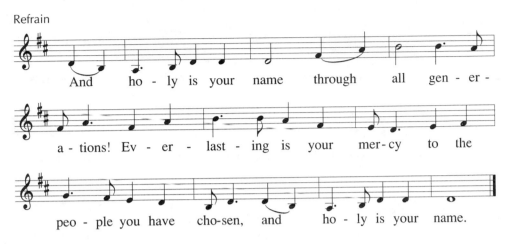

And ho - ly is your name through all gen - er -
a - tions! Ev - er - last - ing is your mer-cy to the
peo - ple you have cho-sen, and ho - ly is your name.

Verses

1. My soul is filled with joy as I sing to God my savior:
   you have looked upon your servant, you have visited your people.

2. I am lowly as a child, but I know from this day forward
   that my name will be remembered, for all will call me blessed.

3. I proclaim the pow'r of God, you do marvels for your servants;
   though you scatter the proud hearted, and destroy the might of princes.

4. To the hungry you give food, send the rich away empty.
   In your mercy you are mindful of the people you have chosen.

5. In your love you now fulfill what you promised to your people.
   I will praise you Lord, my savior, everlasting is your mercy.

Text: Luke 1:46-55, David Haas
Music: WILD MOUNTAIN THYME, Irregular; Irish traditional; arr. by David Haas
© 1989, GIA Publications, Inc.

129 Isaiah 12:2-3, 4, 6

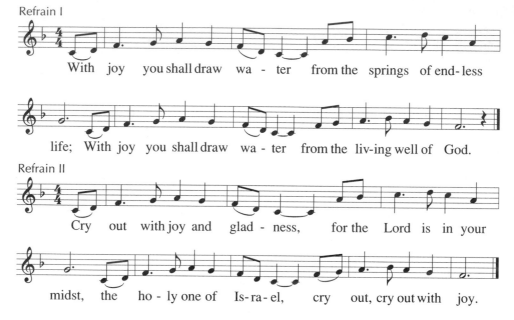

Refrain I

With joy you shall draw wa - ter from the springs of end-less life; With joy you shall draw wa - ter from the liv-ing well of God.

Refrain II

Cry out with joy and glad - ness, for the Lord is in your midst, the ho - ly one of Is-ra-el, cry out, cry out with joy.

Verses

1. God indeed is my Savior, I will never be afraid,
   my strength and courage is the Lord, my Savior and my song.

2. Give thanks and praise the name of God, sing out to all the earth
   the wondrous deeds that God has done, our Savior and our song.

3. Shout with joy, O Zion, for dwelling in your midst
   is the Holy One of Israel, your Savior and your song.

Text: Isaiah 12:2-3, 4, 6; Marty Haugen
Music: Marty Haugen; refrain II adapt. by Diana Kodner
© 1988, 1994, GIA Publications, Inc.

Song of the Three Children / Daniel 3:52-56 130

Refrain

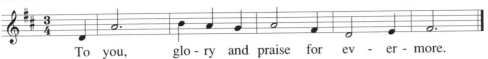

To you, glo - ry and praise for ev - er - more.

Verses

1. You are blest, Lord God of our ancestors.

2. Blest be your glorious holy name.

3. You are blest in the temple of your glory.

4. You are blest on the throne of your kingdom.

5. You are blest who gaze into the depths.

6. You are blest who sit above the cherubim.

7. You are blest in the firmament of heaven.

Text: Daniel 3:52, 53, 54, 55, 56; © 1963, The Grail, GIA Publications, Inc., agent
Music: Michel Guimont, © 1994, GIA Publications, Inc.

The Order of Mass

Each church gathers on the Lord's Day to listen to the Scriptures, to offer prayers, to give thanks and praise to God while recalling God's gifts in creation and saving deeds in Jesus, and to share in holy communion.

In these rites of word and eucharist, the Church keeps Sunday as the Lord's Day, the day of creation and resurrection, the "eighth day" when the fullness of God's kingdom is anticipated. The Mass or eucharistic celebration of the Christian community has rites of gathering, of word, of eucharist, of dismissal. All those who gather constitute the assembly. One member of this assembly who has been ordained to the presbyterate or episcopate, the priesthood, leads the opening and closing prayers and the eucharistic prayer, and presides over the whole assembly. A member ordained to the diaconate may assist, read the gospel, and preach. Other members of the assembly are chosen and trained for various ministries: These are the readers, servers, ushers, musicians, communion ministers. All of these assist the assembly. It is the assembly itself, all those present, that does the liturgy.

The Order of Mass which follows is familiar to all who regularly join in this assembly. It is learned through repetition. This Order of Mass leaves many decisions to the local community and others are determined by the various seasons of the liturgical year.

INTRODUCTORY RITES

The rites which precede the liturgy of the word assist the assembly to gather as a community. They prepare that community to listen to the Scriptures and to celebrate the eucharist together. The procession and entrance song are ways of expressing the unity and spirit of the assembly.

GREETING

All make the sign of the cross.

    Priest: In the name of the Father, and of the Son, and of the Holy Spirit.

    Assembly: **Amen.**

After the sign of the cross one of the greetings is given.

A

Priest: The grace of our Lord Jesus Christ and the love of God and the fellowship of the Holy Spirit be with you all.

Assembly: **And also with you.**

B

Priest: The grace and peace of God our Father and the Lord Jesus Christ be with you.

Assembly: **Blessed be God, the Father of our Lord Jesus Christ.**
or: **And also with you.**

C

Priest: The Lord be with you. (*Bishop:* Peace be with you.)

Assembly: **And also with you.**

132 BLESSING AND SPRINKLING OF HOLY WATER

On Sundays, especially during the season of Easter, instead of the penitential rite below, the blessing and sprinkling of holy water may be done. The following or another appropriate song is sung as the water is sprinkled.

Refrain

If we have died to our-selves in Je-sus, then we shall a - rise to

new life in him. Al - le - lu-ia, al - le-lu - ia!

Verses

1. We   are   fire   and wa-ter,   we   are   sym - bol   and
2. In   the   wa - ter   we seek him,   in   the   well-spring   of
3. In   the   fire   we seek him,   in   the   hun - gers   and
4. In   our   dy - ing   and ris-ing,   we shall   fol - low where
5. Flow-ing   out   of   the des-ert,   roll - ing   down from   the
6. Rain-ing down from the heav-ens,   spring-ing   up   from   the
7. Gift   of   love   and of   mer-cy,   giv - en   free - ly   to

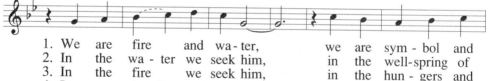

sign   of   grace,   we   are   the   mys - t'ry,
all   that   lives,   all   who   are   thirst - y,
pains   we   bear,   hope   for   the   hope - less,
he   has   gone,   pil - grims   and   lov - ers,
moun - tain   side,   up   from   with - in   you,
dri - est   earth,   sim - ple   and   ho - ly,
all   who   thirst,   gen - tle   and   yield - ing,

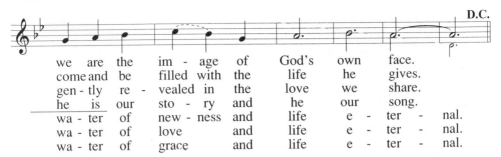

we	are	the	im - age	of	God's	own	face.	
come and	be		filled with	the	life	he	gives.	
gen - tly	re -	vealed in	the	love	we	share.		
he	is	our	sto - ry	and	he	our	song.	
wa - ter	of	new - ness	and	life	e -	ter -	nal.	
wa - ter	of	love	and	life	e -	ter -	nal.	
wa - ter	of	grace	and	life	e -	ter -	nal.	

Text: *Mass of Creation,* Marty Haugen
Music: *Mass of Creation,* Marty Haugen
© 1984, GIA Publications, Inc.

PENITENTIAL RITE

133

The priest invites all to be mindful of their sins and of the great mercy of God.
After a time of silence, one of the following forms is used.

A | *Assembly:* **I confess to almighty God,**
and to you, my brothers and sisters,
that I have sinned through my own fault
in my thoughts and in my words,
in what I have done,
and in what I have failed to do;
and I ask blessed Mary, ever virgin,
all the angels and saints,
and you, my brothers and sisters,
to pray for me to the Lord our God.

B | *Priest:* Lord, we have sinned against you:
Lord, have mercy.

Assembly: **Lord, have mercy.**

Priest: Lord, show us your mercy and love.

Assembly: **And grant us your salvation.**

C | *The priest or another minister makes a series of invocations according*
to the following pattern.

Priest: (Invocation)
Lord, have mercy.

Assembly: **Lord, have mercy.**

Priest: (Invocation)
Christ, have mercy.

Assembly: **Christ, have mercy.**

Priest: (Invocation)
Lord, have mercy.

Assembly: **Lord, have mercy.**

The penitential rite always concludes:

> *Priest:* May almighty God have mercy on us, forgive us our sins, and bring us to everlasting life.
>
> *Assembly:* **Amen.**

134 KYRIE

Unless form C of the penitential rite has been used, the Kyrie follows.

Refrain

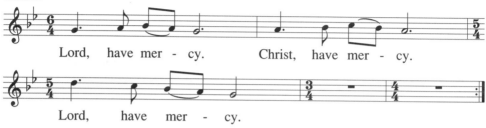

Lord, have mer - cy. Christ, have mer - cy.

Lord, have mer - cy.

Music: *Mass of Creation,* Marty Haugen, © 1984, GIA Publications, Inc.

135 GLORIA

The Gloria is omitted during Advent, Lent, and most weekdays.

Refrain

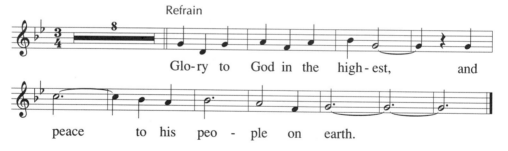

Glo-ry to God in the high-est, and

peace to his peo - ple on earth.

Verses

1. Lord God, heavenly King, almighty God and Father,
   we worship you, we give you thanks,
   we praise you for your glory.

2. Lord Jesus Christ, only Son of the Father,
   Lord God, Lamb of God,
   you take away the sin of the world: have mercy on us;
   you are seated at the right hand of the Father:
   receive our prayer.

3. For you alone are the Holy One,
   you alone are the Lord,
   you alone are the Most High, Jesus Christ,
   with the Holy Spirit,
   in the glory of God, the Father. Amen! Amen!

Music: *Mass of Creation*, Marty Haugen, © 1984, GIA Publications, Inc.

OPENING PRAYER   136

After the invitation from the priest, all pray for a while. The introductory rites conclude with the proper opening prayer and the Amen of the assembly.

LITURGY OF THE WORD   137

When the Church assembles, the book containing the Scriptures (Lectionary) is opened and all listen as the readers and deacon (or priest) read from the places assigned. The first reading is normally from the Hebrew Scriptures (Old Testament), the second from the letters of the New Testament, and the third from the Book of Gospels. Over a three year cycle, the Church reads through the letters and gospels and a portion of the Hebrew Scriptures. During the Sundays of Ordinary Time, the letters and gospels are read in order, each Sunday continuing near the place where the previous Sunday's readings ended. During Advent/Christmas and Lent/Easter, the readings are those which are traditional and appropriate to these seasons.

The Church listens to and—through the weeks and years—is shaped by the Scriptures. Those who have gathered for the Sunday liturgy are to give their full attention to the words of the reader. A time of silence and reflection follows each of the two readings. After the first reading, this reflection continues in the singing of the psalm. A homily, bringing together the Scriptures and the life of the community, follows the gospel. The liturgy of the word concludes with the creed, the dismissal of the catechumens and the prayers of intercession. In the latter, the assembly continues its constant work of recalling and praying for the universal Church and all those in need.

This reading and hearing of the word—simple things that they are—are the foundation of the liturgical celebration. The public reading of the Scriptures and the rituals which surround this—silence and psalm and acclamation, posture and gesture, preaching and litany of intercession—gather the Church generation after generation. They gather and sustain and gradually make of us the image of Christ.

READING I

In conclusion:

      Reader: The word of the Lord.
      Assembly: **Thanks be to God.**

After a period of silence, the responsorial psalm is sung.

READING II

In conclusion:

> *Reader:* The word of the Lord.
>
> *Assembly:* **Thanks be to God.**

A time of silence follows the reading.

138 GOSPEL

Before the gospel, an acclamation is sung.

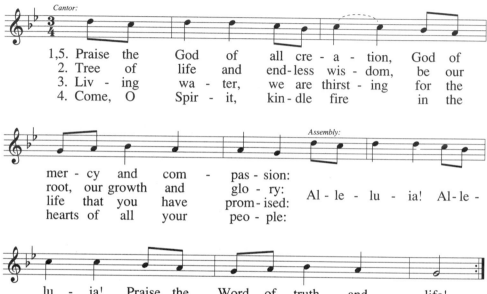

1,5. Praise the God of all cre - a - tion, God of
2. Tree of life and end-less wis - dom, be our
3. Liv - ing wa - ter, we are thirst - ing for the
4. Come, O Spir - it, kin-dle fire in the

mer - cy and com - pas - sion:
root, our growth and glo - ry:
life that you have prom-ised: Al - le - lu - ia! Al-le-
hearts of all your peo - ple:

lu - ia! Praise the Word of truth and life!

Text: *Mass of Creation*, Marty Haugen
Music: *Mass of Creation*, Marty Haugen
© 1984, GIA Publications, Inc.

During Lent one of the following acclamations replaces the alleluia.

| A |

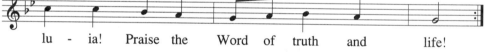

Praise to you, Lord   Je-sus Christ,   king of end-less   glo-ry!

Music: *Mass of Creation*, Marty Haugen, © 1984, GIA Publications, Inc.

Or:

| B | **Praise and honor to you, Lord Jesus Christ!**

| C | **Glory and praise to you, Lord Jesus Christ!**

| D | **Glory to you, Word of God, Lord Jesus Christ!**

Deacon (or priest):   The Lord be with you.

Assembly: **And also with you.**

Deacon: A reading from the holy gospel according to N.

Assembly: **Glory to you, Lord.**

After the reading:

Deacon: The gospel of the Lord.

Assembly: **Praise to you, Lord Jesus Christ.**

HOMILY

PROFESSION OF FAITH   139

We believe in one God,
   the Father, the Almighty,
   maker of heaven and earth,
   of all that is seen and unseen.

We believe in one Lord, Jesus Christ,
   the only Son of God,
   eternally begotten of the Father,
   God from God, Light from Light,
   true God from true God,
   begotten, not made, one in Being with the Father.
   Through him all things were made.
   For us men and for our salvation he came down from heaven:

All bow at the following words up to: and became man.

   by the power of the Holy Spirit
      he was born of the Virgin Mary, and became man.
   For our sake he was crucified under Pontius Pilate;
      he suffered, died, and was buried.
      On the third day he rose again
      in fulfillment of the Scriptures;
      he ascended into heaven
      and is seated at the right hand of the Father.
   He will come again in glory to judge the living and the dead,
      and his kingdom will have no end.

We believe in the Holy Spirit, the Lord, the giver of life,
   who proceeds from the Father and the Son.
   With the Father and the Son he is worshiped and glorified.
   He has spoken through the Prophets.
   We believe in one holy catholic and apostolic Church.
   We acknowledge one baptism for the forgiveness of sins.
   We look for the resurrection of the dead,
      and the life of the world to come. Amen.

140 *At Masses with children, the Apostles' Creed may be used:*

We believe in God, the Father almighty,
    creator of heaven and earth.

We believe in Jesus Christ, his only Son, our Lord.
    He was conceived by the power of the Holy Spirit
        and born of the Virgin Mary.
    He suffered under Pontius Pilate,
        was crucified, died, and was buried.
    He descended to the dead.
    On the third day he arose again.
    He ascended into heaven,
        and is seated at the right hand of the Father.
    He will come again to judge the living and the dead.

We believe in the Holy Spirit,
    the holy catholic Church,
    the communion of saints,
    the forgiveness of sins,
    the resurrection of the body,
    and the life everlasting. Amen.

141 GENERAL INTERCESSIONS

The people respond to each petition as follows, or according to local practice.

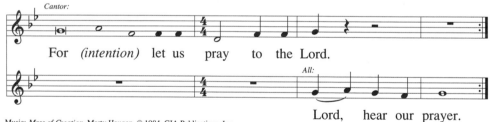

Music: *Mass of Creation*, Marty Haugen, © 1984, GIA Publications, Inc.

LITURGY OF THE EUCHARIST 142

To celebrate the eucharist means to give God thanks and praise. When the table has been prepared with the bread and wine, the assembly joins the priest in remembering the gracious gifts of God in creation and God's saving deeds. The center of this is the paschal mystery, the death of our Lord Jesus Christ which destroyed the power of death and his rising which brings us life. That mystery into which we were baptized we proclaim each Sunday at the eucharist. It is the very shape of Christian life. We find this in the simple bread and wine which stir our remembering and draw forth our prayer of thanksgiving. "Fruit of the earth and work of human hands," the bread and wine become our holy communion in the body and blood of the Lord. We eat and drink and so proclaim that we belong to one another and to the Lord.

The members of the assembly quietly prepare themselves even as the table is prepared. The priest then invites all to lift up their hearts and join in the eucharistic prayer. All do this by giving their full attention and by singing the acclamations from the "Holy, holy" to the great "Amen." Then the assembly joins in the Lord's Prayer, the sign of peace and the "Lamb of God" litany which accompanies the breaking of bread. Ministers of communion assist the assembly to share the bread and wine. A time of silence and prayer concludes the liturgy of the eucharist.

PREPARATION OF THE ALTAR AND THE GIFTS
Bread and wine are brought to the table and the deacon or priest prepares these gifts. If there is no music, the prayers may be said aloud, and all may respond: **"Blessed be God for ever."** *The priest then invites all to pray.*

> *Assembly:* **May the Lord accept the sacrifice at your hands**
> **for the praise and glory of his name,**
> **for our good, and the good of all his Church.**

The priest says the prayer over the gifts and all respond: Amen.

EUCHARISTIC PRAYER 143
The central prayer of the Mass begins with this greeting and invitation between priest and assembly.

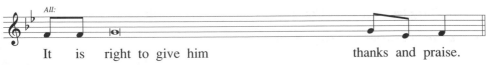

Music: *Mass of Creation,* Marty Haugen, © 1984, GIA Publications, Inc.

144 *The Sanctus acclamation is sung to conclude the introduction to the eucharistic prayer.*

Ho-ly, ho-ly, ho-ly Lord, God of pow-er, God of might, heav-en and earth are full of your glo-ry. Ho-san-na in the high-est. Bless-ed is he who comes in the name of the Lord. Ho-san-na in the high-est, ho-san-na in the high - est.

Music: *Mass of Creation,* Marty Haugen, © 1984, GIA Publications, Inc.

145 *One of the following acclamations follows the priest's invitation: "Let us proclaim the mystery of faith."*

A

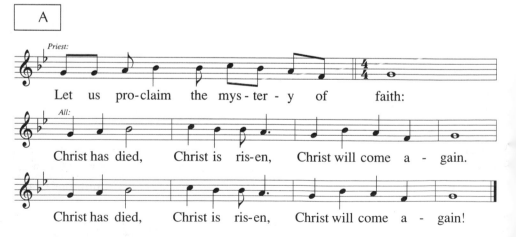

Priest: Let us pro-claim the mys-ter-y of faith:

All: Christ has died, Christ is ris-en, Christ will come a - gain.

Christ has died, Christ is ris-en, Christ will come a - gain!

Music: *Mass of Creation,* Marty Haugen, © 1984, GIA Publications, Inc.

B

Music: *Mass of Creation*, Marty Haugen, ©1990, GIA Publications, Inc.

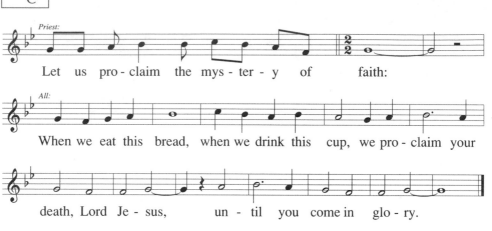

When we eat this bread, when we drink this cup, we proclaim your death, Lord Jesus, until you come in glory.

Music: *Mass of Creation*, Marty Haugen, © 1993, GIA Publications, Inc.

Lord, by your cross and resurrection you have set us free.

You are the Savior of the world. You are the Savior of the world.

Music: *Mass of Creation*, Marty Haugen, © 1993, GIA Publications, Inc.

The eucharistic prayer concludes: **146**

Priest: Through him, with him, in him, in the unity of the Holy Spirit, all glory and honor is yours, almighty Father, for ever and ever.

A - men, a - men, a - men!

A - men, a - men, a - men!

Music: *Mass of Creation*, Marty Haugen, © 1984, GIA Publications, Inc.

147 COMMUNION RITE

The priest invites all to join in the Lord's Prayer.

Our Fa - ther, who art in heav-en,

hal - low-ed be thy name; thy king-dom come; thy

will be done on earth as it is in heav - en.

Give us this day our dai - ly bread; and for - give us our tres-pass-es

as we for - give those who tres - pass a - gainst us; and

lead us not in - to temp - ta - tion, but de -

liv - er us from e - vil.

Priest: Deliver us, Lord...
for the coming our Savior, Jesus Christ.

All:

For the king-dom, the pow - er, and the glo - ry are yours,

now and for ev - er - more. A - men.

Music: *Mass of Creation,* Marty Haugen, © 1984, GIA Publications, Inc.

Following the prayer "Lord, Jesus Christ," the priest invites all to exchange **148**
the sign of peace.

> *Priest:* The peace of the Lord be with you always.
> *Assembly:* **And also with you.**

All exchange a sign of peace. **149**

Then the bread is solemnly broken and the bread and wine are prepared for holy communion. The litany "Lamb of God" is sung during the breaking of the bread.

1. Je-sus, Lamb of
2. Je-sus, Bread of
3. Je-sus, Prince of

God,
Life, you take a-way the sins of the world: have
Peace,

mer-cy on us. Je-sus, Lamb of God; you

take a-way the sins of the world: grant us your peace.

Music: *Mass of Creation*, Marty Haugen, © 1984, GIA Publications, Inc.

The priest then invites all to share in holy communion. **150**

> *Priest:* This is the Lamb of God...his supper.
> *Assembly:* **Lord, I am not worthy to receive you,**
> **but only say the word and I shall be healed.**
> *Minister of communion:* The body (blood) of Christ.
> *Communicant:* **Amen.**

A song or psalm is ordinarily sung during communion. After communion, a time of silence is observed or a song of thanksgiving is sung. The rite concludes with the prayer after communion to which all respond: **Amen.**

151 CONCLUDING RITE

The liturgy of word and eucharist ends very simply. There may be announcements of events and concerns for the community, then the priest gives a blessing and the assembly is dismissed.

GREETING AND BLESSING

> *Priest:* The Lord be with you.
>
> *Assembly:* **And also with you.**

Optional

> *When the bishop blesses the people he adds the following:*
>
> *Bishop:* Blessed be the name of the Lord.
>
> *Assembly:* **Now and for ever.**
>
> *Bishop:* Our help is in the name of the Lord.
>
> *Assembly:* **Who made heaven and earth.**

The blessing may be in a simple or solemn form. All respond to the blessing or to each part of the blessing: **Amen.**

DISMISSAL

The deacon or priest then dismisses the assembly:

Go in the peace of Christ.
or: The Mass is end - ed, go in peace. Thanks be to God.
or: Go in peace to love and serve the Lord.

Setting One

152

KYRIE ELEISON

Ky-ri-e e-le-i-son. Ky-ri-e e-le-i-son.

Chri-ste e-le-i-son. Chri-ste e-le-i-son.

Ky-ri-e e-le-i-son. Ky-ri-e e-le-i-son.

Music: *Mass of Light*, David Haas, © 1987, GIA Publications, Inc.

153 GLORIA

Refrain

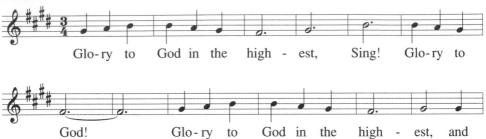

Glo-ry to God in the high - est, Sing! Glo-ry to God! Glo-ry to God in the high - est, and peace to his peo-ple on earth!

Verses

1. Lord God, heavenly King,
   almighty God and Father,
   we worship you, we give you thanks,
   we praise you for your glory!

2. Lord Jesus Christ, only Son of the Father,
   Lord God, Lamb of God,
   you take away the sin of the world:
   have mercy on us;
   you are seated at the right hand of the Father:
   receive our prayer!

3. For you alone are the Holy One,
   you alone are the Lord,
   the Most High, Jesus Christ,
   with the Holy Spirit,
   in the glory of God the Father!

Music: *Mass of Light*, David Haas, © 1988, GIA Publications, Inc.

154 ALLELUIA

Cantor or choir, then all:

Al - le - lu - ia! Al - le - lu - ia! Al - le - lu - ia!

Music: *Mass of Light*, David Haas, © 1988, GIA Publications, Inc.

GOSPEL ACCLAMATION 155

Glo-ry to you, O Word of God, Lord Je-sus Christ!

Music: *Mass of Light*, David Haas, © 1988, GIA Publications, Inc.

PREFACE DIALOG 156

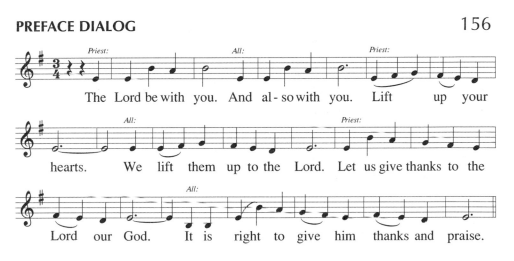

The Lord be with you. And al-so with you. Lift up your

hearts. We lift them up to the Lord. Let us give thanks to the

Lord our God. It is right to give him thanks and praise.

Music: *Mass of Light*, David Haas, © 1988, GIA Publications, Inc.

SANCTUS 157

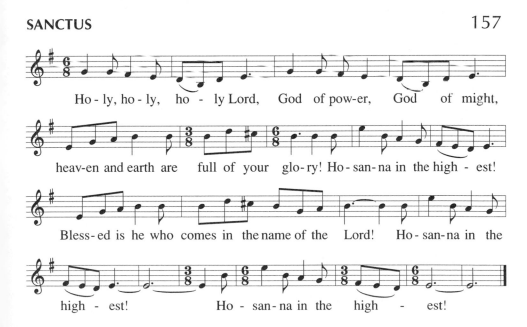

Ho-ly, ho-ly, ho-ly Lord, God of pow-er, God of might,

heav-en and earth are full of your glo-ry! Ho-san-na in the high - est!

Bless-ed is he who comes in the name of the Lord! Ho-san-na in the

high - est! Ho - san-na in the high - est!

Music: *Mass of Light*, David Haas, © 1988, GIA Publications, Inc.

158 EUCHARISTIC ACCLAMATION I (OPTIONAL)*

Ho - san - na in the high - est!

Music: *Mass of Light*, David Haas, © 1988, GIA Publications, Inc.

As in the Eucharistic Prayers for Masses with Children.

159 MEMORIAL ACCLAMATION

Dy- ing you de - stroyed our death, ris- ing you re - stored our life.

Lord Je - sus come! Lord Je - sus come in glo - ry!

Music: *Mass of Light*, David Haas, © 1988, GIA Publications, Inc.

160 EUCHARISTIC ACCLAMATION II (OPTIONAL)

Hear us, hear us. Hear us, hear us.

Music: *Mass of Light*, David Haas, © 1988, GIA Publications, Inc.

161 AMEN

A - men, a - men! A - men, a - men!

Music: *Mass of Light*, David Haas, © 1988, GIA Publications, Inc.

AGNUS DEI

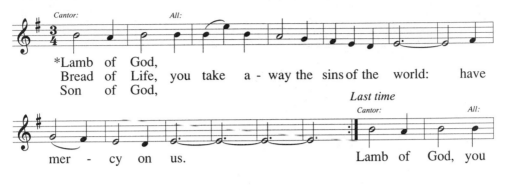

*Lamb of God,
Bread of Life, you take a - way the sins of the world: have
Son of God,

mer - cy on us.   Lamb of God, you

take a - way the sins of the world   grant us your peace.

*"Lamb of God" is sung the first and last times. Alternate intervening invocations include: "Saving Cup," "Hope for all," "Prince of Peace," "Wine of Peace," etc.

Music: *Mass of Light*, David Haas, © 1988, GIA Publications, Inc

Setting Two

163 KYRIE

Ky - ri - e   e - le - i - son,   Chri - ste   e - le - i - son,

Ky - ri - e   e - le - i - son.

Music: *Mass of Remembrance;* Marty Haugen, © 1987, GIA Publications, Inc.

164 GLORIA

Refrain

Priest or cantor:

Glo - ry to God in the high - est,   and peace to his peo - ple on   earth.

All:

Glo - ry to God in the high - est,   and peace to his peo - ple on   earth.

Verses

Choir: Lord God, heavenly King, almighty God and Father,
       we worship you, we give you thanks,
       we praise you for your glory.
                All sing entire refrain

Lord Jesus Christ, only Son of the Father,
Lord God, Lamb of God, you take away the sin of the world:
have mercy on us;
you are seated at the right hand of the Father:
receive our prayer.
All sing entire refrain

For you alone are the Holy One, you alone are the Lord,
you alone are the Most High, Jesus Christ,
with the Holy Spirit, in the glory of God the Father. Amen.
All sing entire refrain

Music: *Mass of Remembrance*, Marty Haugen, © 1987, GIA Publications, Inc.

ALLELUIA 165

Music: *Mass of Remembrance;* Marty Haugen, © 1987, GIA Publications, Inc.

PREFACE DIALOG 166

Music: *Mass of Remembrance*, Marty Haugen, © 1987, GIA Publications, Inc.

167 EUCHARISTIC ACCLAMATION IA (OPTIONAL)*
As in the Eucharistic Prayers for Masses with Children.

Praise, thanks and glo-ry be to you, O God!

Music: *Mass of Remembrance*, Marty Haugen, © 1987, GIA Publications, Inc.

168 SANCTUS

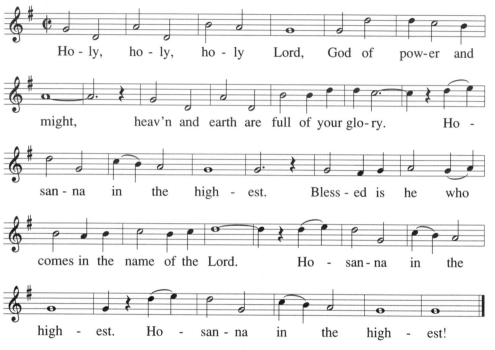

Ho - ly, ho - ly, ho - ly Lord, God of pow-er and might, heav'n and earth are full of your glo-ry. Ho - san - na in the high - est. Bless-ed is he who comes in the name of the Lord. Ho - san - na in the high - est. Ho - san - na in the high - est!

Music: *Mass of Remembrance;* Marty Haugen, © 1987, GIA Publications, Inc.

169 EUCHARISTIC ACCLAMATION IB (OPTIONAL)

Praise, thanks and glo-ry be to you, O Christ!

Music: *Mass of Remembrance;* Marty Haugen, © 1987, GIA Publications, Inc.

MEMORIAL ACCLAMATION 170

When we eat this bread, when we drink this cup, we pro-claim your death, Lord Je-sus, un-til you come, un-til you come in glo - ry!

Music: *Mass of Remembrance*, Marty Haugen, © 1987, GIA Publications, Inc.

EUCHARISTIC ACCLAMATION II (OPTIONAL) 171

We re - mem-ber how you loved us to your death, and still we cel-e-brate, for you are with us here; and we be-lieve that we will see you when you come in your glo-ry, Lord. We re - mem - ber, we cel-e-brate, we be - lieve.

Music: *Mass of Remembrance*, Marty Haugen, © 1987, GIA Publications, Inc.

EUCHARISTIC ACCLAMATION III (OPTIONAL) 172

Hear us, O Lord; hear us, O Lord.

Music: *Mass of Remembrance*, Marty Haugen, © 1987, GIA Publications, Inc.

173 AMEN

Al - le - lu - ia, a - men!
*Praise to you, Lord, a - men!

Al - le - lu - ia, a - men!
Praise to you, Lord, a - men!

* During Lent

Music: *Mass of Remembrance*, Marty Haugen, © 1987, GIA Publications, Inc.

174 AGNUS DEI

1. *Lamb of God,
2. Prince of Peace, you take a-way the sins of the world: have mer-cy on
3. Bread of Life,

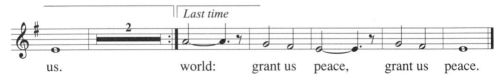

us.　world:　grant us　peace,　grant us　peace.

* "Lamb of God" is sung the first and last times. Alternate intervening invocations
include: Ancient Cup, Bread of Peace, Wine of Hope, Lord of Lords.

Music: *Mass of Remembrance*, Marty Haugen, © 1987, GIA Publications, Inc.

Setting Three

Music: *The Psallite Mass*, Michael Joncas, © 1988, GIA Publications, Inc.

176 GLORIA

Refrain I

Glo-ri-a in ex - cel - sis De-o, glo-ri-a in ex - cel - sis De-o,

glo- ri- a in ex - cel - sis De-o, et in ter- ra pax.

Verses

Choir: Glory to God in the highest, and peace to his people on earth.
Glory to God in the highest, and peace to his people on earth.
Refrain I

Lord, God, heavenly King, almighty God and Father,
we worship you, we give you thanks, we praise you for your glory.
Refrain I

Lord Jesus Christ, only Son of the Father,
Lord Jesus Christ, Lord God, Lamb of God,
Refrain II

Refrain II

Do-mi-ne Je - su Chri- ste, Do-mi-ne Je - su Chri - ste,

mi - se- re - re no - bis, mi - se- re - re.

Verses

You take away the sin of the world: have mercy on us;
you are seated at the right hand of the Father: receive our prayer.
Refrain II

For you alone are the Holy One, you alone are the Lord,
you alone are the Most High, Jesus Christ, *(begin Refrain I)*
with the Holy Spirit, with the Holy Spirit
in the glory of God the Father. Amen.

Music: *The Psallite Mass*, Michael Joncas, © 1988, GIA Publications, Inc.

SANCTUS

177

Ho-ly, ho - ly, ho - ly.

Ho-ly, ho - ly, ho - ly. Ho-san-na,

ho-san-na in the high - est! Ho - ly, ho - ly,

ho - ly. Ho-ly, ho - ly, ho - ly.

Ho-san-na, ho-san-na in the high - est!

MEMORIAL ACCLAMATION

178

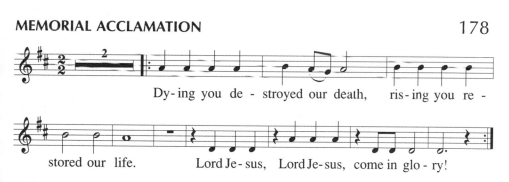

Dy-ing you de - stroyed our death, ris-ing you re -

stored our life. Lord Je-sus, Lord Je-sus, come in glo - ry!

179 AMEN

A - men, a - men, a - men.

Al-le-lu - ia, al-le-lu - ia, al-le-lu - ia!

Music: *The Psallite Mass*, Michael Joncas, © 1988, GIA Publications, Inc.

180 AGNUS DEI

First Invocation

Cantor: Je - sus, Lamb of God, *Assembly:* you take a-way the sins of the world:

have mer - cy, have mer - cy on us.

Invocations

Cantor:
1. Bread of life and sav - ing cup,
2. King of kings and Lord of lords, *All:* you take a - way the
3. Lov - ing Sav - ior, Prince of peace,

sins of the world: have mer - cy, have mer - cy on us.

Last Invocation

Cantor: Je - sus, Lamb of God, *Assembly:* you take a-way the sins of the world:

have mer - cy, and grant us your peace.

Music: *The Psallite Mass*, Michael Joncas, © 1988, GIA Publications, Inc.

Setting Four

O   Lord,   have   mercy,
Se - ñor,   ten   pie - dad,

O   Christ,   have   mer - cy,   O
Cri - sto,   ten   pie - dad,   Se -

Lord,   have   mer - cy   on   us,   O
ñor,   ten   pie - dad de no - so - tros,   Se -

Lord,   have   mer - cy   on   us.
ñor,   ten   pie - dad de no - so - tros.

Music: *Mass for the Life of the World,* Joe Camacho, David Haas; acc. by Rob Glover, © 1993, GIA Publications, Inc.

182 GLORIA / GLORIA A DIOS

Refrain

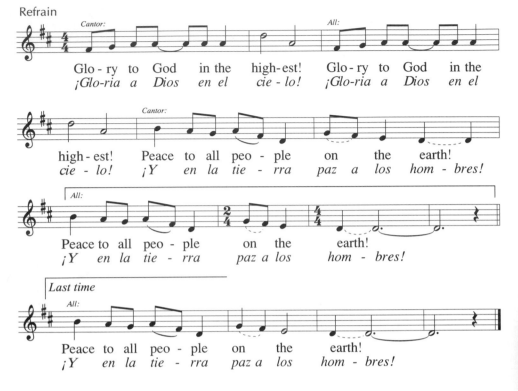

Glo - ry to God in the high-est! Glo - ry to God in the
¡Glo-ria a Dios en el cie - lo! ¡Glo-ria a Dios en el

high - est! Peace to all peo - ple on the earth!
cie - lo! ¡Y en la tie - rra paz a los hom - bres!

Peace to all peo - ple on the earth!
¡Y en la tie - rra paz a los hom - bres!

Last time

Peace to all peo - ple on the earth!
¡Y en la tie - rra paz a los hom - bres!

Verses

1. Lord God, heavenly King,
   almighty God and Father,
   we worship you, we give you thanks,
   we praise you for your glory!

2. Lord Jesus Christ, only Son of the Father,
   Lord God, Lamb of God,
   you take away the sin of the world:
   have mercy on us;
   you are seated at the right hand of the Father:
   receive our prayer.

3. For you alone are the Holy One,
   you alone are the Lord, you alone are the Most High, Jesus Christ,
   with the Holy Spirit, in the glory of God,
   in the glory of God the Father!

Music: *Mass for the Life of the World,* David Haas; acc. by Rob Glover, © 1993, GIA Publications, Inc.

ALLELUIA / ALELUYA 183

Cantor, then all:

Al - le - lu - ia, al - le - lu - ia, al - le - lu -
¡A - le - lu - ya, a - le - lu - ya, a - le - lu -

ia! Al - le - lu - ia, al - le - lu - ia,
ya! ¡A - le - lu - ya, a - le - lu - ya,

al - le - lu - ia!
a - le - lu - ya!

Music: *Mass for the Life of the World,* David Haas, arr. by Rob Glover, © 1993, GIA Publications, Inc.

O LORD, HEAR OUR PRAYER / SEÑOR, OYENOS 184

O Lord, hear our prayer; O
Se - ñor, ó - ye - nos; Se -

Lord, hear our prayer; O Lord, hear our prayer;
ñor, ó - ye - nos; Se - ñor, ó - ye - nos;

To repeat *To end*

O Lord, hear our prayer; O
Se - ñor, ó - ye - nos; Se -

Music: *Mass for the Life of the World,* David Haas, arr. by Rob Glover, © 1993, GIA Publications, Inc.

185 OSTINATO 1 (OPTIONAL)

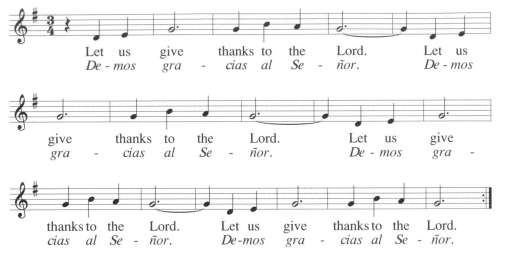

Let us give thanks to the Lord. Let us
De - mos gra - cias al Se - ñor. De - mos

give thanks to the Lord. Let us give
gra - cias al Se - ñor. De - mos gra -

thanks to the Lord. Let us give thanks to the Lord.
cias al Se - ñor. De - mos gra - cias al Se - ñor.

Music: *Mass for the Life of the World,* David Haas; arr. by Rob Glover, © 1993, GIA Publications, Inc.

186 ACCLAMATION 1: SANCTUS

Ho - ly, ho - ly, ho-ly Lord, God of pow'r, God of
San - to, San - to es el Se - ñor, e - res Dios del U - ni -

might, heav - en and earth are full of your glo - ry,
ver - so. Lle - nos es - tán el cie - lo_y la tie - rra de tu glo - ria.

Ho - san - na in the high - est! Blest is he who
¡Ho - san - na en el cie - lo! Ben - di - to él que

comes in the name of the Lord. Ho - san -
vie - ne en nom - bre del Se - ñor. ¡Ho - san -

na! Ho - san - na in the high - est!
na! ¡Ho - san - na en el cie - lo!

Music: *Mass for the Life of the World,* David Haas, arr. by Rob Glover, © 1993, GIA Publications, Inc.

OSTINATO 2 / ACCLAMATION 2 (OPTIONAL)   187

Ho-ly,   ho - ly, ho - ly   Lord.   Ho - ly,   ho -
San-to,   *san - to   es   el   Se - ñor.*   *San-to,*   *san - to*

ly, ho - ly   Lord.   Ho - ly,   ho -   ly, ho - ly   Lord.
es   el   Se - ñor.   *San-to,*   *san - to   es   el   Se - ñor.*

Ho - ly,   ho - ly, ho - ly   Lord.   Ho -   san -
San-to,   *san - to   es   el   Se - ñor.*   *¡Ho -   san -*

na!   Ho - san - na   in   the   high - est!
na!   ¡Ho - san - na   en   el   cie - lo!

Music: *Mass for the Life of the World,* David Haas, arr. by Rob Glover, © 1993, GIA Publications, Inc.

OSTINATO 3 (OPTIONAL)   188

(Hum)

Music: *Mass for the Life of the World,* David Haas, arr. by Rob Glover, © 1993, GIA Publications, Inc.

189 **ACCLAMATION 3: CHRIST HAS DIED**

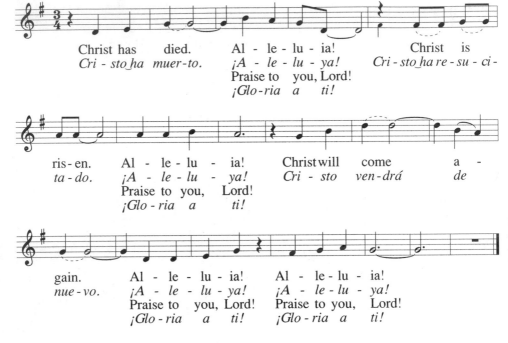

Christ has died.
Cri - sto_ha muer-to.
¡A - le - lu - ya!
Praise to you, Lord!
¡Glo-ria a ti!
Al - le - lu - ia!
Christ is
Cri - sto_ha re - su - ci-

ris- en.
ta - do.
Al - le - lu - ia!
¡A - le - lu - ya!
Praise to you, Lord!
¡Glo - ria a ti!
Christ will come a -
Cri - sto ven-drá de

gain.
nue - vo.
Al - le - lu - ia!
¡A - le - lu - ya!
Praise to you, Lord!
¡Glo - ria a ti!
Al - le - lu - ia!
¡A - le - lu - ya!
Praise to you, Lord!
¡Glo - ria a ti!

Music: *Mass for the Life of the World*, David Haas, arr. by Rob Glover, © 1993, GIA Publications, Inc.

190 **OSTINATO 4 (OPTIONAL)**

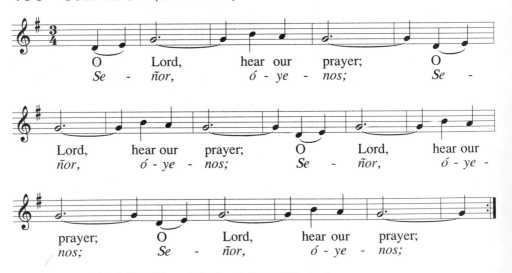

O Lord, hear our prayer; O
Se - ñor, ó - ye - nos; Se -

Lord, hear our prayer; O Lord, hear our
ñor, ó - ye - nos; Se - ñor, ó - ye -

prayer; O Lord, hear our prayer;
nos; Se - ñor, ó - ye - nos;

Music: *Mass for the Life of the World*, David Haas, arr. by Rob Glover, © 1993, GIA Publications, Inc.

ACCLAMATION 4

Al - le - lu - ia!
A - men! ¡A - le - lu - ya! A -
¡A - mén! Praise to you, Lord! ¡A -
¡Glo - ria a ti!

Al - le - lu - ia!
men! ¡A - le - lu - ya! A -
mén! Praise to you, Lord! ¡A -
¡Glo - ria a ti!

Al - le -
men! A - men! ¡A - le -
mén! ¡A - mén! Praise to
¡Glo - ria

lu - ia! Al - le - lu - ia!
lu - ya! ¡A - le - lu - ya! We will
you, Lord! Praise to you, Lord! ¡Es ver -
a ti! ¡Glo - ria a ti!

rise to our cre - a - tor! We will rise with
dad, le - van - tar - e - mos con Je - sús, el

Je - sus, the Son! We will rise through the Spir - it!
hi - jo de Dios! ¡Es ver - dad! ¡A - mén!

Al - le - lu - ia! A - men!
¡A - le - lu - ya! ¡A - mén!
Praise to you, Lord.
¡Glo - ria a ti!

Music: *Mass for the Life of the World,* David Haas, arr. by Rob Glover, © 1993, GIA Publications, Inc.

192 AGNUS DEI

*Lamb   of   God, you take a - way the
*Cor - de - ro de   Dios, que qui - tas el pe -

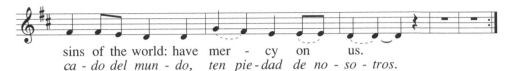

sins of the world: have mer - cy   on   us.
ca - do del mun - do,   ten pie - dad de no - so - tros.

Last time:

Lamb   of   God, you take a - way the   sins of the
Cor - de - ro de   Dios, que qui - tas el pe - ca - do del

world: grant   us   your   peace.
mun - do,   da   nos   la   paz.

*Other invocations may be used: King of kings, Prince of Peace, Bread of Life, Ancient Cup,
Pan de Vida (Bread of Life), Copa de Promesa (Cup of Promise), Sangre de la Cruz,
(Blood of the Cross), Mi Redentor (My Redeemer), etc.*

Music: *Mass for the Life of the World*, David Haas, © 1987, 1993, GIA Publications, Inc.

Service Music

RITE OF SPRINKLING 193

Cleanse us, Lord, from all our sins; wash us and we shall be clean as new snow. Cleanse us, Lord, from all our sins; wash us and we shall be clean as new snow.

Text: Psalm 51:9; Michael Joncas
Music: Michael Joncas
© 1988, GIA Publications, Inc.

RITE OF SPRINKLING 194

Springs of wa-ter, bless the Lord, Give him glo-ry and praise for-ev-er. Al-le-lu-ia! Give him glo-ry and praise!

Text: Refrain trans. © 1973, ICEL; additional text by Marty Haugen, © 1994, GIA Publications, Inc.
Music: Marty Haugen, © 1994, GIA Publications, Inc.

195 RITE OF SPRINKLING

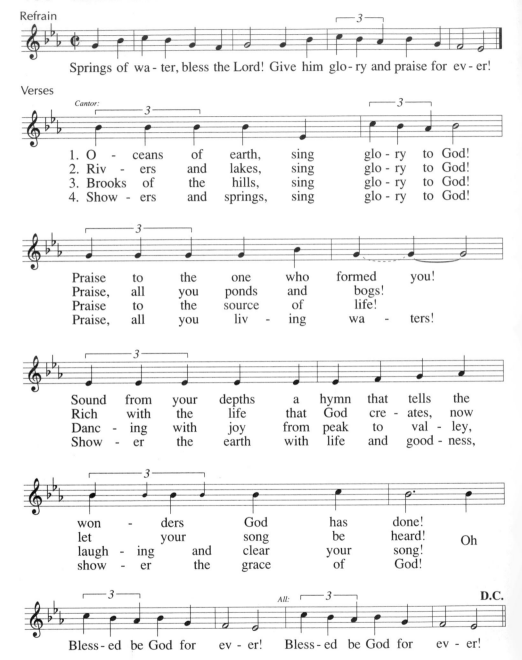

Refrain

Springs of wa - ter, bless the Lord! Give him glo - ry and praise for ev - er!

Verses

Cantor:

1. O - ceans of earth, sing glo - ry to God!
2. Riv - ers and lakes, sing glo - ry to God!
3. Brooks of the hills, sing glo - ry to God!
4. Show - ers and springs, sing glo - ry to God!

Praise to the one who formed you!
Praise, all you ponds and bogs!
Praise to the source of life!
Praise, all you liv - ing wa - ters!

Sound from your depths a hymn that tells the
Rich with the life that God cre - ates, now
Danc - ing with joy from peak to val - ley,
Show - er the earth with life and good - ness,

won - ders God has done!
let your song be heard! Oh
laugh - ing and clear your song!
show - er the grace of God!

All: D.C.

Bless - ed be God for ev - er! Bless - ed be God for ev - er!

Text: Refrain trans. © 1973, ICEL; additional text by Marty Haugen, © 1994, GIA Publications, Inc.
Music: Marty Haugen, © 1994, GIA Publications, Inc.

KYRIE

196

	*Lord	have mer-cy,	Lord	have	mer-cy.
(Invocation)	Christ	have mer-cy,	Christ	have	mer-cy.
	Lord	have mer-cy,	Lord	have	mer-cy.

*Alternate text, "Show us your mercy, be with us now!"

Music: Gary Daigle, © 1993, GIA Publications, Inc.

KYRIE

197

Lord, have mer - cy, Lord, have mer - cy,

Lord, have mer - cy on us.

Christ, have mer - cy, Christ, have mer - cy,

Christ, have mer - cy on us.

Lord, have mer - cy, Lord, have mer - cy,

Lord, have mer - cy, have mer - cy on us.

Music: *Mass of St. Augustine*, Leon C. Roberts, © 1981, GIA Publications, Inc.

198 GLORIA

Refrain

Give glo - ry to God in the high - est, and

peace to his peo - ple on earth.

Verses

1. Lord God, heavenly King,
   almighty God and Father,
   we worship you,
   we give you thanks,
   we praise you for your glory.

2. Lord Jesus Christ,
   only Son of the Father,
   Lord God, Lamb of God,
   you take away the sin of the world:
   have mercy upon us;
   you are seated at the right hand of the Father:
   receive our prayer.

3. You alone are the Holy One,
   you alone are the Lord,
   you alone are the Most High, Jesus Christ,
   with the Holy Spirit, in the glory of God the Father.

Music: John B. Foley, S.J., © 1978, and New Dawn Music

199 GLORIA

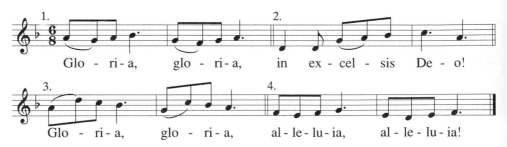

Glo - ri- a, glo - ri- a, in ex - cel - sis De - o!

Glo - ri- a, glo - ri- a, al - le - lu - ia, al - le - lu - ia!

Tune: Jacques Berthier, © 1979, 1988, Les Presses de Taizé, GIA Publications, Inc., agent

GLORIA

Glo-ry to God in the high-est, give glo-ry to our God! Glo-ry to God in the high-est, and peace to all peo-ple on earth.

Verses

1. Lord God, heavenly King,
   almighty God and Father,
   we worship you, we give you thanks,
   we praise you for your glory.

2. Lord Jesus Christ, Son of the Father,
   Lord God, Lamb of God,
   you take away the sin of the world:
   have mercy on us;
   you are seated at the right hand of the Father:
   receive the prayer of your people.

3. You alone are the Most Holy,
   you alone are the Lord Most High, Jesus Christ,
   with the Holy Spirit,
   in the glory of God the Father!

Music: Michel Guimont, © 1992, GIA Publications, Inc.

201 GLORIA

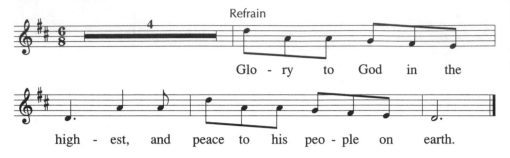

Refrain

Glo - ry to God in the high - est, and peace to his peo - ple on earth.

Verses

1. Lord God, heavenly King,
   almighty God and Father,
   we worship you, we give you thanks,
   we praise you for your glory.

2. Lord Jesus Christ, only Son of the Father,
   Lord God, Lamb of God,
   you take away sin of the world,
   have mercy on us;
   you are seated at the right hand of the Father,
   receive our prayer.

3. You alone are the holy one,
   you alone are the Lord,
   you alone are the Most High, Jesus Christ,
   with the Holy Spirit, in the glory of God the Father.

Music: *Assembly Mass,* Thomas Porter, © 1987, GIA Publications, Inc.

202 ALLELUIA

Al - le - lu - ia, al - le - lu - ia,
al - le - lu - ia, al-le-lu-ia, al-le-lu - ia.

Music: Joe Wise; acc. by Kelly Dobbs Mickus, © 1966, 1973, 1986, GIA Publications, Inc.

ALLELUIA 203

Al - le - lu - ia, al - le - lu - ia, al - le - lu - ia.

Al - le - lu - ia, al - le - lu - ia, al - le - lu - ia!

Music: Alleluia 7; Jacques Berthier, © 1984, Les Presses de Taizé, GIA Publications, Inc., agent

CELTIC ALLELUIA 204

Al - le - lu - ia, al - le - lu - ia!

Al - le - lu - ia, al - le - lu - ia!

Text: Fintan O'Carroll and Christopher Walker
Music: Fintan O'Carroll and Christopher Walker
© 1985, Fintan O'Carroll and Christopher Walker, published by OCP Publications

HALLE, HALLE, HALLE 205

Hal-le, hal-le, hal - le - lu - jah! Hal-le, hal-le, hal-

le - lu - ia! Hal - le, hal - le, hal - le -

lu - jah! Hal-le-lu-jah! Hal-le-lu - jah!

Music: Traditional Carribean, arr. by John L. Bell, © 1990, Iona Community, GIA Publications, Inc., agent; verses and acc. by Marty Haugen, © 1993, GIA Publications, Inc.

206 ALLELUIA

Al - le - lu - ia! Al - le - lu - ia!

Al - le - lu - ia! Al - le - lu - ia!

Text: Normand Gouin and Jennifer Kerr
Music: Normand Gouin and Jennifer Kerr
© 1992, GIA Publications, Inc.

207 LENTEN ACCLAMATION

Praise to you, Lord Je-sus, king of end - less glo-ry,

Sav-ior of the world, Sav-ior of the world.

Text: Marty Haugen
Music: Marty Haugen
© 1983, GIA Publications, Inc.

208 GENERAL INTERCESSIONS

O Lord, hear our prayer.

Text: Ray East
Music: Ray East
© 1987, GIA Publications, Inc.

209 GENERAL INTERCESSIONS

O God, hear us; hear our prayer.

Text: Bob Hurd, © 1984
Music: Bob Hurd, © 1984; acc. by Craig S. Kingsbury, © 1984, OCP Publications
Published by OCP Publications

GENERAL INTERCESSIONS 210

O lov - ing Fa - ther, hear us we pray.

Music: James Moore, © 1983, GIA Publications, Inc.

GENERAL INTERCESSIONS 211

Ky - ri - e, Ky - ri - e, e - le - i - son.

Music: Jacques Berthier, © 1980, Les Presses de Taizé, GIA Publications, Inc., agent

GENERAL INTERCESSIONS 212

Ky - ri - e e - lei - son. Ky - ri - e e - lei - son.
Chri - ste e - lei - son. Chri - ste e - lei - son.

Ky - ri - e e - lei - son.
Chri - ste e - lei - son.

Music: Russian Orthodox; arr. by John L. Bell, © 1990, Iona Community, GIA Publications, Inc., agent

GENERAL INTERCESSIONS 213

Ky - ri - e, e - lei - son. Ky - ri - e e - lei - son.
Chri - ste e - lei - son. Chri - ste e - lei - son.

Ky - ri - e e - lei - son. Ky - ri - e e - lei - son.
Chri - ste e - lei - son. Chri - ste e - lei - son.

Music: Dinah Reindorf, © 1987; arr. by John L. Bell, © 1990, Iona Community, GIA Publications, Inc., agent

214 PREFACE DIALOG

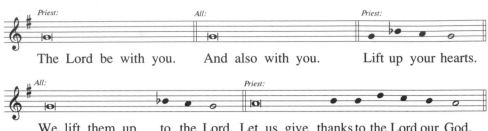

Priest:
The Lord be with you.

All:
And also with you.

Priest:
Lift up your hearts.

All:
We lift them up   to the Lord.

Priest:
Let us give thanks to the Lord our God.

All:
It is right to   give him thanks and   praise.

Music: *Agapé,* Marty Haugen, © 1993, GIA Publications, Inc.

215 EUCHARISTIC ACCLAMATION 1(OPTIONAL)

Ho - ly, ho - ly, ho - ly Lord.

Music: *Agapé,* Marty Haugen, © 1993, GIA Publications, Inc.

216 SANCTUS

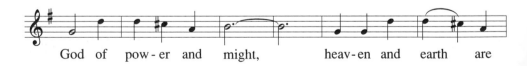

Ho - ly, hol - ly, ho - ly, Lord,

God of pow - er and might,   heav-en and earth are

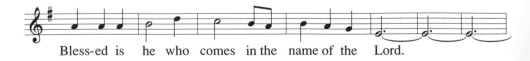

full of your glo-ry! Ho - san - na   in the high - est!

Bless-ed is he who comes in the name of the Lord.

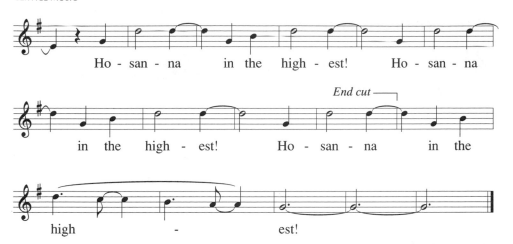

Ho - san - na in the high - est! Ho - san - na

in the high - est! Ho - san - na in the

End cut

high - est!

Music: *Agapé*, Marty Haugen, © 1993, GIA Publications, Inc.

EUCHARISTIC ACCLAMATION 2 (OPTIONAL)   217

We re - mem - ber, O God, we re - mem - ber, O God.

Music: *Agapé*, Marty Haugen, © 1993, GIA Publications, Inc.

MEMORIAL ACCLAMATION   218

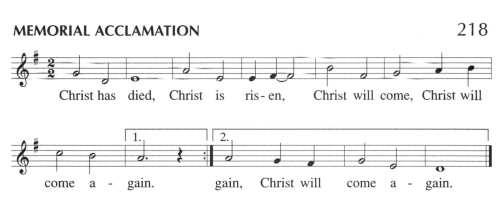

Christ has died, Christ is ris - en, Christ will come, Christ will

1.

2.

come a - gain. gain, Christ will come a - gain.

Music: *Agapé*, Marty Haugen, © 1993, GIA Publications, Inc.

EUCHARISTIC ACCLAMATION 3 (OPTIONAL)   219

Re - mem - ber, O God, re - mem - ber, O God.

Music: *Agapé*, Marty Haugen, © 1993, GIA Publications, Inc.

220 DOXOLOGY AND GREAT AMEN

A - men! Al - le - lu - ia! A -

men! Al - le - lu - ia! ia! A - men! A - men!

Music: *Agapé,* Marty Haugen, © 1993, GIA Publications, Inc.

221 EUCHARISTIC PRAYER FOR CHILDREN

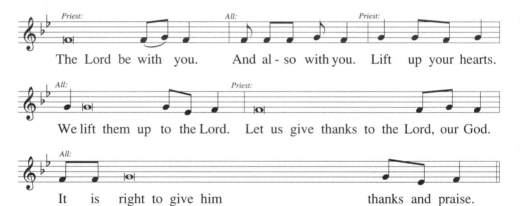

The Lord be with you. And al - so with you. Lift up your hearts.

We lift them up to the Lord. Let us give thanks to the Lord, our God.

It is right to give him thanks and praise.

Music: *Mass of Creation,* Marty Haugen, © 1984, GIA Publications, Inc.

222 ACCLAMATION 1

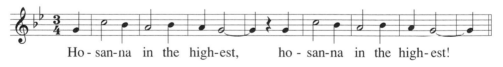

Ho - san-na in the high-est, ho - san-na in the high-est!

Music: Eucharistic Prayer for Children, *Mass of Creation,* Marty Haugen, adapt. by Rob Glover, © 1989, GIA Publications, Inc.

SANCTUS

Ho-ly, ho-ly, ho-ly Lord, God of pow-er,
God of might, heav-en and earth are full of your glo-ry. Ho-
san-na in the high-est. Bless-ed is he who comes in the
name of the Lord. Ho-san-na in the high-est,
ho-san-na in the high - est.

Music: *Mass of Creation,* Marty Haugen, © 1984, GIA Publications, Inc.

ACCLAMATION 2

223

224

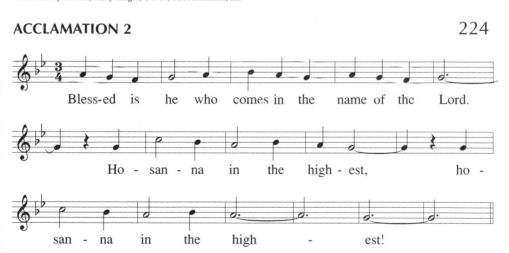

Bless-ed is he who comes in the name of the Lord.
Ho-san-na in the high-est, ho-
san-na in the high - est!

Music: Eucharistic Prayer for Children, *Mass of Creation,* Marty Haugen, adapt. by Rob Glover, © 1989, GIA Publications, Inc.

225 ACCLAMATION 3

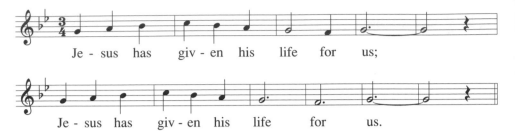

Je - sus has giv - en his life for us;

Je - sus has giv - en his life for us.

Music: Eucharistic Prayer for Children, *Mass of Creation,* Marty Haugen, adapt. by Rob Glover, © 1989, GIA Publications, Inc.

226 ACCLAMATION 4

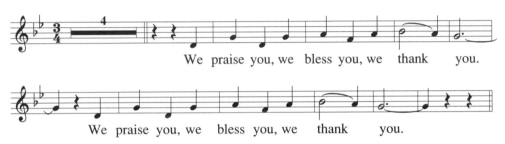

We praise you, we bless you, we thank you.

We praise you, we bless you, we thank you.

Music: Eucharistic Prayer for Children, *Mass of Creation,* Marty Haugen, adapt. by Rob Glover, © 1989, GIA Publications, Inc.

227 DOXOLOGY AND GREAT AMEN

A - men, a - men, a - men!

A - men, a - men, a - men!

Music: *Mass of Creation*, Marty Haugen, © 1984, GIA Publications, Inc.

EUCHARISTIC PRAYER II: PREFACE DIALOG 228

Music: *Eucharistic Prayer II*, Marty Haugen, © 1990, GIA Publications, Inc.

ADDITIONAL ACCLAMATION 1 (OPTIONAL) 229

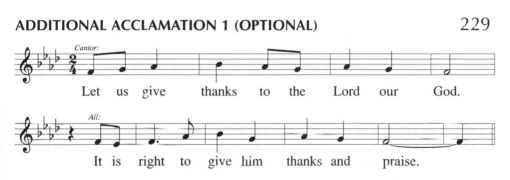

Music: *Eucharistic Prayer II*, Marty Haugen, © 1990, GIA Publications, Inc.

230 SANCTUS

Ho - ly, ho - ly, ho - ly Lord, God of pow-er and might; heav-en and earth are full of your glo - ry: Ho - san - na in the high - est! Bless-ed is he, bless-ed is he who comes in the name of the Lord. Ho - san - na in the high - est! Ho - san - na in the high - est!

Music: *Eucharistic Prayer II,* Marty Haugen, © 1990, GIA Publications, Inc.

231 ADDITIONAL ACCLAMATION 2 (OPTIONAL)

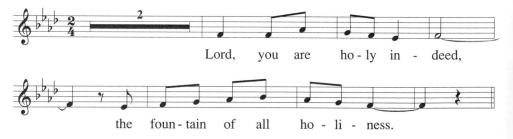

Lord, you are ho - ly in - deed, the foun - tain of all ho - li - ness.

Music: *Eucharistic Prayer II,* Marty Haugen, © 1990, GIA Publications, Inc.

ADDITIONAL ACCLAMATION 3 (OPTIONAL)

232

Cantor, then all:

Glo- ry and praise to you, O Christ! Sav - ior of the world!

Music: *Eucharistic Prayer II,* Marty Haugen, © 1990, GIA Publications, Inc.

MEMORIAL ACCLAMATION

233

Priest:

Let us pro- claim the mys- ter - y of faith:

Cantor:

Dy - ing you de -

Cantor:

stroyed our death, ris- ing you re -

All:

Dy- ing you de - stroyed our death,

stored our life. Lord Je - sus, come in

ris- ing you re - stored our life. Lord

glo - ry.

Je - sus, come in glo - ry.

Music: *Eucharistic Prayer II,* Marty Haugen, ©1990, GIA Publications, Inc.

234 ADDITIONAL ACCLAMATION 4 (OPTIONAL)

Cantor, then all:

Good and gra-cious God, hear and re-mem-ber us.

Music: *Eucharistic Prayer II,* Marty Haugen, © 1990, GIA Publications, Inc.

235 DOXOLOGY AND GREAT AMEN

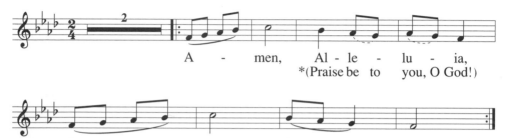

A - men, Al - le - lu - ia,
*(Praise be to you, O God!)

A - men, A - men!

*During Lent

Music: *Eucharistic Prayer II,* Marty Haugen, © 1990, GIA Publications, Inc.

236 SANCTUS

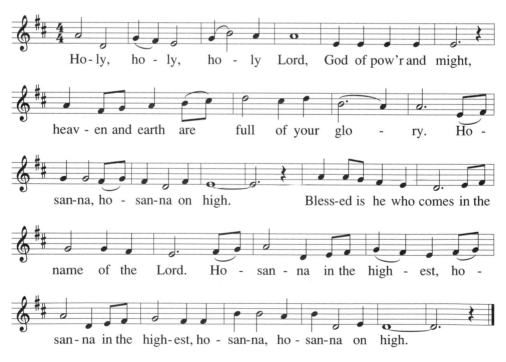

Ho - ly, ho - ly, ho - ly Lord, God of pow'r and might,

heav - en and earth are full of your glo - ry. Ho -

san-na, ho - san-na on high. Bless-ed is he who comes in the

name of the Lord. Ho - san - na in the high - est, ho -

san - na in the high-est, ho - san-na, ho - san-na on high.

Music: *St. Louis Jesuits Mass;* Robert J. Dufford, SJ, and Daniel L. Schutte, © 1973, administered by New Dawn Music; acc. by Diana Kodner, © 1993, GIA Publications, Inc.

WHEN WE EAT THIS BREAD 237

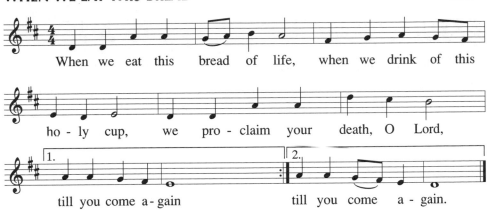

When we eat this bread of life, when we drink of this
ho - ly cup, we pro - claim your death, O Lord,
1. till you come a - gain
2. till you come a - gain.

Music: *St. Louis Jesuits Mass;* Robert J. Dufford, SJ, and Daniel L. Schutte, © 1977, 1979, administered by New Dawn Music

AMEN 238

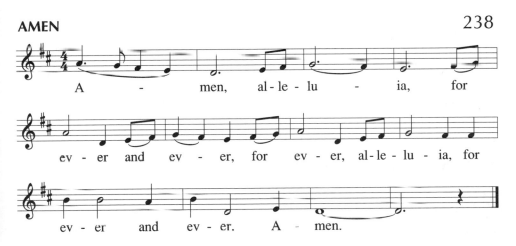

A - men, al - le - lu - ia, for
ev - er and ev - er, for ev - er, al - le - lu - ia, for
ev - er and ev - er. A - men.

Music: *St. Louis Jesuits Mass,* Robert J. Dufford, SJ, and Daniel L. Schutte, © 1973, administered by New Dawn Music; acc. by Diana Kodner, © 1993,
   GIA Publications, Inc.

239 SANCTUS

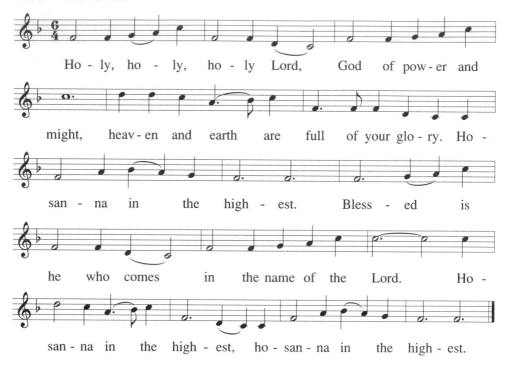

Ho - ly, ho - ly, ho - ly Lord, God of pow - er and might, heav - en and earth are full of your glo - ry. Ho - san - na in the high - est. Bless - ed is he who comes in the name of the Lord. Ho - san - na in the high - est, ho - san - na in the high - est.

Music: *Land of Rest;* adapt. by Marcia Pruner, © 1980, Church Pension Fund; acc. by Richard Proulx, © 1986, GIA Publications, Inc.

240 MEMORIAL ACCLAMATION

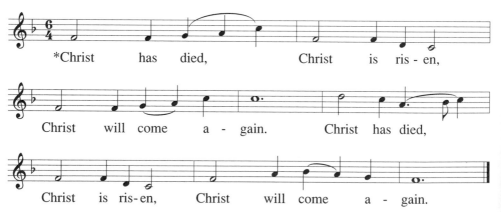

*Christ has died, Christ is ris - en, Christ will come a - gain. Christ has died, Christ is ris - en, Christ will come a - gain.

*For a shorter version of this acclamation, sing the first two measures and the last two measures.

Music: *Land of Rest,* adapt. by Richard Proulx, © 1986, GIA Publications, Inc.

AMEN

241

A - men, a - men, a - men.

Music: *Land of Rest,* adapt. by Richard Proulx, GIA Publications, Inc.

MEMORIAL ACCLAMATION

242

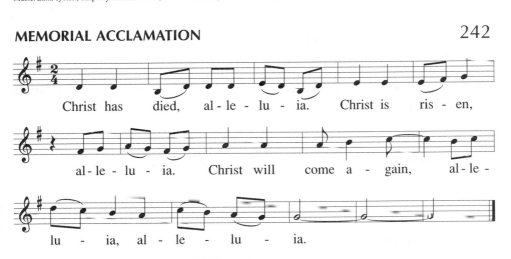

Christ has died, al - le - lu - ia. Christ is ris - en,

al - le - lu - ia. Christ will come a - gain, al - le -

lu - ia, al - le - lu - ia.

Music: Joe Wise; acc. by T.F. and R.P., © 1971, 1972, GIA Publications, Inc.

243 LAMB OF GOD

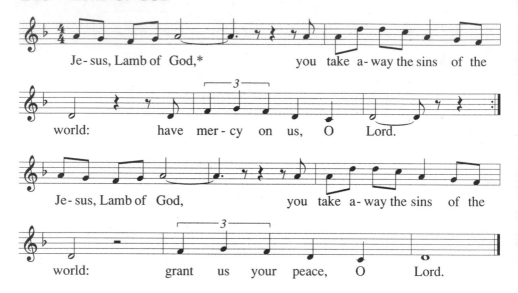

Je- sus, Lamb of God,* you take a- way the sins of the

world: have mer - cy on us, O Lord.

Je- sus, Lamb of God, you take a- way the sins of the

world: grant us your peace, O Lord.

Alternate invocations:

Jesus, Word of God...
Jesus, Bread of Life...
Jesus, Cup of Life...
Jesus, Light of Peace...
Jesus, Hope of all...

Music: *Agapé,* Marty Haugen, © 1993, GIA Publications, Inc.

244 LAMB OF GOD

1. Lamb of God, you take a - way the sin of the
2. Lamb of God, you break the chains of ha - tred and
3. Lamb of God, you are the way of jus - tice and
4. Lamb of God, you are the way of mer - cy and

world;
fear; have mer-cy on us, mer-cy on us, mer-cy on us.
peace:
love:

Lamb of God, you take a-way the sin of the world:

grant us peace, grant us peace, grant us peace.

Text: ICET; additional text by Marty Haugen, © 1990, GIA Publications, Inc.
Music: *Now the Feast and Celebration*, Marty Haugen, © 1990, GIA Publications, Inc.

LAMB OF GOD

245

1. Je - sus, Lamb of God you
2. Je - sus, Pas - chal vic - tim you

take a - way the sins of the world, have mer - cy on us.

Last time

Je - sus, Lamb of God you take a - way the

sins of the world, grant us peace, grant us peace.

Additional invocations:

3. Jesus, Food of Pilgrims...
4. Jesus, True Bread from Heaven...
5. Jesus, Wine of Peace...
6. Jesus, Good Shepherd...

Music: Tony Way, © 1993

246 LAMB OF GOD: MAY WE BE ONE

Cantor(s):

1. Lamb of God, you
2. Lamb of God, un -
3. Lamb of God, de -
4. Lamb of God, whose
5. Lamb of God, our
6. Lamb of God, our

take a - way the sins of the world:
blem - ished of - f'ring made for our sin:
stroyed that all who eat might be healed:
blood will save your peo - ple from death:
com - mon mem - 'ry, cov - e - nant feast:
free - dom won, re - mem- bered for ev - er:

All:

have mer - cy on us, have mer - cy on us.

Last time

Cantor(s):

Lamb of God, you take a- way the sins of the world,

All:

grant us peace, grant us peace.

Additional invocations:

Lamb of God, the shepherd of all who hunger and thirst...
Lamb of God, joy of the martyrs, song of the saints...
Lamb of God, all peoples will sing your victory song...
Lamb of God, unconquered light of the city of God...
Lamb of God, how blessed are those who are called to your feast...

Text: *Agnus Dei;* additional text by Rory Cooney
Music: Gary Daigle
© 1993, GIA Publications, Inc.

MAY WE BE ONE (COMMUNION HYMN)

247

Refrain

When we eat this bread and drink this cup,

we pro-claim your death, Lord Je - sus. So as we

share this feast may we be - come, heal-ing and

To verses | Last time

light and peace. May we be one. one.

Verses

A - men, a - men.

A - men, a - men. A - men, a -

D.C.

men. A - men, a - men.

248 The King Shall Come When Morning Dawns

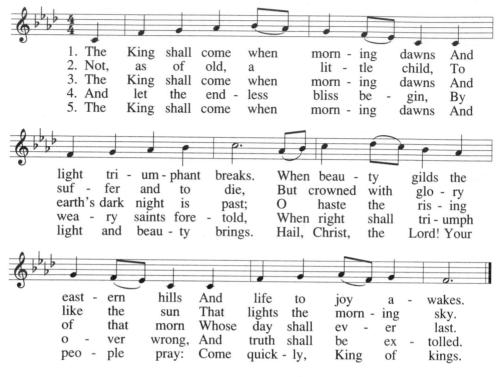

1. The King shall come when morn - ing dawns And light tri - um - phant breaks. When beau - ty gilds the east - ern hills And life to joy a - wakes.
2. Not, as of old, a lit - tle child, To suf - fer and to die, But crowned with glo - ry like the sun That lights the morn - ing sky.
3. The King shall come when morn - ing dawns And earth's dark night is past; O haste the ris - ing of that morn Whose day shall ev - er last.
4. And let the end - less bliss be - gin, By wea - ry saints fore - told, When right shall tri - umph o - ver wrong, And truth shall be ex - tolled.
5. The King shall come when morn - ing dawns And light and beau - ty brings. Hail, Christ, the Lord! Your peo - ple pray: Come quick - ly, King of kings.

Text: John Brownlie, 1857-1925
Tune: CONSOLATION, CM; John Wyeth, 1770-1858; arr. by Robert J. Batastini, b.1942, © 1994, GIA Publications, Inc.

249 Walk in the Reign

Refrain

Close as to - mor - row the sun shall ap - pear.
Free - dom is com - ing and heal - ing is near. And I shall be
with you in laugh - ter and pain to stand in the wind and

walk in the reign, to walk in the reign.

Verses

1. In days to come the des-ert shall bloom.
2. Com-fort each oth-er, for pain soon must end. A
3. A cur-tain of fear is be-ing torn down.
4. The streets of So-we-to, the docks at G-dansk, Ti-

Riv-ers will run there, soon, ver-y soon. So
day comes when li-on and lamb shall be friends. The
Pris-ons are o-pened; the lost have been found. So
en-an-men Square, the slums of The Bronx, When

what shall we fear, though death do its
sight-less shall see then, the speech-less sing
go tell the seek-er what we've seen and
we stand to-geth-er to stand a-gainst

worst? The word of our God is the
songs. The name of our God is the
heard: The name of our God is the
hell, The name of this peo-ple is

D.C.

last shall be first, the last shall be first.
right-er of wrongs, the right-er of wrongs.
keep-er of word, the keep-er of word.
"Em-man-u-el," is "Em-man-u-el."

Text: Rory Cooney, b.1952
Tune: Rory Cooney, b.1952
© 1990, GIA Publications, Inc.

250   Advent Gathering

Verses

1. Here in this world where dark-ness sur - rounds us,
2. Where is the peace you prom-ised the wid - ow?
3. Where is the road you prom-ise the ex - ile?
4. Where is the heart whose "yes" is sal - va - tion?

Show us your

face, O prom-ise of dawn.

We seek a sign that
Where is the home you
Where is the good news
Where is the child whose

you are a - mong us.
prom - ised the or - phan?
preached to the low - ly?
life is our fu - ture?

Show us your face, O Lord Je-sus come.

Refrain

Come, O hope of your peo-ple. Come a-mong us and

Come, O hope of your peo-ple.

stay. Lead us in mer - cy up from the

Come a - mong us and stay.

shad - ows, Shine in our dark - ness, be here to - day.

Text: Rory Cooney, b.1952
Tune: Gary Daigle, b.1957
© 1993, GIA Publications, Inc.

Like a Shepherd 251

Refrain

Like a shep-herd he feeds his flock and gath-ers the
lambs in his arms, hold-ing them care-ful-ly
close to his heart, lead-ing them home.

Verses 1, 2

1. Say to the cit-ies of Ju-dah; Pre-pare the
2. I my-self will shep-herd them, for oth-ers have

way of the Lord. Go to the moun-tain top,
led them a-stray. The lost I will res-cue and

D.C.

lift your voice; Je-ru-sa-lem, here is your God.
heal their wounds and pas-ture them, giv-ing them rest.

Verse 3

3. Come un-to me if you are

heav-i-ly bur-dened, and take my yoke up-

D.C.

on your shoul-ders, I will give you rest.

Text: Isaiah 40:9ff, Ezekiel 34:11, Matthew 11:28ff; Bob Dufford, SJ, b.1943
Tune: Bob Dufford, SJ, b.1943; acc. by Sr. Theophane Hytrek, OSF, 1915-1992, alt.
© 1976, Robert J. Dufford, SJ, and New Dawn Music

252 My Soul in Stillness Waits

Refrain

For you, O Lord, my soul in still - ness waits, tru - ly my hope is in you.

Verses

1. O Lord of Light, our on - ly hope of glo - ry, your ra - diance shines in all who look to you, come, light the hearts of all in dark and shad - ow.

2. O Spring of Joy, rain down up - on our spir - its, our thirst - y hearts are yearn - ing for your Word, come, make us whole, be com - fort to our hearts.

3. O Root of Life, im - plant your seed with - in us, and in your ad - vent, draw us all to you, our hope re - born in dy - ing and in ris - ing.

4. O Key of Knowl - edge, guide us in our pil - grim - age, we ev - er seek, yet un - ful - filled re - main, o - pen to us the path - way of your peace.

5. Come, let us bow be - fore the God who made us, let ev - 'ry heart be o - pened to the Lord, for we are all the peo - ple of his hand.

6. Here we shall meet the Mak - er of the heav - ens, Cre - a - tor of the moun - tains and the seas, Lord of the stars, and pres - ent to us now.

D.C.

Text: Psalm 95 and "O" Antiphons; Marty Haugen, b.1950
Tune: Marty Haugen, b.1950
© 1982, GIA Publications, Inc.

Within Our Hearts Be Born 253

1. O an-cient love, pro-cess-ing through the
2. O home-less love, that dwells a-mong the
3. O gen-tle love, car-ess-ing those in
4. O suf-f'ring love, that bears our hu-man

a - ges: O hid-den love, re-vealed in hu-man
stran - ger: O low-ly love, that knows the might-y's
sor - row: O ten-der love, that com-forts those for-
weak - ness: O bound-less love, that ris-es with the

form: O prom-ised love, the dream of seers and
scorn: O hun-gry love, that lay with-in a
lorn: O hope-ful love, that prom-is-es to-
morn: O might-y love, con-cealed in in-fant

sa - ges:
man - ger: O liv-ing Love, with-in our hearts be
mor - row:
meek - ness:

born, O liv-ing Love, with-in our hearts be borne.

Text: Michael Joncas, b.1951
Tune: BEDFORD ABBEY, 11 10 11 10 10; Michael Joncas, b.1951
© 1994, GIA Publications, Inc.

254 Your Mercy Like Rain

Refrain

Let me taste your mer - cy like rain on my face; here in my life, show me your peace. Let us see with our own eyes your day break - ing bright. Come, O Morn - ing; come, O Light!

Verses

1. What God has spoken I will declare:
   Peace to the people of God ev'rywhere.
   God's saving presence is close at hand:
   glory as near as our land!

2. Here faithful love and truth will embrace;
   here peace and justice will come face to face.
   God's truth shall water the earth like a spring,
   while justice will bend down and sing.

3. God will keep the promise indeed;
   our land will yield the food that we need.
   Justice shall walk before you that day,
   clearing a path, preparing your way.

Text: Psalm 85; Rory Cooney, b.1952
Tune: Rory Cooney, b.1952
© 1993, GIA Publications, Inc.

God of All People 255

1. God of all plac - es: pres-ent, un - seen; Voice in our
2. God of all dream-ing, near and yet far. Vi - sion un -
3. God of all peo - ple, dust and the clay. Breath of a

si - lence, song in our midst. We are your peo-ple, know-ing, un -
heard of, wake us to rest. We are your pres-ence, sent forth a -
new wind, fire in our hearts. Light born of heav-en, peace on the

sure.   Come, Lord Je - sus, come!
fraid.   Come, Lord Je - sus, come!
earth.   Come, Lord Je - sus, come!

Text: David Haas, b.1957
Tune: KINGDOM, 9 9 9 6; David Haas, b.1957
© 1988, GIA Publications, Inc.

Wait for the Lord 256

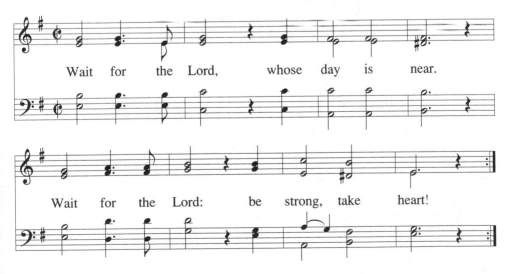

Wait for the Lord, whose day is near.

Wait for the Lord: be strong, take heart!

Text: Isaiah 40, Philippians 4, Matthew 6-7; Taizé Community, 1984
Tune: Jacques Berthier, b.1923
© 1984, Les Presses de Taizé, GIA Publications, Inc., agent

257 Come to Set Us Free

Refrain

Come to set us free, come to make us your own.

Come to show the way to your peo-ple, your cho - sen.

O - pen our lives to the light of your prom - ise.

Come to our hearts with heal-ing, come to our minds with pow-er,

come to us and bring us your life.

Verses

1. You are light which shines in dark - ness, Morn - ing
2. You are hope which brings us cour - age, you are
3. You are prom - ise of sal - va - tion, you are

3

Star which nev-er sets. O - pen our eyes which on - ly dim-ly
strength which nev-er fails. O - pen our minds to ways we do not
God in hu-man form. Bring to our world of emp - ti - ness and

D.C.

see the truth which sets us free.
know, but where your Spir - it grows.
fear the Word we long to hear.

Text: Bernadette Farrell, b.1957
Tune: Bernadette Farrell, b.1957
© 1982, Bernadette Farrell, published by OCP Publications

Each Winter As the Year Grows Older 258

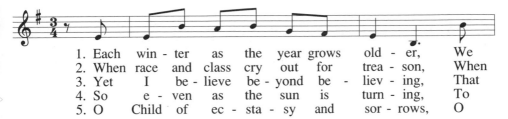

1. Each win-ter as the year grows old-er, We
2. When race and class cry out for trea-son, When
3. Yet I be-lieve be-yond be-liev-ing, That
4. So e-ven as the sun is turn-ing, To
5. O Child of ec-sta-sy and sor-rows, O

each grow old-er too. The chill sets in a lit-tle
si-rens call for war, They o-ver-shout the voice of
life can spring from death; That growth can flow-er from our
jour-ney to the north, The liv-ing flame, in se-cret
Prince of peace and pain, Bright-en to-day's world by to-

cold-er; The ver-i-ties we knew Seem
rea-son, And scream till we ig-nore All
griev-ing; That we can catch our breath And
burn-ing, Can kin-dle on the earth, And
mor-row's, Re-new our lives a-gain; Lord

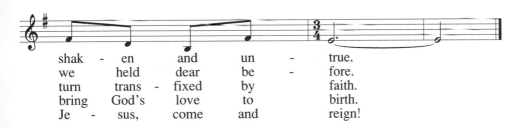

shak-en and un-true.
we held dear be-fore.
turn trans-fixed by faith.
bring God's love to birth.
Je-sus, come and reign!

Text: William Gay, fl. 1969, © 1971, United Church Press
Tune: CAROL OF HOPE, 9 6 9 66; Annabeth Gay, b.1925, © 1971, United Church Press; acc. by Marty Haugen, b.1950, alt.,
© 1987, GIA Publications, Inc.

259 People of the Night

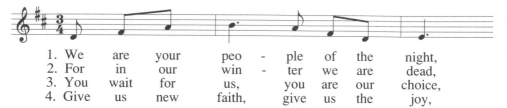

1. We are your peo - ple of the night,
2. For in our win - ter we are dead,
3. You wait for us, you are our choice,
4. Give us new faith, give us the joy,

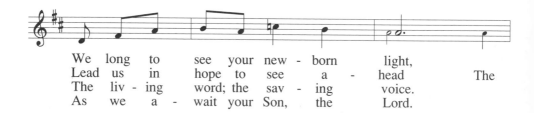

We long to see your new - born light,
Lead us in hope to see a - head   The
The liv - ing word; the sav - ing voice.
As we a - wait your Son, the Lord.

Dis - tant glim - mer; ris - ing from a - far.
spring-time and the gift that is to come.
Break the si - lence, lis - ten to our call.
In our pres - ence, child born of your breath,

We a - wait you, ho - ly morn-ing star.
Come and save us, be God's on - ly Son.
Be our an - swer, new life for us all.
Sav - ior broth - er; life that shat-ters death.

Text: David Haas, b.1957
Tune: SHEPHERD'S SONG, 88 99; David Haas, b.1957
© 1983, GIA Publications, Inc.

On Jordan's Bank 260

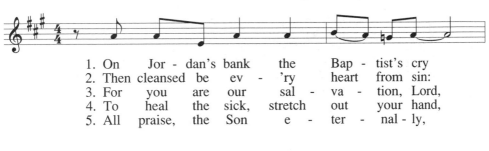

1. On   Jor - dan's bank   the   Bap - tist's cry
2. Then cleansed be   ev - 'ry   heart   from sin:
3. For   you   are   our   sal - va - tion, Lord,
4. To   heal   the   sick,   stretch   out   your hand,
5. All   praise, the   Son   e - ter - nal - ly,

An - noun - ces that   the   Lord   is   nigh;   A -
Make straight the   way   for   God   with - in,   And
Our   ref - uge, and   our   great   re - ward;   With -
And   bid   the   fall - en   sin - ner   stand;   Shine
Whose ad - vent sets   all   peo - ple   free;   Whom

wake   and   heark - en   for   he   brings   Glad
let   each   heart   pre - pare   a   home   Where
out   your   grace   we   waste   a - way   Like
forth,   and   let   your   light   re - store   Earth's
with   the   Fa - ther   we   a - dore   And

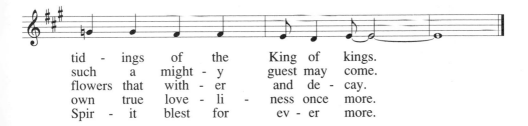

tid - ings   of   the   King of   kings.
such   a   might - y   guest may come.
flowers that   with - er   and de - cay.
own   true   love - li - ness once more.
Spir - it   blest   for   ev - er   more.

Text: *Jordanis oras praevia*; Charles Coffin, 1676-1749; tr. by John Chandler, 1806-1876
Tune: ST. JOHN THE BAPTIST, LM; Gary Miles, © 1974, 1975, Celebration

261 Night of Silence

1. Cold are the peo-ple, win-ter of life, We trem-ble in
2. Voice in the dis-tance, call in the night, On wind you en-
3. Spir-it a-mong us, shine like the star, Your light that guides

shad-ows this cold end-less night, Fro-zen in the snow lie
fold us, you speak of the light, Gen-tle on the ear you
shep-herds and kings from a-far, Shim-mer in the sky so

ros-es sleep-ing, Flow-ers that will ech-o the sun-
whis-per soft-ly, Ru-mors of a dawn so em-brac-
emp-ty, lone-ly, Ris-ing in the warmth of your Son's

rise, Fire of hope is our on-ly warmth,
ing, Breath-less love a-waits dark-ened souls,
love, Star un-know-ing of night and day,

Wea-ry, its flame will be dy-ing soon.
Soon will we know of the morn-ing.
Spir-it we wait for your lov-ing Son.

Text: Daniel Kantor, b.1960
Tune: Daniel Kantor, b.1960
© 1984, GIA Publications, Inc.

262 Silent Night

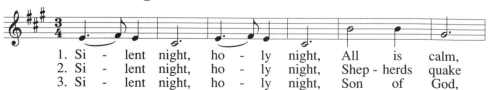

1. Si - lent night, ho - ly night, All is calm,
2. Si - lent night, ho - ly night, Shep - herds quake
3. Si - lent night, ho - ly night, Son of God,

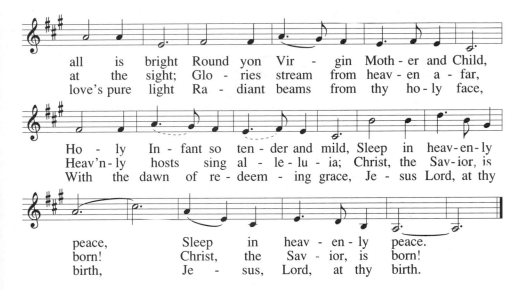

all   is   bright Round yon Vir - gin Moth - er and Child,
at   the   sight; Glo - ries stream from heav - en a - far,
love's pure light Ra - diant beams from thy ho - ly face,

Ho - ly In - fant so ten - der and mild, Sleep in heav-en-ly
Heav'n-ly hosts sing al - le - lu - ia; Christ, the Sav-ior, is
With the dawn of re - deem - ing grace, Je - sus Lord, at thy

peace,   Sleep   in   heav - en - ly peace.
born!   Christ,   the   Sav - ior, is born!
birth,   Je -   sus,   Lord, at thy birth.

This version is included for use with "Night of Silence."

Text: *Stille Nacht, heilige Nacht;* Joseph Mohr, 1792-1849; trans. by John F. Young, 1820-1885
Tune: STILLE NACHT, 66 89 66; Franz X. Gruber, 1787-1863

Gloria 263

¡Glo - ria, glo - ria, glo - ria   en las al - tur - as a Dios!
Glo - ry, glo - ry, glo - ry,   glo - ry be to God on high!

Y en la tie - rra paz pa-ra a - que-llos que a - ma el Se - ñor.
And on earth peace to the peo - ple in whom God is well pleased.

Text: Luke 2:14
Tune: Pablo Sosa, © 1990

264 The Virgin Mary Had a Baby Boy

Verses

1. The virgin Mary had a baby boy, the virgin Mary had a baby boy, the virgin Mary had a baby boy, and they say that his name was Jesus.
2. The angels sang when the baby born, the angels sang when the baby born, the angels sang when the baby born, and they say that his name was Jesus.
3. The wise men saw where the baby born, the wise men saw where the baby born, the wise men went where the baby born, and they say that his name was Jesus.

Refrain

He come from the glory, he come from the glorious kingdom. Oh, yes! believer! Oh, yes! believer! He come from the glory, he come from the glorious kingdom.

Text: West Indian carol, © 1945, Boosey and Co., Ltd.
Tune: West Indian carol, © 1945, Boosey and Co., Ltd.; acc. by Diana Kodner, b. 1957, © 1993, GIA Publications, Inc.

Awake, Awake, and Greet the New Morn   265

1. A - wake! a - wake, and greet the new morn, For
2. To us, to all in sor - row and fear, Em -
3. In dark - est night his com - ing shall be, When
4. Re - joice, re - joice, take heart in the night, Though

an - gels her - ald its dawn - ing, Sing out your joy, for
man - u - el comes a - sing - ing, His hum - ble song is
all the world is de - spair - ing, As morn - ing light so
dark the win - ter and cheer - less, The ris - ing sun shall

now he is born, Be - hold! the Child of our long - ing.
qui - et and near, Yet fills the earth with its ring - ing;
qui - et and free, So warm and gen - tle and car - ing.
crown you with light, Be strong and lov - ing and fear - less;

Come as a ba - by weak and poor, To bring all hearts to -
Mu - sic to heal the bro - ken soul And hymns of lov - ing
Then shall the mute break forth in song, The lame shall leap in
Love be our song and love our prayer, And love, our end - less

geth - er, He o - pens wide the heav'n - ly door And
kind - ness, The thun - der of his an - thems roll To
won - der, The weak be raised a - bove the strong, And
sto - ry, May God fill ev - 'ry day we share, And

lives now in - side us for ev - er.
shat - ter all ha - tred and blind - ness.
weap - ons be bro - ken a - sun - der.
bring us at last in - to glo - ry.

Text: Marty Haugen, b.1950
Tune: REJOICE, REJOICE, 9 8 9 8 8 7 8 9; Marty Haugen, b.1950
© 1983, GIA Publications, Inc.

266 The Age of Expectation

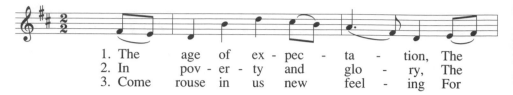

1. The age of ex - pec - ta - tion, The
2. In pov - er - ty and glo - ry, The
3. Come rouse in us new feel - ing For

heav - y years have passed. The light of God's sal -
sta - ble and the stars Be - gin to sing your
what we have seen and known. Come give all peo - ple

va - tion Now dawns for us at last.
sto - ry And how you come to ours.
heal - ing And make us as your own.

Our God now pierc - es his - to - ry And
Hu - mil - i - ty now teach - es us Be -
No per - son is a stran - ger, For

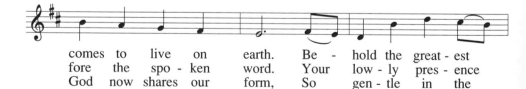

comes to live on earth. Be - hold the great - est
fore the spo - ken word. Your low - ly pres - ence
God now shares our form, So gen - tle in the

mys - ter - y, A God of hu - man birth.
reach - es us. No heart is left un - stirred.
man - ger, So meek and hu - man born.

Text: Todd Flowerday
Tune: ASHWOOD, 7 6 7 6 D; Bobby Fisher, b.1952
© 1992, GIA Publications, Inc.

God's Surprise 267

1. Who would think that what was need-ed To trans-
2. Shep - herds watch and wise men won-der, Mon - archs
3. Cen - tu - ries of skill and sci-ence Span the

form and save the earth Might not be a
scorn and an - gels sing; Such a place as
past from which we move, Yet ex - pe - rience

plan or ar - my, Proud in pur - pose, proved in
none would reck - on Hosts a ho - ly help - less
ques - tions wheth-er, With such pro - gress, we im -

worth? Who would think, de - spite de - ri - sion,
thing; Sta - ble beasts and by - passed stran-gers
prove. While the hu - man lot we pon - der,

That a child should lead the way? God sur - pris - es
Watch a ba - by laid in hay:
Lest our hopes and hu - mor fray,

earth with heav-en, Com - ing here on Christ - mas Day.

Text: John L. Bell, b.1949
Tune: SCARLET RIBBONS, 8 7 8 7 D; English traditional; arr. by John L. Bell, b.1949
© 1987, Iona Community, GIA Publications, Inc., agent

268 The Tiny Child to Bethlehem Came

1. The ti - ny child to Beth - le-hem came That
2. When truth be - comes the light of our way, When
3. And see with - in his shin - ing eyes A
4. Let all cre - a - tion e - cho and ring In

all of the world might turn And care for ev - 'ry
peace is the gift we share, When love is more than
God who is near at hand, A God whose wis - dom
praise of the In - fant small, Now lift your hearts and

crea - ture the same, The way of com - pas - sion to learn.
words that we say, The spir - it of Je - sus is there.
baf - fles the wise, So on - ly the child un - der - stands.
voic - es to sing, And wel - come the child in us all.

Text: Marty Haugen, b.1950
Tune: TINY CHILD, 9 7 9 8; Marty Haugen, b.1950
© 1992, GIA Publications, Inc.

A Stable Lamp Is Lighted 269

1. A sta - ble lamp is light-ed Whose glow shall wake the
2. This child through Da-vid's cit - y Shall ride in tri - umph
3. Yet he shall be for - sak - en, And yield-ed up to
4. But now, as at the end-ing, The low is lift - ed

sky; The stars shall bend their voic - es, And
by; The palm shall strew its branch - es, And
die; The sky shall groan and dark - en, And
high; The stars shall bend their voic - es, And

ev - 'ry stone shall cry. And ev - 'ry stone shall cry, And
ev - 'ry stone shall cry. And ev - 'ry stone shall cry, Though
ev - 'ry stone shall cry. And ev - 'ry stone shall cry, For
ev - 'ry stone shall cry. And ev - 'ry stone shall cry, In

straw like gold shall shine; A barn shall har - bor
heav - y, dull, and dumb, And lie with - in the
hearts made hard by sin: God's blood up - on the
prais - es of the child By whose de - scent a -

heav - en, A stall be - come a shrine.
road - way To pave the king - dom come.
spear - head, God's love re - fused a - gain.
mong us The worlds are rec - on - ciled.

Text: Richard Wilbur, © 1961
Tune: ANNIKA, 7 6 7 66 6 7 6; Marty Haugen, b.1950, © 1992, GIA Publications, Inc.

270 Child of Mercy

Refrain

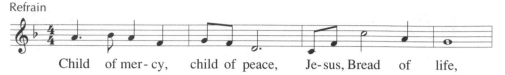

Child of mer-cy, child of peace, Je-sus, Bread of life,

food to fill our long-ing. Child of jus-tice, child of light,

Je-sus, sav-ing cup, Em-man-u-el, God with us.

Verses

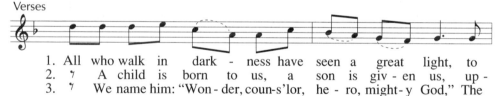

1. All who walk in dark - ness have seen a great light, to
2. ⁊ A child is born to us, a son is giv-en us, up -
3. ⁊ We name him: "Won-der, coun-s'lor, he - ro, might-y God," The
4. We pro-claim good news to you, great ti - dings of joy: To

D.C.

those who dwell in fear, a light has shone!
on his shoul - der glo - ry rests!
Ho - ly One for ev - er: Prince of peace!
you is born a sav - ior: Christ the Lord!

Text: Isaiah 9:1, 5; David Haas, b.1957
Tune: David Haas, b.1957
© 1991, GIA Publications, Inc.

Rise Up, Shepherd, and Follow   271

Verses

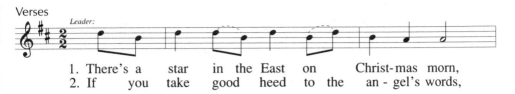

1. There's a star in the East on Christ-mas morn,
2. If you take good heed to the an - gel's words,

Rise up, shep-herd, and fol-low, It will lead to the place where the
Rise up, shep-herd, and fol-low, You'll for-get your flocks, you'll for-

Christ was born, Rise up, shep-herd, and fol - low.
get your herds, Rise up, shep-herd, and fol - low.

Refrain

Fol - low, fol - low, Rise up, shep-herd, and fol-low,

Fol- low the Star of Beth- le - hem, Rise up, shep-herd, and fol- low.

Text: Traditional
Tune: African-American spiritual

272 'Twas in the Moon of Wintertime

1. 'Twas in the moon of win - ter - time, When all the birds had
2. The ear - liest moon of win - ter - time Is not so round and
3. Oh, chil - dren of the for - est free, The an - gel song is

fled, That God the Lord of all the earth Sent
fair As was the ring of glo - ry 'round The
true; The ho - ly child of earth and sky Is

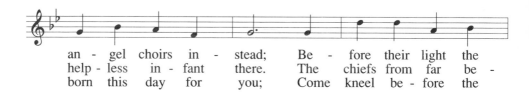

an - gel choirs in - stead; Be - fore their light the
help - less in - fant there. The chiefs from far be -
born this day for you; Come kneel be - fore the

stars grew dim, And wan - d'ring hunt - ers heard the hymn:
fore him knelt With gifts of fox and bea - ver pelt.
ra - diant boy, Who brings you beau - ty, peace, and joy.

Je - sus your king is born; Je - sus is born, in ex -

cel - sis glo - ri - a.

Text: Jean de Brebeuf, 1593-1649; trans. by Jesse E. Middleton, 1872-1960, © 1927, Frederick Harris Music Co. Ltd.
Tune: UNE JEUNE PUCELLE, 8 6 8 6 88 with refrain; French melody; arr. by Marty Haugen, b.1950, © 1992, GIA Publications, Inc.

Song of the Stable   273

1. Chill of the night-fall, Lamps in the win-dows,
2. Si - lence of mid-night, Voic - es of an - gels,
3. Splen - dor of star - light High on the hill - side,
4. Glo - ry of day-break! Sor - rows and shad-ows,

Let - ting their light fall Clear on the snow;
Sing - ing to bid night Yield to the dawn;
Faint is the far light Burn - ing be - low;
Sud - den - ly they break Forth in - to morn;

Bit - ter De - cem - ber Bids us re - mem - ber
Dark - ness is end - ed, Sin - ners be - friend - ed,
Kneel - ing be - fore him Shep - herds a - dore him,
Sing out and tell now All shall be well now;

Christ in the sta-ble Long, long a - go.
Where in the sta-ble Je - sus is born.
Christ in the sta-ble Long, long a - go.
For in the sta-ble Je - sus is born!

Text: *Chill of the Nightfall*, Timothy Dudley-Smith, b.1926, © 1980, Hope Publishing Co.
Tune: PRIOR LAKE, 5 5 5 4; David Haas, b.1957, © 1985, GIA Publications, Inc.

274　Nativity Carol

1. Si - lent, in the chill of mid - night,
2. "Fear not," said an - gel - ic voic - es;
3. Je - sus, Lord of all cre - a - tion,

star - light shines up - on a low - ly man - ger.
"ti - dings of a won - drous love we bring you.
sleep now close be - side your moth - er, Mar - y.

Won - der, won - der of the a - ges;
Go now, find him in a man - ger;
Bring us light a - mid the dark - ness,

heav - en breaks forth on the earth.
vis - it God's home on the earth."
prom - ise of life with - out end.

Refrain

For a child is born, the world re - joic - es! Shep-herds and

an - gels pro - claim his birth. This is Je - sus the Lord, our

Sav - ior and broth - er, bear - ing God's peace to the earth.

Text: Francis Patrick O'Brien, b.1958
Tune: Francis Patrick O'Brien, b.1958
© 1992, GIA Publications, Inc.

Carol at the Manger 275

1. Ho - ly Child with - in the man - ger, Long a -
2. Once a - gain we tell the sto - ry— How your
3. Ho - ly Child with - in the man - ger, Lead us

go yet ev - er near; Come as friend to ev - 'ry
love for us was shown, When the Im - age of your
ev - er in your way, So we see in ev - 'ry

stran - ger, Come as hope for ev - 'ry fear. As you
glo - ry Wore an im - age like our own. Come, en
stran - ger How you come to us to - day. In our

lived to heal the bro - ken, Greet the
light - en with your wis - dom, Come, and
lives and in our liv - ing Give us

out - cast, free the bound, As you taught us love un -
fill us with your grace, May the fire of your com -
strength to live as you, That our hearts might be for -

spo - ken, Teach us now where you are found.
pas - sion Kin - dle ev - 'ry land and race.
giv - ing And our spir - its strong and true.

Text: Marty Haugen, b.1950
Tune: JOYOUS LIGHT, 8 7 8 7 D; Marty Haugen, b.1950
© 1987, GIA Publications, Inc.

276 He Came Down

1. He came down that we may have love; He came down that we may have love; He came down that we may have love, Hal-le - lu-jah for ev-er-more.

2. He came down that we may have peace; He came down that we may have peace; He came down that we may have peace, Hal-le - lu-jah for ev-er-more.

3. He came down that we may have joy; He came down that we may have joy; He came down that we may have joy; Hal-le - lu-jah for ev-er-more.

Cantor: Why did he come?

Text: Cameroon traditional
Tune: Cameroon traditional; transcribed and arr. by John L. Bell, b. 1949, © 1990, Iona Community, GIA Publications, Inc., agent

The Aye Carol 277

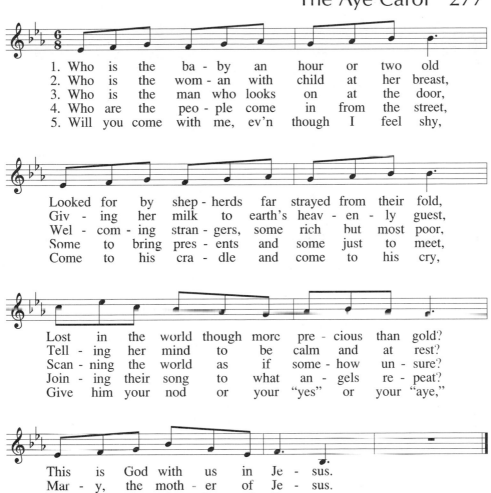

1. Who is the ba-by an hour or two old
2. Who is the wom-an with child at her breast,
3. Who is the man who looks on at the door,
4. Who are the peo-ple come in from the street,
5. Will you come with me, ev'n though I feel shy,

Looked for by shep-herds far strayed from their fold,
Giv-ing her milk to earth's heav-en-ly guest,
Wel-com-ing stran-gers, some rich but most poor,
Some to bring pres-ents and some just to meet,
Come to his cra-dle and come to his cry,

Lost in the world though more pre-cious than gold?
Tell-ing her mind to be calm and at rest?
Scan-ning the world as if some-how un-sure?
Join-ing their song to what an-gels re-peat?
Give him your nod or your "yes" or your "aye,"

This is God with us in Je-sus.
Mar-y, the moth-er of Je-sus.
Jo-seph, the fa-ther of Je-sus.
These are the new friends of Je-sus.
Give what you can give to Je-sus?

Text: John L. Bell, b.1949
Tune: AYE CAROL; 10 10 10 8; John L. Bell, b.1949
© 1987, Iona Community, GIA Publications, Inc., agent

278 Brightest and Best

1. Bright - est and best of the stars of the morn - ing,
2. Cold on his cra - dle the dew - drops are shin - ing,
3. Shall we then yield him, in cost - ly de - vo - tion,
4. Vain - ly we of - fer each am - ple o - bla - tion,
5. Bright - est and best of the stars of the morn - ing,

Dawn on our dark - ness, and lend us thine aid;
Low lies his head with the beasts of the stall;
O - dors of E - dom, and of - f'rings di - vine,
Vain - ly with gifts would his fa - vor se - cure,
Dawn on our dark - ness, and lend us thine aid;

Star of the east, the hor - i - zon a - dorn - ing,
An - gels a - dore him in slum - ber re - clin - ing,
Gems of the moun - tain, and pearls of the o - cean,
Rich - er by far is the heart's ad - o - ra - tion,
Star of the east, the ho - ri - zon a - dorn - ing,

Guide where our in - fant Re - deem - er is laid.
Mak - er and Mon - arch and Sav - ior of all.
Myrrh from the for - est, and gold from the mine?
Dear - er to God are the pray'rs of the poor.
Guide where our in - fant Re - deem - er is laid.

Bright - est and best of the stars of the morn - ing,

Dawn on our dark - ness, and lend us thine aid;

Star of the east, the ho - ri - zon a - dorn - ing,

Guide where our in - fant Re - deem - er is laid.

Text: Reginald Heber, 1783-1826, alt.
Tune: STAR IN THE EAST, 11 10 11 10 with refrain; *Southern Harmony*, 1835; harm. by Marty Haugen, b.1950, © 1987, GIA Publications, Inc.

Lord, Today 279

Refrain

Lord, to-day we have seen your glo-ry, dawn
fol-lows the night. We, your peo-ple who walked in
dark-ness now have seen a great light.

Verses

1. A child is born, a Son giv-en
2. The Lord is king, the na-tions re-
3. O Beth-le-hem, you are from of
4. The days will come, the Lord prom-ised
5. New light has dawned up-on all the

us, on him do-min-ion shall rest.
joice, let all God's peo-ple be glad. The
old, too small a-mong Ju-dah's clans.
us, when God would raise up a shoot
just, glad-ness for up-right of heart. Re-

His name shall be Won-der-ful God,
heav-ens pro-claim jus-tice for all.
From you shall come a rul-er this day,
to rule the land, reign as a king,
joice in the Lord, you faith-ful ones.

D.C.

Coun-sel-or, Prince of Peace.
Glo-ry has filled the land.
shep-herd to guide the land.
whose name is Lord the Just.
Give thanks to God's great name.

Text: Mike Balhoff, b.1946
Tune: Darryl Ducote, b.1945, Gary Daigle, b.1957
© 1978, Damean Music. Distributed by GIA Publications, Inc.

280 Dust and Ashes

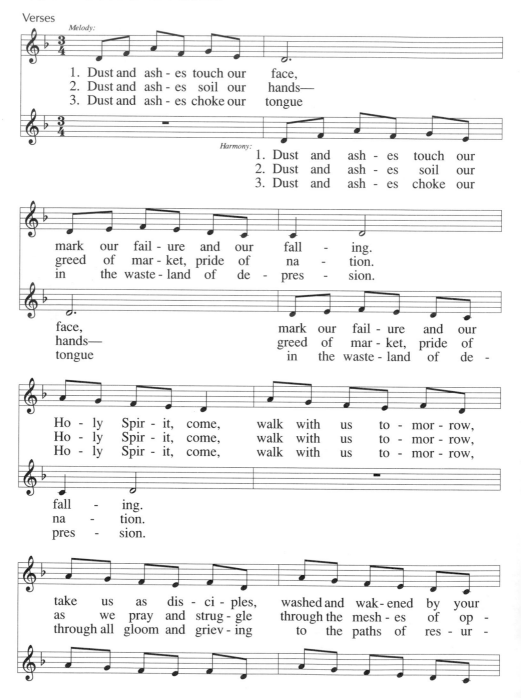

Verses

Melody:

1. Dust and ash - es touch our face,
2. Dust and ash - es soil our hands—
3. Dust and ash - es choke our tongue

Harmony:

1. Dust and ash - es touch our
2. Dust and ash - es soil our
3. Dust and ash - es choke our

mark our fail - ure and our fall - ing.
greed of mar - ket, pride of na - tion.
in the waste - land of de - pres - sion.

face,
hands—
tongue

mark our fail - ure and our
greed of mar - ket, pride of
in the waste - land of de -

Ho - ly Spir - it, come, walk with us to - mor - row,
Ho - ly Spir - it, come, walk with us to - mor - row,
Ho - ly Spir - it, come, walk with us to - mor - row,

fall - ing.
na - tion.
pres - sion.

take us as dis - ci - ples, washed and wak - ened by your
as we pray and strug - gle through the mesh - es of op -
through all gloom and griev - ing to the paths of res - ur -

call - ing.
pres - sion.
rec - tion.

Refrain

Take us by the hand and lead us,

Take us by the hand and

lead us through the des - ert sands,

lead us, lead us through the des - ert

bring us liv - ing wa - ter,

sands, bring us liv - ing

Ho - ly Spir - it, come.

wa - ter, Ho - ly Spir - it, come.

281 Eternal Lord of Love

1. E - ter - nal Lord of love, be - hold your Church,
2. So dai - ly dy - ing to the way of self,
3. If dead in you, so in you we a - rise,

Walk - ing once more the pil - grim way of Lent,
So dai - ly liv - ing to your way of love,
You the first - born of all the faith - ful dead;

Led by your cloud by day, by night your fire,
We walk the road, Lord Je - sus, that you trod,
And as through ston - y ground the green shoots break,

Moved by your love and t'ward your pres - ence bent:
Know - ing our - selves bap - tized in - to your death:
Glo - rious in spring - time dress of leaf and flower,

Far off yet here the goal of all de - sire.
So we are dead and live with you in God.
So in the Fa - ther's glo - ry shall we wake.

Text: Thomas H. Cain, b.1931, © 1982
Tune: FENN HOUSE, 10 10 10 10 10; Michael Joncas, b.1951, © 1988; GIA Publications, Inc.

Hosea 282

Verses

1. Come back to me with all your heart.
   ⸱ Trees do bend, 'though straight and tall;
2. The wil - der - ness will lead you
   In - teg - ri - ty and jus - tice,
3. ⸱ You shall sleep se - cure with peace;

   Don't let fear keep us a - part.
   so must we to oth - ers' call.
   to your heart where I will speak.
   With ten - der - ness, ⸱ you shall know.
   faith - ful - ness will be your joy. *(To refrain)*

Refrain

Long have I wait-ed for your com - ing home to me and

D.C.

liv - ing deep - ly our new life.

Text: Based on Hosea 6:1, 3:3, 2:16,21; Joel 2:12; Gregory Norbet, b.1940
Tune: Gregory Norbet, b.1940; arr. by Mary David Callahan, b 1923
© 1972, 1980, The Benedictine Foundation of the State of Vermont, Inc.

283   Return to God

Refrain

Re - turn to God with all your heart, the source of grace and mer - cy; come seek the ten - der faith - ful - ness of God.

Verses

1. Now the time of grace has come,
   the day of salvation;
   come and learn now the way of our God.

2. I will take your heart of stone
   and place a heart within you,
   a heart of compassion and love.

3. If you break the chains of oppression,
   if you set the pris'ner free;
   if you share your bread with the hungry,
   give protection to the lost;
   give a shelter to the homeless,
   clothe the naked in your midst,
   then your light shall break forth like the dawn.

Text: Marty Haugen, b.1950
Tune: Marty Haugen, b.1950
© 1990, 1991, GIA Publications, Inc.

Jerusalem, My Destiny 284

Refrain

I have fixed my eyes on your hills, Je-ru-sa-lem, my des-ti-ny! Though I can-not see the end for me, I can-not turn a-way. We have set our hearts for the way; this jour-ney is our des-ti-ny. Let no-one walk a-lone. The jour-ney makes us one.

Verses

1. Oth - er spir - its, less - er gods, have court-ed me with lies. Here a-mong you I have found a truth which bids me rise.
2. See, I leave the past be - hind; a new land calls to me. Here a-mong you now I find a glimpse of what might be.
3. In my thirst, you let me drink the wa - ters of your life. Here a-mong you I have met the sa - viour, Je - sus Christ.
4. All the worlds I have not seen you o - pen to my view. Here a-mong you I have found a vi - sion, bright and new.
5. To the tombs I went to mourn the hope I thought was gone. Here a-mong you I a - woke to un - ex - pect - ed dawn.

D.C.

Text: Rory Cooney, b.1952
Tune: Rory Cooney, b.1952
© 1990, GIA Publications, Inc.

285 Change Our Hearts

Refrain

Change our hearts this time, Your word says it can
be. Change our minds, this time, Your life could make us
free. We are the peo - ple Your call set a - part,
Lord, this time change our hearts.

Verses

1. Brought by your hand to the edge of our dreams.
2. Now as we watch you stretch out your hands,
3. Show us the way that leads to your side,

One foot in par - a - dise, one in the waste.
of - 'fring a - bun - dan - ces, full - ness of joy.
o - ver the moun - tains and sands of the soul.

Drawn by your prom - is - es, still we are
Your milk and hon - ey seem dis - tant, un -
Be for us man - na, wa - ter from

D.C.

lured by the shad - ows and the chains we leave be - hind. But
real, when we have bread and wa - ter in our hands. But
stone, light which says we nev - er walk a - lone. And

Text: Rory Cooney, b.1952
Tune: Rory Cooney, b.1952
© 1984, North American Liturgy Resources

God of Abraham 286

(Invocation) Lead us to your king - dom.

(Invocation) Lead us to-geth-er, lead us to free-dom.

Last time

lead us to free-dom. Lead us to free-dom now.

Text: Bernadette Farrell, b.1957
Tune: Bernadette Farrell, b.1957
© 1990, Bernadette Farrell, published by OCP Publications

287 Adoramus Te Christe

Canon Refrain

A - do - ra - mus te Chri - ste, a - do - ra - mus te Chri - ste,

a - do - ra - mus te Chri - ste, a - do - ra - mus Chri - ste.

Verses

1. A - do - ra - mus te Chri - ste, et be - ne -

di - ci - mus ti - bi, 2. Qui - a per san - ctam

Cru - cem tu - am re - de - mi - sti mun - dum.

Text: Antiphon from Good Friday Liturgy; *We adore you, O Christ, and we bless you, because by your holy cross you have redeemed the world.*
Tune: Marty Haugen, b.1950, © 1984, GIA Publications, Inc.

288 Tree of Life

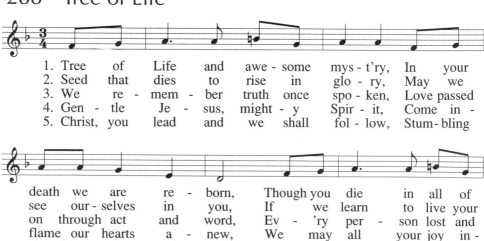

1. Tree of Life and awe - some mys - t'ry, In your
2. Seed that dies to rise in glo - ry, May we
3. We re - mem - ber truth once spo - ken, Love passed
4. Gen - tle Je - sus, might - y Spir - it, Come in -
5. Christ, you lead and we shall fol - low, Stum - bling

death we are re - born, Though you die in all of
see our - selves in you, If we learn to live your
on through act and word, Ev - 'ry per - son lost and
flame our hearts a - new, We may all your joy in -
though our steps may be, One with you in joy and

his - t'ry,   Still   you   rise with   ev - 'ry   morn,   Still   you
sto - ry   We   may   die   to   rise   a - new,   We   may
bro - ken   Wears the   bod - y   of   our   Lord,   Wears the
her - it   If   we   bear the   cross   with   you,   If   we
sor - row,   We   the   riv - er,   you   the   sea,   We   the

rise with ev - 'ry   morn.
die   to   rise   a - new.
bod - y   of   our   Lord.
bear the cross with   you.
riv - er,   you   the   sea.

Lenten Verses:

General: Light of life beyond conceiving, Mighty Spirit of our Lord;
Give new strength to our believing, Give us faith to live your word.

1st Sunday: From the dawning of creation, You have loved us as your own;
Stay with us through all temptation, Make us turn to you alone.

2nd Sunday: In our call to be a blessing, May we be a blessing true;
May we live and die confessing Christ as Lord of all we do.

3rd Sunday: Living Water of salvation, Be the fountain of each soul;
Springing up in new creation, Flow in us and make us whole.

4th Sunday: Give us eyes to see you clearly, Make us children of your light;
Give us hearts to live more nearly As your gospel shining bright.

5th Sunday: God of all our fear and sorrow, God who lives beyond our death;
Hold us close through each tomorrow, Love as near as every breath.

Text: Marty Haugen, b.1950
Tune: THOMAS, 8 7 8 77; Marty Haugen, b.1950
© 1984, GIA Publications, Inc.

289 Hold Us in Your Mercy: Penitential Litany

Hold us in your mer - cy. Hold us in your mer - cy.

Hold us in your mer - cy. Hold us in your mer - cy.

(Invocation) Hold us in your mer - cy.

(Invocation) Hold us in your mer - cy.

Hold us in your mer - cy. Hold us in your mer - cy.

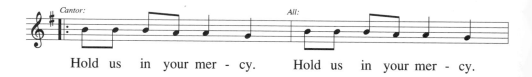

Hold us in your mer - cy. Hold us in your mer - cy.

Hold us in your mer - cy Hold us in your mer - cy.

Text: Rory Cooney, b.1952
Tune: Gary Daigle, b.1957
© 1993, GIA Publications, Inc.

Deep Within 290

Refrain

Deep with - in I will plant my law, not on stone, but in your heart. Fol - low me, I will bring you back, you will be my own, and I will be your God.

Verses

D.C.

1. I will give you a new heart, a new spir - it with-
2. Seek my face, and see your
3. Re - turn to me, with all your

in you, for I will be your strength.
God, for I will be your hope.
heart, and I will bring you back.

Text: Jeremiah 31:33, Ezekiel 36:26, Joel 2:12; David Haas, b.1957
Tune: David Haas, b.1957; acc. by Jeanne Cotter, b.1964
© 1987, GIA Publications, Inc.

291 Wash Me, Cleanse Me

Verses

1. Wash me, cleanse me and I shall be bright-er than the snow. For my soul is long-ing for your pres-ence, Lord, and my bro-ken heart you know.

2. Ash to ash, dust to dust, ev-'ry-thing re-turn-ing to your heart. You are al-ways mer-ci-ful and gra-cious, Lord, slow to an-ger, just and kind.

3. Fear-ful, faith-ful, I a-wait new heav-en and new earth. Yet a day to you is as a thou-sand years, and a thou-sand years a day.

4. Hear me, spare me, do not face me sud-den-ly with death. Give me grace to heal my sin and ig-no-rance, and the time to change my heart.

Refrain

O Lord, please wash me, cleanse me and I shall be bright-er than the snow. Wash me, cleanse me and I shall be bright-er than the snow.

Text: Jeremy Young, b.1948
Tune: Jeremy Young, b.1948
© 1990, GIA Publications, Inc.

Hosanna 292

Refrain

Ho - san - na, ho - san - na, ho - san - na! Ho - san - na, ho - san - na, ho - san - na, ho - san - na!

Verses

1. Blessed is he,
   blessed is he who comes in the name of the Lord!
   Blessed is he,
   blessed is he who comes in the name of the Lord!

2. Blessed is the reign of our father, David.
   Blessed is the reign of our father, David, to come!

Text: Mark 11:9-10; David Haas, b.1957
Tune: David Haas, b.1957
© 1988, GIA Publications, Inc.

293 Jesus, Remember Me

Ostinato Refrain

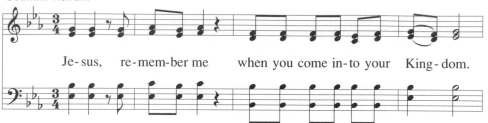

Je-sus, re-mem-ber me when you come in-to your King-dom.

Je-sus, re-mem-ber me when you come in-to your King-dom.

Text: Luke 23:42; Taizé Community, 1981
Tune: Jacques Berthier, b.1923
© 1981, Les Presses de Taizé, GIA Publications, Inc., agent

Ride On, Jesus, Ride 294

Ride on, Je - sus, ride. Ride on, Je - sus, ride.

Ride on, Je - sus, con - quering King, Ride on, Je - sus ride.

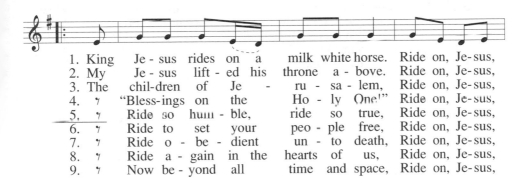

1. King Je - sus rides on a milk white horse. Ride on, Je - sus,
2. My Je - sus lift - ed his throne a - bove. Ride on, Je - sus,
3. The chil-dren of Je - ru - sa - lem, Ride on, Je - sus,
4. ' "Bless-ings on the Ho - ly One!" Ride on, Je - sus,
5. ' Ride so hum - ble, ride so true, Ride on, Je - sus,
6. ' Ride to set your peo - ple free, Ride on, Je - sus,
7. ' Ride o - be - dient un - to death, Ride on, Je - sus,
8. ' Ride a - gain in the hearts of us, Ride on, Je - sus,
9. ' Now be - yond all time and space, Ride on, Je - sus,

ride. The riv - er Jor - dan he did cross.
ride. ' See his mer - cy and his love.
ride, ' strewed their branch - es on his way.
ride. ' "Bless - ings on the Sav - ing One!"
ride. ' Ride to bring the world to you, Ride on, Je - sus,
ride. ' Ride the road to Cal - va - ry,
ride. ' Ride to break the chains of death,
ride. ' Ride a - gain in the hands of us,
ride. ' Now in ev - 'ry land and race,

ride. Ride on, Je - sus, con - quering King. Ride on, Je - sus ride.

Text: African-American spiritual; verses 3-9, Marty Haugen, b.1950, © 1991, GIA Publications, Inc.
Tune: African-American spiritual; harm. by Barbara Jackson Martin, © 1987, GIA Publications, Inc.

295 Triduum Hymn: Wondrous Love

Holy Thursday Verses

1. What won-drous love is this, O my soul, O my
2. The night be - fore the end of his life, of his
3. "The ones who share this feast in my name, in my
4. As ser - vant, then, he knelt at their feet, at their
5. "What I have done for you in my love, in my
6. They sang a hymn of praise un - to you, un - to

soul? What won-drous love is this, O my soul? What
life, The night be - fore the end of his life; The
name, The ones who share this feast in my name; The
feet, As ser - vant, then, he knelt at their feet; As
love, What I have done for you in my love; What
you, They sang a hymn of praise un - to you; They

won - drous love is this that caused the Lord of
night be - fore the end my Lord sat with his
ones who share this feast shall know their joy in -
ser - vant, then, he knelt, a ser - vant's towel for
I have done for you, so you are called to
sang a hymn of praise, their hearts and voic - es

bliss To bear the dread-ful curse for my soul, for my
friends, And of - fered them the meal of his death and his
creased, The reign of grace and peace in my name, in my
belt, He showed the love he felt at their feet, at their
do, To be a ser - vant true in your love, in your
raised, Then he went to his death— un - to you, un - to

soul, To bear the dread - ful curse for my soul?
life, He of - fered them a share in his life.
name, The reign of grace and peace in my name."
feet, He showed the love he felt at their feet.
love, To be a ser - vant true in your love."
you, Then he went to his death— un - to you.

Text: St. 1, Alexander Means, 1801-1853; remainder, Marty Haugen, b.1950, © 1987, GIA Publications, Inc.
Tune: WONDROUS LOVE, 12 9 12 12 9; *Southern Harmony,* 1835; acc. by Marty Haugen, b.1950, © 1987, GIA Publications, Inc.

Good Friday Verses

What wondrous love is this, O my
  soul, O my soul?
What wondrous love is this, O my soul?
What wondrous love is this that
  caused the Lord of bliss
To bear the dreadful curse for my soul,
  for my soul,
To bear the dreadful curse for my soul?

As you have shown the way, let us
  love, let us love,
As you have shown the way, let us love;
As you have shown the way, so teach
  us ev'ry day
To simply be the way of your love, of
  your love,
To simply be the way of your love.

Wherever you are found, may we be,
  may we be,
Wherever you are found, may we be;
Wherever you are found in souls and
  bodies bound,
Where suffering is found, may we be,
  may we be,
Where suffering is found, may we be.

As instruments of peace, may we
  grow, may we grow,
As instruments of peace, may we grow;
As instruments of peace to bring the
  bound release,
And make oppression cease, help us
  grow, help us grow,
To make oppression cease,
  help us grow.

O let us hear your call to be love,
  to be love,
O let us hear your call to be love;
O let us hear your call, great servant
  of us all,
To be the least of all, as your love, as
  your love,
To be the least of all, as your love.

Easter Vigil Verses

No more within the grave does he lie,
  does he lie,
No more within the grave does he lie;
No more within the grave, but risen
  now to save,
No more within the earth does he lie,
  does he lie
No more within the earth does he lie.

The God who raised my Lord will raise
  me, will raise me,
The God who raised my Lord will
  raise me;
The God who raised my Lord, who
  spoke the living word
Will shout into my tomb and raise me,
  and raise me,
Will shout into my tomb and raise me.

Up from the holy flood, I will rise, I
  will rise,
Up from the holy flood, I will rise;
Up from the holy flood, the water and
  the blood,
To praise the living God, I will rise, I
  will rise,
To praise the living God, I will rise.

To God and to the lamb I will sing, I
  will sing,
To God and to the lamb I will sing;
To God and to the lamb, who is the
  great "I am,"
While millions join the theme, I will
  sing, I will sing,
While millions join the theme, I will sing.

And when from death I'm free, I'll
  sing on, I'll sing on,
And when from death I'm free, I'll sing on;
And when from death I'm free, I'll sing
  and joyful be,
And through eternity I'll sing on,
  I'll sing on,
And through eternity I'll sing on.

Text: St. 1, Alexander Means, 1801-1853; remainder, Marty Haugen, b.1950, © 1987, GIA Publications, Inc.
Tune: WONDROUS LOVE, 12 9 12 12 9; *Southern Harmony*, 1835; acc. by Marty Haugen, b.1950, © 1987, GIA Publications, Inc.

296 Jesu, Jesu

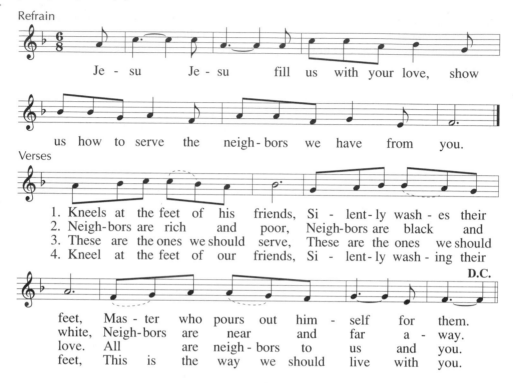

Refrain

Je - su Je - su fill us with your love, show
us how to serve the neigh - bors we have from you.

Verses

1. Kneels at the feet of his friends, Si - lent-ly wash - es their
2. Neigh-bors are rich and poor, Neigh-bors are black and
3. These are the ones we should serve, These are the ones we should
4. Kneel at the feet of our friends, Si - lent-ly wash - ing their

D.C.

feet, Mas - ter who pours out him - self for them.
white, Neigh-bors are near and far a - way.
love. All are neigh - bors to us and you.
feet, This is the way we should live with you.

Text: John 13:3-5; Ghana folk song; tr. by Tom Colvin, b.1925
Tune: CHEREPONI, Irregular; Ghana folk song; Tom Colvin, b.1925; acc. by Jane M. Marshall, b.1924, © 1982, Hope Publishing Co.

297 Serving You

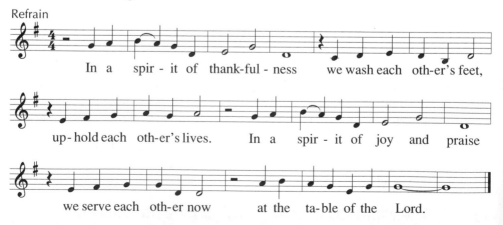

Refrain

In a spir - it of thank-ful - ness we wash each oth-er's feet,
up - hold each oth-er's lives. In a spir - it of joy and praise
we serve each oth-er now at the ta-ble of the Lord.

Verses

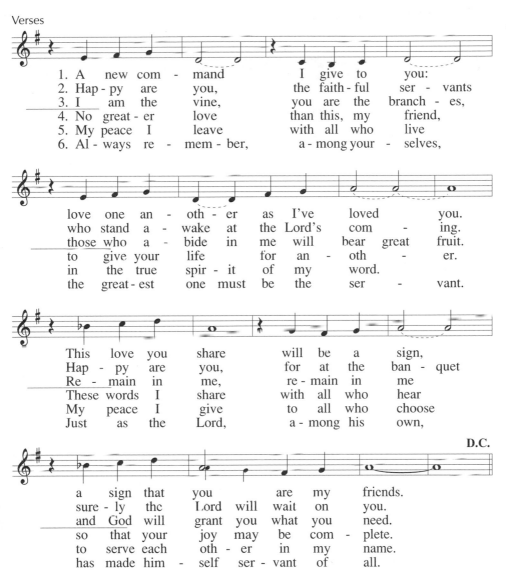

1. A new com - mand I give to you:
2. Hap - py are you, the faith - ful ser - vants
3. I am the vine, you are the branch - es,
4. No great - er love than this, my friend,
5. My peace I leave with all who live
6. Al - ways re - mem - ber, a - mong your - selves,

love one an - oth - er as I've loved you.
who stand a - wake at the Lord's com - ing.
those who a - bide in me will bear great fruit.
to give your life for an - oth - er.
in the true spir - it of my word.
the great - est one must be the ser - vant.

This love you share will be a sign,
Hap - py are you, for at the ban - quet
Re - main in me, re - main in me
These words I share with all who hear
My peace I give to all who choose
Just as the Lord, a - mong his own,

D.C.

a sign that you are my friends.
sure - ly the Lord will wait on you.
and God will grant you what you need.
so that your joy may be com - plete.
to serve each oth - er in my name.
has made him - self ser - vant of all.

Text: Michel Guimont, b.1950
Tune: Michel Guimont, b.1950
© 1992, GIA Publications, Inc.

298 Stay Here and Keep Watch

Ostinato Refrain

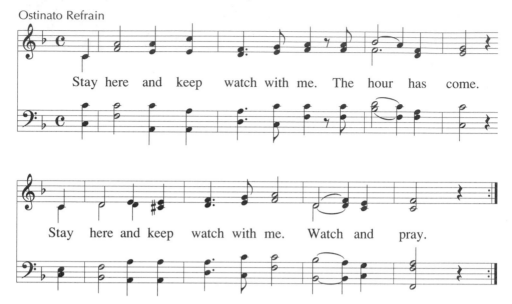

Stay here and keep watch with me. The hour has come.

Stay here and keep watch with me. Watch and pray.

Text: from Matthew 26; Taizé Community
Tune: Jacques Berthier, b.1923
© 1984, Les Presses de Taizé, GIA Publications, Inc., agent

299 Song of the Lord's Supper

1. We re - mem - ber one who loved us well,
2. We re - mem - ber how he spoke of you,
3. On the night be - fore he suf - fered death,
4. As they sat at ta - ble he took bread,
5. Now we take these gifts of field and vine,

Shared our life, its joy and sor - row, Walked a - mong us as the
Taught us to be - lieve your prom - ise, Showed us all what you are
Je - sus gath - ered his dis - ci - ples, Knelt be - fore them as a
Blest it, broke it, gave it free - ly: "Take this bread and eat it,
Bless and share them in his mem - 'ry: Bread of life and cup of

least of all, Gave him - self in - to our keep - ing.
real - ly like— Faith - ful, ten - der, God of peo - ple:
ser - vant might, Washed their feet and bid them wel - come:
all of you; Take and eat, this is my bod - y."
cov - e - nant, King - dom - feast in pledge and prom - ise.

He is light that dawns for blind - ed eyes,
Not a God to break the wound - ed heart,
"Do you know what I have done for you,
Then he took the cup and passed it round:
When we eat this bread and drink this cup

He is hope for the de - spair - ing; All on earth can find a
Not the thun - der of the might - y, But a God that wel - comes
I who am your Lord and Mas - ter? If I bend to you and
"Take and drink, this is my life - blood, Shed for you and for all
We pro-claim the death of Je - sus, Taste his pres-ence, liv - ing

place with him, Saint and sin - ner at his ta - ble.
sin - ners home, Meets the low - ly with com - pas- sion.
wash your feet, So must you for one an - oth - er."
hu - man - kind, Shed that sins may be for - giv - en"
in our midst, Look for him to come in glo - ry

Text: Michael Joncas, b.1951
Tune: Michael Joncas, b.1951
© 1988, GIA Publications, Inc.

300 Faithful Family

Refrain

Be like our God, who chose to live and learn our ways, and die in deep, un-bound-ed love. For-give each oth - er ten - der - ly. The faith-ful fam-'ly of our God.

Verses

1. Where ev - er there is char - i - ty, self - less, giv - ing care,
2. And let us love the Liv - ing God, mer - ci - ful, and kind,
3. When we are to - geth - er, let us act as one,
4. One day in the com - pan - y of the saints in light,

sure - ly our God is there.
bod - y and heart and mind.
ways of greed and con - flict done.
may we see your face shine bright;

The love of Christ has gath - ered us to one from is - land ways:
Let us love each oth - er well, hold the stran - ger dear,
Let there be no bit - ter - ness, quar - rel - ing, nor strife.
Bright up - on your fam - i - ly, faith - ful, hu - man, flawed.

D.C.

let us sing for joy all our days.
reach - ing out to all with - out fear.
In our midst is Christ, our life.
Shine in glo - ry, Christ, our God.

Text: Verses based on *Ubi Caritas;* Rory Cooney, b.1952
Tune: Rory Cooney, b.1952
© 1986, North American Liturgy Resources

Ubi Caritas 301

Refrain

U - bi ca - ri - tas et a - mor,
Live in char - i - ty and stead - fast love,

u - bi ca - ri - tas De - us i - bi est.
live in char - i - ty; God will dwell with you.

Text: I Corinthians 13;2-8; *Where charity and love are found, God is there;* Taizé Community, 1978
Tune: Jacques Berthier, 1923-1994
© 1979, Les Presses de Taizé, GIA Publications, Inc., agent

302 Were You There

1. Were you there when they cru - ci - fied my Lord?
2. Were you there when they nailed him to the tree?
3. Were you there when they pierced him in the side?
4. Were you there when the sun re - fused to shine?
5. Were you there when they laid him in the tomb?
6. Were you there when they rolled the stone a - way?

Were you there when they cru - ci - fied my Lord?
Were you there when they nailed him to the tree?
Were you there when they pierced him in the side?
Were you there when the sun re - fused to shine?
Were you there when they laid him in the tomb?
Were you there when they rolled the stone a - way?

Oh!   Some-times   it   caus - es   me   to

trem-ble,   trem-ble,   trem - ble,   Were you

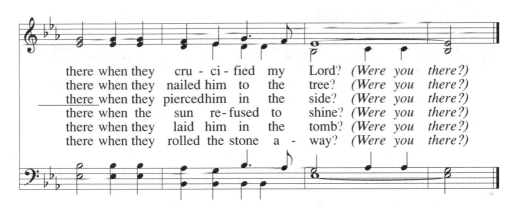

there when they cru - ci - fied my Lord? *(Were you there?)*
there when they nailed him to the tree? *(Were you there?)*
there when they pierced him in the side? *(Were you there?)*
there when the sun re-fused to shine? *(Were you there?)*
there when they laid him in the tomb? *(Were you there?)*
there when they rolled the stone a - way? *(Were you there?)*

Text: African-American spiritual
Tune: WERE YOU THERE, 10 10 with refrain; African-American spiritual; harm. by Robert J. Batastini, b.1942, © 1987, GIA Publications, Inc.

303 Crucem Tuam / O Lord, Your Cross

Cru - cem tu - am a - do - ra - mus Do - mi -
O Lord, your cross, we a - dore and glo - ri -

ne, re - sur - re - cti - o - nem tu - am lau - da - mus Do - mi -
fy, for your ho - ly re - sur - rec - tion, we praise you Lord of

ne. Lau - da - mus et glo - ri - fi - ca - mus.
life. We praise you and we glo - ri - fy you.

Re - sur - re - cti - o - nem tu - am lau - da - mus Do - mi - ne.
For your ho - ly re - sur - rec - tion, we praise you Lord of life.

Text: Taizé Community, 1991
Tune: Jacques Berthier, b.1923
© 1991, Les Presses de Taizé, GIA Publications, Inc., agent

Jesus, the Lord   304

Refrain

Je - sus.   Je - sus.   Let all cre - a - tion bend the knee to the Lord.

Verse 1

1. In him we live, we move and have our be - ing; in him the Christ, in him the King. Je - sus, the Lord.

D.C.

Verses 2, 3

2. Though Son, he did not cling to god - li - ness; but emp - tied him - self, be - came a slave!

3. He lived o - be - dient - ly his Fa - ther's will ac - cept - ing his death, death on a tree!

Je - sus, the Lord.

D.C.

Text: *Jesus Prayer*, Philippians 2:5-11; Acts 17:28; Roc O'Connor, SJ, b.1949
Tune: Roc O'Connor, SJ, b.1949; arr. by John Foley, SJ, b.1939, alt.
© 1981, Robert F. O'Connor, SJ, and New Dawn Music

305 Calvary

Refrain

Cal - va - ry,   Cal - va - ry,   Cal - va -

ry,   Cal - va - ry,   Cal - va - ry,

Cal - va - ry,   Sure - ly he died on   Cal - va - ry.

Verses

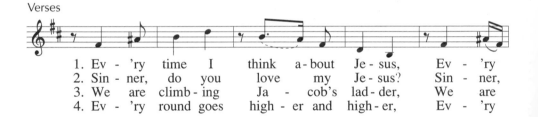

1. Ev - 'ry time I think a - bout Je - sus,   Ev - 'ry
2. Sin - ner, do you love my Je - sus?   Sin - ner,
3. We are climb - ing Ja - cob's lad - der,   We are
4. Ev - 'ry round goes high - er and high - er,   Ev - 'ry

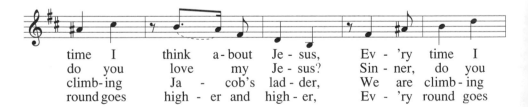

time I think a - bout Je - sus,   Ev - 'ry time I
do you love my Je - sus?   Sin - ner, do you
climb - ing Ja - cob's lad - der,   We are climb - ing
round goes high - er and high - er,   Ev - 'ry round goes

D.C.

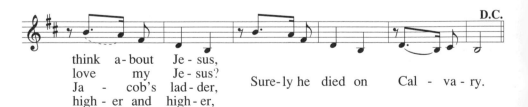

think a - bout Je - sus,
love my Je - sus?   Sure - ly he died on   Cal - va - ry.
Ja - cob's lad - der,
high - er and high - er,

Text: African-American spiritual
Tune: African-American spiritual

Behold the Wood 306

Refrain

Be - hold, be - hold the wood of the cross, on which is hung our sal - va - tion.

O come, let us a - dore.

Verses

1. Un - less a grain of wheat shall fall up -
2. And when my hour of glo - ry comes as
3. For there can be no great - er love
4. My Fa - ther, if it be your plan, this
5. For sure - ly he has borne our tears, is
6. My bod - y now is torn with pain, my

on the ground and die, it shall re - main but a
all was meant to be, you shall see me
shown up - on this land than in the one who
cup might pass me by, yet let it hap - pen
wound - ed by our sin, and yet he o - pens
friends have left and gone. O lov - ing Fa - ther,

D.C.

sin - gle grain and not give life.
lift - ed up up - on a tree.
came to die that we might live.
as you will if I must die.
not his mouth that we might live.
take my life in - to your hands.

Text: John 12; Dan Schutte, b.1947
Tune: Dan Schutte, b.1947
© 1976, Daniel L. Schutte and New Dawn Music

307 Easter Alleluia

Refrain

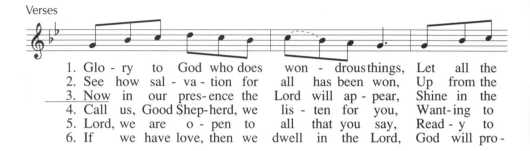

Al - le - lu - ia, al - le - lu - ia, al - le - lu - ia!

Verses

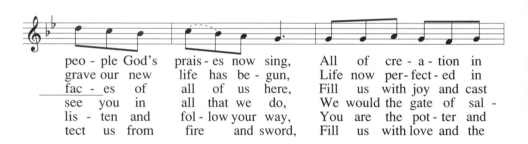

1. Glo - ry to God who does won - drous things, Let all the
2. See how sal - va - tion for all has been won, Up from the
3. Now in our pres - ence the Lord will ap - pear, Shine in the
4. Call us, Good Shep - herd, we lis - ten for you, Want - ing to
5. Lord, we are o - pen to all that you say, Read - y to
6. If we have love, then we dwell in the Lord, God will pro -

peo - ple God's prais - es now sing, All of cre - a - tion in
grave our new life has be - gun, Life now per - fect - ed in
fac - es of all of us here, Fill us with joy and cast
see you in all that we do, We would the gate of sal -
lis - ten and fol - low your way, You are the pot - ter and
tect us from fire and sword, Fill us with love and the

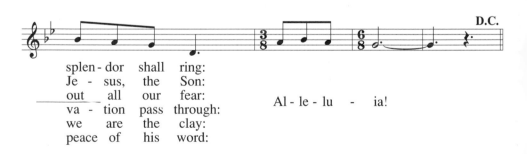

D.C.

splen - dor shall ring:
Je - sus, the Son:
out all our fear:
va - tion pass through:
we are the clay:
peace of his word:

Al - le - lu - ia!

Text: Marty Haugen, b.1950
Tune: O FILII ET FILIAE; 10 10 10 with alleluias; adapt. by Marty Haugen, b.1950
© 1986, GIA Publications, Inc.

Christ Has Risen   308

1. Christ has ris - en while earth slum - bers, Christ has
2. Christ has ris - en for the peo - ple Whom he
3. Christ has ris - en to com - pan - ion For - mer
4. Christ has ris - en and for ev - er Lives to

ris - en where hope died, As he said and as he
died to love and save; Christ has ris - en for the
friends who fear the night, Sens - ing loss and lim - i -
chal - lenge and to change All whose lives are messed or

prom - ised, As we doubt - ed and de -
wom - en Bring - ing flowers to grace his
la - tion Where their faith had once burned
man - gled, All who find re - li - gion

nied. Let the moon em - brace the bless - ing; Let the
grave. Christ has ris - en for dis - ci - ples Hud - dled
bright. They be - moan what is no long - er, They ex -
strange. Christ is ris - en, Christ is pres - ent Mak - ing

sun sus - tain the cheer; Let the world con - firm the
in an up - stairs room. He whose word in - spired cre -
pect no hope - ful sign Till Christ ends their con - ver -
us what he has been— Ev - i - dence of trans - for -

ru - mor: Christ is ris - en, God is here!
a - tion Can't be si - lenced by the tomb.
sa - tion, Break - ing bread and shar - ing wine.
ma - tion In which God is known and seen.

Text: John L. Bell, b.1949
Tune: TRANSFORMATION, 8 7 8 7 D; John L. Bell, b.1949

309 All Things New

Refrain

Sing a new song! Re - joice! The dawn is break-ing,

the earth is wak-ing, its dreams come true. And do you

hear the voice, dark - ness sur - pris - ing, sing in its

ris - ing: "See, I am mak - ing all things new!"

Verses

1. Whom shall we live for? Whose might - y hand
2. Who found us wan - der-ers, and made us in - to one?
3. Who is known to ev - 'ry heart and called by man - y names?

made the moon, the sun and stars on high?
Who is ev - er near with strength to save?
Who has called the low - ly ones "My own,"

Who made a way for us through
Whose love a - dopt - ed us as
Breathes a dream of jus - tice in - to

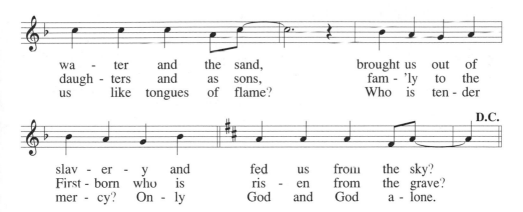

wa - ter and the sand, brought us out of
daugh - ters and as sons, fam - 'ly to the
us like tongues of flame? Who is ten - der

D.C.

slav - er - y and fed us from the sky?
First - born who is ris - en from the grave?
mer - cy? On - ly God and God a - lone.

Text: Rory Cooney, b. 1952
Tune: Rory Cooney, b. 1952
© 1993, GIA Publications, Inc.

Surrexit Dominus Vere II 310

Canon—*4 voices*

1. Sur - re - xit Do - mi - nus ve - re.
2. Al - le - lu - ia, al - le - lu - ia.
3. Sur - re - xit Chri - stus ho - di - e,
4. Al - le - lu - ia, al - le - lu - ia.

Text: *The Lord is truly risen! Christ is risen today!* Taizé Community, 1978
Tune: Jacques Berthier, 1923-1994
© 1978, Les Presses de Taizé, GIA Publications, Inc., agent

311 Christ Is Risen! Shout Hosanna!

1. Christ is ris - en! Shout Ho - san - na! Cel - e - brate this
2. Christ is ris - en! Raise your spir - its From the cav - erns
3. Christ is ris - en! Earth and heav - en Nev - er - more shall

day of days! Christ is ris - en! Hush in won - der:
of des - pair. Walk with glad - ness in the morn - ing.
be the same. Break the bread of new cre - a - tion

All cre - a - tion is a - mazed. In the des - ert
See what love can do and dare. Drink the wine of
Where the world is still in pain. Tell its grim, de -

all sur - round - ing, See, a spread - ing tree has grown.
res - ur - rec - tion, Not a ser - vant, but a friend.
mon - ic cho - rus: "Christ is ris - en! Get you gone!"

Heal - ing leaves of grace a - bound - ing
Je - sus is our strong com - pan - ion.
God the First and Last is with us.

Bring a taste of love un - known.
Joy and peace shall nev - er end.
Sing Ho - san - na ev - 'ry one!

Text: Brian Wren, b.1936, © 1986, Hope Publishing Co.
Tune: HOSANNA, 8 7 8 7 D; David Haas, b.1957, © 1991, GIA Publications, Inc.

Resucitó 312

Refrain

Re - su - ci - tó,   re - su - ci - tó,   re - su - ci -
A - le - lu - ya,   a - le - lu - ya,   a - le - lu -

Final ending

tó,   a - le - lu - ya.   A - le - lu - ya.
ya,   re - su - ci - tó.

Verses

1.   La   muer - te   ¿dón - de_es - tá la
2.   Gra - cias se - an   da - das al
3.   A - le - grí - a,   a - le - grí - a_her -
4. Si con Él mo - ri - mos   γ con Él vi -
1. *   And death now,   van ished is the*
2. *   The king - dom,   praise to God, the*
3. *   Our glad - ness,   bliss - ful in our*
4. *   With him then,   die and live with*

muer - te?   ¿Dón - de_es - tá mi
Pa - dre   que nos pa - só_a su
ma - nos,   que si hoy nos que -
vi - mos,   γ con Él can -
fear now,   ban - ished are my
king - dom!   Raised up to the
glad - ness,   this will be our
him then,   rise and sing our

D.C.

muer - te?   ¿Dón - de su vic - to - ria?
rei - no.   ¿Dón - de se vi - ve de_a - mor?
re - mos.   Es que re - su - ci - tó.
ta - mos.   γ A - le - lu - ya.
tears now,   death has passed a - way.
king - dom,   we shall live in love.
glad - ness,   that he is a - live.
hymn then,   sing al - le - lu - ia.

Text: Kiko Argüello, © 1972, Ediciones Musical PAX, U.S. agent: OCP Publications; trans. by Robert C. Trupia, © 1988, OCP Publications
Tune: Kiko Argüello, © 1972, Ediciones Musical PAX, U.S. agent: OCP Publications; acc. by Diana Kodner, © 1993, GIA Publications, Inc.

313 Sing to the Mountains

Refrain

Sing to the moun-tains, sing to the sea. Raise your
voic - es, lift your hearts. This is the day the
Lord has made. Let all the earth re - joice.

Verse 1

1. I will give thanks to you, my Lord. You have
an - swered my plea. You have saved my
soul from death. You are my strength and my song.

Verse 2

2. Ho - ly, ho - ly, ho - ly Lord,
heav - en and earth are full of your glo - ry.

Verse 3

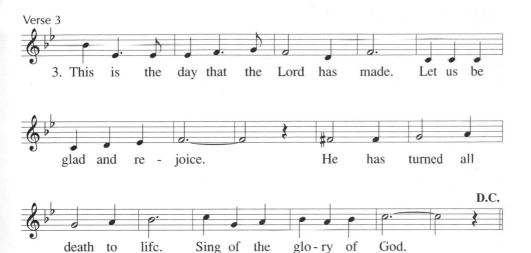

3. This is the day that the Lord has made. Let us be

glad and re - joice. He has turned all

D.C.

death to life. Sing of the glo - ry of God.

Text: Psalm 118; Bob Dufford, SJ, b.1943
Tune: Bob Dufford, SJ, b.1943; acc. by Sr. Theophane Hytrek, OSF, 1915-1992, alt.
© 1975, Robert J. Dufford, SJ, and New Dawn Music

Surrexit Christus 314

Ostinato Refrain

(hum) Sur - re - xit Chri-stus, al - le - lu - ia!

(hum) Can - ta - te Do - mi - no, al - le - lu - ia!

Text: *Christ is risen, sing to the Lord;* Daniel 3; Taizé Community, 1984
Tune: Jacques Berthier, 1923-1994
© 1984, Les Presses de Taizé, GIA Publications, Inc., agent

315 Christ the Lord Is Risen!

1. Christ the Lord is ris'n! Christ the Lord is ris'n!
2. He has con - quered death. He has con - quered death.
3. Sin has done its worst. Sin has done its worst.
4. He is King of kings. He is King of kings.
5. He is Lord of lords. He is Lord of lords.
6. All the world is his. All the world is his.
7. Come and wor - ship him. Come and wor - ship him.
8. Christ our Lord is ris'n! Christ our Lord is ris'n!
9. Hal - le - lu - jah! Hal - le - lu - jah!

Je - su. Christ the Lord is ris'n!
Je - su. He has con - quered death.
Je - su. Sin has done its worst.
Je - su. He is King of kings.
Je - su. He is Lord of lords.
Je - su. All the world is his.
Je - su. Come and wor - ship him.
Je - su. Christ our Lord is ris'n!
Je - su. Hal - le - lu - jah!

Christ the Lord is ris'n! Je - su.
He has con - quered death. Je - su.
Sin has done its worst. Je - su.
He is King of kings. Je - su.
He is Lord of lords. Je - su.
All the world is his. Je - su.
Come and wor - ship him. Je - su.
Christ our Lord is ris'n! Je - su.
Hal - le - lu - jah! Je - su.

Text: Tom Colvin, b.1925
Tune: Garu, Ghanian folk song, arr. by Kevin R. Hackett
© 1969, Hope Publishing Company

Come Away to the Skies 316

1. Come a - way to the skies, My be -
2. Now with sing - ing and praise, Let us
3. For the glo - ry we were First cre -
4. We with thanks do ap - prove The de -
5. Hal - le - lu - jah we sing, To our

lov - ed, a - rise And re - joice in the
spend all the days, By our heav - en - ly
at - ed to share, Both the na - ture and
sign of that love Which has joined us to
Fa - ther and King, And his rap - tu - rous

day you were born; On this
Fa - ther be - stowed, While his
king - dom di - vine! Now cre -
Je - sus' name; So u -
prais - es, re - peat: To the

fes - ti - val day, Come ex - ult - ing a -
grace we re - ceive From his boun - ty, and
at - ed a - gain That our lives may re -
nit - ed in heart, Let us nev - er - more
Lamb that was slain, Hal - le - lu - jah a -

way, And with sing - ing to Zi - on re - turn.
live To the hon - or and glo - ry of God.
main, Through-out time and e - ter - ni - ty, thine.
part, Till we meet at the feast of the Lamb.
gain, Sing, all heav - en, and fall at his feet.

Text: Anonymous, *Southern Harmony*, 1835, alt.
Tune: MIDDLEBURY, 66 9 66 9; *Southern Harmony*, 1835; harm. by Jack W. Burnam, b.1946, © 1984

317 Alleluia, Alleluia, Give Thanks

Refrain

Al - le - lu - ia, al - le - lu - ia, give
thanks to the ris - en Lord. Al - le - lu - ia, al - le -
lu - ia, give praise to his Name.

Verses

1. Je - sus is Lord of all the earth.
2. Spread the good news o'er all the earth:
3. We have been cru - ci - fied with Christ.
4. God has pro - claimed his gra - cious gift:
5. Come, let us praise the liv - ing God,

D.C.

He is the King of cre - a - tion.
Je - sus has died and has ris - en.
Now we shall live for ev - er.
Life e - ter - nal for all who be - lieve.
Joy - ful - ly sing to our Sav - ior.

Text: Donald Fishel, b.1950, © 1973, Word of God Music
Tune: ALLELUIA NO. 1, 8 8 with refrain; Donald Fishel, b.1950, © 1973, Word of God Music; descant harm. by Betty Pulkingham, b.1929,
    Charles Mallory, b.1953, and George Mims, b.1938, © 1979, Celebration

Now the Green Blade Rises 318

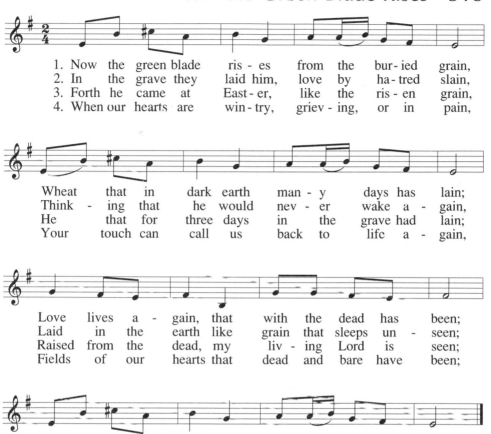

1. Now the green blade ris - es from the bur- ied grain,
2. In the grave they laid him, love by ha - tred slain,
3. Forth he came at East - er, like the ris - en grain,
4. When our hearts are win - try, griev - ing, or in pain,

Wheat that in dark earth man - y days has lain;
Think - ing that he would nev - er wake a - gain,
He that for three days in the grave had lain;
Your touch can call us back to life a - gain,

Love lives a - gain, that with the dead has been;
Laid in the earth like grain that sleeps un - seen;
Raised from the dead, my liv - ing Lord is seen;
Fields of our hearts that dead and bare have been;

Love is come a - gain like wheat a - ris - ing green.

Text: John M.C. Crum, 1872-1958, *Oxford Book of Carols,* © Oxford University Press
Tune: NOEL NOUVELET, 11 10 11 10; French Carol; acc. by Marty Haugen, b.1950, © 1987, GIA Publications, Inc.

319 Darkness Is Gone

1. Dark-ness is gone, day-light has come: The
2. See now the cross, see now the grave: They,
3. Green-er the grass, bright-er the sun, The
4. The need-ed trust, the longed-for peace Are
5. "The King-dom comes!" the King pro-claims: Jus-
6. En-roll the drum, en-list the gong To

Son of God and man a-ris-es with the
va-cant, cel-e-brate how God's fool-ish-ness can
God-loved world pro-claims a new age has be-
passed as hands from sword and shack-le are re-
tice and joy a-bound where Christ-filled faith per-
cel-e-brate in sound that right has con-quered

dawn. Death los-es its sin-is-ter sting: God's
save. The crim-i-nal nailed as a fraud Is
gun. Cre-a-tion is decked for her guest Who,
leased. The vio-lence of hate reigns no more: The
tains. Re-li-gion, re-mote and type-cast, Is
wrong. Join hands with the neigh-bor un-known, U-

prom-ise to do a new thing Is done, and Hal-le-
raised by the pow-er of God And lives. So, Hal-le-
freed from his grave clothes, is dressed In light and, Hal-le-
vic-t'ry of love is the core Of hope and, Hal-le-
gone and the fu-ture is vast. New tongues sing, "Hal-le-
nite through the love that is shown In Christ, for, Hal-le-

lu-jah! Earth joins heav'n to sing.
lu-jah! Scat-ter the news a-broad.
lu-jah! Tells that the earth is blessed.
lu-jah! Love means an o-pen door.
lu-jah! God is for us at last!"
lu-jah! Christ is our Lord a-lone.

Text: John L. Bell, b.1949
Tune: DAYLIGHT; Irregular; John L. Bell, b.1949
© 1988, Iona Community, GIA Publications, Inc. agent

This Is the Day 320

Refrain

This is the day that the Lord has made,

Let us re - joice and be glad, and be glad.

This is the day that the Lord has made, al - le -

lu - ia, al - le - lu - ia.

Verses

1. Let us sing un - to the Lord,
2. Let the heav - ens be glad,
3. Bring your gifts be - fore the Lord,

praise God's name with our joy - ful shouts,
let the earth now re - joice and sing,
bring your of - f'rings in - to his court;

en - ter in with our joy - ful hearts, to the
let the fields and the trees cry out and the
tell God's glo - ry to all the earth and God's

D.C.

God of our sal - va - tion.
o - ceans thun - der praise.
won - ders for all time.

Text: Psalm 95, 96; Marty Haugen, b.1950
Tune: Marty Haugen, b.1950
© 1980, GIA Publications, Inc.

321 Up from the Earth

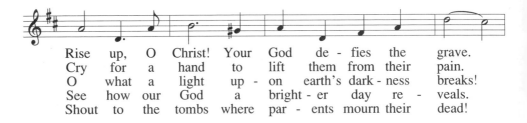

1. Up from the earth, and surg-ing like a wave,
2. Up from the cross a bil-lion voic-es strain,
3. Up from the night Christ Morn-ing-star a - wakes.
4. Up from the tomb of all the past con - ceals!
5. Cry to the cross where ty - rants work their dread!

Rise up, O Christ! Your God de - fies the grave.
Cry for a hand to lift them from their pain.
O what a light up - on earth's dark - ness breaks!
See how our God a bright - er day re - veals.
Shout to the tombs where par - ents mourn their dead!

Up from the earth push blade and leaf and stem. They
Up from the cross but scarred in limbs and side, A
Up from the night Christ sows his life like wheat, And
Up from the tomb! Though death had bound us tight, Like
Sing to the earth, for God all new-ness gives! Al -

rise for Christ, and we shall rise with them!
wound-ed church brings heal-ing far and wide!
death it - self lies fal - low at his feet!
Laz - a - rus, we stum-ble in - to light!
le - lu - ia! Christ Lib - er - a - tor lives!

Text: Rory Cooney, b.1952
Tune: LIBERATOR, 10 10 10 10; Rory Cooney, b.1952
© 1987, North American Liturgy Resources

I Will Be with You   322

Refrain

"I will be with you!"   That is my prom-ise.

"I will be with you   for ev - er - more."

Trust in my   love.   Bring me all your

cares,   for   I   will   be   with   you   for ev - er - more.

Verses

1. You are my   peo - ple,   and I   am your
2. You have re - ceived me,   now go and spread my

God.   I made you   a   prom-ise,   to   be with you al -
word.   You are with - in   me   and   I   am in

ways,   be - cause   I   real - ly   love you.   I   real - ly
you,

D.S.

love you,   and   I   will   be   with   you   for ev - er - more.

Text: James E. Moore, Jr., b.1951
Tune: James E. Moore, Jr., b.1951
© 1983, GIA Publications, Inc.

323 Go

1. Go ye there-fore and teach all na - tions,
2. If you love me, real - ly love me,

go, go, go. Go ye
feed my sheep. If you

there - fore and teach all na - tions, go,
love me, real - ly love me, feed

go, go. Bap - tiz - ing them in the
my sheep. And lo, I'll be with you for

name of the Fa - ther and Son and Ho - ly
ev - er and ev - er un - til the ends of the

Ghost. Go, go,
world, go, go,

go.
go.

Text: Leon Patillo
Tune: Leon Patillo
© 1981, 1982, Word Music, Inc.

Envía Tu Espíritu 324

Refrain

En - ví - a tu Es-pí - ri - tu, en - ví - a tu Es-pí- ri - tu,

en - ví - a tu Es-pí - ri - tu, se - a re-no-va-

da la faz de la tie - rra. Se-a re-no-va-

da la faz de la tie - rra.

Verses

1. Spir - it of the liv - ing God,
2. Wind of prom - ise, wind of change,
3. Breath of life and ho - li - ness,

burn in our hearts, and make us a peo -
friend of the poor, em - pow - er your peo -
heal ev - 'ry wound, and lead us be - yond

D.C.

ple of hope and com - pas - sion.
ple to make peace and jus - tice.
ev - 'ry sin that di - vides us.

Text: *Send out your spirit and renew the face of the earth;* Psalm 104:30; the Sequence of Pentecost; Bob Hurd, b.1950, © 1988
Tune: Bob Hurd, b.1950, © 1988; acc. by Craig Kingsbury, b.1952, © 1988, OCP Publications; arr. © 1988, OCP Publications
Published by OCP Publications

325 Spirit Blowing through Creation

Verses

1. Spir - it blow - ing through cre - a - tion,
2. As you moved up - on the wa - ters,
3. Love that sends the riv - ers danc - ing,
4. All the crea - tures you have fash - ioned,

Spir - it burn - ing in the skies,
As you ride up - on the wind,
Love that wa - ters all that lives,
All that live and breathe in you,

Let the hope of your sal - va - tion fill our eyes;
Move us all, your sons and daugh-ters deep with - in;
Love that heals and holds and rous - es and for - gives;
Find their hope in your com - pas - sion, strong and true;

God of splen - dor, God of glo - ry,
As you shaped the hills and moun-tains,
You are food for all your crea - tures,
You, O Spir - it of sal - va - tion,

You who light the stars a - bove,
Formed the land and filled the deep,
You are hun - ger in the soul,
You a - lone, be - neath, a - bove,

All the heav - ens tell the sto - ry of your love. *(To verse 2)*
Let your hand re - new and wak - en all who sleep. *(To refrain)*
In your hands the bro - ken - heart-ed are made whole. *(To verse 4)*
Come, re - new your whole cre - a - tion in your love. *(To refrain)*

Refrain

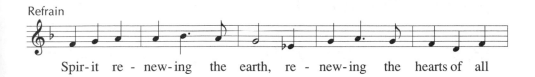

Spir-it re - new-ing the earth, re - new-ing the hearts of all

peo - ple; Burn in the wea - ry souls,

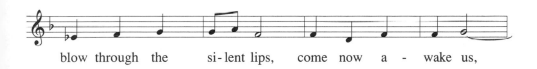

blow through the si - lent lips, come now a - wake us,

Spir-it of God.

Text: Marty Haugen, b.1950
Tune: Marty Haugen, b.1950
© 1987, GIA Publications, Inc.

Veni Sancte Spiritus 326

Ostinato Refrain

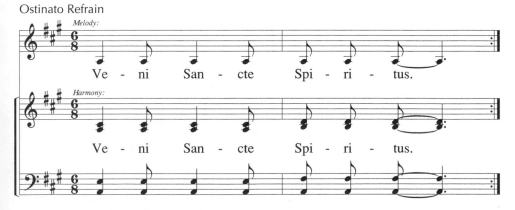

Ve - ni San - cte Spi - ri - tus.

Ve - ni San - cte Spi - ri - tus.

Text: *Come Holy Spirit;* Verses drawn form the Pentecost Sequence; Taizé Community, 1978
Tune: Jacques Berthier, 1923-1994
© 1979, Les Presses de Taizé, GIA Publications, Inc., agent

327 Send Down the Fire

Refrain

Send down the fire of your jus - tice,

Send down the rains of your love; Come,

send down the Spir - it, breathe life in your peo - ple, and

we shall be peo - ple of God.

Verses

1. Call us to be your com - pas - sion,
2. Call us to learn of your mer - cy,
3. Call us to an - swer op - pres - sion,
4. Call us to wit - ness your King - dom,

Teach us the song of your love; Give us
Teach us the way of your peace; Give us
Teach us the fire of your truth; Give us
Give us the pres - ence of Christ; May your

hearts that sing, Give us deeds that ring, Make us
hearts that feel, Give us hands that heal, Make us
right - eous souls, 'Til your jus - tice rolls, Make us
ho - ly light Keep us shin - ing bright, Ev - er

ring with the song of your love.
walk in the way of your peace.
burn with the fire of your truth.
shine with the pres - ence of Christ.

Text: Marty Haugen, b.1950
Tune: Marty Haugen, b.1950
© 1989, GIA Publications, Inc.

Spirit-Friend 328

1. God sends us his Spir - it   to be-friend and help us.
2. Dark-ened roads are clear - er,   heav - y bur - dens light - er,
3. Now we are God's peo - ple,   bond-ed by God's pres - ence,

Re - cre - ate and guide us,   Spir - it - Friend.
When we're walk - ing with our   Spir - it - Friend.
A - gents of God's pur - pose,   Spir - it - Friend.

Spir it who en liv ens,   sanc ti fies, en light ens,
Now we need not fear the   pow - ers of the dark - ness.
Lead us for-ward ev - er,   slip - ping back-ward nev - er,

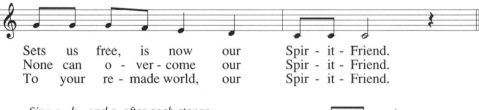

Sets us free, is now our   Spir - it - Friend.
None can o - ver-come our   Spir - it - Friend.
To your re - made world, our   Spir - it - Friend.

Sing a., b., and c. after each stanza.   *Hand claps*

a. Spir - it of our Mak - er,   Spir - it - Friend.
b. Spir - it of our Je - su,   Spir - it - Friend.
c. Spir - it of God's peo - ple,   Spir - it - Friend.

Text: Tom Colvin, b.1925
Tune: NATOMAH, 12 9 12 9 with refrain; Gonja folk song; adapt. by Tom Colvin, b.1925; acc. by Marty Haugen, b. 1950
© 1969, 1987, Hope Publishing Co.

329 Send Us Your Spirit

Refrain

Come Lord Je-sus, send us your Spir-it, re-new the face of the earth. Come Lord Je-sus, send us your Spir-it, re-new the face of the earth.

Verses

1. Come to us, Spir-it of God, breathe in us now, we sing to-geth-er. Spir-it of hope and of light, fill our lives, come to us, Spir-it of God.
2. Fill us with the fire of your love, burn in us now, bring us to-geth-er. Come to us, dwell in us, change our lives, O Lord, come to us, Spir-it of God.
3. Send us the wings of new birth, fill all the earth with the love you have taught us. Let all cre-a-tion now be shak-en with love, come to us, Spir-it of God.

D.C.

May be sung in canon.

Text: David Haas, b.1957
Tune: David Haas, b.1957; acc. by Jeanne Cotter, b.1964
© 1981, 1982, 1987, GIA Publications, Inc.

Wa Wa Wa Emimimo / Come, O Holy Spirit   330

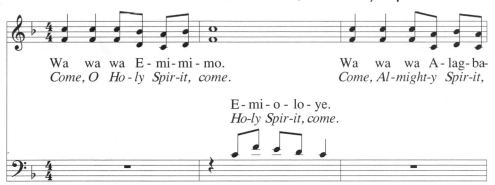

Wa   wa   wa   E - mi - mi - mo.
Come, O   Ho - ly   Spir-it,   come.

Wa   wa   wa   A - lag-ba-
Come, Al - might-y   Spir-it,

E - mi - o - lo - ye.
Ho-ly Spir-it, come.

ra.
come.

Wa - o,   wa - o,   wa - o.
Come,   come,   come.

A - lag - ba - ra - me - ta.
Al - might-y Spir-it, come.

E - mi - mi - mo.
O Spir-it, come.

Text: Nigerian traditional
Tune: As taught by Samuel Solanke; transcription and paraphrase © 1990, I-to-Loh

331   How Wonderful the Three-in-One

1. How won - der - ful the Three — in — One, Whose
2. Be - fore the flow of dawn and dark, Cre -
3. The Lov - er's own Be - lov'd, in time, Be -
4. Their E - qual Friend all life sus - tains With
5. How won - der - ful the Liv - ing God: Di -

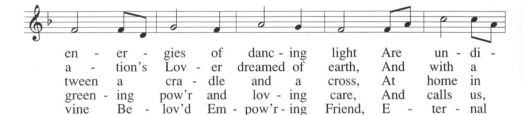

en - er - gies of danc - ing light Are un - di -
a - tion's Lov - er dreamed of earth, And with a
tween a cra - dle and a cross, At home in
green - ing pow'r and lov - ing care, And calls us,
vine Be - lov'd Em - pow'r - ing Friend, E - ter - nal

vid - ed, pure and good, Com - mun - ing
car - ing deep and wise, All things con -
flesh, gave love and life To heal our
born a - gain by grace, In Love's com -
Lov - er, Three - in - One, Our hope's be -

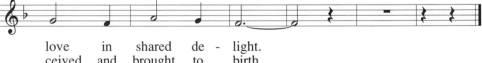

love in shared de - light.
ceived and brought to birth.
bro - ken - ness and loss.
mun - ing life to share.
gin - ning, way and end.

Text: Brian Wren, b.1936, © 1989, Hope Publishing Co.
Tune: PROSPECT, 8 8 8 8; *Southern Harmony*; arr. by Marty Haugen, b.1950, © 1991, GIA Publications, Inc.

Alleluia, Sing! 332

1. Bless - ed be our God! Bless - ed be our
2. Gift of love and peace! Gift of love and
3. Come, O Spir - it of truth! Come, O Spir - it of

God! Joy of our hearts, source of all life and
peace! Je - sus the Christ, Je - sus our hope and
truth! Prom - ise of hope, kind - ness and mer -

love! God of heav - en and
light! A flame of faith in our
cy! Come and dwell in our

earth! God of heav - en and earth!
hearts! A flame of faith in our hearts! Pro -
hearts! Come and dwell in our hearts!

Dwell - ing with - in, call - ing us all by name!
claim - ing the day, shin - ing through - out the night!
Jus - tice and peace, the king - dom of God in us!

Al - le - lu - ia, sing!

Al - le - lu - ia, sing!

Text: David Haas, b.1957
Tune: David Haas, b.1957
© 1988, GIA Publications, Inc.

333 God Is One, Unique and Holy

1.,4. God is One, u - nique and ho - ly,
2. God is One - ness - by - Com - mun - ion,
3. God is One through des - o - la - tion—

end - less dance of love and light,
nev - er sin - gle or a - lone;
blind - ness, trea - son, blood and gall;

on - ly source of mind and bod - y,
all to - geth - er - ness in - clud - ing
One, though torn by sep - a - ra - tion

star - cloud, a - tom, day or night:
friend - ship, fam - i - ly, and home,
in the Son's for - sa - ken call;

ev - 'ry thing that is or could be
com - mon mind and shared a - gree - ment,
One through death and res - ur - rec - tion;

tells God's an - guish and de - light.
com - mon loaf and sung Sha - lom.
One in Spir - it, One for all.

Text: Brian Wren, b.1936, © 1983, Hope Publishing Co.
Tune: Gary Daigle, b.1957, © 1994, GIA Publications, Inc.

Blessed Be God   334

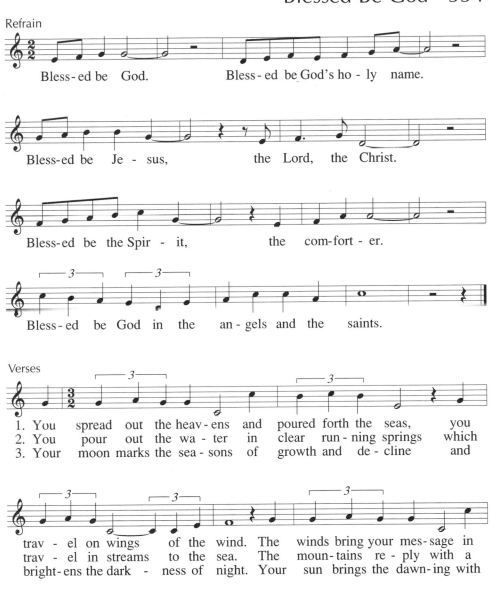

Refrain

Bless-ed be God. Bless-ed be God's ho-ly name.

Bless-ed be Je-sus, the Lord, the Christ.

Bless-ed be the Spir-it, the com-fort-er.

Bless-ed be God in the an-gels and the saints.

Verses

1. You spread out the heav-ens and poured forth the seas, you
2. You pour out the wa-ter in clear run-ning springs which
3. Your moon marks the sea-sons of growth and de-cline and

1. trav-el on wings of the wind. The winds bring your mes-sage in
2. trav-el in streams to the sea. The moun-tains re-ply with a
3. bright-ens the dark - ness of night. Your sun brings the dawn-ing with

D.C.

1. whis-per-ing breath and fire bright-ly glows with your word.
2. blan-ket of green and val - leys bear fruit in due time.
3. pow-er-ful light, a bea - con of life and of hope.

Text: Based on *The Divine Praises* and Psalm 103; Michael Connolly, b.1955
Tune: Michael Connolly, b.1955
© 1988, GIA Publications, Inc.

335 Stand Up Friends

Verses

1. Praise the God who chang - es plac - es, Leaves the loft - y seat,
2. Praise the Rab - bi, speak - ing, do - ing All that God in - tends,
3. Praise the Breath of Love, whose free-dom Spreads our wak-ing wings,
4. Praise, un - til we join the sing-ing Far be-yond our sight,

Wel - comes us with warm em - bra - ces, Stoops to wash our feet.
Dy - ing, ris - ing, faith re - new-ing, Call - ing us his friends.
Lift - ing ev - 'ry blight and bur - den Till the spir - it sings;
With the End-ing and Be - gin-ning Danc - ing in the light.

Refrain

Stand up, friends! Hold your heads high! Free-dom is our song! Al -

le - lu - ia! Free-dom is our song! Al - le - lu - ia!

ia!

D.C. *Final ending*

Text: Brian Wren, b. 1936, © 1986, Hope Publishing Co.
Tune: David Haas, b. 1957, © 1993, GIA Publications, Inc.

The Carpenter 336

Refrain

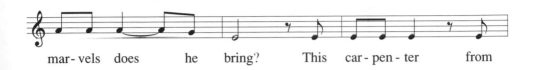

This Je - sus Christ, who can he be, what

mar- vels does he bring? This car - pen - ter from

Gal - i - lee, we know him as our king.

Verses

1. They brought their sick, he made them well.
   He told their dead to rise.
   But on his cross few words he'd tell
   Till death announced its prize.

2. He brought glad tidings to the poor,
   And healed them in their fears.
   But Laz'rus died too soon for cure;
   And Jesus too shed tears.

3. He'd taken on our poverty,
   A migrant's life he led. But said to God,
   "All comes from thee.
   A banquet you have spread."

4. "O yes, a banquet's spread for me,
   In sight of ev'ry foe:
   For love has grown from death's high tree:
   O let that love now flow."

Text: John Foley, SJ, b.1939
Tune: John Foley, SJ, b.1939
© 1993, GIA Publications, Inc.

337 Sing Out Earth and Skies

Verses

Cantor: ... *All:*

1. Come, O God of all the earth: Come to us, O
2. Come, O God of wind and flame: Fill the earth with
3. Come, O God of flash-ing light: Twin-kling star and
4. Come, O God of snow and rain: Show-er down up-
5. Come, O Jus-tice, Come, O Peace: Come and shape our

Cantor:

Right - eous One; Come, and bring our love to birth:
right - eous - ness; Teach us all to sing your name:
burn - ing sun; God of day and God of night:
on the earth; Come, O God of joy and pain:
hearts a - new; Come and make op - pres - sion cease:

All:

In the glo - ry of your Son.
May our lives your love con - fess.
In your light we all are one.
God of sor - row, God of mirth.
Bring us all to life in you.

Refrain

Sing out, earth and skies! Sing of the God who

loves you! Raise your joy - ful cries!

Dance to the life a - round you!

Text: Marty Haugen, b.1950
Tune: SING OUT, 7 7 7 7 with refrain; Marty Haugen, b.1950
© 1985, GIA Publications, Inc.

Many and Great   338

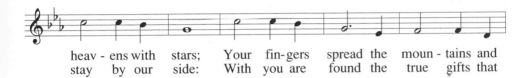

1. Man - y and great, O God, are your works, Mak - er of
2. Grant us com - mun - ion with you, our God, Though you tran -

earth and   sky;   Your hands have   set   the
scend the   stars.   Come close to   us   and

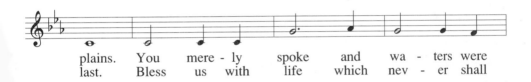

heav - ens with   stars;   Your fin-gers spread the moun - tains and
stay   by our   side: With you are   found the   true   gifts that

plains.   You   mere - ly   spoke   and   wa - ters were
last.   Bless   us   with   life   which   nev - er shall

formed; Deep   seas o - bey your   voice.
end,   E -   ter - nal life with   you.

Text: *Wakantanka tuku nitawa;* Dakota hymn; para. by Philip Frazier, 1892-1964, © 1916, Walton Music Corp.
Tune: LACQUIPARLE, 9 6 9 9 9 6; *Dakota Odowan,* 1879; acc. by John L. Bell, b.1949, © 1993, Iona Community, GIA Publications, Inc., agent

339 God, beyond All Names

Verses

1. God, be - yond our dreams, you have
2. God, be - yond all names, you have
3. God, be - yond all words, all cre -
4. God, be - yond all time, you are
5. God of ten - der care, you have

stirred in us a mem - 'ry; you have placed your pow'r - ful
made us in your im - age; we are like you, we re -
a - tion tells your sto - ry; you have shak - en with our
la - bor - ing with - in us; we are mov - ing, we are
cra - dled us in good-ness, you have moth - ered us in

spir - it in the hearts of hu - man - kind.
flect you, we are wo - man, we are man.
laugh - ter, you have trem - bled with our tears.
chang - ing in your spir - it ev - er new.
whole - ness, you have loved us in - to birth.

Refrain

All a - round us we have known you, all cre -

a - tion lives to hold you. In our liv - ing and our

dy - ing we are bring - ing you to birth.

Text: Bernadette Farrell, b.1957
Tune: Bernadette Farrell, b.1957
© 1990, Bernadette Farrell, published by OCP Publications

All You Works of God 340

Refrain

All you works of God, ev-'ry moun-tain, star and tree, bless the One who shapes your beau-ty, who has caused you all to be one great song of love and grace, ev-er an - cient, ev-er new. Raise your voic - es, all you works of God!

Verses

Soloist: / *All:* / *Soloist:*

1. Sun   and   moon: Stars   of heav-en:
2. Winds of   God: Cold   and win-ter:
3. Night   and   day: Light   and dark-ness:
4. All   the   earth: Bless your Mak - er!   Hills   and moun-tains:
5. Wells   and springs: Seas   and riv - ers:
6. Fly -   ing   birds: Beasts and cat - tle:
7. All   who   live: Men   and wom-en:

All: / *Soloist:*

Show - ers   and   dew:
Snow - storms   and   ice:
Light - nings   and   clouds:
Green   things   that   grow:
Whales   in   the   deep:
Chil - dren   at   play:
Ser   - vants   of   God:

Chant   your   praise!

D.C.

All:

Raise   up   your   joy - ful   song.

Text: Marty Haugen, b.1950
Tune: Marty Haugen, b.1950
© 1989, GIA Publications, Inc.

341 The Earth Is the Lord's

1. Lord, your hands have formed this world, Ev - 'ry
2. Yours the soil that holds the seed, You give
3. Like a mat you roll out land, Space to

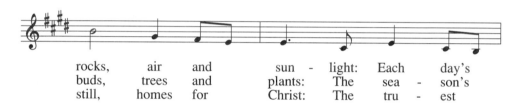

part is shaped by you— Wa - ter tum - bling o - ver
warmth and mois - ture too. Sprout-ing blos - soms, crops and
build, for us and you Earth - ly homes and, bet - ter

rocks, air and sun - light: Each day's
buds, trees and plants: The sea - son's
still, homes for Christ: The tru - est

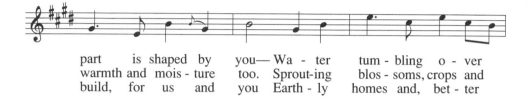

signs that you make all things new.
signs that you make all things new.
sign that you make all things new.

Text: Ramon and Sario Oliano; para. by James Minchin; trans. by Delebert Rice; © 1991, Ramon and Sario Oliano
Tune: GAYOM NI HIGAMI, 7 7 7 13; trad. Ikalahan melody; harm. © 1991, Iona Community, GIA Publications, Inc., agent

Canticle of the Sun 342

Refrain

The heav-ens are tell-ing the glo-ry of God, and all cre-a-tion is shout-ing for joy. Come, dance in the for-est, come, play in the field, and sing, sing to the glo-ry of the Lord.

Verses

1. Praise for the sun, the bring-er of day, He car-ries the light of the Lord in his rays; The moon and the stars who light up the way Un-to your throne.
2. Praise for the wind that blows through the trees, The seas might-y storms, ⁊ the gen-tl-est breeze; They blow where they will, they blow where they please To please the Lord.
3. Praise for the rain that wa-ters our fields, And bless-es our crops ⁊ so all the earth yields; From death un-to life her mys-t'ry re-vealed Springs forth in joy.
4. Praise for the fire who gives us his light, The warmth of the sun ⁊ to bright-en our night; He danc-es with joy, his spir-it so bright, He sings of you.
5. Praise for the earth who makes life to grow, The crea-tures you made ⁊ to let your life show; The flow-ers and trees that help us to know The heart of love.
6. Praise for our death that makes our life real, The knowl-edge of loss ⁊ that helps us to feel; The gift of your-self, your pres-ence re-vealed To lead us home.

D.C.

Text: Marty Haugen, b.1950
Tune: Marty Haugen, b.1950
© 1980, GIA Publications, Inc.

343 God of All Creation

1. God of the o - cean and sea! Bathe us a - new with
2. God of the wind and the breeze! Breathe in our hearts the
3. God of the for - ests and trees! Col - or our lives with
4. God of the morn - ing and night! Gift all our days with
5. God of the plan - ets and stars! Pow - er our dreams and

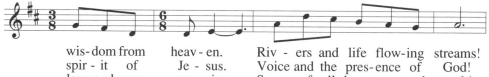

wis-dom from heav - en. Riv - ers and life flow-ing streams!
spir - it of Je - sus. Voice and the pres-ence of God!
love and com - pas - sion. Source of all beau - ty and truth!
signs of your prom - ise. Sun - light and dark-ness are yours!
lift us to glo - ry. Je - sus, the light of the world!

Call us a - gain to be liv - ing wa - ter,
Guide us to hear the call of cre - a - tion,
Help us to live as shade for the wea - ry,
In death and life may we know your ris - ing,
Shine in our lives and be "God a - mong us,"

Flood-ing and fill - ing the earth with new life!
Sing - ing and danc-ing the cry of de - light!
Hope for the bro - ken and home for the lost!
Al - pha, O - me - ga: be - gin-ning and end!
Build-ing your king-dom, the cit - y of peace!

Text: David Haas, b.1957
Tune: CREATION, 7 10 7 10 10; David Haas, b. 1957; acc. by Jeanne Cotter, b.1964, alt.
© 1987, GIA Publications, Inc.

The Stars Declare His Glory 344

1. The stars de-clare his glo - ry; The vault of heav - en
2. The dawn re - turns in splen - dor, The heav-ens burn and
3. So shine the Lord's com - mand - ments To make the sim - ple
4. So or - der too this life of mine, Di - rect it all my

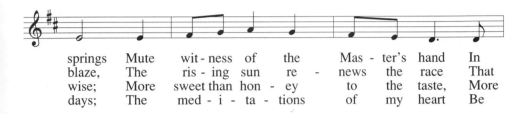

springs Mute wit - ness of the Mas - ter's hand In
blaze, The ris - ing sun re - news the race That
wise; More sweet than hon - ey to the taste, More
days; The med - i - ta - tions of my heart Be

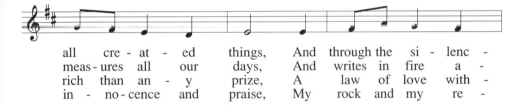

all cre - at - ed things, And through the si - lenc -
meas - ures all our days, And writes in fire a -
rich than an - y prize, A law of love with -
in - no-cence and praise, My rock and my re -

es of space Their sound - less mu - sic sings.
cross the skies God's maj - es - ty and praise.
in our hearts, A light be - fore our eyes.
deem-ing Lord, In all my words and ways.

Text: Psalm 19; Timothy Dudley-Smith, b.1926, © 1981, Hope Publishing Co.
Tune: DEERFIELD, 7 6 8 6 8 6; David Haas, b.1957, © 1986, GIA Publications, Inc.

345 Song at the Center

Refrain

From the cor-ners of cre - a - tion to the cen-ter where we stand, Let all

things be blessed and ho - ly, all is fash-ioned by your hand; Broth-er

wind and sis - ter wa - ter, moth-er earth and fa - ther sky, Sa-cred

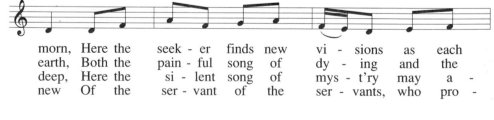

plants and sa-cred crea - tures, sa-cred peo - ple of the land.

Verses

1. In the east, the place of dawn-ing, there is beau - ty in the
2. In the south, the place of grow-ing, there is wis-dom in the
3. In the north, the place of wis - dom, there is ho - ly dark-ness
4. In the west, the place of see - ing, there is born a vi - sion

morn, Here the seek - er finds new vi - sions as each
earth, Both the pain - ful song of dy - ing and the
deep, Here the si - lent song of mys - t'ry may a -
new Of the ser - vant of the ser - vants, who pro -

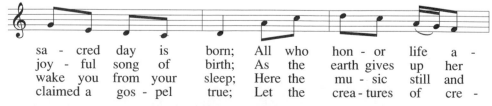

sa - cred day is born; All who hon - or life a -
joy - ful song of birth; As the earth gives up her
wake you from your sleep; Here the mu - sic still and
claimed a gos - pel true; Let the crea - tures of cre -

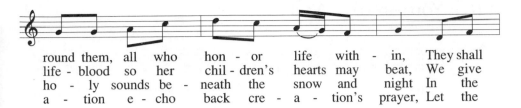

round them,   all   who   hon - or   life   with - in,   They shall
life - blood so   her   chil - dren's hearts may   beat, We give
ho - ly sounds be - neath the   snow and   night In   the
a   - tion e - cho   back cre - a - tion's prayer, Let the

D.C.

shine with light and   glo - ry when the morn - ing breaks a - gain.
back to   her   our   rev - 'rence ho - ly ground be - neath our   feet.
ones who wait with   pa - tience for the com - ing of   the   light.
Spir - it now breathe through us and   re - store the sa - cred there.

Text: Marty Haugen, b.1950
Tune: DEBORAH, 8 7 8 7 D with refrain; Marty Haugen, b.1950
© 1993, GIA Publications, Inc.

346 You Are All We Have

Refrain

You are all we have. You give us what we need. Our

lives are in your hands, O Lord, our lives are in your hands.

Verses

1. Protect me, Lord; I come to you for safety.
   I say, "You are my God."
   All good things, Lord, all good things
   that I have come from you,
   the God of my salvation.

2. How wonderful are your gifts to me,
   how good they are!
   I praise the Lord who guides me
   and teaches me the way of truth and life.

3. You are near, the God I seek.
   Nothing can take me from your side.
   All my days I rest secure;
   you will show me the path that leads to life.

Text: Francis Patrick O'Brien, b.1958
Tune: Francis Patrick O'Brien, b.1958
© 1992, GIA Publications, Inc.

I Will Lift Up My Eyes   347

Refrain

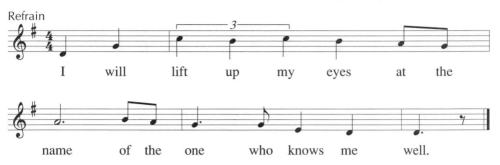

I will lift up my eyes at the

name of the one who knows me well.

Verses

1. You are my God, whom I seek with my life;
   for you I thirst, as the dry earth for water.
   Lifeless and parched,
   without you I am nowhere, no one at all.

2. Thus have I seen you in your ho-ly house,
   with my own eyes, how faithful and sure.
   More than my life, your mercy endures
   longer than time.

3. Thus shall I bless you while I am alive;
   calling on you, my breath and my bread.
   And with a song through day and the darkness
   clinging to you.

4. And I shall see that day when his justice and pow'r
   will break the chains that bind me.
   And mine enemies' lies strewn broken and empty:
   his mighty hand, that awful grace.

Text: Psalm 63; Tom Conry, b.1951, alt.
Tune: Tom Conry, b.1951
© 1984, TEAM Publications, published by OCP Publications

348 All You Who Are Thirsty

Refrain

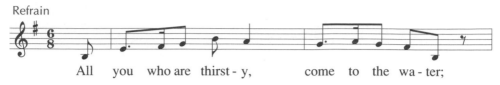

All you who are thirst-y, come to the wa-ter;

All you who hun-ger, come, re-ceive grain; All with-out mon-ey,

come with-out pay-ing; All you who heed me, come for rich fare.

Verses

Cantor or choir:

1. Come now and lis-ten that you may have life; my
2. Why spend your mon-ey for what is not bread, your
3. Drink of this wa-ter a - bun-dant with life and

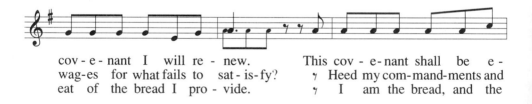

cov-e-nant I will re - new. This cov-e-nant shall be e-
wag-es for what fails to sat-is-fy? Heed my com-mand-ments and
eat of the bread I pro - vide. I am the bread, and the

D.C.

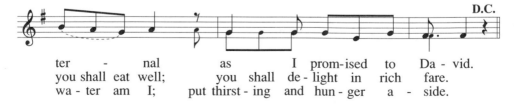

ter - nal as I prom-ised to Da - vid.
you shall eat well; you shall de - light in rich fare.
wa - ter am I; put thirst-ing and hun-ger a - side.

Come to the Water 349

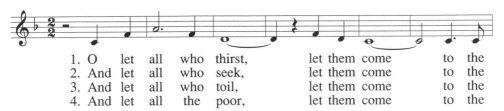

1. O let all who thirst,   let them come   to the
2. And let all who seek,   let them come   to the
3. And let all who toil,   let them come   to the
4. And let all the poor,   let them come   to the

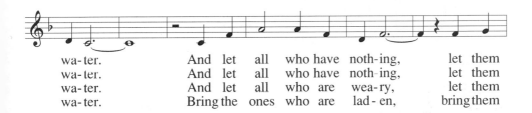

wa-ter.   And let all who have noth-ing,   let them
wa-ter.   And let all who have noth-ing,   let them
wa-ter.   And let all who are wea-ry,   let them
wa-ter.   Bring the ones who are lad-en,   bring them

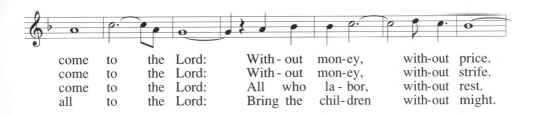

come to the Lord: With-out mon-ey,   with-out price.
come to the Lord: With-out mon-ey,   with-out strife.
come to the Lord: All who la-bor,   with-out rest.
all to the Lord: Bring the chil-dren   with-out might.

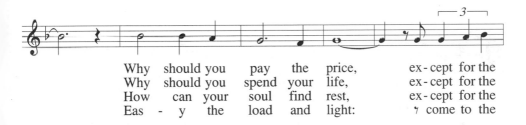

Why should you pay the price,   ex-cept for the
Why should you spend your life,   ex-cept for the
How can your soul find rest,   ex-cept for the
Eas-y the load and light: come to the

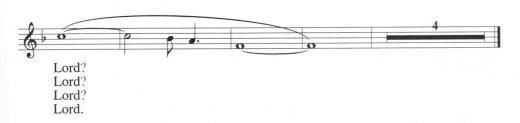

Lord?
Lord?
Lord?
Lord.

Text: Isaiah 55:1,2, Matthew 11:28-30; John Foley, SJ, b.1939
Tune: John Foley, SJ, b.1939
© 1978, John B. Foley, SJ, and New Dawn Music

350 Come to the Feast

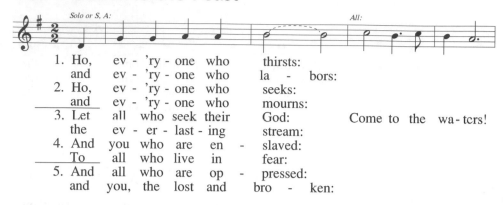

1. Ho,   ev - 'ry - one who   thirsts:
   and   ev - 'ry - one who   la - bors:
2. Ho,   ev - 'ry - one who   seeks:
   and   ev - 'ry - one who   mourns:
3. Let   all   who seek their   God: Come to the wa - ters!
   the   ev - er - last - ing   stream:
4. And   you who are   en - slaved:
   To   all   who live   in   fear:
5. And   all   who are   op - pressed:
   and   you, the lost and   bro - ken:

here   is   an   end   to hun - ger:
all   you who have no mon - ey:
hear   me   and share the rich - es:
now   is   an   end   to sad - ness:
heed now the One who calls you: Come to the feast!   Come to the
drink deep the Cup that saves you:
this   is   the feast of free - dom:
join   in   the feast with cour - age:
this   is   the feast of jus - tice:
this   is   the feast of heal - ing:

feast! For this   is   life: 1. the   wa - ters of the   Jor - dan:
                            2. the streams of joy and   glad - ness:
                            3. the floods that o - ver - whelm you: For
                            4. the   wa - ters that have freed you:
                            5. to   die   and rise in   Je - sus:

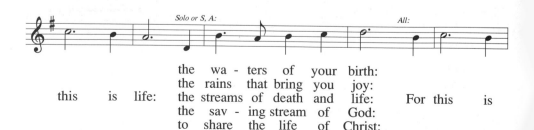

                  the   wa - ters of   your   birth:
                  the   rains that bring you   joy:
this   is   life: the streams of death and life: For this   is
                  the   sav - ing stream of   God:
                  to   share the life of   Christ:

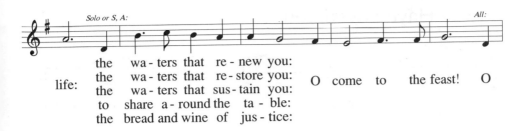

Solo or S, A: *All:*

life: the wa-ters that re-new you: O come to the feast! O
       the wa-ters that re-store you:
       the wa-ters that sus-tain you:
       to share a-round the ta-ble:
       the bread and wine of jus-tice:

[1.-4. D.C.] [5.]

come to the feast!   feast! O come to the feast!

Text: Isaiah 55; Marty Haugen, b.1950
Tune: Marty Haugen, b.1950

351 I Have Loved You

Refrain

I have loved you   with an   ev - er - last-ing love, I have

called you   and you are mine;   I have loved you   with an

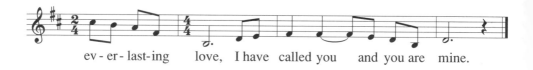

ev - er - last-ing   love, I have called you   and you are mine.

Verses

1. Seek   the face   of   the   Lord   and long   for
2. Seek   the face   of   the   Lord   and long   for
3. Seek   the face   of   the   Lord   and long   for

D.C.

him: He will   bring   you his light   and his   peace.
him: He will   bring   you his joy   and his   hope.
him: He will   bring   you his care   and his   love.

Text: Jeremiah 31:3, Psalm 24:3; Michael Joncas, b.1951
Tune: Michael Joncas, b.1951
© 1979, New Dawn Music

I Want to Walk as a Child of the Light 352

1. I want to walk as a child of the light.
2. I want to see the bright-ness of God.
3. I'm look - ing for the com - ing of Christ.

I want to fol - low Je - sus.
I want to look at Je - sus.
I want to be with Je - sus.

God set the stars to give light to the world. The
Clear sun of right-eous-ness shine on my path, And
When we have run with pa - tience the race, We

star of my life is Je - sus.
show me the way to the Fa - ther.
shall know the joy of Je - sus.

In him there is no dark - ness at all. The

night and the day are both a - like. The

Lamb is the light of the cit - y of God.

Shine in my heart, Lord Je - sus.

Text: Ephesians 5:8-10, Revelation 21:23, John 12: 46, 1 John 1:5, Hebrews 12:1; Kathleen Thomerson, b.1934, © 1970, 1975, Celebration
Tune: HOUSTON, 10 7 10 8 9 9 10 7; Kathleen Thomerson, b.1934, © 1970, 1975, Celebration; acc. by Robert J. Batastini, b.1942, © 1987, GIA
Publications, Inc.

353 We Are the Light of the World

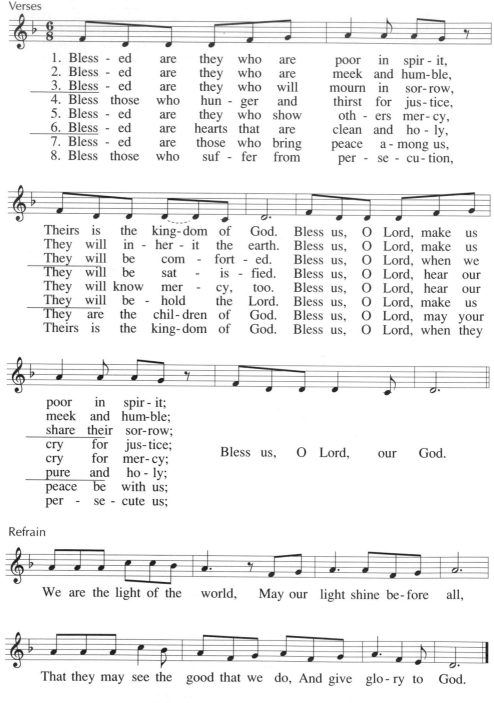

Verses

1. Bless - ed are they who are poor in spir - it,
2. Bless - ed are they who are meek and hum-ble,
3. Bless - ed are they who will mourn in sor-row,
4. Bless those who hun - ger and thirst for jus-tice,
5. Bless - ed are they who show oth - ers mer-cy,
6. Bless - ed are hearts that are clean and ho - ly,
7. Bless - ed are those who bring peace a - mong us,
8. Bless those who suf - fer from per - se - cu-tion,

Theirs is the king-dom of God. Bless us, O Lord, make us
They will in - her - it the earth. Bless us, O Lord, make us
They will be com - fort - ed. Bless us, O Lord, when we
They will be sat - is - fied. Bless us, O Lord, hear our
They will know mer - cy, too. Bless us, O Lord, hear our
They will be - hold the Lord. Bless us, O Lord, make us
They are the chil-dren of God. Bless us, O Lord, may your
Theirs is the king-dom of God. Bless us, O Lord, when they

poor in spir - it;
meek and hum-ble;
share their sor-row;
cry for jus-tice;
cry for mer-cy;   Bless us, O Lord, our God.
pure and ho - ly;
peace be with us;
per - se - cute us;

Refrain

We are the light of the world, May our light shine be-fore all,

That they may see the good that we do, And give glo-ry to God.

Text: Matthew 5:3-11, 14-16; Jean A. Greif, 1898-1981
Tune: Jean A. Greif, 1898-1981

Be Light for Our Eyes 354

Refrain

Come and be light for our eyes; be the air we breathe, be the voice we speak! Come, be the song we sing, be the path we seek!

Verses

1. Your life was giv - en; food for all peo - ple,
2. We hold your pres - ence, ris - en for ev - er!
3. Lead us to jus - tice, light in the dark - ness;

bod - y and blood, new life in our midst!
Your name now names us peo - ple of God!
sing - ing, pro - claim - ing Je - sus is Lord!

Death is no long - er, life is our fu - ture;
Filled with your vi - sion, peo - ple of mis - sion,
Teach us to speak, and help us to lis - ten

D.C.

Je - sus, Mes - si - ah, name of all names!
heal - ing, for - giv - ing; light for the world!
for when your truth and our dreams em - brace!

Text: David Haas, b.1957
Tune: David Haas, b.1957; keyboard arr. by David Haas, b.1957, and Marty Haugen, b.1950
© 1985, GIA Publications, Inc.

355 I Am the Light of the World

Refrain

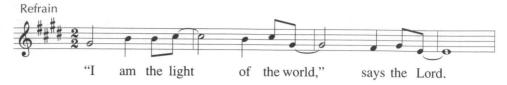

"I am the light of the world," says the Lord.

"They who fol-low me will have the light of life."

Verses

1. "A-rise," says the Lord, "Have no fear with-
2. "Walk in the light; there is no cause to
3. "Lis-ten to my words; they are from the one who

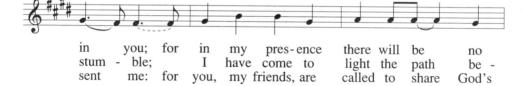

in you; for in my pres-ence there will be no
stum - ble; I have come to light the path be -
sent me: for you, my friends, are called to share God's

D.C.

dark - ness. I am the light of the world."
fore you. I am the light of the world."
glo - ry. You are the light of the world."

Text: John 8:12, Matthew 5:14; Ephesians 5:14, I John 2:10; Greg Hayakawa, b.1953, © 1978, 1979
Tune: Greg Hayakawa, b.1953, © 1978, 1979; acc. by Craig S. Kingsbury, b.1952, © 1985, OCP Publications
Published by OCP Publications

Light of Christ / Exsultet 356

Refrain

All:

The light of Christ sur - rounds us, the love of Christ en - folds us, the pow'r of Christ pro - tects us, the pres - ence of Christ watch - es o - ver us.

To verses

Last time

us, for ev - er, and ev - er, for ev - er, and ev - er. A - men.

Verses 1, 2, 3

Cantor or schola:

1. All the earth is a - blaze with the glo - ry of
2. Let us fill ev - 'ry space with the sound of our
3. As this can - dle shines out through the dark - ness of

D.C.

God, for the Light has come to burn a - way the dark - ness.
joy, prais - ing Christ, who is liv - ing now a - mong us.
night, may the love of Christ burn ev - er in our hearts.

Verse 4

4. In the east, the Morn - ing Star ris - es bright up - on you,

D.C.

in its peace - ful light shines the glo - ry of the Lord.

Text: Based on a prayer by James Dillet Freeman and the *Exsultet;* Marty Haugen, b.1950
Tune: Marty Haugen, b.1950
© 1987, GIA Publications, Inc.

357 We Are Marching

We are march - ing* in the light of God, we are

1. march-ing in the light of God.
2. march-ing in the light of God, march-ing in the light of the march-ing in the light of God,

we are march - ing,

light of God, we are march - ing, march - ing, we are

Oo we are

march - ing, march-ing, we are march-ing in the light of God.

Alternate text: dancing, singing, praying

Text: South African
Tune: South African
© 1984, Utryck, Walton Music Corporation, agent

This Little Light of Mine   358

1. This lit - tle light of mine   I'm gon - na let it shine,
2. Ev - 'ry - where I go,   I'm gon - na let it shine,
3. Je - sus gave it to me,   I'm gon - na let it shine,

This lit - tle light of mine   I'm gon - na let it shine;
Ev - 'ry - where I go,   I'm gon - na let it shine;
Je - sus gave it to me,   I'm gon - na let it shine;

This lit - tle light of mine   I'm gon - na let it shine,
Ev - 'ry - where I go,   I'm gon - na let it shine,
Je - sus gave it to me,   I'm gon - na let it shine,

Let it shine, let it shine, let it shine.
Let it shine, let it shine, let it shine.
Let it shine, let it shine, let it shine.

Text: African-American spiritual
Tune: African-American spiritual; harm. by Horace Clarence Boyer

359 The Word of Life

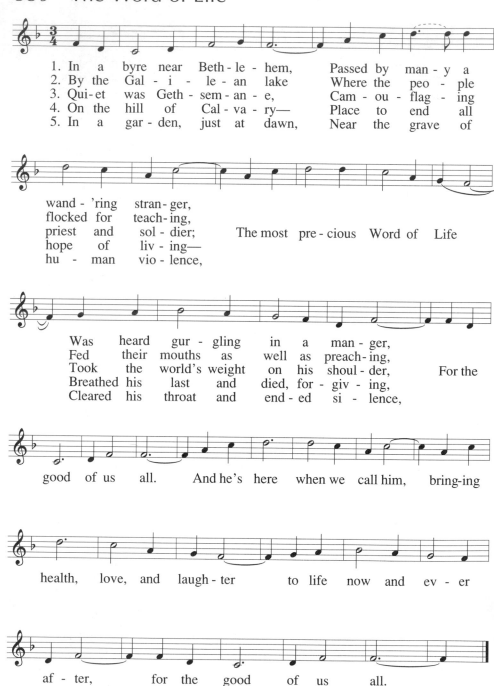

1. In a byre near Beth-le-hem, Passed by man-y a
2. By the Gal-i-le-an lake Where the peo-ple
3. Qui-et was Geth-sem-an-e, Cam-ou-flag-ing
4. On the hill of Cal-va-ry— Place to end all
5. In a gar-den, just at dawn, Near the grave of

wand-'ring stran-ger,
flocked for teach-ing,
priest and sol-dier; The most pre-cious Word of Life
hope of liv-ing—
hu-man vio-lence,

Was heard gur-gling in a man-ger,
Fed their mouths as well as preach-ing,
Took the world's weight on his shoul-der, For the
Breathed his last and died, for-giv-ing,
Cleared his throat and end-ed si-lence,

good of us all. And he's here when we call him, bring-ing

health, love, and laugh-ter to life now and ev-er

af-ter, for the good of us all.

Text: John L. Bell, b.1949
Tune: WILD MOUNTAIN THYME, irregular; Irish traditional; arr. by John L. Bell, b.1949
© 1987, Iona Community, GIA Publications, Inc., agent

Praise to You, O Christ, Our Savior 360

Refrain

Praise to you, O Christ, our Sav-ior, Word of the Fa-ther,

call-ing us to life; Son of God who

leads us to free-dom: glo-ry to you, Lord Je-sus Christ!

Verses

1. You are the Word who calls us out of dark-ness;
2. You are the one whom proph-ets hoped and longed for;
3. You arc thc Word who calls us to be ser-vants;
4. You are the Word who binds us and u-nites us;

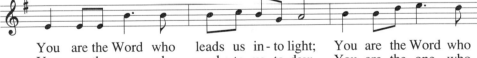

You are the Word who leads us in-to light; You are the Word who
You are the one who speaks to us to-day; You are the one who
You are the Word whose on-ly law is love; You are the Word made
You are the Word who calls us to be one; You are the Word who

D.C.

brings us through the des-ert: Glo-ry to you, Lord Je-sus Christ!
leads us to our fu-ture: Glo-ry to you, Lord Je-sus Christ!
flesh who lives a-mong us: Glo-ry to you, Lord Je-sus Christ!
teach-es us for-give-ness: Glo-ry to you, Lord Je-sus Christ!

Text: Bernadette Farrell, b.1957
Tune: Bernadette Farrell, b.1957
© 1986, Bernadette Farrell, published by OCP Publications

361 Sow the Word

Refrain

So the Word came to the world, so the

Word came to stretch his arms and die for the world. As he

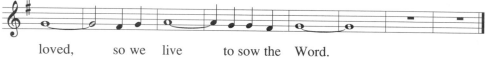

loved, so we live to sow the Word.

Verses

1. As the rain and the snow come down from heaven
   and do not return without watering the earth,
   making it yield and giving it growth
   to provide seed for the sower and bread for the world:

2. This is the word that we have tasted with our eyes,
   and our lips speak the love in its passing on to you.
   God is light. If we live our love in light,
   we will reap the grain of the sower and be bread for the world.

3. We are God's lovers. Give it all away.
   We must be love to the hungry at our doors.
   Open the bread! Bring the robes and rings!
   Lavish the hungry with the plenty we have known in the word.

Text: Isaiah 55:10-11; J. Keith Zavelli, b.1958, Steven R. Janco, b.1961
Tune: J. Keith Zavelli, b.1958, Steven R. Janco, b.1961; harm. by Steven R. Janco, b.1961
© 1986, GIA Publications, Inc.

Not by Bread Alone 362

Refrain

We do not live by bread a - lone, but by ev - 'ry
word that comes from the mouth of God.

Verses 1, 3

1. Lead our hearts a - way from world-ly gain, turn our
3. When the snares of e - vil hem us in, and op -

eyes from see - ing what is vain, teach us your wis - dom.
pres - sion weighs us down, lib - er - a - tion

D.C.

Give us knowl-edge; in your word we hope and trust.
and sal - va - tion come as prom-ised through your word.

Verse 2

2. A lamp to our feet, a light to our path, sweet-er than

hon - ey, pre-cious as gold, your word is our de - light;

D.C.

it brings e - ter - nal life.

Text: Matthew 4:4, Psalm 119; Donald J. Reagan, b.1923
Tune: Donald J. Reagan, b.1923
© 1983, GIA Publications, Inc.

363 The Word Is in Your Heart

Refrain

The Word is near you, deep with-in you. The Word is

on your lips. The Word who made you yet will

save you. The Word is in your heart.

Verses

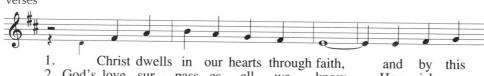

1. Christ dwells in our hearts through faith, and by this
2. God's love sur - pass - es all we know. How rich are
3. God's Spir - it fills each faith - ful heart, and as God's

D.C.

pres - ence may we come to know the full - ness of God's love.
we whom God has cho - sen to be - come his ver - y own!
ves - sels we are called to live in ho - li - ness and love.

Text: Bob Moore, b. 1962
Tune: Bob Moore, b. 1962
© 1993, GIA Publications, Inc.

Laudate Dominum 364

Ostinato Refrain

Lau-da-te Do-mi-num, lau-da-te Do-mi-num om-nes

1. gen-tes, al-le-lu - ia.
2. al-le-lu - ia.

Text: Psalm 117, *Praise the Lord, all you peoples;* Taizé Community, 1980
Tune: Jacques Berthier, b.1923, © 1980, Les Presses de Taizé, GIA Publications, Inc., agent

Cantai ao Senhor 365

Can-tai ao Sen-hor um can-ti-co no-vo, can-tai ao Sen-
O sing to the Lord, O sing God a new song, O sing to the
Can-tar al Se-ñor un can-ti-co nue-vo, can-tar al Se-

hor um can-ti-co no-vo, can - tai ao Sen - hor um
Lord, O sing God a new song, O sing to the Lord, O
ñor un can-ti-co nue-vo, can - tar al Se - ñor un

can-ti-co no-vo, can-tai ao Sen-hor, can-tai ao Sen-hor.
sing God a newsong, O sing to the Lord, O sing to the Lord.
can-ti-co nue-vo, can-tar al Se-ñor, can-tar al Se-ñor.

Text: Psalm 98; Anonymous
Tune: Tradtional Brazilian, © Editora Sinodal, Sao Leopoldo; arr. by John L. Bell, b. 1949, © 1991, Iona Community, GIA Publications, Inc., agent

366 Shake Up the Morning

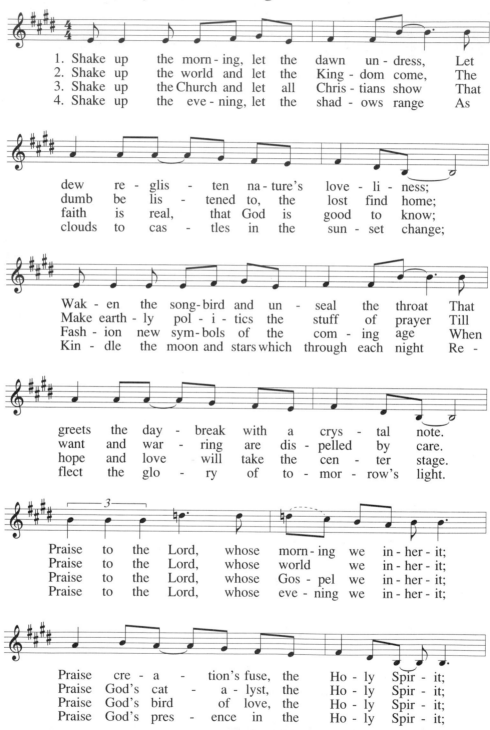

1. Shake up the morn-ing, let the dawn un-dress, Let
2. Shake up the world and let the King-dom come, The
3. Shake up the Church and let all Chris-tians show That
4. Shake up the eve-ning, let the shad-ows range As

dew re - glis - ten na-ture's love - li - ness;
dumb be lis - tened to, the lost find home;
faith is real, that God is good to know;
clouds to cas - tles in the sun - set change;

Wak - en the song-bird and un - seal the throat That
Make earth - ly pol - i - tics the stuff of prayer Till
Fash - ion new sym-bols of the com - ing age When
Kin - dle the moon and stars which through each night Re -

greets the day - break with a crys - tal note.
want and war - ring are dis - pelled by care.
hope and love will take the cen - ter stage.
flect the glo - ry of to - mor - row's light.

Praise to the Lord, whose morn-ing we in-her-it;
Praise to the Lord, whose world we in-her-it;
Praise to the Lord, whose Gos-pel we in-her-it;
Praise to the Lord, whose eve-ning we in-her-it;

Praise cre - a - tion's fuse, the Ho - ly Spir - it;
Praise God's cat - a - lyst, the Ho - ly Spir - it;
Praise God's bird of love, the Ho - ly Spir - it;
Praise God's pres - ence in the Ho - ly Spir - it;

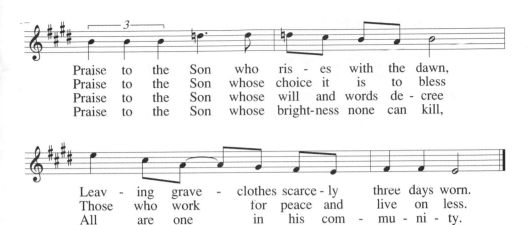

Praise to the Son who ris - es with the dawn,
Praise to the Son whose choice it is to bless
Praise to the Son whose will and words de - cree
Praise to the Son whose bright-ness none can kill,

Leav - ing grave - clothes scarce - ly three days worn.
Those who work for peace and live on less.
All are one in his com - mu - ni - ty.
Light - ing paths for those who seek his will.

Text: John L. Bell, b.1949
Tune: SHAKE UP, irregular; John L. Bell, b.1949
© 1987, Iona Community, GIA Publications, Inc., agent

A New Song 367

I will sing the Lord a new song, a new song. I will sing his

prais - es while I live. I will sing his prais - es for ev - er more.

1. Sing God a new song, Make it loud and clear.
2. Sing God a new song ⅞ For all he's done.
3. Sing God a new song, Spread his love a - round.

D.C.

Sing God a new song For all the world to hear.
Sing God a new song, ⅞ Help to make us one.
Sing God a new song, ⅞ Make a joy - ful sound.

Text: James E. Moore, Jr., b.1951
Tune: James E. Moore, Jr., b.1951
© 1983, GIA Publications, Inc.

368 To God with Gladness Sing

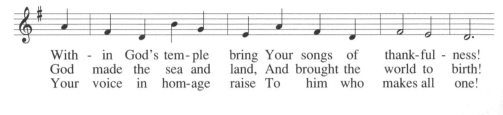

1. To God with glad - ness sing, Your Rock and Sav - ior bless;
2. God cra - dles in his hand The heights and depths of earth;
3. Your heav'n - ly Fa - ther praise, Ac - claim his on - ly Son,

With - in God's tem - ple bring Your songs of thank-ful - ness!
God made the sea and land, And brought the world to birth!
Your voice in hom-age raise To him who makes all one!

O Lord of might, To you we sing,
O Lord most high, We are your sheep,
O Dove of peace, On us de - scend,

En - throned as King On heav - en's height!
On us you keep Your Shep - herd's eye!
That strife may end And joy in - crease!

Text: Psalm 95; James Quinn, SJ, b.1919, © 1969. Used by permission of Selah Publishing., Inc., Kingston, N.Y.
Tune: CYMBALA, 6 6 6 6 4 44 4; Michael Joncas, b.1951, © 1979, GIA Publications, Inc.

Amen Siakudumisa 369

A-men si - a-ku-du-mi - sa.   A-men si-a-ku-du-mi -

sa.   A-men ba-wo,   A-men ba-wo,

A - men si - a - ku - du - mi - sa.

Text: *Amen. Praise the name of the Lord*. South African traditional
Tune: Attributed to S.C. Molefe as taught by George Mxadana; arr. by John L. Bell, b.1949, © 1990, Iona Community, GIA Publications, Inc., agent

370   We Praise You

Refrain

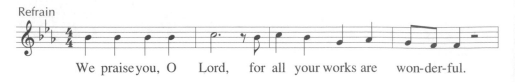

We praise you, O Lord, for all your works are won-der-ful.

We praise you, O Lord, for ev-er is your love.

Verses

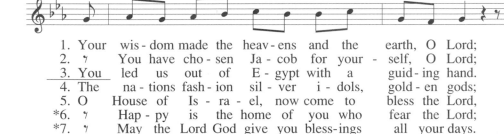

1. Your wis-dom made the heav-ens and the earth, O Lord;
2. ⸗ You have cho-sen Ja-cob for your-self, O Lord;
3. You led us out of E-gypt with a guid-ing hand.
4. The na-tions fash-ion sil-ver i-dols, gold-en gods;
5. O House of Is-ra-el, now come to bless the Lord,
*6. ⸗ Hap-py is the home of you who fear the Lord;
*7. ⸗ May the Lord God give you bless-ings all your days.

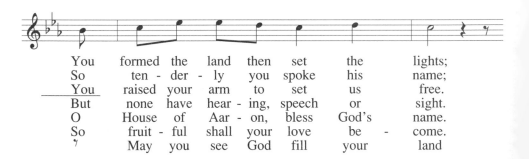

You   formed the land then set the lights;
So   ten-der-ly you spoke his name;
You   raised your arm to set us free.
But   none have hear-ing, speech or sight.
O   House of Aar-on, bless God's name.
So   fruit-ful shall your love be-come.
⸗   May you see God fill your land

And   like your love the sun will rule the day,
Then   called a ho-ly na-tion, Is-ra-el,
And   like a ten-der vine you plant-ed us
Their   mak-ers shall be like their emp-ty gods,
O   bless the Lord, all you who hon-or God,
Your   chil-dren flour-ish like the ol-ive plants,
Un -   til your chil-dren bring their chil-dren home

wedding verses

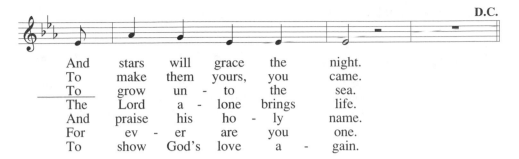

And stars will grace the night.
To make them yours, you came.
To grow un - to the sea.
The Lord a - lone brings life.
And praise his ho - ly name.
For ev - er are you one.
To show God's love a - gain.

Text: Mike Balhoff, b.1946
Tune: Darryl Ducote, b.1945, Gary Daigle, b.1957
© 1978, Damean Music. Distributed by GIA Publications, Inc.

Alabaré 371

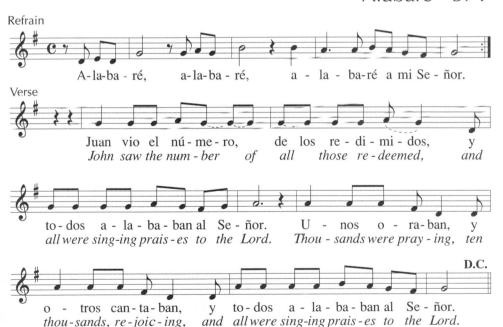

Refrain

A-la-ba - ré, a-la-ba - ré, a - la - ba-ré a mi Se - ñor.

Verse

Juan vio el nú - me - ro, de los re - di - mi - dos, y
John saw the num - ber of all those re - deemed, and

to - dos a - la - ba - ban al Se - ñor. U - nos o - ra - ban, y
all were sing-ing prais - es to the Lord. Thou - sands were pray - ing, ten

o - tros can - ta - ban, y to - dos a - la - ba - ban al Se - ñor.
thou - sands, re - joic - ing, and all were sing-ing prais - es to the Lord.

Text: *I will praise the Lord;* Manuel José Alonso, José Pagán, © 1979 and Ediciones Musical PAX, published by OCP Publications;
  trans. unknown
Tune: Manuel José Alonso, José Pagán, © 1979 and Ediciones Musical PAX, published by OCP Publications; acc. by Diana Kodner,
  © 1994, GIA Publications, Inc.

372 O God of Matchless Glory

1. O God of match-less glo-ry, Of all-sur-pass-ing
2. With Wis-dom as your part-ner You formed the earth and
3. Your word gives life for - ev-er; Our fear of death is

worth, You fill the world with won - der; You
sea; And still she calls the sim - ple, "Be
stilled. With liv - ing bread and wa - ter Our

bring the stars to birth. To whom shall we sing
wise and learn from me." Who else gives rest in
deep - est need is filled. To whom shall we go

prais-es? To whom, O God, but you? Al-le-lu - ia! Al-le-
la - bor? Who else, O God, but you? Al-le-lu - ia! Al-le-
seek-ing? To whom, O God, but you? Al-le-lu - ia! Al-le-

lu - ia! You are our God; We be - long to you.
lu - ia! We share your yoke; We be - long to you.
lu - ia! You are our God; We be - long to you.

Text: Ruth Duck, b. 1947
Tune: MATCHLESS GLORY, 7 6 7 6 7 6 4 4 4 5; Ruth Duck, b. 1947; acc. by Randall Sensmeier, b.1948
© 1992, GIA Publications, Inc.

Sing of the Lord's Goodness 373

1. Sing of the Lord's good-ness, Fa-ther of all wis-dom,
2. Pow - er he has wield-ed, hon - or is his gar-ment,
3. Cour - age in our dark-ness, com - fort in our sor - row,
4. Praise him with your sing-ing, praise him with the trum-pet,

come to him and bless his name. Mer - cy he has shown us,
ris - en from the snares of death. His word he has spo - ken,
Spir - it of our God most high; sol - ace for the wea - ry,
praise God with the lute and harp; praise him with the cym - bals,

his love is for ev er, faith - ful to the end of days.
one bread he has bro-ken, new life he now gives to all.
par - don for the sin - ner, splen - dor of the liv-ing God.
praise him with your danc-ing, praise God till the end of days.

Come, then, all you na - tions, sing of your Lord's good - ness,

mel - o - dies of praise and thanks to God.

Ring out the Lord's glo - ry, praise him with your mu - sic,

wor - ship him and bless his name.

Text: Ernest Sands, b.1949, © 1981
Tune: Ernest Sands, b.1949, © 1981; acc. by Paul Inwood, b.1947, © 1986
Published by OCP Publications

374 All the Earth, Proclaim God's Glory

Refrain

All the earth, pro - claim God's glo - ry. Sing with songs of

love. Mus - ic, danc - ing, new songs ris - ing, God of beau - ty,

God of splen - dor, God of won - der and love.

Verses 1, 2

1. Lov - ing kind - ness to all na - tions. Peace a - cross the land and sea.
2. For the God of liv - ing splen - dor, God of might - y deeds,

D.C.

Harps and cym - bals sound the mes - sage, blend in har - mo - ny.
keeps the prom - ise to the faith - ful, breath - ing Spir - it's peace.

Verse 3

3. Pour on us new clean wa - ter. Cleanse, re - fresh our souls.

D.C.

Give to us a will - ing spir - it. Heal us, make us whole.

Text: Mark Friedman and Bobby Fisher, b. 1952
Tune: Bobby Fisher, b.1952

Cantemos al Señor / Let's Sing unto the Lord   375

1. Can - te - mos al Se - ñor   Un him - no de a - le - grí - a,   Un
2. Can - te - mos al Se - ñor   Un him - no de a - la - ban - za   Que ex -
1. Let's sing un - to the Lord   A hymn of glad re - joic - ing,   Let's
2. Let's sing un - to the Lord   A hymn of a - do - ra - tion,   Ex -

cán - ti - co de a - mor   Al na - cer   el nue - vo dí - a.   El
pre - se nues-tro a - mor,   Nues-tra fe y   nues-tra es - pe - ran - za,   En
sing a hymn of love,   Join-ing hearts and hap - py voic - es.   God
press un - to the Lord   Our   songs   of faith and hope.   Cre -

hi - zo el cie - lo el mar,   El sol y las es - tre - llas   Y
to - da la crea - ción   Pre - go - na su gran - de - za,   A -
made the sky a - bove,   The stars, the sun, the   o - ceans.   Their
a - tion's broad dis - play   Pro - claims the work of gran-deur,   The

vio en   e - llos bon - dad,   Pues sus   o - bras e - ran   be - llas.
sí   nues-tro can - tar   Va a-nun - cian - do su   be - lle - za.
good - ness does pro - claim   The   glo - ry of God's name.
bound - less love of One   Who   bless - es us with   beau - ty.

¡A - le - lu - ya!   ¡A - le - lu - ya!   Can - te - mos al Se -
Al - le - lu - ia!   Al - le - lu - ia!   Let's sing un - to the

|1.| |2.|

ñor.   ¡A - le - lu   -   ya!   lu   -   ya!
Lord.   Al - le - lu   -   ia!   lu   -   ia!

Text: Based on Psalm 19; Carlos Rosas, b.1939; trans. by Roberto Escamilla, Elise Eslinger, and George Lockwood, 1983,
    © 1976, Resource Publications, Inc.
Tune: ROSAS, 6 7 6 8 D with refrain; Carlos Rosas, b.1939, © 1976, Resource Publications, Inc.; acc. by Diana Kodner, b.1957,
    © 1993, GIA Publications, Inc.

376 Canticle of the Turning

Verses

1. My soul cries out with a joy - ful shout that the
2. Though I am small, my God, my all, you
3. From the halls of power to the for - tress tower, not a
4. Though the na - tions rage from age to age, we re -

God of my heart is great, And my spir - it sings of the
work great things in me, And your mer - cy will last from the
stone will be left on stone. Let the king be - ware for your
mem - ber who holds us fast: God's mer - cy must de -

won - drous things that you bring to the ones who wait. You
depths of the past to the end of the age to be. Your
jus - tice tears ev - 'ry ty - rant from his throne. The
liv - er us from the con - quer - or's crush - ing grasp. This

fixed your sight on your ser - vant's plight, and my
ver - y name puts the proud to shame, and to
hun - gry poor shall weep no more, for the
sav - ing word that our fore - bears heard is the

weak - ness you did not spurn, So from east to west shall my
those who would for you yearn, You will show your might, put the
food they can nev - er earn; There are ta - bles spread, ev - 'ry
prom - ise which holds us bound, 'Til the spear and rod can be

name be blest. Could the world be a - bout to turn?
strong to flight, for the world is a - bout to turn.
mouth be fed, for the world is a - bout to turn.
crushed by God, who is turn - ing the world a - round.

Refrain

My heart shall sing of the day you bring. Let the

fires of your jus - tice burn. Wipe a - way all tears, for the

dawn draws near, and the world is a - bout to turn!

Text: Luke 1:46-58; Rory Cooney, b.1952
Tune: STAR OF THE COUNTY DOWN; Irish traditional; arr. by Rory Cooney, b.1952
© 1990, GIA Publications, Inc.

Jubilate Servite 377

Canon— 2 voices

Ju - bi - la - te De - o om - nis ter - ra.

Ser - vi - te Do - mi - no in lae - ti - ti - a.

Al - le - lu - ia, al - le - lu - ia, in lae - ti - ti - a.

Al - le - lu - ia, al - le - lu - ia, in lae - ti - ti - a!

Text: Psalm 100, *Rejoice in God, all the earth, Serve the Lord with gladness;* Taizé Community, 1978
Tune: Jacques Berthier, b.1923
© 1979, Les Presses de Taizé, GIA Publications, Inc., agent

378　All the Ends of the Earth

Refrain

All the ends of the earth, all you crea-tures of the sea, lift up your

eyes to the won-ders of the Lord. For the Lord of the earth, the

Mas-ter of the sea, has come with jus-tice for the world.

Verse 1

1. Break in-to song at the deeds of the Lord, the

D.C.

won-ders he has done in ev-'ry age.

Verse 2

2. Heav-en and earth shall re-joice in his might; ev-'ry heart,

D.C.

ev-'ry na-tion call him Lord.

Verse 3

3. The Lord has made sal-va-tion known, faith-ful to the prom-

is-es of old. Let the ends of the earth, let the

D.C.

sea and all it holds make mu-sic be-fore our King!

Text: Psalm 98; Bob Dufford, SJ, b.1943
Tune: Bob Dufford, SJ, b.1943; acc. by Bob Dufford and Chris Morash, alt.
© 1981, Robert J. Dufford, SJ, and New Dawn Music

Sing a New Song to the Lord 379

1. Sing a new song to the Lord,
2. Now to the ends of the earth
3. Sing a new song and re - joice,
4. Join with the hills and the sea

He to whom won - ders be - long! Re -
See his sal - va - tion is shown; And
Pub - lish his prais - es a - broad! Let
Thun - ders of praise to pro - long! In

joice in his tri - umph and
still he re - mem - bers his
voic - es in cho - rus, with
judge - ment and jus - tice he

tell of his power, O sing to the
mer - cy and truth, Un - chang - ing in
trum - pet and horn, Re - sound for the
comes to the earth, O sing to the

Lord a new song!
love to his own.
joy of the Lord!
Lord a new song!

Text: Psalm 98; Timothy Dudley-Smith, b.1926
Tune: CANTATE DOMINO (ONSLOW SQUARE), Irregular; David G. Wilson, b.1940
© 1973, Hope Publishing Co.

380 Glory and Praise to Our God

Refrain

Glo-ry and praise to our God, who a-lone gives light to our days. Man-y are the bless-ings he bears to those who trust in his ways.

Verses 1-3

1. We, the daugh-ters and sons of him who built the val-leys and plains, Praise the won-ders our God has done in ev-'ry heart that sings.
2. In his wis-dom he strength-ens us, like gold that's test-ed in fire. Though the pow-er of sin pre-vails, our God is there to save.
3. Ev-'ry mom-ent of ev-'ry day our God is wait-ing to save, Al-ways read-y to seek the lost, to an-swer those who pray.

D.C.

Verse 4

4. God has wa-tered our bar-ren land and spent his mer-ci-ful rain. Now the riv-ers of life run full for an-y-one to drink.

D.C.

Text: Psalm 65, 66; Dan Schutte, b. 1947
Tune: Dan Schutte, b. 1947; acc. by Sr. Theophane Hytrek, OSF, 1915-1992, alt.

Sing Our God Together   381

After each verse, repeat key word in the refrain: (Dance/Dance our; Serve/Serve our;
Shine/Shine in; Teach/Teach our; Seek/ Seek our; Live/Live our)

Text: David Haas, b. 1957, and Marty Haugen, b. 1950
Tune: David Haas, b. 1957, and Marty Haugen, b. 1950
© 1993, GIA Publications, Inc.

382 I Want to Praise Your Name

Verses

1. Praise with the trum - pet, Praise with the harp,
2. Moun - tains and val - leys, Riv - ers and seas,
3. Moth - ers and fa - thers, Daugh - ters and sons,

Praise with the tim - brel, the dance and the lyre; Let ev - 'ry -
Stars in the heav - ens and fish in the deep; Let all cre -
All of God's peo - ple, the old and the young; Let all who

thing that has breath give praise to God.
a - tion give praise to God on high.
hun - ger to do God's will give praise.

Refrain

I want to praise your name. I want to sing your

1.,2.   D.C.

good - ness. Glo - ry, O God; Glo - ry.

3.

Glo - ry.

Text: Psalm 148, 149, 150; adapt. by Bob Hurd, b. 1950, © 1984
Tune: Bob Hurd, b. 1950, © 1984, acc. by Craig S. Kingsbury, b. 1952, © 1984, OCP Publications
Published by OCP Publications

World without End 383

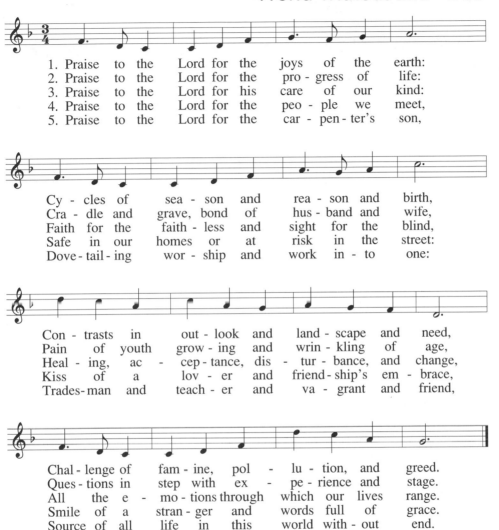

1. Praise to the Lord for the joys of the earth:
2. Praise to the Lord for the pro - gress of life:
3. Praise to the Lord for his care of our kind:
4. Praise to the Lord for the peo - ple we meet,
5. Praise to the Lord for the car - pen - ter's son,

Cy - cles of sea - son and rea - son and birth,
Cra - dle and grave, bond of hus - band and wife,
Faith for the faith - less and sight for the blind,
Safe in our homes or at risk in the street:
Dove - tail - ing wor - ship and work in - to one:

Con - trasts in out - look and land - scape and need,
Pain of youth grow - ing and wrin - kling of age,
Heal - ing, ac - cep - tance, dis - tur - bance, and change,
Kiss of a lov - er and friend - ship's em - brace,
Trades - man and teach - er and va - grant and friend,

Chal - lenge of fam - ine, pol - lu - tion, and greed.
Ques - tions in step with ex - pe - rience and stage.
All the e - mo - tions through which our lives range.
Smile of a stran - ger and words full of grace.
Source of all life in this world with - out end.

Text: John L. Bell, b.1949, © 1987, Iona Community, GIA Publications, Inc., agent
Tune: BONNIE GEORGE CAMPBELL, 10 10 10 10; Scottish Folk Song; acc. by John L. Bell, b.1949, © 1993, Iona Community,
GIA Publications, Inc., agent

384　Sing a New Song

Refrain

Sing a new song un - to the Lord; let your song be
sung from moun - tains high. Sing a new song
un - to the Lord, sing - ing al - le - lu - ia.

Verses

1. Yah - weh's peo - ple dance for joy. O come be -
2. Rise, O chil - dren, from your sleep; your Sav - ior
3. Glad my soul for I have seen the glo - ry

fore the Lord. And play for him on
now has come. He has turned your
of the Lord. The trum - pet sounds; the

D.C.

glad tam - bou - rines, and let your trum - pet sound.
sor - row to joy, and filled your soul with song.
dead shall be raised. I know my Sav - ior lives.

Text: Psalm 98; Dan Schutte, b. 1947
Tune: Dan Schutte, b. 1947
© 1972, Daniel L. Schutte, administered by New Dawn Music

Let Heaven Your Wonders Proclaim 385

1. Let heav - en your won - ders pro - claim, Let
2. Your strength rules the rage of the sea, Your
3. The heav - ens are yours and the earth: You
4. { Tough - ness and val - or are yours, {
5. So, glad are the peo - ple who praise you, Who

an - gels your faith - ful - ness praise, For
faith - ful - ness calms its wild waves, You
found - ed the world and its wealth; The
Strong is your hand lift - ed high; Yet
walk in the light of your love; In

who in the heights or the depths Can
quell ev - 'ry ter - ror of the deep And
north and the south show your skill. The
jus - tice is found at your throne And
you, God a - lone, is their strength, Their

e - qual your maj - es - ty, O God?
scat - ter your en - e - mies a - far.
east and the west at - test your fame.
love is for ev - er by your side.
hon - or, their jus - tice, and their joy.

Text: Psalm 89: 1-16; John L. Bell, b.1949, © 1991, Iona Community, GIA Publications, Inc., agent
Tune: Salvador T. Martinez, © 1989, Salvador T. Martinez; arr. by John L. Bell, b.1949, © 1991, Iona Community, GIA Publications, Inc., agent

386 I Will Sing, I Will Sing

Verses 1, 2, 3, 6

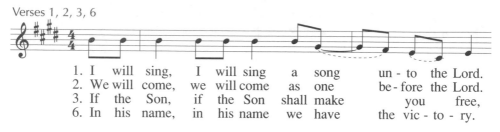

1. I will sing, I will sing a song un - to the Lord.
2. We will come, we will come as one be - fore the Lord.
3. If the Son, if the Son shall make you free,
6. In his name, in his name we have the vic - to - ry.

I will sing, I will sing a song un - to the Lord.
We will come, we will come as one be - fore the Lord.
If the Son, if the Son shall make you free,
In his name, in his name we have the vic - to - ry.

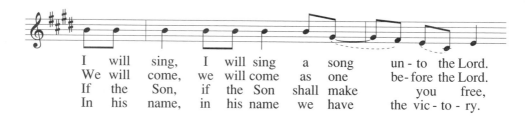

I will sing, I will sing a song un - to the Lord.
We will come, we will come as one be - fore the Lord.
If the Son, if the Son shall make you free,
In his name, in his name we have the vic - to - ry.

To refrain

Al - le - lu - ia, glo - ry to the Lord.
Al - le - lu - ia, glo - ry to the Lord.
You shall be free in - deed.
Al - le - lu - ia, glo - ry to the Lord.

Refrain

Al - le - lu, al - le - lu - ia, glo - ry to the Lord. Al - le -

lu, al-le-lu-ia, glo - ry to the Lord. Al-le-lu, al-le-lu-ia, glo

To verses

ry to the Lord. Al - le - lu - ia, glo - ry to the Lord.

Verses 4, 5

4. They that sow in tears shall reap in joy. They that
5. Ev - 'ry knee shall bow and ev-'ry tongue con - fess, Ev - 'ry

sow in tears shall reap in joy. They that
knee shall bow and ev-'ry tongue con - fess, Ev - 'ry

sow in tears shall reap in joy. Al - le -
knee shall bow and ev-'ry tongue con - fess, That

To refrain

lu - ia, glo - ry to the Lord.
Je - sus Christ is Lord.

Text: Max Dyer
Tune: PULKINGHAM, Irregular; Max Dyer
© 1974, 1975, Celebration

387 Lift Up Your Hearts

Refrain

Lift up your hearts to the Lord, praise God's gra-cious mer-cy!

Sing out your joy to the Lord, whose love is en - dur - ing.

Verses

1. Shout with joy to the Lord, all the earth!
2. Let the earth wor - ship, sing - ing your praise.
3. God's right hand made a path through the night,
4. Lis - ten now, all you ser - vants of God,

Praise the name a - bove all names! Say to God, "How
Praise the glo - ry of your name! Come and see what
split the wa - ters of the sea. All cre - a - tion,
As I tell of these great works. Bless - ed be the

D.C.

won - drous your works, how glo - rious your name!"
God has re-vealed, bless God's ho - ly name!
lift up your voice: Our God set us free.
Lord of my life, whose love shall en - dure!

Text: Psalm 66; Roc O'Connor, SJ, b. 1949, © 1981, 1993, and New Dawn Music, alt.
Tune: Roc O'Connor, SJ, b. 1949, © 1981 and New Dawn Music; acc. by Robert J. Batastini, b. 1942, © 1994, GIA Publications, Inc.

Shout for Joy 388

Verses

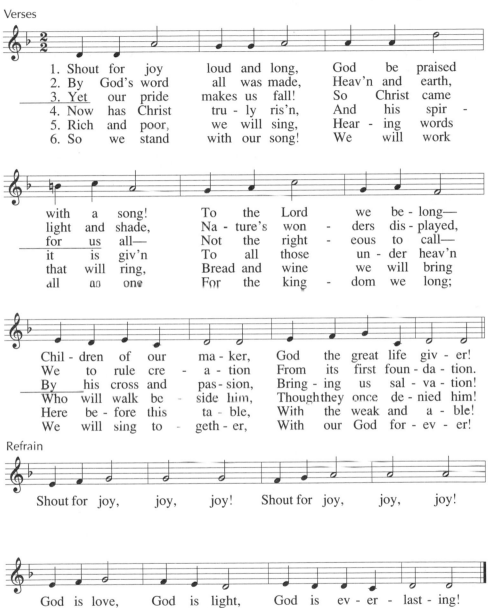

1. Shout for joy loud and long, God be praised
2. By God's word all was made, Heav'n and earth,
3. Yet our pride makes us fall! So Christ came
4. Now has Christ tru - ly ris'n, And his spir -
5. Rich and poor, we will sing, Hear - ing words
6. So we stand with our song! We will work

with a song! To the Lord we be - long—
light and shade, Na - ture's won - ders dis - played,
for us all— Not the right - eous to call—
it is giv'n To all those un - der heav'n
that will ring, Bread and wine we will bring
all as one For the king - dom we long;

Chil - dren of our ma - ker, God the great life giv - er!
We to rule cre - a - tion From its first foun - da - tion.
By his cross and pas - sion, Bring - ing us sal - va - tion!
Who will walk be - side him, Though they once de - nied him!
Here be - fore this ta - ble, With the weak and a - ble!
We will sing to - geth - er, With our God for - ev - er!

Refrain

Shout for joy, joy, joy! Shout for joy, joy, joy!

God is love, God is light, God is ev - er - last - ing!

Text: Stanzas 1-4, David Mowbray, © 1982, Hope Publishing Co.; stanzas 5-6, David Haas, b.1957, © 1993, GIA Publications, Inc.
Tune: PERSONET HODIE 666 66 with refrain, *Piae cantiones*, Griefswald, 1582; harm. by Diana Kodner, b.1957, © 1992, GIA Publications, Inc.

389 Joyfully Singing

Verses

1. Joy-ful-ly sing-ing to the Lord,
2. God, in your mer-cy, free our hearts to
3. Gath-er the na-tions to you, Lord,

prais-ing God on high, all of the earth in thank-
praise your ho-ly name, help-ing the poor and low-
draw them to your care, com-ing from all the dis-

ful-ness joins in glad re-ply.
ly ones faith-ful-ly pro-claim.
tant lands glad-ly to de-clare.

Refrain

Bless-ed are your days, ho-ly are your nights,

won-drous is your love all of our lives.

Lord, bring us to-geth-er from east and from the west.

Show us your moun-tain, your dwell-ing place, your

D.C.

life of ho-li-ness.

Text: Mike Balhoff, b. 1946, Gary Daigle, b.1957, Darryl Ducote, b.1945
Tune: Mike Balhoff, b. 1946, Gary Daigle, b.1957, Darryl Ducote, b.1945
© 1985, Damean Music. Distributed by GIA Publications, Inc.

391 When, in Our Music, God Is Glorified

1. When, in our mu - sic, God is glo - ri - fied,
2. How of - ten, mak - ing mu - sic, we have found
3. So has the Church, in lit - ur - gy and song,
4. And did not Je - sus sing a psalm that night
5. Let ev - 'ry in - stru-ment be tuned for praise!

And ad - o - ra - tion leaves no room for pride,
A new di - men - sion in the world of sound,
In faith and love, through cen - tu - ries of wrong,
When ut - most e - vil strove a - gainst the Light?
Let all re - joice who have a voice to raise!

It is as though the whole cre - a - tion cried:
As wor-ship moved us to a more pro - found
Borne wit-ness to the truth in ev - 'ry tongue: Al-le-lu -
Then let us sing, for whom he won the fight:
And may God give us faith to sing al - ways;

ia! Al-le-lu - ia! Al-le-lu - ia!

Text: Fred Pratt Green, b.1903, © 1972, Hope Publishing Co.
Tune: MAYFLOWER, 10 10 10 with alleluias; Marty Haugen, b.1950, © 1989, GIA Publications, Inc.

You Are the Voice   390

Refrain

You are the voice of the liv - ing God,

call- ing us now to live in your love, to be

chil- dren of God once a - gain!

Verses

Cantor:

1. Praise for the light that shines through the night, from
2. Praise for the wa - ter that springs from the sea, the
3. Praise for the sing- ing and praise for the dance, with

dark - ness to light, from death to new life, and
seed that gives life to all who be - lieve, God's
new heart and voice, all raise the song of

praise to the morn- ing that brings forth the sun, to
love o - ver - flow- ing, our hearts know the joy to be
praise to cre - a - tion; all heav - en and earth, come

All:

o - pen our eyes to the Lord! To
daugh- ters and sons of the Lord! To be
sing of the glo - ry of God! Come

D.C.

o - pen our eyes to the Lord! For
daugh- ters and sons of the Lord! For
sing of the glo - ry of God! For

Text: David Haas, b.1957
Tune: David Haas, b.1957; acc. by Jeanne Cotter, b.1964
© 1983, 1987, GIA Publications, Inc.

May We Praise You 392

1. May we praise you, O Lord, With heart and hand and
2. May our liv-ing be true. May all re-turn to
3. Let your step guide our path. Let shades of dark not
4. To the Fa-ther be praise; To Son and Spir-it,

voice. And since life it-self is your gift to us, Then may
you. And when life is done let our pass-ing be Like a
last. May the sun of jus-tice re - turn on high, And your
praise. Un-to God the one let all praise be done, Till the

1.- 3.

all that we are be yours.
birth in-to light of day.
love be our road and guide.
dawn of the last - ing

4.

day, may we praise.

Text: Vs. 1 from *The Liturgy of the Hours;* John Foley, SJ, b.1939
Tune: John Foley, SJ, b.1939
© 1981, John Foley, SJ, and New Dawn Music

393 Praise the Lord, My Soul

Praise the Lord, my soul! Sing al-le - lu - ia, bless God's name.

Verses 1, 3, 5, 7

1. All prais - es to the Fa - ther of our Lord, a
3. How great the sign of God's love for us in
5. And now we are God's work of art, a
7. We come to you with hearts full of faith, your

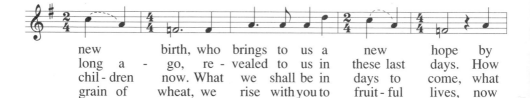

God so mer - ci - ful and kind, who gives to us a
giv - ing us his Son to be our bread: as prom-ised us so
new cre - a - tion formed in Christ the Lord. We know we are his
voice is call-ing us so deep with - in. We died with you as

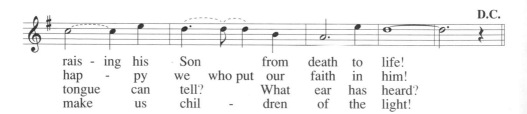

new birth, who brings to us a new hope by
long a - go, re - vealed to us in these last days. How
chil - dren now. What we shall be in days to come, what
grain of wheat, we rise with you to fruit - ful lives, now

D.C.

rais - ing his Son from death to life!
hap - py we who put our faith in him!
tongue can tell? What ear has heard?
make us chil - dren of the light!

Verses 2, 4, 6

2. On this moun - tain God will pre - pare a ban - quet for all
4. Ev - 'ry tear shall be wiped a - way and shame shall be no
6. Taste and see the good-ness of God! Hap-py those who take their

peo - ples: rich food and fin - est wine. On this moun - tain
more for God's own cho - sen friends. Then they shall say:
shel - ter be - neath his watch-ful care. Fear the Lord!

God will re-move the mourn - ing veil that cov-ers all peo - ples
"This is the one we hoped for to bring us sal - va - tion.
Proud and rich may find them-selves sent emp - ty a - way;

D.C.

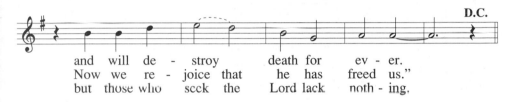

and will de - stroy death for ev - er.
Now we re - joice that he has freed us."
but those who seek the Lord lack noth - ing.

394 Halleluya! We Sing Your Praises

Refrain

Hal - le - lu - ya! We sing your prais-es, all our hearts are filled with glad - ness. Hal - le - lu - ya! We sing your prais-es, all our hearts are filled with glad - ness.

Verses

1. Christ the Lord to us said: I am
2. Now he sends us all out, strong in

wine, I am bread, I am wine, I am
faith, free of doubt, strong in faith, free of

bread, give to all who thirst and hun - ger.
doubt, to pro - claim the joy - ful Gos - pel.

Text: South African
Tune: South African

395 Santo, Santo, Santo / Holy, Holy, Holy

1. San - to, san - to, san - to, san - to, san - to,
2. san - to, san - to, san - to, san - to,
1. *Ho - ly, ho - ly, ho - ly, ho - ly, ho - ly,*
2. *ho - ly, ho - ly, ho - ly, ho - ly,*

san - to_es nues - tro Dios, Se - ñor de to - da la
san - to_es nues - tro Dios, Se - ñor de to - da la_his -
ho - ly is our God, God, the Lord of earth and
ho - ly is our God, God, the Lord of all of

tie - rra. San-to, san - to_es nues - tro Dios. San-to,
to - ria. San-to, san - to_es nues - tro Dios.
heav - en. Ho-ly, ho - ly is our God. Ho-ly,
his - t'ry. Ho-ly, ho - ly is our God.

Que_a - com̧ - pa - ña_a nues - tro pue - blo, que vi - ve_en
Ben - di - tos los que_en su nom - bre el e - van -
Who ac - com - pa - nies our peo - ple, who lives with-
Bless - ed those who in the Lord's name an - nounce the

nues - tras lu - chas, del u - ni - ver - so_en -
ge - lio_a - nun - cian, la bue - na_y gran no -
in our strug - gles, of all the earth and
ho - ly gos - pel, pro - claim - ing the good

te - ro el ú - ni - co Se - ñor.
ti - cia de la li - be - ra - ción.
heav - en the one and on - ly Lord.
news that our lib - er - a - tion comes.

Text: Guillermo Cuellar; trans. by Linda McCrae
Tune: Guillermo Cuellar; acc. by Diana Kodner, b.1957
© 1993, 1994, GIA Publications, Inc.

In the Lord I'll Be Ever Thankful 396

Ostinato Refrain

In the Lord I'll be ev - er thank - ful, in the Lord I will re - joice! Look to God, do not be a - fraid; lift up your voic - es, the Lord is near; lift up your voic - es, the Lord is near.

Text: Taizé Community
Tune: Jacques Berthier, b.1923
© 1986, 1991, Les Presses de Taizé, GIA Publications, Inc., agent

397 Thanks Be to You

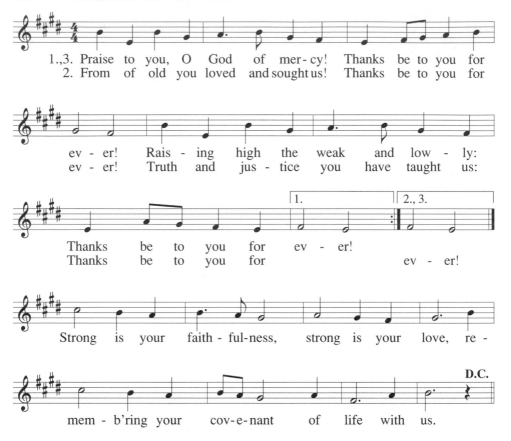

1.,3. Praise to you, O God of mer-cy! Thanks be to you for
2. From of old you loved and sought us! Thanks be to you for

ev - er! Rais - ing high the weak and low - ly:
ev - er! Truth and jus - tice you have taught us:

1.
Thanks be to you for ev - er!
2., 3.
Thanks be to you for ev - er!

Strong is your faith - ful-ness, strong is your love, re -

D.C.

mem - b'ring your cov-e-nant of life with us.

Text: Marty Haugen, b.1950
Tune: Marty Haugen, b.1950
© 1990, GIA Publications, Inc.

Confitemini Domino / Come and Fill   398

Ostinato Refrain

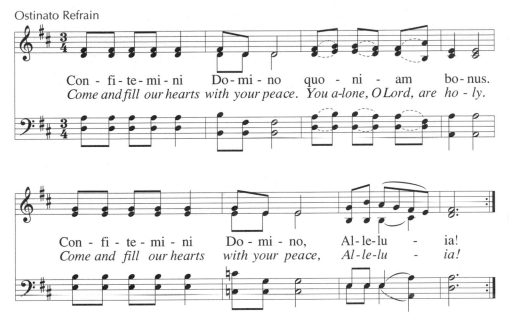

Con - fi - te - mi - ni   Do - mi - no   quo - ni - am   bo - nus.
Come and fill our hearts with your peace. You a-lone, O Lord, are ho - ly.

Con - fi - te - mi - ni   Do - mi - no,   Al - le - lu - ia!
Come and fill our hearts   with your peace,   Al - le - lu - ia!

Text: Psalm 137, *Give thanks to the Lord for he is good;* Taizé Community, 1982
Tune: Jacques Berthier, b.1923
© 1982, 1991, Les Presses de Taizé, GIA Publications, Inc., agent

399 Table Prayer

Choir or cantor:

1. The ta - ble which you set has the
2. The peo - ple whom you call come to
3. The sa - cred food you give is the

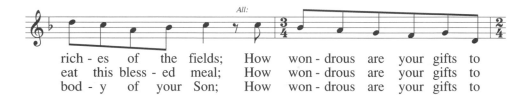

rich - es of the fields; How won - drous are your gifts to
eat this bless - ed meal; How won - drous are your gifts to
bod - y of your Son; How won - drous are your gifts to

Choir or cantor:

us. You share the fin - est por - tion, Lord, with rev-'rence and with
us. We raise our hearts in thanks to you, a sin - gle prayer of
us. You nour - ish us with ho - ly wine to sat - is - fy our

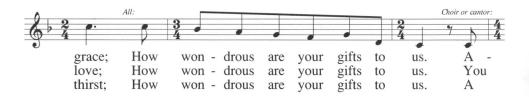

All: *Choir or cantor:*

grace; How won - drous are your gifts to us. A -
love; How won - drous are your gifts to us. You
thirst; How won - drous are your gifts to us. A

All:

bun - dant is your love; How won - drous are your gifts to us.
gath - er us as one; How won - drous are your gifts to us.
ban - quet for all time; How won - drous are your gifts to us.

Text: Mike Balhoff, b.1946, Gary Daigle, b.1957, Darryl Ducote, b.1945
Tune: Mike Balhoff, b.1946, Gary Daigle, b.1957, Darryl Ducote, b.1945
© 1985, Damean Music. Distributed by GIA Publications, Inc.

Lead Me, Guide Me 400

Refrain

Lead me, guide me, a - long the way, For if you

lead me, I can-not stray. Lord, let me walk each

day with thee. Lead me, oh Lord, lead me.

Verses

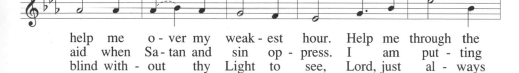

1. I am weak and I need thy strength and power to
2. Help me tread in the paths of right - eous - ness, Be my
3. I am lost if you take your hand from me, I am

help me o - ver my weak - est hour. Help me through the
aid when Sa - tan and sin op - press. I am put - ting
blind with - out thy Light to see, Lord, just al - ways

D.C.

dark-ness thy face to see, Lead me, oh Lord, lead me.
all my trust in thee. Lead me, oh Lord, lead me.
let me thy ser - vant be. Lead me, oh Lord, lead me.

Text: Doris M. Akers, b.1922
Tune: Doris M. Akers, b.1922, harm. by Richard Smallwood
© 1953, Doris M. Akers, All rights administered by Unichappell Music, Inc.

401   We Cannot Measure How You Heal

1. We can - not meas - ure how you heal Or
2. The pain that will not go a - way, The
3. So some have come who need your help And

an - swer ev - 'ry suf - f'rer's prayer, Yet
guilt that clings from things long past, The
some have come to make a - mends, As

we be - lieve your grace re - sponds Where faith and
fear of what the fu - ture holds, Are pres - ent
hands which shaped and saved the world Are pres - ent

doubt u - nite to care. Your hands, though blood - ied
as if meant to last. But pres - ent too is
in the touch of friends. Lord, let your Spir - it

on the cross, Sur - vive to hold and heal and
love which tends The hurt we nev - er hoped to
meet us here To mend the bod - y, mind, and

warn, To car - ry all through death to
find, The pri - vate ag - o - nies in -
soul, To dis - en - tan - gle peace from

life And cra - dle chil - dren yet un - born.
side, The mem - o - ries that haunt the mind.
pain, And make your bro - ken peo - ple whole.

Text: John L. Bell, b.1949
Tune: YE BANKS AND BRAES, 8 8 8 8 D; Scottish tradtional; arr. by John L. Bell, b.1949
© 1989, Iona Community, GIA Publications, Inc., agent

Come to Us, Creative Spirit   402

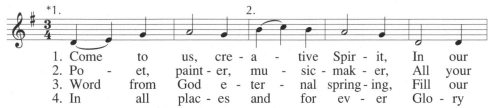

1. Come to us, cre - a - tive Spir - it, In our
2. Po - et, paint - er, mu - sic - mak - er, All your
3. Word from God e - ter - nal spring - ing, Fill our
4. In all plac - es and for ev - er Glo - ry

Fa - ther's house; Ev - 'ry hu - man tal - ent
treas - ures bring; Crafts - man, ac - tor, grace - ful
minds, we pray; And in all ar - tis - tic
be ex - pressed To the Son, with God the

hal - low, Hid - den skills a - rouse,
danc - er, Make your of - fer - ing;
vi - sion Give in - teg - ri - ty:
Fa - ther And the Spir - it blessed:

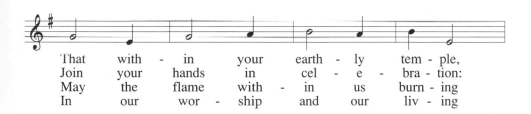

That with - in your earth - ly tem - ple,
Join your hands in cel - e - bra - tion:
May the flame with - in us burn - ing
In our wor - ship and our liv - ing

Wise and sim - ple, may re - joice.
Let cre - a - tion shout and sing!
Kin - dle yearn - ing day by day.
Keep us striv - ing for the best.

May be sung in canon.

Text: David Mowbray, b.1938, © 1979, Stainer and Bell, Ltd., London, England
Tune: CREATOR SPIRITUS, 8 5 8 5 84 3; Thomas F. Savoy, b.1955, © 1987, GIA Publications, Inc.

403 Standin' in the Need of Prayer

1. Not my broth-er, nor my sis-ter, but it's me, Oh Lord,
2. Not the preach-er, nor the dea-con, but it's me, Oh Lord,
3. Not my fa-ther, nor my moth-er, but it's me, Oh Lord,
4. Not the stran-ger, nor my neigh-bor, but it's me, Oh Lord,

Stand-in' in the need of prayer; Not my broth-er, nor my sis-ter,
Stand-in' in the need of prayer; Not the preach-er, nor the dea-con,
Stand-in' in the need of prayer; Not my fa-ther, nor my moth-er,
Stand-in' in the need of prayer; Not the stran-ger, nor my neigh-bor,

but it's me, Oh Lord, Stand-in' in the need of prayer.
but it's me, Oh Lord, Stand-in' in the need of prayer.
but it's me, Oh Lord, Stand-in' in the need of prayer. It's
but it's me, Oh Lord, Stand-in' in the need of prayer.

me, it's me, Oh Lord, Stand-in' in the need of prayer. It's

me, it's me, Oh Lord, Stand-in' in the need of prayer.

Text: African-American spiritual
Tune: African-American spiritual

Creating God   404

1. Cre - at - ing God, your fin - gers
2. Sus - tain - ing God, your hands up -
3. Re - deem - ing God, your arms em -
4. In - dwel - ling God, your gos - pel

trace The bold de - signs of far - thest space;
hold Earth's mys - t'ries known or yet un - told;
brace All now de - spised for creed or race;
claims One fam - 'ly with a bil - lion names;

Let sun and moon and stars and light And
Let wa - ters frag - ile blend with air, En -
Let peace, de - scend - ing like a dove, Make
Let ev - 'ry life be touched by grace Un -

what lies hid - den praise your might.
a - bling life, pro - claim your care.
known on earth your heal - ing love.
til we praise you face to face.

Text: Jeffrey Rowthorn, b.1934, © 1979, Hymn Society of America, alt.
Tune: PRESENCE, LM; David Haas, b.1957, © 1989, GIA Publications, Inc.

405 Kyrie Guarany

1. O - ré mbo - ria - jú ve - re - kó Nan - de - ya - ra. O - ré mbo - ria - jú ve - re - kó Nan - de - ya - ra.
2. O - ré mbo - ria - jú ve - re - kó Je - su - cris - to. O - ré mbo - ria - jú ve - re - kó Je - su - cris - to.

1. *On the poor, on the poor, show your mer - cy, O Lord. On the poor, on the poor, show your mer - cy, O Lord.*
2. *On the poor, on the poor, show your mer - cy, O Christ. On the poor, on the poor, show your mer - cy, O Christ.*

Text: Adapt. liturgical text; traditional Paraguayan
Tune: As taught by Pablo Sosa; arr. by John L. Bell b.1949, © 1991, Iona Community, GIA Publications, Inc., agent

I Need You to Listen 406

Refrain

I need you to lis-ten. I need you to an-swer.

I need you to lis-ten. I need you to an - swer.

Verses

1. O God, I need you to. I want to see your face.
   It is this love I have. It makes me search for you.

2. Do not avoid my eyes or let me anger you.
   Do not toss me aside. O God, do not drop me.

3. You are the only hope I have; father, mother, they can leave me orphaned,
   but your love must never. Lead me to you, O God, along the smoothest road.

4. There are those who hate me. Do not leave me to them.
   They eat my life away by lying under oath or twisting evidence.

5. I trust your love. I will see your beauty after death in your land of life.
   My love will wait for you. It will be strong waiting. O God, my love will wait!

Text: Based on Psalm 27; Francis Patrick Sullivan, © 1983, The Pastoral Press
Tune: Marty Haugen, b.1950, © 1991, GIA Publications, Inc.

407 Gifts That Last

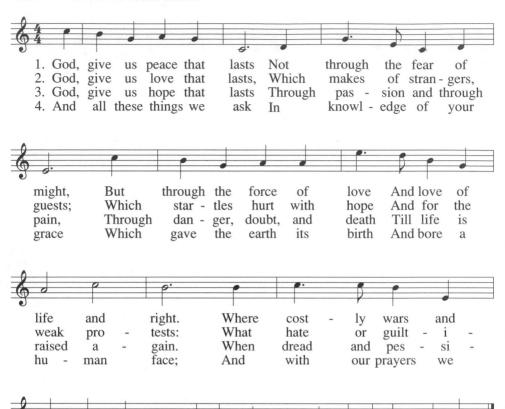

1. God, give us peace that lasts Not through the fear of
2. God, give us love that lasts, Which makes of stran - gers,
3. God, give us hope that lasts Through pas - sion and through
4. And all these things we ask In knowl - edge of your

might, But through the force of love And love of
guests; Which star - tles hurt with hope And for the
pain, Through dan - ger, doubt, and death Till life is
grace Which gave the earth its birth And bore a

life and right. Where cost - ly wars and
weak pro - tests: What hate or guilt - i -
raised a - gain. When dread and pes - si -
hu - man face; And with our prayers we

weap - ons lure, Show us our Lord a - mong the poor.
ness em - boss, Con - front with Je - sus and the cross.
mism loom, Di - rect us to the emp - ty tomb.
give our word To serve and fol - low Christ our Lord.

Text: John L. Bell, b.1949
Tune: ARKLET ROAD, 6 6 6 6 88; John L. Bell, b.1949
© 1989, Iona Community, GIA Publications, Inc., agent

Healing River   408

Cantor:*

1. O heal - ing riv - er, send down your
2. This land is parch - ing, this land is
3. Let the seed of free - dom, a - wake and

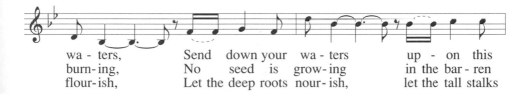

wa - ters, Send down your wa - ters up - on this
burn - ing, No seed is grow - ing in the bar - ren
flour - ish, Let the deep roots nour - ish, let the tall stalks

land. O heal - ing riv - er, send down your
ground. O heal - ing riv - er, send down your
rise. O heal - ing riv - er, send down your

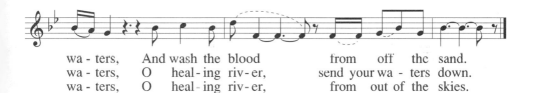

wa - ters, And wash the blood from off the sand.
wa - ters, O heal - ing riv - er, send your wa - ters down.
wa - ters, O heal - ing riv - er, from out of the skies.

*The assembly echoes each phrase of the cantor at the interval of one half measure.

Text: Fran Minkoff.
Tune: Fred Hellerman; arr. by Michael Joncas, b.1951
© 1964, Appleseed Music, Inc.

409 Song over the Waters

Refrain

God, you have moved up-on the wa-ters, you have sung in the rush of wind and flame; and in your love, you have called us sons and daugh-ters, make us peo-ple of the wa-ter and your name.

Verses

1. Come fill our wait-ing hearts with the
2. Give us a thirst for love, give us a
3. You are the breath of life, you are the
4. Come, o-pen ev-'ry heart, come now and

spir - it of Je - sus, let us shine with your
hun - ger for jus - tice, make us one with the
hope of the hope - less, come and fill us with
wake us to won - der, make us ves - sels of

D.C.

light and peace.
mind of Christ.
light and peace.
light and peace.

Sprinkling Rite

Cantor: All:
(Invocation)   Re - new us!

Cantor: All: D.C.
(Invocation)   Re - new us!

Text: Marty Haugen, b.1950
Tune: Marty Haugen, b.1950
© 1987, GIA Publications, Inc.

O Lord, Hear My Prayer   410

Ostinato Chorale

O Lord, hear my prayer, O Lord, hear my prayer:
when I call an-swer me. O Lord, hear my prayer, O
Lord, hear my prayer. Come and lis-ten to me. O

Text: Psalm 102; Taizé Community, 1982
Tune: Jacques Berthier, b.1923

411 Bwana Awabariki / May God Grant You a Blessing

Bwa - na a-wa-ba-ri - ki, Bwa - na
May God grant you a bless-ing, may God

a - wa - ba - ri - ki, Bwa - na a-wa-ba-ri - ki
grant you a bless-ing, may God grant you a bless-ing

mi - le - le. U - ki - mcha Bwa - na.
ev - er - more. Re - vere the Lord.

Bwa - na a-wa-ba-ri - ki.
May God grant you a bless - ing.

Text: Swahili folk hymn
Tune: Swahili melody

Blest Are You 412

Cantor or choir;

1., 5. Blest are you who made the u - ni - verse,
2. Through your good - ness we have bread to eat,
3. Through your good - ness we have wine to drink,
4. Here the stran - ger is a wel-come guest

You who see be - yond our death. Blest are you who dwells in
Seeds that died to bring life new. As the sep - 'rate grains be -
Fruit of vine-yard, work of hands. Let the fruits of all we
Here all hun - gers shall be fed. Come, and know the one who

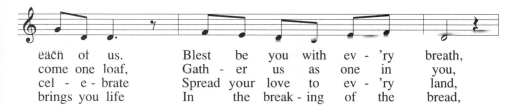

each of us. Blest be you with ev - 'ry breath,
come one loaf, Gath - er us as one in you,
cel - e - brate Spread your love to ev - 'ry land,
brings you life In the break - ing of the bread,

All:

Blest be you with ev - 'ry breath.
Gath - er us as one in you.
Spread your love to ev - 'ry land.
In the break - ing of the bread.

Text: Berakhot and *Didache*; Marty Haugen, b.1950
Tune: Marty Haugen, b.1950
© 1993, GIA Publications, Inc.

413 May the Lord, Mighty God

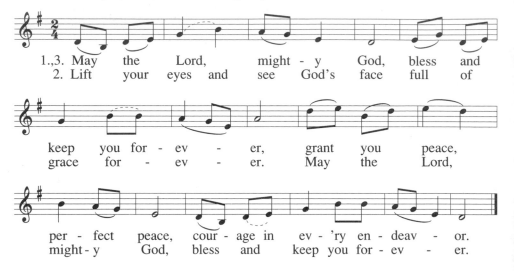

1.,3. May the Lord, might - y God, bless and
2. Lift your eyes and see God's face full of

keep you for - ev - er, grant you peace,
grace for - ev - er. May the Lord,

per - fect peace, cour - age in ev - 'ry en - deav - or.
might - y God, bless and keep you for - ev - er.

Text: Numbers 6:24-26; unknown
Tune: WEN-TI, Irregular; Chinese, Pao-chen Li; adapted by I-to Loh, © 1983, Abingdon Press; acc. by Diana Kodner, b.1957, © 1993,
    GIA Publications, Inc.

414 We Walk by Faith

1., 5. We walk by faith, and not by sight: No
2. We may not touch his hands and side, Nor
3. Help then, O Lord, our un - be - lief, And
4. That when our life of faith is done In

gra - cious words we hear Of him who spoke as
fol - low where he trod; Yet in his prom - ise
may our faith a - bound; To call on you when
realms of clear - er light We may be - hold you

none e'er spoke, But we be-lieve him near.
we re-joice, And cry "My Lord and God!"
you are near, And seek where you are found:
as you are In full and end-less sight.

Text: Henry Alford, 1810-1871, alt.
Tune: SHANTI, CM; Marty Haugen, b.1950, © 1984, GIA Publications, Inc.

How Shall I Sing to God?   415

1. How shall I sing to God when life is filled with
2. How shall I sing to God when life is filled with
3. How shall I sing to God and tell my Sav-ior's

glad-ness, lov-ing and birth, won - der and worth? I'll
bleak-ness, emp-ty and chill, break-ing my will? I'll
sto-ry: pass-o-ver bread, life from the dead? I'll

sing from the heart, thank-ful-ly re-ceiv-ing, joy-ful in be-liev-ing.
sing through my pain, an-gri-ly or ach-ing, cry-ing or com-plain-ing.
sing with my life, wit-ness-ing and giv-ing, risk-ing and for-giv-ing.

This is my song, I'll sing it with love.
This is my song, I'll sing it with love.
This is my song, I'll sing it with love.

Text: Brian Wren, b.1936, © 1986, Hope Publishing Co.
Tune: HOPE, Irregular; David Haas, b.1957, © 1990, GIA Publications, Inc.

416 Mayenziwe / Your Will Be Done

Ma - ye-(Ma - ye) nzi - we 'nta - ndo ya - kho. Ma-
Your will (Your will) be done on earth, O Lord. Your

ye-(Ma - ye) nzi - we 'nta-ndo ya - kho. Ma - ye - nzi-
will (Your will) be done on earth, O Lord. Your will be

we 'nta - ndo ya - kho. Ma - ye-nzi-we 'nta -
done on earth, O Lord. Your will be done on

ndo ya - kho. Ma - ye-nzi-we 'nta - ndo ya - kho.
earth, O Lord. Your will be done on earth, O Lord.

Text: from the Lord's Prayer, South African
Tune: South African traditional, as taught by George Mxadana; transcribed by John L. Bell, b.1949; © 1990, Iona Community,
  GIA Publications, Inc., agent

We Remember 417

Refrain

We re - mem-ber how you loved us to your death, and still we

cel-e-brate, for you are with us here; and we be-lieve that we will

see you when you come in your glo-ry, Lord. We re -

mem-ber, we cel-e-brate, we be - lieve.

Verses

1. Here, a mil - lion wound - ed souls are
2. Now we re - cre - ate your love, we
3. Christ, the Fa - ther's great "A - men" to
4. See the face of Christ re - vealed in

yearn-ing just to touch you and be healed.
bring the bread and wine to share a meal.
all the hopes and dreams of ev - 'ry heart,
ev - 'ry per - son stand-ing by your side,

D.C.

Gath - er all your peo-ple, and hold them to your heart.
Sign of grace and mer-cy, the pres-ence of the Lord.
Peace be - yond all tell-ing, and free - dom from all fear.
Gift to one an - oth-er, and tem-ples of your love.

Text: Marty Haugen, b.1950
Tune: Marty Haugen, b.1950
© 1980, GIA Publications, Inc.

418 Dwelling Place

Verses 1, 2, 4

1.,4. I fall on my knees to the Fa - ther of Je - sus, the
2. May Christ in his love give us strength for our liv - ing, the

Lord who has shown us the glo - ry of God. *(To verse 2)*
strength of the Spir - it the glo - ry of God.

Refrain

May Christ find a dwell - ing place of faith in our hearts.

May our lives be root - ed in love,

root-ed in love.

Verse 3

3. May grace and peace be yours in God our Fa - ther,

D.S.

and in the Son.

Text: Ephesians 3:14-17; 1:2; John Foley, SJ, b.1939
Tune: John Foley, SJ, b.1939
© 1976 by John B. Foley, SJ, administered by New Dawn Music

We Live a Mystery 419

Refrain

We live a mys-ter-y of ev-er - last-ing love:

Je - sus the liv-ing Lord, the God who came to earth to die and

rise a - gain; We live your mys - t'ry Lord.

Verses

1. This truth we car - ry, this faith we cling to:
2. He came as broth - er, he came as sav - ior.
3. No eye has seen it, no ear has heard it:

that Je - sus came to live as one of us, and die for
Son though he was, he learned o - be-di-ence, a harsh in -
what God has planned for those who hope in him, who put their

D.C.

all of us.
her - i - tance. We wait for your re - turn.
trust in him.

Text: Michael Connolly, b.1955
Tune: Michael Connolly, b.1955
© 1988, GIA Publications, Inc.

420 Do Not Fear to Hope

Refrain

Do not fear to hope tho' the wick-ed rage and rise, our

God sees not as we see, suc-cess is not the prize. Do not

fear to hope for tho' the night be long, the race shall not be

to the swift, the fight not to the strong.

Verses

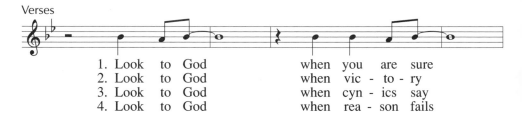

1. Look to God when you are sure
2. Look to God when vic-to-ry
3. Look to God when cyn-ics say
4. Look to God when rea-son fails

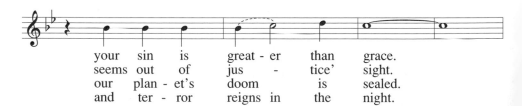

your sin is great-er than grace.
seems out of jus - tice' sight.
our plan-et's doom is sealed.
and ter-ror reigns in the night.

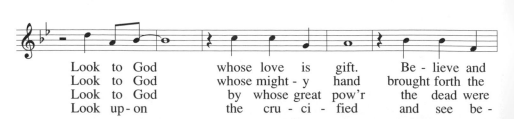

Look to God whose love is gift. Be-lieve and
Look to God whose might-y hand brought forth the
Look to God by whose great pow'r the dead were
Look up-on the cru-ci-fied and see be-

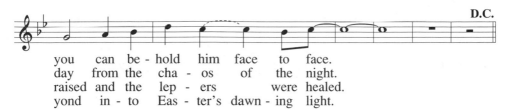

you can be - hold him face to face.
day from the cha - os of the night.
raised and the lep - ers were healed.
yond in - to Eas - ter's dawn - ing light.

Text: Rory Cooney, b. 1952
Tune: Rory Cooney, b. 1952
© 1986, North American Liturgy Resources

I Say "Yes," Lord / Digo "Sí," Señor   421

Verses

(Invocation)   I say "Yes," my Lord. I say "Yes," my Lord.
Di - go "Sí," Se - ñor. Di-go "Sí," Se-ñor.

Refrain

I say "Yes," my Lord, in all the good times, through
Di - go "Sí," Se - ñor, en tiem-pos mal - os, en

all the bad times, I say "Yes," my Lord to
tiem - pos bue - nos, Di - go "Sí," Se - ñor a

ev - 'ry word you speak.
to - do lo que ha - blas.

Text: Donna Peña, b.1955
Tune: Donna Peña, b.1955; arr. by Marty Haugen, b.1950
© 1989, GIA Publications, Inc.

422 Center of My Life

Refrain

O Lord, you are the cen-ter of my life: I will al-ways praise you,

I will al-ways serve you, I will al-ways keep you in my sight.

Verses 1- 3

1. Keep me safe, O God, I take ref-uge in you. I
2. I will bless the Lord who gives me coun - sel, who
3. And so my heart re - joic - es, my soul is glad;

say to the Lord, "You are my God. My
e - ven at night di - rects my heart. I
e - ven in safe - ty shall my bod - y rest. For

hap - pi - ness lies in you a - lone; my
keep the Lord ev - er in my sight: since
you will not leave my soul a - mong the dead, nor

D.C.

hap-pi - ness lies in you a - lone."
he is at my right hand, I shall stand firm.
let your be - lov - ed know de - cay.

Verse 4

4. You will show me the path of life, the

full - ness of joy in your pres-ence, at your right hand,

at your right hand   hap-pi-ness for ev-er.

Text: Psalm 16; verses trans. © 1963, The Grail, GIA Publications, Inc., agent; refrain, Paul Inwood, b.1947, © 1985
Tune: Paul Inwood, b.1947, © 1985
Published by OCP Publications

Hold Me in Life   423

Refrain

Hold me in life for you are my safe - ty,

al - ways my eyes are look - ing for you.

Verses

1. Be - cause you are just who you are,
2. Are you the one who is to come,
3. You gave your Word to this, our world:

don't pass me by, but show me your mer - cy;
or must we wait and fol - low some oth - er?
you are my song, the God of my glad - ness;

D.C.

I will wait for you all my life.
Lord, my God, I am cer - tain of you.
my de - sire goes out to you.

Text: Psalm 25; Huub Oosterhuis, b.1933; trans. by David Smith, b.1933, and Forrest Ingram
Tune: Bernard Huijbers, b.1922
© 1967, Gooi en Sticht, bv., Baarn, The Netherlands, Exclusive English-language agent: OCP Publications

424 Only in God

Refrain

On - ly in God will my soul be at rest. From him comes my

hope, my sal - va - tion. He a - lone is my rock of

safe - ty, my strength, my glo - ry, my God.

Verses

1. Trust in him at all times, O peo - ple, and pour out
2. Man - y times have I heard him tell of his long last -

your hearts. God him - self is a ref - uge for
ing love. You your - self, Lord, re - ward all who

D.C.

us and a strong - hold for our fear.
la - bor for love of your name.

Text: Psalm 62:1, 2 8, 11, 12; John Foley, SJ, b.1939
Tune: John Foley, SJ, b.1939
© 1976, John B. Foley, SJ and New Dawn Music

All That We Have   425

Refrain

All that we have and all that we of-fer Comes from a
heart both fright-ened and free. Take what we bring now and
give what we need, All done in his name.

Verses

1. Some would re - ly on their pow - er,
2. Some - times the road may be lone - some,
3. Some - times when trou - bles are man - y,

Oth - ers put trust in their gold.
Of - ten we may lose our way;
Life can seem emp - ty, it's true,

Some have on - ly their Sav - ior,
Take cour - age and al - ways re - mem - ber
But look at the life of the Mas - ter,

D.C.

Whose faith-ful-ness nev - er grows old.
Love is - n't just for a day.
Who lov - ing - ly suf - fered for you.

Text: Gary Ault, b.1944
Tune: Gary Ault b.1944; acc. by Gary Daigle, b.1957, alt.
© 1969, 1979, Damean Music. Distributed by GIA Publications, Inc.

426 Though the Mountains May Fall

Refrain

Though the moun - tains may fall and the hills turn to dust,

yet the love of the Lord will stand

as a shel - ter for all who will call on his name.

Sing the praise and the glo - ry of God.

Verses

1. Could the Lord ev - er leave you? Could the Lord for -
2. Should you turn and for - sake him, he will gent - ly
3. Go to him when you're wea - ry; he will give you
4. As he swore to your fa - thers, when the flood de -

get his love? Though a moth - er for -
call your name. Should you wan - der a -
ea - gle's wings. You will run, nev - er
stroyed the land; He will nev - er for -

D.C.

sake her child, he will not a - ban - don you.
way from him, he will al - ways take you back.
tire, for your God will be your strength.
sake you; he will swear to you a - gain.

Text: Isaiah 54:6-10, 49:15, 40:31-32; Dan Schutte, b.1947
Tune: Dan Schutte, b.1947; acc. by Michael Pope, SJ
© 1975, Daniel L. Schutte and New Dawn Music

How Can I Keep from Singing 427

Verses

1. My life flows on in end-less song A-
2. Through all the tu-mult and the strife, I
3. What though the tem-pest 'round me roar, I
4. When ty-rants trem-ble, sick with fear, And
5. The peace of Christ makes fresh my heart, A

bove earth's lam-en-ta-tion. I hear the real though
hear that mu-sic ring-ing; It sounds and ech-oes
hear the truth it liv-eth. What though the dark-ness
hear their death knells ring-ing; When friends re-joice both
foun-tain ev-er spring-ing. All things are mine since

far-off hymn That hails a new cre-a-tion.
in my soul; How can I keep from sing-ing?
'round me close, Songs in the night it giv-eth.
far and near, How can I keep from sing-ing?
I am his; How can I keep from sing-ing?

Refrain

No storm can shake my in-most calm, While to that rock I'm

cling-ing. Since love is Lord of heav-en and earth,

How can I keep from sing-ing?

Text: Robert Lowry, 1826-1899; adapted with additional text by Doris Plenn
Tune: HOW CAN I KEEP FROM SINGING, 8 7 8 7 with refrain; Robert Lowry, 1826-1899; harm. by Robert J. Batastini, b.1942
© 1957, 1964, Sanga Music, Inc.

428 You Are Near

Refrain

Yah-weh, I know you are near, stand-ing al - ways at my side. You guard me from the foe, and you lead me in ways ev - er - last - ing.

Verses

1. Lord, you have searched my heart, and you
2. Where can I run from your love? If I
3. You know my heart and its ways, you who
4. Mar - vel - ous to me are your works; how pro -

know when I sit and when I stand. Your
climb to the heav - ens you are there; if I
formed me be - fore I was born in the
found are your thoughts, my Lord. E - ven

hand is up - on me pro - tect - ing me from death,
fly to the sun - rise or sail be - yond the sea,
se - cret of dark - ness be - fore I saw the sun
if I could count them, they num - ber as the stars,

D.C.

keep - ing me from harm.
still I'd find you there.
in my moth - er's womb.
you would still be there.

Text: Psalm 139; Dan Schutte, b.1947
Tune: Dan Schutte, b.1947; acc. by Sr. Theophane Hytrek, OSF, 1915-1992
© 1971, Daniel L. Schutte, administered by New Dawn Music

The Lord Is My Light 429

Verses 1, 3

1. The Lord is my light   and   my   sal - va - tion, the Lord is my
3. ⸢ Wait on the Lord   and   be   of good cour - age, O   wait on the

light   and   my   sal - va - tion, the Lord is my   light   and
Lord   and   be of good   cour - age, ⸢   wait on the Lord   and

my   sal - va - tion;   whom   shall   I   fear?
be of good   cour - age.   He   shall strength - en thine   heart.

Refrain

Whom shall I   fear,   whom shall I   fear?   The Lord is the

strength   of   my   life;   whom   shall I   fear?

Verse 2

2. In   the time   of   trou - ble   he shall   hide me, O   in the time of

trou - ble,   he shall   hide me,   in the time of   trou - ble,

D.S.

he shall   hide me;   whom   shall I   fear?

Text: Lillian Bouknight
Tune: Lillian Bouknight; arr. by Paul Gainer
© 1980, Savgos Music, Inc.

430 Be Not Afraid

Verse 1

1. You shall cross the bar-ren des-ert, but you shall not die of thirst. You shall wan-der far in safe-ty though you do not know the way. You shall speak your words in for-eign lands and all will un-der-stand. You shall see the face of God and live.

Refrain 𝄋

Be not a-fraid. I go be-fore you al-ways. Come, fol-low me, and I will give you rest.

Verse 2

2. If you pass through rag-ing wa-ters in the sea, you shall not drown. If you walk a-mid the burn-ing flames, you shall not be harmed. If you stand be-fore the

pow'r of hell and death is at your side, know that I am

D.S.

with you through it all.

Verse 3

3. Bless - ed are your poor, for the king-dom shall be theirs.

Blest are you that weep and mourn, for one day you shall

laugh. And if wick-ed tongues in - sult and hate you

all be - cause of me, bless ed,

D.S.

bless - ed are you!

Text: Isaiah 43:2-3, Luke 6:20ff; Bob Dufford, SJ, b.1943
Tune: Bob Dufford, SJ, b.1943; acc. by Sr. Theophane Hytrek, OSF, 1915-1992
© 1975, Robert J. Dufford, SJ, and New Dawn Music

431 The Lord Is Near

Refrain

The Lord is near to all who call, rest in God a - lone, rest in God a - lone.

Verses

1. God will guard your com - ing and your go - ing;
2. God has seen a thou - sand years go past;
3. Lord, in you I come to take my ref - uge;
4. Trust in God for ev - er, O my peo - ple;

And will be the one to guard your life. The
Swift - ly as a morn - ing fades to night. So
Through the night you ev - er coun - sel me. O
Pour out all your hearts be - fore the Lord. Your

sun will not harm you in the day - light, And the
come, and be filled with God's wis - dom, To
Lord, you have formed me to be ho - ly And to
God is a rock of strength, your glo - ry; In the

D.C.

Lord will watch you through the night.
num - ber all your days a - right.
rest with - in you peace - ful - ly.
Lord is all your hope re - stored.

Text: Psalm 62; Mike Balhoff, b.1946
Tune: Darryl Ducote, b.1945, Gary Daigle, b.1957
© 1978, Damean Music. Distributed by GIA Publications, Inc.

My Refuge   432

Refrain

In you, O God, my re-fuge I take;

I will not be a-fraid.

Verses

1. In your jus - tice save me;
2. You, O God, are my rock, my
3. I will re - joice in the Lord, be
4. You will free me, O Lord, from
5. In - to your hands, O Lord, I com -

turn your ear to me. O
for - tress, and my strength; for
glad of your kind - ness to me.
out of my cap - tor's snares; for
mend my spir - it to you. For

Lord make haste to an -
your name's sake you will lead
Lord, let your face shine up -
you are my ref - uge
you will re - deem me,

D.C.

swer me.
and guide me.
on me, your ser - vant.
you are my hope.
faith - ful God.

Text: Psalm 31; Dennis Vessels, b.1953
Tune: Dennis Vessels, b.1953; arr. by Sheryl Soderberg
© 1982, Dennis Vessels

433 On Eagle's Wings

Verse 1

1. You who dwell in the shel - ter of the Lord, who a -
bide in his shad - ow for life, say to the Lord: "My
ref - uge, my rock in whom I trust!"

Refrain 𝄋

And he will raise you up on ea - gle's wings,
bear you on the breath of dawn, make you to shine like the sun, and

Last time to coda 𝄌   *To verses*

hold you in the palm of his hand.   2. The

Verse 2

snare of the fowl - er will nev - er cap - ture you, and
fam - ine will bring you no fear: un - der his wings your

D.S.

ref - uge, his faith - ful - ness your shield.

Verse 3

3. You need not fear the ter - ror of the night, nor the

ar - row that flies by day; though thou - sands fall a -

D.S.

bout you, near you it shall not come.

Verse 4

4. For to his an - gels he's giv - en a com - mand to

guard you in all of your ways; up - on their hands they will

D.S.

bear you up, lest you dash your foot a - gainst a stone.

Coda

And hold you, hold you in the palm of his hand.

Text: Psalm 91; Michael Joncas, b.1951
Tune: Michael Joncas, b.1951
© 1979, New Dawn Music

434 Amazing Grace

1. A - maz - ing grace! how sweet the sound, That saved a wretch like me! I once was lost, but now am found, Was blind, but now I see.
2. 'Twas grace that taught my heart to fear, And grace my fears re- lieved; How pre - cious did that grace ap - pear The hour I first be - lieved!
3. The Lord has prom - ised good to me, His word my hope se- cures; He will my shield and por - tion be As long as life en - dures.
4. Through man - y dan - gers, toils, and snares, I have al - read - y come; 'Tis grace has brought me safe thus far, And grace will lead me home.
5. When we've been there ten - thou - sand years, Bright shin - ing as the sun, We've no less days to sing God's praise Than when we'd first be - gun.

Text: St. 1-4 John Newton, 1725-1807; st. 5 attr. to John Rees, fl.1859
Tune: NEW BRITAIN, CM; *Virginia Harmony*, 1831; acc. by Diana Kodner, b.1957, © 1993, GIA Publications, Inc.

436 For You Are My God

Refrain

For you are my God; you a - lone are my joy.

Last time

De - fend me, O Lord.

Verses 1,2

1. You give mar - vel-ous com - rades to me: the
2. You are my por - tion and cup; it is

faith - ful who dwell in your land. Those who choose
you that I claim for my prize. Your her - it - age

a - li - en gods have cho - sen an
is my de - light, the lot you have

D.C.

a - li - en band.
giv - en to me.

Verses 3, 4

3. Glad are my heart and my soul;
4. You show me the path for my life;

se - cure - ly my bod - y shall rest.
in your pres - ence the full - ness of joy.

The Lord Is My Hope 435

Refrain

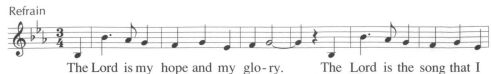

The Lord is my hope and my glo-ry. The Lord is the song that I

sing: so ten-der and lov-ing a shep-herd, so

root-ed in jus-tice, a king. When shad-ow con-fus-es my vi-sion,

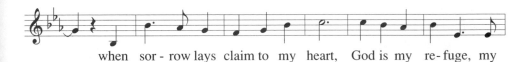

when sor-row lays claim to my heart, God is my re-fuge, my

rock and my shield. I will re-ly on the Lord.

Verses

1. Near to death, I cried "Save me!" and you heard.
2. King - doms fall; na-tions trem - ble at your pow'r.
3. Jus - tice reigns, and the wick - ed are cast down.
4. All who trust in your prom - ise will be saved,
5. Morn - ing comes: I will praise you with my life,

D.C.

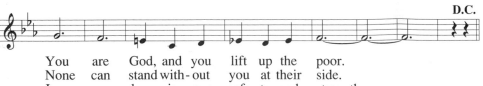

You are God, and you lift up the poor.
None can stand with-out you at their side.
In your love is our safe-ty and strength.
for your word has been test-ed in fire.
ev - er faith-ful and true to your word.

Text: 2 Samuel 22; M. D. Ridge, b.1938, © 1989
Tune: M. D. Ridge, b.1938, © 1989; acc. by Patrick Loomis, 1951-1990, © 1990, OCP Publications
Published by OCP Publications

For you   will   not   leave me   for   dead,
To   be   at   your   right hand for - ev - er

nor   lead   your   be - lov - ed   a -
for   me   would   be   hap - pi - ness

D.C.

stray.
al -   ways.

Text: Psalm 16; John Foley, SJ, b.1939
Tune: John Foley, SJ, b.1939
© 1970, John B. Foley, SJ, administered by New Dawn Music

437 Blest Be the Lord

Refrain

Blest be the Lord; blest be the Lord, the God of mer-cy, the God who saves. I shall not fear the dark of night, nor the ar - row that flies by day.

Verses

1. He will re - lease me from the nets of all my foes. He will pro - tect me from their wick-ed hands. Be - neath the shad-ow of his wings
2. I need not shrink be - fore the ter - rors of the night nor stand a - lone be - fore the light of day. No harm shall come to me, no
3. Al - though a thou - sand strong have fall - en at my side, I'll not be shak-en with the Lord at hand. His faith - ful love is all the

I will re - joice
ar - row strike me down,
ar - mor that I need

to find a dwell - ing place se - cure.
no e - vil set - tle in my soul.
to wage my bat - tle with the foe.

Text: Psalm 91; Dan Schutte, b.1947, alt.
Tune: Dan Schutte, b.1947; arr. by Sr. Theophane Hytrek, OSF, 1915-1992
© 1976, 1979, Daniel L. Schutte and New Dawn Music

Be Still, and Know That I Am God 438

Canon

Be still and know that I am God. Be still and

know that I am God.

Text: Psalm 46:10; John L. Bell, b.1949
Tune: John L. Bell, b.1949
© 1989, Iona Community, GIA Publications, Inc., agent

439 The Lord Is Near

*Refrain

O the Lord is near to all who call on him; he is
** May the an - gels lead you in - to par - a - dise; may the

close to all who seek his face, slow to an - ger and full of com -
mar - tyrs come to wel-come you, and take you to the ho - ly

pas-sion and a-bound-ing in mer-ci - ful love.
cit - y, the new and e - ter - nal Je - ru - sa - lem.

Verse 1

1. The Lord is my light and my sal - va - tion, there is

noth - ing at all I fear; the Lord is the

ref - uge of my life; of whom should I be a - fraid?

Verse 2

2. One thing I ask of the Lord; there is

on - ly one thing I seek: to dwell in the

house of the Lord all the days of my life.

Verse 3

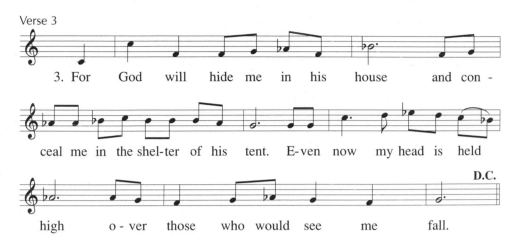

3. For God will hide me in his house and con -

ceal me in the shel-ter of his tent. E-ven now my head is held

D.C.

high o - ver those who would see me fall.

The refrain may be sung in a two-voice canon at a distance of one measure, or a three-voice canon at a distance of one-half measure.

** *Alternate refrain for funerals*

Text: Psalm 27; Michael Joncas, b.1951
Tune: Michael Joncas, b.1951
© 1979, New Dawn Music

440 You Will Draw Water

You will draw wa - ter from the

well of the king - dom of God. You will draw

wa - ter from the well of the king - dom of God.

Verses

1. God alone is my rock;
   how then should I be afraid?

2. God alone is my strength;
   who then can stand before me?

3. God alone is my rest;
   the Lord God is my safety.

4. God alone is my peace;
   God shatters steel and nations.

5. God alone is my day;
   God's name will shine before me.

6. God alone is my prize;
   though mountains fall to pieces.

7. God alone is my life,
   living, now and for ever.

Not for Tongues of Heaven's Angels 441

1. Not for tongues of heav - en's an - gels,
2. Love is hum - ble, love is gen - tle,
3. Nev - er jeal - ous, nev - er self - ish,
4. Soon will fade the word of wis - dom,

Not for wis - dom to dis - cern,
Love is ten - der, true, and kind;
Love will not re - joice in wrong;
Faith and hope be one day past:

Not for faith that mas - ters moun - tains,
Love is gra - cious, ev - er pa - tient,
Nev - er boast - ful nor re - sent - ful,
When we see our Sav - ior clear - ly,

For this bet - ter gift we yearn:
Gen - er - ous of heart and mind—
Love be - lieves and suf - fers long—
Love it is a - lone will last

May love be ours, Lord; may love be ours.

May love be ours, O Lord.

Text: Timothy Dudley-Smith, b.1926, © 1985, Hope Publishing Co.
Tune: COMFORT, 8 7 8 7 with refrain; Michael Joncas, b.1951, © 1988, GIA Publications, Inc.

442 Faith, Hope and Love

Refrain

Faith, hope and love, let these en-dure a - mong you;

and the great - est of these is love.

The great - est of these is love.

Verses

1. Come, let us love, for love is of God, in
2. Come, let us love, for love is of God, and
3. Come, let us love, for love is of God, for
4. Come, let us love, for love is of God, and
5. Come, let us love, for love is of God, where

D.C.

God a - lone will love be our truth!
we will be - come God's own chil - dren!
those who do not love will not find God!
we shall see our God, who first loved us!
love may be found, God is there!

Text: 1 Corinthians 13:13, 1 John 4:7; David Haas, b. 1957
Tune: David Haas, b. 1957
© 1992, GIA Publications, Inc.

Where Charity and Love Prevail   443

1. Where char - i - ty and love pre - vail,
2. With grate - ful joy and ho - ly fear
3. For - give we now each oth - er's faults
4. Let strife a - mong us be un - known,
5. Let us re - call that in our midst
6. No race nor creed can love ex - clude,

There God is ev - er found; Brought here to - geth - er
God's char - i - ty we learn; Let us with heart and
As we our faults con - fess; And let us love each
Let all con - ten - tion cease; Be God's the glo - ry
Dwells God's be - got - ten Son; As mem - bers of his
If hon - ored be God's name; Our fam - i - ly em -

by Christ's love, By love are we thus bound.
mind and soul Now love him in re - turn.
oth - er well In Chris - tian ho - li - ness.
that we seek, Be ours God's ho - ly peace.
bod - y joined, We are in him made one.
brac - es all Whose Fa - ther is the same.

Text: *Ubi caritas;* trans. by Omer Westendorf, b.1916
Tune: CHRISTIAN LOVE, CM; Paul Benoit, OSB, 1893-1979
© 1961, 1962, World Library Publications, Inc.

444 No Greater Love

Refrain

There is no great-er love, says the Lord, than to

lay down your life for a friend; there is no great-er love,

no great-er love, than to lay down your life for a friend.

Verse 1

1. As the Fa-ther has loved me, so I have loved you.

Live on in my love. You will live in my love if you

keep my com-mands, ev-en as I have kept my Fa-ther's.   **D.C.**

Verse 2

2. All this I tell you that my joy may be yours and

your joy may be com-plete. Love one an-oth-er as

I have loved you: This is my com - mand.

Verse 3

3. You are my friends if you keep my com - mands;

no long-er slaves but friends to me. All I heard from my Fa - ther,

I have made known to you: Now I call you friends.

Verse 4

4. It was not you who chose me, it was I who chose you, chose

you to go forth and bear fruit. Your fruit must en - dure, so

you will re - ceive all you ask the Fa - ther in my name.

Text: John 15: 9-17; Michael Joncas, b.1951
Tune: Michael Joncas, b. 1951

445 God Is Love

Refrain

God is love, and all who live in love, live in God.

Verse 1

1. God is light, in God there is no dark-ness. Come

D.C.

live in the love of the Lord.

Verse 2

2. Come to the Lord, re-ceive the light, and

D.C.

live in the love of the Lord.

Verse 3

3. We are called to be God's own chil-dren, to

D.C.

live in the love of the Lord.

Verse 4

4. All of you are one, u-nit-ed in Je-sus, to

D.C.

live in the love of the Lord.

Text: 1 John 1:5, 3:2, 4:15, Psalm 33:6, Galatians, 3:28; David Haas, b.1957
Tune: David Haas, b.1957
© 1987, GIA Publications, Inc.

Love One Another 446

Refrain

Love one an - oth - er, for love is of God.

Love one an - oth - er, for God is love.

Verses

1. God loved the world so much he sent us his only son,
   that all who believe in him might have eternal life.

2. Since God has given his love to us, therefore let us love one another.
   If we love one another, God will love us, and live in us in perfect love.

3. Ev'ryone who loves is begotten of God and knows him as the Father.
   But they who do not love do not know God, for God is love.

4. Let not your hearts be troubled, for love has no room for fear.
   In love all fear is forgotten, for God is here with us.

5. God is love, and they who abide in love,
   abide in God, and God in them.

Text:1 John 4; James J. Chepponis, b.1956
Tune: James J. Chepponis, b.1956
© 1983, GIA Publications, Inc.

447 Song of Thanksgiving

Refrain

Love that's free-ly giv - en wants to free-ly be re - ceived.

All the love you've poured on us can hard-ly be be - lieved, And

all that we can of - fer you is thanks.

All that we can of - fer you is thanks.

Verses

1. Cre - a - tion tells a sto - ry that be -
2. Your care called out a peo - ple; Your
3. Our hearts for - got your sto - ry, So your
4. So now we stand in won - der of

1. gan so long a - go, of love that longed to
2. love made them your own. You freed their hearts and
3. Son be - came its Word and gave a sign in
4. all your love has done: to hear your tale and

1. share its life in hope that love would grow. The
2. calmed their fears and fi - nally brought them home. It's
3. bread and wine to be sure that we had heard. We
4. of - fer thanks that we are not a - lone. Just

sun re - peats each morn - ing, the
when our trials are end - ed we me -
tried to kill his mem - 'ry but your
fill us with your Spir - it to

sto - ry is re - told, and
eas - i - ly for - get, but your
love re - fused to die, now
make your peo - ple one, so

just in love's re - tell - ing new
friend - ship nev - er ceas - es, Your
ev - 'ry time we break this bread love's
we can join your sto - ry to the

D.C.

chap - ters yet un - fold.
love shows no re - gret.
mean - ing comes a - live.
one told through your son.

Text: Darryl Ducote, b.1945, © 1973, Damean Music, Distributed by GIA Publications, Inc.
Tune: Darryl Ducote, b.1945, © 1973, Damean Music, Distributed by GIA Publications, Inc.; acc. by Diana Kodner, b.1957, © 1993,
   GIA Publications, Inc.

448 Lover of Us All

Refrain

With all the earth we sing your praise!
With sun and moon we dance for joy!

We come to give you thanks, O Lov-er of us
We are your work of art, the glo-ry of your

1.
all, and Giv-er of our lov-ing.
hand, the chil-dren of your

2.
lov-ing.

Verses 1-3

1. I am Mak-er of moun-tains; I am
2. As I know of your la-bor, so I
3. If the night would sur-round you and the

God of the earth. Like a moth-er in
watch while you sleep. Ev-er close at your
sun fall from sight, yet my hand will pro-

D.C.

la-bor I bring all to birth.
call-ing so my love will be.
tect you; I will be your light.

Verses 4-6

4. Long be-fore there were mead-ows, or
5. If you trav-el the heav-ens, or
6. In the womb of my wis-dom, I

wa - ters on the shore, I laughed and I
sail the far - thest shore, I stand there be -
fash - ioned ev - 'ry star, I formed you in

D.C.

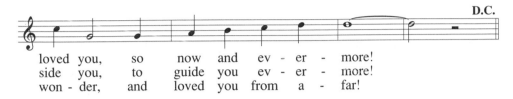

loved you, so now and ev - er - more!
side you, to guide you ev - er - more!
won - der, and loved you from a - far!

Text: Ephesians 2:7-10; 5:19-20; Dan Schutte, b.1947
Tune: Dan Schutte, b.1947; acc. alt.
© 1987, 1989, Daniel L. Schutte, published by OCP Publications

Shelter Me, O God 449

Refrain

Shel-ter me, O God; hide me in the shad-ow of your

wings. You a-lone are my hope.

Verses

1. When my foes sur-round me, set me high a-bove their
2. As a moth-er gath-ers her young be-neath her
3. Though I walk in dark-ness, through the nee-dle's eye of

D.C.

reach. Hear me when I call your name.
care, gath-er me in-to your arms.
death, you will nev-er leave my side.

Text: Psalm 16, 61, Luke 13:34; Bob Hurd, b. 1950, © 1984
Tune: Bob Hurd, b. 1950, © 1984; harm. by Craig S. Kingsbury, b. 1952, © 1984, OCP Publications
Published by OCP Publications

450   Eye Has Not Seen

Refrain

Eye has not seen, ear has not heard what God has read-y for those who love him; Spir-it of love, come, give us the mind of Je - sus, teach us the wis-dom of God.

Verses 1-3

1. When   pain and sor - row   weigh us down, be   near to us, O
2. Our   lives are but   a   sin - gle breath, we   flow-er and we
3. To   those who see with   eyes of faith, the   Lord is ev - er

Lord, for - give the weak-ness   of our faith, and   bear us up   with-
fade, yet   all our days are   in your hands, so   we re-turn   in
near, re - flect-ed in the   fac - es   of   all the poor and

D.C.

in   your peace - ful   word.
love what love   has   made.
low - ly   of the   world.

Verse 4

4. We   sing a mys-t'ry   from the past   in halls where saints have

trod, yet ev-er new the mu-sic rings to Je-sus, Liv-ing

D.C.

Song of God.

Text: 1 Corinthians 2:9-10; Marty Haugen, b.1950
Tune: Marty Haugen, b.1950
© 1982, GIA Publications, Inc.

Nada Te Turbe / Nothing Can Trouble 451

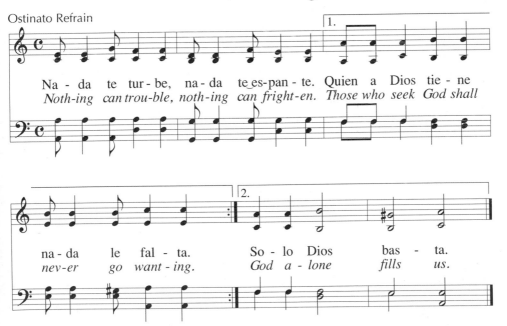

Ostinato Refrain

1.

Na - da te tur - be, na - da te_es-pan - te. Quien a Dios tie - ne
Noth-ing can trou-ble, noth-ing can fright-en. Those who seek God shall

2.

na - da le fal - ta.   So - lo Dios bas - ta.
nev-er go want-ing.   God a - lone fills us.

Text: St. Teresa of Jesus; Taizé Community, 1986, 1991
Tune: Jacques Berthier, b.1923
© 1986, 1991, Les Presses de Taizé, GIA Publications, Inc., agent

452 A Touching Place

Verses

1. Christ's is the world in which we move,
2. Feel for the peo-ple we most a-void,
3. Feel for the par-ents who've lost their child,
4. Feel for the lives by life con-fused,

Christ's are the folk we're sum-moned to love,
Strange or be-reaved or nev-er em-ployed;
Feel for the wom-en whom men have de-filed,
Rid-dled with doubt, in lov-ing a-bused;

Christ's is the voice which calls us to care, And
Feel for the wom-en, and feel for the men Who
Feel for the ba-by for whom there's no breast, And
Feel for the lone-ly heart, con-scious of sin, Which

Christ is the one who meets us here.
fear that their liv-ing is all in vain.
feel for the wea-ry who find no rest.
longs to be pure but fears to be-gin.

Refrain

To the lost Christ shows his face; To the un-loved he

gives his em-brace; To those who cry in pain or dis-

grace, Christ makes, with his friends, a touch-ing place.

Text: John L. Bell, b.1949, © 1989, Iona Community, GIA Publications, Inc., agent
Tune: DREAM ANGUS, Irregular; Scottish folk song; acc. by John L. Bell, b.1949, © 1993, Iona Community, GIA Publications, Inc., agent

Shepherd of My Heart 453

Verses

1. My shep-herd is the Lord, for noth-ing shall I want;
2. If I should walk one day in - to the vale of dark-ness,
3. You a-noint my head with oil; my cup is o - ver-flow-ing;

green are the pas - tures where I'm led to re - pose.
no e - vil shall I fear with God at my side.
good-ness and kind-ness crown the days of my life.

Near wa - ters still and deep God will re - fresh my soul.
There with your crook and staff you give me strength and com - fort;
With - in the Lord's own house I dwell in peace for ev - er;

I am led on-ward in ways true to the Name.
you spread a ban-quet in the sight of my foes.
with - in the house of God my soul is at rest.

Refrain

Guide me, O shep-herd of my heart; lead me home-ward through the

dark, in - to ev - er-last-ing, day. Show me the way of truth and

light; keep me al - ways in your sight. May my life nev - er

D.C.

part from the shep - herd of my heart.

Text: Psalm 23; Francis Patrick O'Brien, b.1958
Tune: Francis Patrick O'Brien, b.1958
© 1992, GIA Publications, Inc.

454 Come to Me, O Weary Traveler

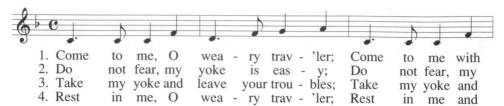

1. Come to me, O wea - ry trav - 'ler; Come to me with
2. Do not fear, my yoke is eas - y; Do not fear, my
3. Take my yoke and leave your trou - bles; Take my yoke and
4. Rest in me, O wea - ry trav - 'ler; Rest in me and

your dis - tress; Come to me, you heav - y bur-dened;
bur - den's light; Do not fear the path be - fore you;
come with me. Take my yoke, I am be - side you;
do not fear. Rest in me, my heart is gen - tle;

Come to me and find your rest.
Do not run from me in fright.
Take and learn hu - mil - i - ty.
Rest and cast a - way your care.

Text: Matthew 11:28-30; Sylvia G. Dunstan, 1955-1993, © 1991, GIA Publications, Inc.
Tune: DUNSTAN, 8 7 8 7; Bob Moore, b.1962, © 1993, GIA Publications, Inc.

456 Within Our Darkest Night

Within our dark-est night, you kin-dle the
fire that nev-er dies a - way, nev-er dies a -
way. With-in our dark-est night, you kin - dle the
fire that nev-er dies a - way, nev-er dies a - way.

Text: Taizé Community, 1991
Tune: Jacques Berthier, b.1923
© 1991, Les Presses de Taizé, GIA Publications, Inc., agent

The Lord Is My Shepherd 455

Verses

1. The Lord is my shep-herd, my shield and my strong-hold, de - fend - ing me sound - ly, re - deem-ing my shame.
2. If I walk in the val - ley of dark - ness, the shad - ow of death, then no fear will I have, you are there
3. Sure-ly good-ness and kind - ness will al - ways pur - sue me. My ta - ble is full now; my cup o - ver - flows.
4. The Lord is my shep-herd, green pas - tures, cool wa - ter; He ten - ders me al - ways, love ev - er the same.

He will an - swer my call 'til the fall of the moun - tains, the fall of the cit - ies; he's true to his name.
with your staff and your rod, O my God, give me com - fort, O God give me com-fort, as al - ways you have.
point - ed; for - ev - er I live in the house of the Lord.
He will an - swer my call 'til the fall of the moun - tains, the fall of the cit - ies; he's true to his name.

While my head is a - noint-ed the time is ap -

Refrain

Al - le - lu - ia, al - le - lu - ia, the Lord is my shep-herd and ev-er the same. Al - le - lu - ia, al - le - lu - ia, the Lord is my shep-herd; he's true to his name.

Text: Psalm 23; Joe Wise, b.1939
Tune: Joe Wise, b.1939; acc. by Marty Haugen, b.1950
© 1979, 1987, GIA Publications, Inc.

Show Us the Path of Life 457

Refrain

Lord, come show us the path of life, we will walk ev - er joy - ful, near to your side.

Verse 1

1. Keep me safe, O Lord, with - out you I am noth - ing, run-ning af-ter shad-ows, fol-low-ing an emp-ty dream.

Verse 2

2. Let us tell the sto-ry of how our God has loved us. God has been our cup of life, for ev - er true and faith - ful.

Verses 3, 4

3. Glo-ry in God's coun-sel, the wis-dom of e - ter - ni-ty,
4. I re-joice in you, Lord, your love and light sur - round me;

lead-ing us through dark-ness, sing-ing in each si-lent heart.
nev-er shall you leave me, ev - er will I trust in you.

Text: Psalm 16; Marty Haugen, b.1950
Tune: Marty Haugen, b.1950
© 1982, GIA Publications, Inc.

458 With a Shepherd's Care

Refrain

With a shep-herd's care, God leads us. With a fa-ther's strength, God guides us. With a moth-er's love, God nur-tures us, and cra-dles us in gen-tle arms.

Verses

1. When we are lost, and can - not find the way, God
2. When we are weak, and cares press all a-round, God
3. When we are scared, and feel so all a-lone, God

cares for us and keeps us safe. For
strength-ens us to face each day. For
loves us and is by our side. For

God is our light and our faith - ful guide, and
God is our rock and our sav - ing help, and
God is our hope and our con - stant friend, and

D.C.

leads us with a shep - herd's care.
guides us with a fa - ther's strength.
nur - tures with a moth - er's love.

Text: James J. Chepponis, b.1956
Tune: James J. Chepponis, b.1956
© 1992, GIA Publications, Inc.

Come to Me 459

Refrain

Come to me, come to me, come when you are wea-ry; come to me, come to me, and I will give you rest.

Verses 1,2

1. All who la-bor and are bur-dened,
2. Take my yoke up-on your shoul-ders,

all who la-bor and are bur-dened, let them come to me,
take my yoke up-on your shoul-ders, come and learn from me,

D.C.

come to me, and I will give them rest.
learn from me, for I am gen-tle of heart.

Verse 3

3. For the heart I hold is hum-ble,

yes, the heart I hold is hum-ble, and my yoke is eas-y, my

D.C.

bur-den light, and you will find rest for your souls.

Text: Matthew 11:28-30; Michael Joncas, b.1951
Tune: Michael Joncas, b.1951
© 1989, GIA Publications, Inc.

460 There Is a Balm in Gilead

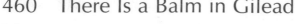

Refrain

There is a balm in Gil-e-ad To make the wound-ed whole,

There is a balm in Gil-e-ad To heal the sin-sick soul.

Verses

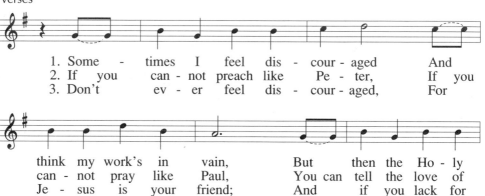

1. Some - times I feel dis - cour - aged And
2. If you can - not preach like Pe - ter, If you
3. Don't ev - er feel dis - cour - aged, For

think my work's in vain, But then the Ho - ly
can - not pray like Paul, You can tell the love of
Je - sus is your friend; And if you lack for

D.C.

Spir - it Re - vives my soul a - gain.
Je - sus, And say, "He died for all!"
knowl - edge He'll ne'er re - fuse to lend.

Text: Jeremiah 8:22, African-American spiritual
Tune: BALM IN GILEAD, Irregular; African-American spiritual; acc. by Robert J. Batastini, b.1942, © 1987, GIA Publications, Inc.

You Are Mine 461

Verses

1. I will come to you in the si - lence,
2. I am hope for all who are hope-less,
3. I am strength for all the des - pair-ing,
4. am the Word that leads all to free-dom, I

I will lift you from all your fear.
I am eyes for all who long to see. In the
heal - ing for the ones who dwell in shame.
am the peace the world can - not give.

You will hear my voice, I claim you as my choice, be
shad-ows of the night, I will be your light,
All the blind will see, the lame will all run free, and
I will call your name, em - brac-ing all your pain, stand

still and know I am here. *(To verse 2)*
come and rest in me. *(To refrain)*
all will know my name. *(To refrain)*
up, now walk, and live! *(To refrain)*

Refrain

Do not be a-fraid, I am with you. I have called you each by

name. Come and fol-low me, I will bring you home; I

D.C.

love you and you are mine.

4. I

Text: David Haas, b.1957
Tune: David Haas, b.1957
© 1991, GIA Publications, Inc.

462 Come to Me

Refrain

Come to me, all you wea-ry. I will re-fresh you, learn from me. My yoke is eas-y, my bur-den light.

Verses

1. Ask and you shall receive; seek and you shall find.
   Knock, it shall be opened, the goodness of the Lord.
   For the one who asks, receives, the one who seeks shall find.
   The one who knocks will enter, and see the face of God.

2. See the birds in the sky, they neither sow nor reap,
   and still our God cares for them, will not the Lord care for you?
   See the lilies of the field, they do not work or spin;
   if they are clothed in splendor, God will provide for you.

3. Do not worry about your life, what to eat or wear.
   Is not your life for greater things?
   Is not your life for the Lord?
   Seek the one who knows your need, and all things will be yours.
   Worry not of tomorrow, let tomorrow find its way.

Text: Matthew 6:26, 28, 30-31, 33-34; 7: 7-8; David Haas, b.1957
Tune: David Haas, b.1957
© 1989, GIA Publications, Inc.

So the Day Dawn for Me   463

1. So the day dawn for me, so the day
2. Be the day shine to me, be the day
3. Be the day dark to me, be the day
4. Be the day swift to me, be the day
5. So the day close for me, so the night

break, Christ watch-ing o - ver me,
bright, Christ my com - pan - ion be,
drear, Christ shall my com - fort be,
long, Christ my con - tent - ment be,
fall, Christ watch-ing o - ver me,

Christ as I wake, Christ watch - ing
Christ be my light, Christ my com -
Christ be my cheer, Christ shall my
Christ be my song, Christ my con -
Christ be my all, Christ watch - ing

o - ver me, Christ as I wake.
pan - ion be, Christ be my light.
com - fort be, Christ be my cheer.
tent - ment be, Christ be my song.
o - ver me, Christ be my all.

Text: Timothy Dudley-Smith, b.1926, © 1993, Hope Publishing Co.
Tune: NEW FREEDOM, 6 4 6 4 6 4; David Haas, b.1957, © 1994, GIA Publications, Inc.

464 Our God Is Rich in Love

Refrain

Our God is ten-der,   ten-der and car-ing,

slow to an-ger   so rich in love.

God shows com-pas-sion,   kind-ness and mer-cy.

God is gen-tle.   Our God is rich in love.

Verses

1. Our God is merciful. God's gentle kindness knows no end.
   And though our sins be great or small, God's love is our reward.

2. Our God is tender as a parent to a child.
   God remembers how we were made, remembers that we are dust.

3. God's love is eternal for those who live the law;
   for those who live the covenant; for those who keep the faith.

Text: Psalm 103: Bob Moore, b. 1962
Tune: Bob Moore, b. 1962
© 1993, GIA Publications, Inc.

The People of God 465

Come to me all who are bur - dened;

come and rest in my love. Re -

joice and be glad, your hope lies in heav - en, your

home with the peo - ple of God.

Verses

1. Blessed, blessed are the poor in spirit, blessed be the Lord's own children,
theirs is the kingdom of God.
Blessed, blessed are they who walk in sorrow, blessed be the Lord's own children;
they are embraced by God.

2. Blessed, blessed the ones who are lowly, blessed be the Lord's own children;
they shall inherit the land.
Blessed, blessed the ones who thirst for righteousness,
blessed be the Lord's own children; all of their dreams will come true.

3. Blessed, blessed are they who show mercy, blessed be the Lord's own children;
mercy from God shall be theirs.
Blessed, blessed the ones with a pure heart, blessed be the Lord's own children;
for they shall see God.

4. Blessed, blessed the ones who make peace. Blessed are they who know pain
for the sake of righteousness.
Blessed, blessed are you who know suff'ring, blessed are you who know insult
because of your God.

Text: Matthew 5:3-12; Francis Patrick O'Brien, b.1958
Tune: Francis Patrick O'Brien, b.1958
© 1992, GIA Publications, Inc.

466 Thy Kingdom Come

Verses

1. O you who taught the mud to dream,
   Did spin like tops the stars in space,
2. Like seed and rain your word goes out,
   The blooms that grow there shall re - main,
3. From hearts of stone, O Lord, you drew, O
   And won your King - ship with that sword,
4. And ev - 'ry heart that's sick with sin,
   The wound - ed spir - it he shall dress,
5. And when the skies you break at last,
   Then shall there be a joy - ful noise:

Lord, thy king - dom come.

And make the world with
Did guide their paths with
In gar - dens of the
Their scent the sign of your
The sword of sin that
That cut you down, O
The Heal - er King has
With balms of love and
Your king - dom come to
Your king - dom praise you

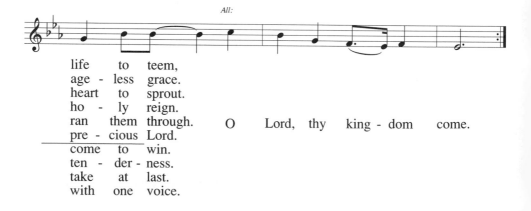

All:

life to teem,
age - less grace.
heart to sprout.
ho - ly reign.
ran them through. O Lord, thy king - dom come.
pre - cious Lord.
come to win.
ten - der - ness.
take at last.
with one voice.

Refrain

We wait in joy, we wait in joy,

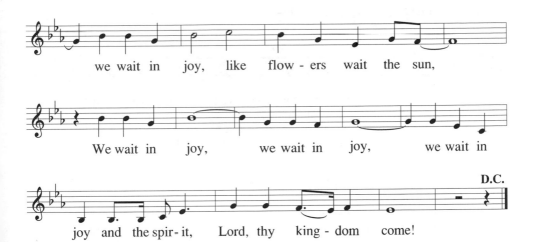

we wait in joy, like flow - ers wait the sun,

We wait in joy, we wait in joy, we wait in

D.C.

joy and the spir - it, Lord, thy king - dom come!

Text: Rory Cooney, b.1952
Tune: Rory Cooney, b.1952
© 1984, North American Liturgy Resources

467 I Will Not Die

Verses

1., 5. I will not die be-fore I've lived to see that land;
2. I will not rest un-til your dawn is in my eyes;
3. And I will breathe in that might-y wind of jus-tice;
4. You will stand up for the poor and the need-y;

firm as the earth, your own prom-ise.
that frag-ile light, new like morn-ing.
I'll know my name and rise up sing-ing.
you'll break the chains that bind your peo-ple.

I'll not let go un-til I've held it in my hand;
I will not sleep be-fore I've wak-ened to that sun-rise;
And I will call un-til my words bring on the thun-der;
For you are home for the lost and the des-p'rate;

that word of hope, and gen-tle laugh-ter.
and all the world knows your glo-ry.
washed in that rain, then I'll know you.
your strong right hand goes be-fore us.

Refrain

For your right hand has de-liv-ered us from death;

You have re-gard-ed our tears,

D.C.

you who are good-ness and grace.

Text: Tom Conry, b.1951, alt.
Tune: Tom Conry, b.1951
© 1984, 1990, TEAM Publications, published by OCP Publications

Bring Forth the Kingdom 468

Verses

Cantor:

1. You are salt for the earth, O peo-ple:
2. You are a light on the hill, O peo-ple:
3. You are a seed of the Word, O peo-ple:
4. We are a blest and a pil-grim peo-ple:

All: *Cantor:*

Salt for the King-dom of God! Share the fla-vor of
Light for the Cit-y of God! Shine so ho-ly and
Bring forth the King-dom of God! Seeds of mer-cy and
Bound for the King-dom of God! Love our jour-ney and

All:

life, O peo-ple: Life in the King-dom of God!
bright, O peo-ple: Shine for the King-dom of God!
seeds of jus-tice, Grow in the King-dom of God!
love our home-land: Love is the King-dom of God!

Refrain

Bring forth the King-dom of mer-cy, Bring forth the

King-dom of peace; Bring forth the King-dom of jus-tice,

Bring forth the Cit-y of God!

Text: Marty Haugen, b.1950
Tune: Marty Haugen, b.1950

469 Blest Are They

Verses 1-3

1. Blest are they, the poor in spir - it,
2. Blest are they, the low - ly ones,
3. Blest are they who show mer - cy,

theirs is the king - dom of God.
they shall in - her - it the earth.
mer - cy shall be theirs.

Blest are they, full of sor - row,
Blest are they who hun - ger and thirst,
Blest are they, the pure of heart,

they shall be con - soled.
they shall have their fill.
they shall see God!

Refrain

Re - joice and be glad! Bless-ed are you,

ho - ly are you! Re - joice and be glad!

Yours is the king-dom of God!

Verses 4, 5

4. Blest are they who seek peace;
5. Blest are you who suf - fer hate,

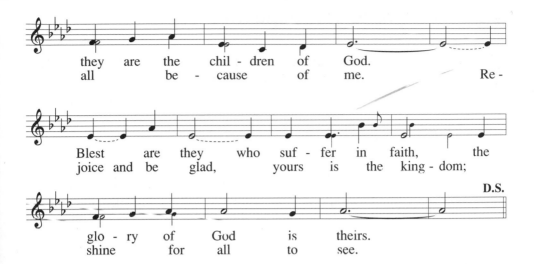

they are the chil - dren of God.
all be - cause of me. Re -

Blest are they who suf - fer in faith, the
joice and be glad, yours is the king - dom;

D.S.

glo - ry of God is theirs.
shine for all to see.

Text: Matthew 5:3-12; David Haas, b.1957
Tune: David Haas, b.1957; vocal arr. by David Haas, b.1957, Michael Joncas, b.1951
© 1985 GIA Publications, Inc.

470 Onward to the Kingdom

Refrain

Sing we now, and on we go; God a-bove, and God be-low;

Arm in arm, in love we go on-ward to the king-dom.

Verses

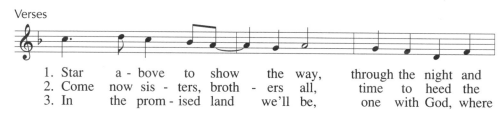

1. Star a-bove to show the way, through the night and
2. Come now sis-ters, broth-ers all, time to heed the
3. In the prom-ised land we'll be, one with God, where

in - to day, with the light we won't
Lord's call, we will tra - vel stand-
all are free, the deaf will hear, the blind

D.C.

de - lay on - ward to the king - dom.
ing tall on - ward to the king - dom.
will see when we reach the king - dom.

Text: David Haas, b. 1957, © 1993, GIA Publications, Inc.
Tune: MARIE'S WEDDING, 7 7 7 6 with refrain; Irish traditional; arr. by David Haas, b. 1957, © 1993, GIA Publications, Inc.

As a Fire Is Meant for Burning 471

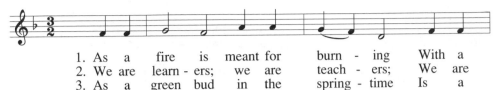

1. As a fire is meant for burn-ing With a
2. We are learn-ers; we are teach-ers; We are
3. As a green bud in the spring-time Is a

bright and warm-ing flame, So the church is meant for
pil-grims on the way. We are seek-ers; we are
sign of life re-newed, So may we be signs of

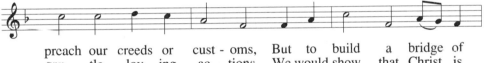

mis - sion, Giv-ing glo - ry to God's name. Not to
giv - ers; We are ves - sels made of clay. By our
one - ness 'Mid earth's peo - ples, man-y hued. As a

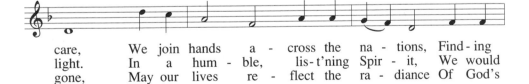

preach our creeds or cust-oms, But to build a bridge of
gen - tle, lov-ing ac - tions, We would show that Christ is
rain - bow lights the heav-ens When a storm is past and

care, We join hands a - cross the na - tions, Find-ing
light. In a hum - ble, lis-t'ning Spir - it, We would
gone, May our lives re - flect the ra - diance Of God's

neigh - bors ev - 'ry - where.
live to God's de - light.
new and glor - ious dawn.

Text: Ruth Duck, b.1947, © 1992, GIA Publications, Inc.
Tune: BEACH SPRING, 8 7 8 7 D; *The Sacred Harp*, 1844; harm. by Marty Haugen, b.1950, © 1985, GIA Publications, Inc.

472 Church of God

Refrain

Church of God, cho-sen peo-ple, sing your praise to God.

He has called you out of dark-ness in-to his mar-vel-ous light.

Verses

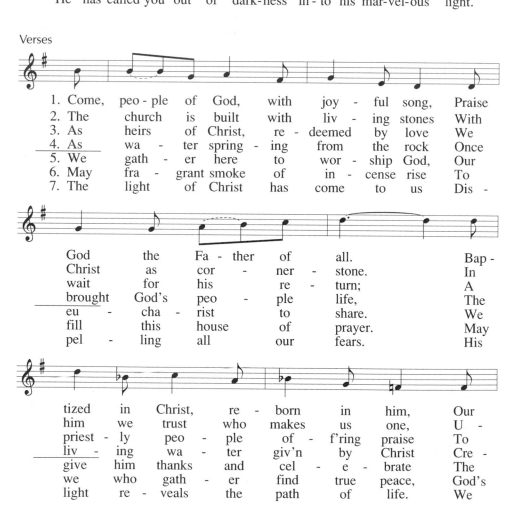

1. Come, peo-ple of God, with joy - ful song, Praise
2. The church is built with liv - ing stones With
3. As heirs of Christ, re - deemed by love We
4. As wa - ter spring - ing from the rock Once
5. We gath - er here to wor - ship God, Our
6. May fra - grant smoke of in - cense rise To
7. The light of Christ has come to us Dis -

God the Fa - ther of all. Bap -
Christ as cor - ner - stone. In
wait for his re - turn; A
brought God's peo - ple life, The
eu - cha - rist to share. We
fill this house of prayer. May
pel - ling all our fears. His

tized in Christ, re - born in him, Our
him we trust who makes us one, U -
priest - ly peo - ple of - f'ring praise To
liv - ing wa - ter giv'n by Christ Cre -
give him thanks and cel - e - brate The
we who gath - er find true peace, God's
light re - veals the path of life. We

hearts	are	filled	with	joy.	He	cleans - es	our
nit - ing	us	in	love.	We	build	on the
God,	the	source	of	hope.	For	Je - sus	is
ates	our	lives	a - new.	So	come	you who
mys - t'ry	of	his	love;	The	Word	is made
pres - ence	fill - ing	our	lives.	Our	hearts	lift with
fol - low	him	with	joy,	The	glo - ry	of

D.C.

sin,	Re - new - ing	our	lives.
rock	Of	faith	in	Christ.
Lord,	Our	Sav - ior	and	God.
thirst	To	springs	of	new	life.
flesh	And	giv - en	for	us.
praise,	Our	lips	sing	in	joy.
God,	The	light	of	the	world.

Text: Sr. Pamela Stotter
Tune: Margaret Daly
© 1980, International Commission on English in the Liturgy, Inc.

473 We Will Serve the Lord

Verses

1. Wealth can be an i-dol built of gleam-ing gold,
2. Plea-sure is a si-ren, prom-is-ing the flesh
3. Pow-er is a hun-ger, burn-ing in the breast, to
4. Fath-er of all mer-cy, Giv-er of all life,

bring-ing dreams of par-a-dise, ⁊ fu-tures bought and sold.
brief re-lief from emp-ti-ness, a hid-ing place from death.
walk a-mong the might-y and tram-ple on the rest.
here we speak our cov-e-nant a-bove the nois-y strife.

Some will choose to gath-er it, all that they can hoard, but
Some will choose to chase it, un-til it leaves them bored, but
Some will choose to gain it by lie or guile, or sword, but
Hear us shout in glo-ry a-bove the pa-gan horde, ⁊

1.
2.-4.

as for me and my house, we will serve the Lord!
as for me and my house, we will serve the Lord!
as for me and my house, we will serve the Lord!
as for me and my house, we will serve the Lord!

Refrain

Melody:

As for me and my house, we will serve the Lord,

we will serve the Lord, we will serve the Lord!

Text: Rory Cooney, b.1952
Tune: Rory Cooney, b.1952
© 1986, North American Liturgy Resources

Pues Si Vivimos / If We Are Living   474

1. Pues si vi - vi - mos pa - ra Él vi - vi - mos,
1. *If we are liv - ing we are in the Lord,*
2. En es - ta vi - da, fru - tos he - mos de dar;
2. *Through-out our lives we have fruit to bear.*
3. En la tris - te - za y en el do - lor,
3. *When there is sad - ness, when there is pain*
4. En es - te mun - do, he - mos de en - con - trar
4. *And in this world we will al - ways find*

y si mo - ri - mos pa - ra Él mo - ri - mos.
and if we die we are in the Lord,
las o - bras bue - nas son pa - ra of - ren - dar.
All of our good works are for us to share.
en la be - lle - za y en el a - mor
in Christ the Lord, we have love to gain.
gen - te que llo - ra y sin con - so - lar.
those who are weep - ing, sick in heart and mind.

Sea que vi - va - mos o que mu - ra - mos,
for if we live or if we die
Ya sea que de - mos o que re - ci - ba - mos,
Whe - ther we give, or we re - ceive
Sea que su - fra - mos o que go - ce - mos,
Whe - ther we suf - fer or we re - joice,
Sea que a - yu - de - mos o que al - i - men - te - mos,
They need our help, they need our care.

so - mos del Señ - or, so - mos del Señ - or.
we be - long to God, we be - long to God.

Text: Verse 1, Romans 14:8; traditional Spanish; translation by Deborah L. Schmitz, b.1969, © 1994, GIA Publications, Inc.
Tune: Traditional Spanish; arr. by Diana Kodner, b.1957, © 1994, GIA Publications, Inc.

475 Jesus in the Morning

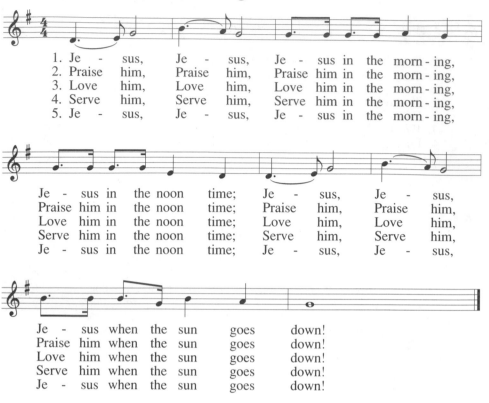

1. Je - sus, Je - sus, Je - sus in the morn - ing,
2. Praise him, Praise him, Praise him in the morn - ing,
3. Love him, Love him, Love him in the morn - ing,
4. Serve him, Serve him, Serve him in the morn - ing,
5. Je - sus, Je - sus, Je - sus in the morn - ing,

Je - sus in the noon time; Je - sus, Je - sus,
Praise him in the noon time; Praise him, Praise him,
Love him in the noon time; Love him, Love him,
Serve him in the noon time; Serve him, Serve him,
Je - sus in the noon time; Je - sus, Je - sus,

Je - sus when the sun goes down!
Praise him when the sun goes down!
Love him when the sun goes down!
Serve him when the sun goes down!
Je - sus when the sun goes down!

Text: African-American folk song
Tune: African-American folk song

The Servant Song   476

1.,6. Will you let me be your ser - vant,
2. We are pil - grims on a jour - ney,
3. I will hold the Christ - light for you
4. I will weep when you are weep - ing;
5. When we sing to God in heav - en

Let me be as Christ to you; Pray that I may
We are trav - 'lers on the road; We are here to
In the night - time of your fear; I will hold my
When you laugh I'll laugh with you. I will share your
We shall find such har - mo - ny, Born of all we've

have the grace to Let you be my ser - vant, too.
help each oth - er Walk the mile and bear the load.
hand out to you, Speak the peace you long to hear.
joy and sor - row 'Til we've seen this jour - ney through.
known to - geth - er Of Christ's love and ag - o - ny.

Text: Richard Gillard
Tune: Richard Gillard; harm. by Betty Pulkingham, b.1929
© 1977, Scripture in Song

477 Whatsoever You Do

Refrain

What-so-ev-er you do to the least of my peo-ple, that you do un-to me.

Verses

1. When I was hun-gry, you gave me to eat;
2. When I was home-less, you o-pened your door;
3. When I was wea-ry, you helped me find rest;
4. When I was lit-tle, you taught me to read;
5. When in a pris-on, you came to my cell;
6. In a strange coun-try, you made me at home;
7. Hurt in a bat-tle, you bound up my wounds;
8. When I was Black, or La-ti-no, or white;
9. When I was a-ged, you both-ered to smile;
10. You saw me cov-ered with spit-tle and blood;
11. When I was laughed at, you stood by my side;

When I was thirst-y, you gave me to drink.
When I was na-ked, you gave me your coat.
When I was anx-ious, you calmed all my fears.
When I was lone-ly, you gave me your love.
When on a sick-bed, you cared for my needs.
Seek-ing em-ploy-ment, you found me a job.
Search-ing for kind-ness, you held out your hand.
Mocked and in-sult-ed, you car-ried my cross.
When I was rest-less, you lis-tened and cared.
You knew my fea-tures, though grim-y with sweat.
When I was hap-py, you shared in my joy.

D.C.

Now en-ter in-to the home of my Fa-ther.

Text: Matthew 5:3-12; Willard F. Jabusch, b.1930, © 1966, 1979
Tune: WHATSOEVER YOU DO, 10 10 11 with refrain; Willard F. Jabusch, b.1930, © 1966, 1979; harm. by Robert J. Batastini, b.1942, © 1975, GIA
Publications, Inc.

Glorious in Majesty 478

Verses

1. Glo - ri - ous in maj - es - ty, Ho - ly in his prais - es,
2. Vic - to - ry he won for us, Free - ing us from dark - ness,
3. One in love, as fam - i - ly, Liv - ing with each oth - er,

Je - sus, our Sav - ior and our King. Born a man, yet God of old,
Dy - ing and ris - ing from the dead. Liv - ing with the Fa - ther now,
Glad - ly we share each oth - er's pain. Yet he will not leave us so,

Let us all a - dore him: Filled with his Spir - it, let us sing.
Yet he is a - mong us: We are the bod - y, he the head.
Soon he is re - turn - ing, Tak - ing us back with him to reign.

Refrain

Liv - ing is to love him, serv - ing him to know his free - dom.

Come a - long with us to join the praise of Je - sus.

Come to Je - sus now, Go to live his word re - joic - ing.

Text: Jeff Cothran, fl.1972, © 1972, GIA Publications, Inc.
Tune: SHIBBOLET BASADEH, 7 6 7 8 D with refrain; Jewish melody; harm. by Jeff Cothran, fl.1972, © 1972, GIA Publications, Inc.

479 I Am the Vine

Refrain

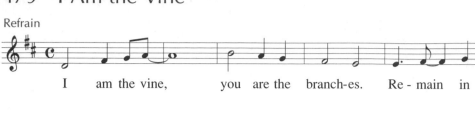

I am the vine, you are the branch-es. Re - main in

me, you shall be fruit - ful. Love for the world,

hope for the hope - less.

Verses

1. If you love, then you must root your - self
2. If you give, then you must give your - self

in me; For the branch will
to me; For the well will

D.C.

fail and die with-out the tree.
soon run dry with-out the sea.

Text: John 15:1-10; Bob Hurd, b.1950, © 1979
Tune: Bob Hurd, b.1950, © 1979; acc. by Craig Kingsbury, b.1952, © 1983, OCP Publications
Published by OCP Publications

Take This Moment 480

1. Take this mo - ment, sign, and space;
2. Take the time to call my name,
3. Take the tired - ness of my days,
4. Take the lit - tle child in me,
5. Take my tal - ents, take my skills,

Take my friends a - round; Here a -
Take the time to mend Who I
Take my past re - gret, Let - ting
Scared of grow - ing old; Help him/her
Take what's yet to be; Let my

mong us make the place Where your
am and what I've been, All I've
your for - give - ness touch All I
here to find his/her worth Made in
life be yours, and yet, Let it

love is found.
failed to tend.
can't for - get.
Christ's own mold.
still be me.

Text: John L. Bell, b.1949
Tune: TAKE THIS MOMENT, 7 5 7 5; John L. Bell, b.1949
© 1989, Iona Community, GIA Publications, agent

481 I Bind My Heart

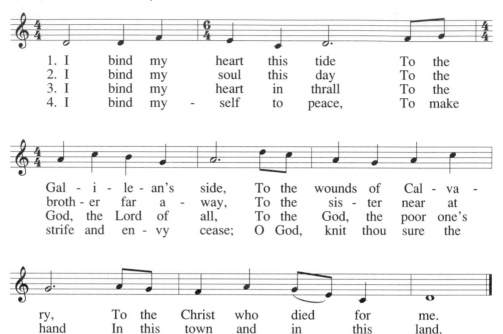

1. I bind my heart this tide To the Gal - i - le - an's side, To the wounds of Cal - va - ry, To the Christ who died for me.

2. I bind my soul this day To the broth - er far a - way, To the sis - ter near at hand, In this town and in this land.

3. I bind my heart in thrall To the God, the Lord of all, To the God, the poor one's friend, And the Christ whom he did send.

4. I bind my - self to peace, To make strife and en - vy cease; O God, knit thou sure the cord Of my thrall - dom to my Lord.

Text: "Thraldom," *The Tryst,* 1907, Lauchlan McLean Watt, 1853-1931
Tune: Suzanne Toolan, SM, b.1927, © 1979, Resource Publications, Inc.

The God Who Sends Us Forth   482

1. The God who sends us forth,
2. The road a-head is filled
3. So let us bless our God,

u-nit-ed
by trav-'lers
the send-er

in our pray'r,
with-out end:
and the one,

Has strength-ened us and
The way-ward and the
And let us bless the

tend-ed us with shep - herd's care.
wan-der-er, the mi - grant friend.
ser-vant, Je - sus Christ the Son.

God's Je-sus makes us bold,
And we are Je-sus' flesh,
The Spir-it let us thank,

his bod-y
his wel-come
whose love is

is our bread;
and his home
bright in-deed,

His wine of life is
We go from here to
Who lights a gen-tle

full-ness for the road a - head.
love and serve, to tend God's own.
path-way for a world in need.

483   You Have Anointed Me

Verse 1

1. To bring glad tid - ings to the low - ly, to heal the bro-ken heart, You have a - noint - ed me. To pro - claim lib - er - ty to cap - tives, re - lease to pris - on - ers, You have a - noint - ed me.

Refrain

Your Spir - it, O God, is up - on me, You have a - noint - ed me.

Verse 2

2. To an - nounce a year of fa - vor, to com - fort those who mourn, You have a - noint - ed me. To give to them the oil of glad-ness, and

D.S.

share   a man-tle   of joy,   You   have   a - noint - ed   me.

Text: Mike Balhoff, b.1946, Gary Daigle, b.1957, Darryl Ducote, b.1945
Tune: Mike Balhoff, b.1946, Gary Daigle, b.1957, Darryl Ducote, b.1945; acc. by Gary Daigle, b.1945
© 1981, Damean Music. Distributed by GIA Publications, Inc.

Thuma Mina / Send Me, Jesus   484

1. Thu-ma   mi - na,   Thu-ma   mi - na,   Thu - ma
   Je - sus,   send me,   Je - sus,   send   me,
   Je - sus,   lead me,   Je - sus,   lead   me,
   Je - sus,   fill me,   Je - sus   fill   me,

|1.- 3.| |4.|

mi - na   So - man - dla.   2. Send   me,
Je - sus,   send   me,   Lord.   3. Lead   me,
Je - sus,   lead   me,   Lord.   4. Fill   me,
Je - sus,   fill   me,   Lord.

Text: South African
Tune: THUMA MINA, South African
© 1984, Utryck

485   City of God

Verses 1, 2

1. A-wake from your slum-ber! A - rise from your
2. We are sons of the morn-ing; we are daugh-ters of

sleep! A new day is dawn - ing
day. The One who has loved us

for all those who weep. The peo - ple in
has bright-ened our way. The Lord of all

dark - ness have seen a great light. The Lord of our
kind - ness has called us to be a light for his

long - ing has con-quered the night.
peo - ple to set their hearts free.

Refrain 𝄉

Let us build the cit-y of God. May our tears be

turned in - to danc - ing! For the Lord, our light and our

love, has turned the night in - to day!

Verse 3

3. God is light; in him there is no dark-ness. Let us walk in his light, his chil-dren, one and all.

O com-fort my peo-ple; make gen-tle your words. Pro-claim to my cit-y

D.S.

the day of her birth.

Verse 4

4. O cit-y of glad-ness, now lift up your voice. Pro-claim the good tid-ings

D.S.

that all may re - joice!

Text: Dan Schutte, b.1947, © 1981, Daniel L. Schutte and New Dawn Music
Tune: Dan Schutte, b.1947, © 1981, Daniel L. Schutte and New Dawn Music; acc. by Robert J. Batastini, b.1942, © 1994, GIA Publications, Inc.

486 Good News

Verses

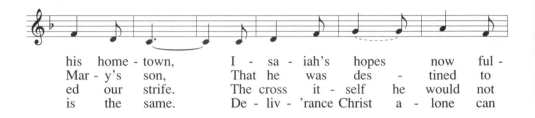

1. When Je - sus worked here on earth he preached in
2. The eld - ers of the syn - a - gogue were shocked by
3. The way he lived was proof of it: he qui - et -
4. So pass it on to - day, good friend: the mes - sage

his home - town, I - sa - iah's hopes now ful -
Mar - y's son, That he was des - tined to
ed our strife. The cross it - self he would not
is the same. De - liv - 'rance Christ a - lone can

filled, those claims of great re - nown.
be the Christ for ev - 'ry - one.
flee e'en though it cost his life.
give, for this to earth he came.

Refrain

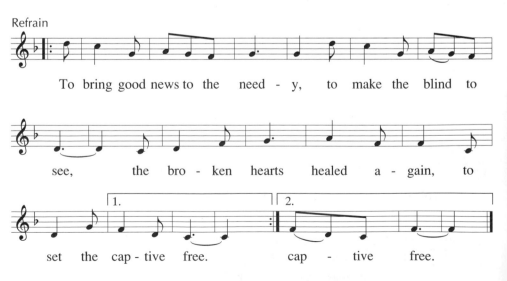

To bring good news to the need - y, to make the blind to

see, the bro - ken hearts healed a - gain, to

1.
set the cap - tive free.

2.
cap - tive free.

Text: Howard S. Olson
Tune: Almaz Belihu; Yemissrach Dimts Literature Program, Ethiopia
© 1993, Howard S. Olson

You Are Called to Tell the Story 487

1. You are called to tell the sto - ry, pass - ing
2. You are called to teach the rhy - thm of the
3. You are called to set the ta - ble, bless - ing
4. May the One whose love is broad - er than the

words of life a - long, Then to
dance that nev - er ends, Then to
bread as Je - sus blessed, Then to
meas - ure of all space Give us

blend your voice with oth - ers as you
move with - in the cir - cle, hand in
come with thirst and hun - ger, need - ing
words to sing the sto - ry, move a -

sing the sa - cred song. Christ be
hand with stran - gers, friends, Christ be
care like all the rest, Christ be
mong us in this place. Christ be

known in all our sing - ing,
known in all our danc - ing,
known in all our shar - ing,
known in all our liv - ing,

fill - ing all with songs of love.
touch - ing all with hands of love.
feed - ing all with signs of love.
fill - ing all with gifts of love.

Text: Ruth Duck, b.1947, © 1992, GIA Publications, Inc.
Tune: GHENT, 8 7 8 7 8 7; M.D. Ridge, b.1938; acc. by Patrick Loomis, 1951-1990, © 1987, GIA Publications, Inc.

488 God Has Chosen Me

Verses

1. God has cho-sen me, God has cho-sen me to
2. God has cho-sen me, God has cho-sen me to
3. God is call-ing me, God is call-ing me in

1. bring good news to the poor. God has cho-sen me,
2. set a - light a new fire. God has cho-sen me,
3. all whose cry is un - heard. God is call-ing me,

1. God has cho-sen me to bring new sight to those
2. God has cho-sen me to bring to birth a new
3. God is call-ing me to raise up the voice with no

1. search-ing for light. God has cho - sen me, cho - sen me:
2. king - dom on earth. God has cho - sen me, cho - sen me:
3. pow - er or choice. God is call - ing me, call - ing me:

Refrain

And to tell the world that God's king-dom is near, to re -

move op - pres - sion and break down fear, yes, God's

[1.] time is near, God's time is near, God's [2.] time is near.

Text: Bernadette Farrell, b.1957
Tune: Bernadette Farrell, b.1957
© 1990, Bernadette Farrell, published by OCP Publications

Servant Song   489

Refrain

Be fair and just. Be mer-ci-ful and true.

These are the things I am ask-ing of you. Walk

hum-bly with your God, in ev-'ry-thing you do.

This is the way that will lead you to the truth.

Verses

1. To you, O Lord, we lift our souls. To
2. Lead us on the path of truth.
3. Breathe in us the spir-it of life. A-
4. Mold our hearts for all that is good. Let

you, O Lord, we pray. For we
Guide us a-long the way. Re-
wak-en our sens-es this day to
kind-ness be our guide. May

o-pen our hearts to you, O God, a-
mem-ber your kind-ness and mer-cy, O God.
feel your pres-ence in all of the earth.
we be your voice to oth-ers in need, your

D.C.

wak-en us, show us the way.
Give us your wis-dom to-day.
Move in us, lead us to you.
shel-ter where friends can a-bide.

Text: Micah 6:8, Psalm 25; Ziggy Stardust and Bobby Fisher, b.1952
Tune: Bobby Fisher, b.1952
© 1992, GIA Publications, Inc.

490 Great Is the Lord

Refrain

Great is the Lord, wor-thy of praise, tell all the na-tions

God is King! Spread the news of God's love! [1.-3. *To verses*] [4.] love!

Verses

1. The Spir-it of the Lord is up-on me be-cause the
2. How beau-ti-ful up-on the moun-tains, the feet of
3. Give glo-ry to the Fa-ther, the Son and

Lord has a-noint-ed me. God has
those who bring glad tid-ings, an-nounc-ing
Ho-ly Spir-it blest, the God who

sent me to bring glad tid-ings to the
peace, bear-ing good news that the
is, who was, who will be, for

D.C.

low-ly, to the low-ly.
Lord God is King!
ev-er, A-men.

Text: Isaiah 61:1 - 4; 52:7; Suzanne Toolan, SM, b.1927
Tune: Suzanne Toolan, SM, b.1927
© 1974, GIA Publications, Inc.

Moved by the Gospel, Let Us Move 491

1. Moved by the Gos - pel, let us move With
2. Let weav - ers form from bro - ken strands A
3. O Spir - it, breathe a - mong us here; In -

ev - 'ry gift and art. The im - age of cre -
tap - es - try of prayer. Let art - ists paint with
spire the work we do. May hands and voic - es,

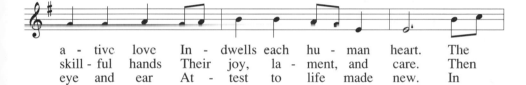

a - tive love In - dwells each hu - man heart. The
skill - ful hands Their joy, la - ment, and care. Then
eye and ear At - test to life made new. In

Mak - er calls cre - a - tion good, So
mime the sto - ry: Christ has come. With
wor - ship and in dai - ly strife Cre -

let us now ex - press With sound and col - or,
rev - 'rence dance the word. With flute and or - gan,
ate a - mong us still. Great Art - ist, form our

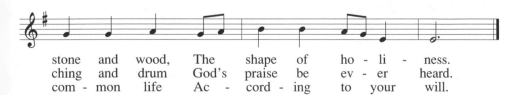

stone and wood, The shape of ho - li - ness.
ching and drum God's praise be ev - er heard.
com - mon life Ac - cord - ing to your will.

Text: Ruth Duck, b. 1947, © 1992, GIA Publications, Inc.
Tune: KINGSFOLD, CMD; English; harm. by Ralph Vaughan Williams, 1872-1958

492 Here I Am, Lord

Verses

1. I, the Lord of sea and sky, I have heard my
2. I, the Lord of snow and rain, I have borne my
3. I, the Lord of wind and flame, I will tend the

peo - ple cry. All who dwell in dark and sin
peo - ple's pain. I have wept for love of them.
poor and lame. I will set a feast for them.

My hand will save. I who made the
They turn a - way. I will break their
My hand will save. Fin - est bread I

stars of night, I will make their dark-ness bright. Who will bear my
hearts of stone, Give them hearts for love a - lone. I will speak my
will pro - vide Till their hearts be sat - is - fied. I will give my

light to them? Whom shall I send?
word to them. Whom shall I send?
life to them. Whom shall I send?

Refrain

Here I am, Lord. Is it I, Lord? I have heard you

call-ing in the night. I will go, Lord, if you lead me.

I will hold your peo - ple in my heart.

Text: Isaiah 6; Dan Schutte. b.1947
Tune: Dan Schutte. b.1947; arr. by Michael Pope, SJ, John Weissrock
© 1981, Daniel L. Schutte and New Dawn Music

Out of Darkness 493

Refrain

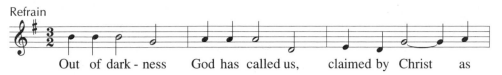

Out of dark-ness God has called us, claimed by Christ as

God's own peo - ple. Ho-ly na - tion, roy - al priest - hood,

1.- 3. *To verse* | *Last time*

walk-ing in God's marv'-lous light. A - men.

Verses

1. Let us take the words you give,
2. Let us take the Christ you give,
3. Let us take the love you give,

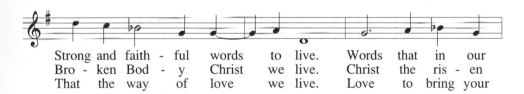

Strong and faith - ful words to live. Words that in our
Bro - ken Bod - y Christ we live. Christ the ris - en
That the way of love we live. Love to bring your

D.C.

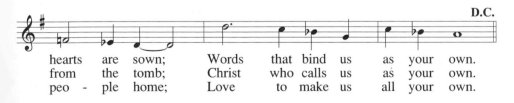

hearts are sown; Words that bind us as your own.
from the tomb; Christ who calls us as your own.
peo - ple home; Love to make us all your own.

Text: Christopher Walker, b.1947
Tune: Christopher Walker, b.1947
© 1989, Christopher Walker, published by OCP Publications

494 Anthem

Refrain

We are called, we are cho-sen. We are Christ for one an-oth-er. We are prom-ised to to-mor-row, while we are for him to-day. We are sign, we are won-der. We are sow-er, we are seed. We are har-vest, we are hun-ger. We are ques-tion, we are creed.

Verses

1. Then where can we stand jus-ti-fied? In what can we be-
2. Then how are we to stand at all, this world of bend-ed
3. Then shall we not stand emp-ty at the al-tar of our

lieve? In no one else but Christ who suf-fered, noth-ing
knee? In noth-ing more than bar-ren shad-ows. No one
dreams? When Christ prom-ised us our-selves. Who mark

more than Christ who rose. Who was jus-tice for the poor.
else but Christ could save us. Who was jus-tice for the poor.
time a-gainst to-mor-row. Who are jus-tice for the poor.

Who was rage a-gainst the night. Who was
Who was rage a-gainst the night. Who was
Who are rage a-gainst the night. Who are

D.C.

hope for peace-ful peo-ple. Who was light.
hope for peace-ful peo-ple. Who was light.
hope for peace-ful peo-ple. Who are light.

Text: Tom Conry, b.1951, © 1978, New Dawn Music, alt.
Tune: Tom Conry, b.1951, © 1978, New Dawn Music; acc. by Robert J. Batastini, b.1942, © 1994, GIA Publications, Inc.

Now Go Forward 495

Now go for-ward, press toward the goal. Plen-ti-ful har - vest

waits for you. Faith - ful ser - vants, fear not death,

toil and la - bor for the Lord. Come, be - hold, your

days pass a - way. Look a - head, the

cross leads the way. While you have breath

on this day, give your - self. For - ward go!

Text: Unknown; trans. © 1986, Evelyn Chiu
Tune: Traditional Chinese melody; acc. by Diana Kodner, b. 1957, © 1994, GIA Publications, Inc.

496 Sing Hey for the Carpenter

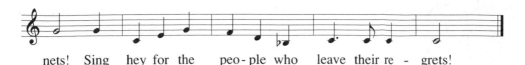

nets! Sing hey for the peo-ple who leave their re - grets!

Text: John L. Bell, b.1949
Tune: SING HEY, Irregular; John L. Bell, b.1949
© 1987, The Iona Community, GIA Publications, Inc., agent

We Are Climbing Jacob's Ladder 497

1. We are climb-ing Ja - cob's lad - der, We are
2. Ev - 'ry round goes high - er, high - er, Ev - 'ry
3. Sin - ner, do you love my Je - sus? Sin - ner,
4. If you love him, why not serve him? If you
5. We are climb-ing high - er, high - er, We are

climb - ing Ja - cob's lad - der, We are climb - ing
round goes high - er, high - er, Ev - 'ry round goes
do you love my Je - sus? Sin - ner, do you
love him, why not serve him? If you love him,
climb - ing high - er, high - er, We are climb - ing

Ja - cob's lad - der, Sol - diers of the cross.
high - er, high - er, Sol - diers of the cross.
love my Je - sus? Sol - diers of the cross.
why not serve him? Sol - diers of the cross.
high - er, high - er, Sol - diers of the cross.

Text: African-American spiritual
Tune: JACOB'S LADDER, 8 8 8 5; African-American spiritual

498 Now We Remain

Refrain

We hold the death of the Lord deep in our hearts. Liv-ing; now we re - main with Je - sus the Christ.

Verses

1. Once we were peo - ple a - fraid, lost in the night.
2. Some-thing which we have known, some-thing we've touched,
3. He chose to give of him - self, be - came our bread.
4. We are the pres - ence of God; this is our call.

Then by your cross we were saved; Dead be - came liv-ing, Life from your giv - ing.
What we have seen with our eyes: This we have heard; Life giv - ing word.
Bro - ken, that we might live. Love be - yond love, Pain for our pain.
Now to be - come bread and wine: Food for the hun-gry, Life for the wea - ry,

1.- 3.   **D.C.**   *4.* for to live with the

500 Lord, When You Came / Pescador de Hombres

Verses

1. Lord, when you came to the sea - shore
2. Lord, you knew what my boat car - ried:
3. Lord, have you need of my la - bor,
4. Lord, send me where you would have me,
1. Tú has ve - ni - do_a la_o - ri - lla,
2. Tú sa - bes bien lo que ten - go,
3. Tú ne - ce - si - tas mis ma - nos,
4. Tú pes - ca - dor de_o - tros, ma - res,

You weren't seek - ing the wise or the
Nei - ther mon - ey nor weap - ons for
Hands for ser - vice, a heart made for
To a vil - lage, or heart of the
no_has bus - ca - do ni_a sa - bios, ni_a
en mi bar - ca no_hay o - ro ni_es -
mi can - san - cio que_a o - tros des -
an - sia_e - ter - na, al - mas que es -

wealth - y, But on - ly ask - ing
fight - ing, But nets for fish - ing,
lov - ing, My arms for lift - ing
cit - y; I will re - mem - ber
ri - cos, tan só - lo quie - res
pa - das, tan só - lo re - des
can - se, a - mor que quie - ra
pe - ran. A - mi - go bue - no,

that I might fol - low.
my dai - ly la - bor.
the poor and bro - ken?
that you are with me.
que yo te si - ga.
y mi tra - ba - jo.
se - guir a - man - do.
que_a - sí me lla - mas.

Lord, we must die with the Lord.

Text: Corinthians, 1 John, 2 Timothy; David Haas, b.1957
Tune: David Haas, b.1957
© 1983, GIA Publications, Inc.

Only This I Want 499

Refrain

On-ly this I want: but to know the Lord,

and to bear his cross so to wear the crown he wore.

Verses

1. All but this is loss, worth-less ref-use to me,
2. I will run the race; I will fight the good fight,
3. Let your heart be glad, al-ways glad in the Lord,

1. for to gain the Lord is to gain all I need.
2. so to win the prize of the King-dom of my Lord.
3. so to shine like stars in the dark-ness of the night.

Text: Philippians 3:7-16; 2:15, 18; Dan Schutte, b.1947
Tune: Dan Schutte, b.1947; arr. by Michael Pope, SJ
© 1981, Daniel L. Schutte and New Dawn Music

Refrain

O Lord,   in my eyes you were   gaz - ing,
Se - ñor   me̮has mi - ra-do̮a los   o - jos,

Kind-ly smil - ing,   my   name you were
son - ri - en - do   has   di - cho mi

say - ing;   All I   treas - ured,
nom - bre,   en la̮a   re - ña

I have left on the   sand   there;   Close to
he de - ja - do mi   bar - ca,   jun - to̮a

you,   I will find oth - er   seas.
ti   bus - ca - ré o - tro   mar.

Text: *Pescador de Hombres,* Cesáreo Gabaráin; trans. by Willard Francis Jabusch, b.1930, © 1979, published by OCP Publications
Tune: Cesáreo Gabaráin, © 1979, published by OCP Publications; acc. by Diana Kodner, b.1957, © 1994, GIA Publications, Inc.

501　We Have Been Told

Refrain

We have been told, we've seen his face, and heard his voice a-live in our hearts;

"Live in my love with all your heart, as the Fa-ther has loved me, so I have loved you."

Verse 1

1. "I am the vine, you are the branch-es, and all who live in me will bear great fruit."

D.C.

Verses 2, 3

2. "You are my friends, if you keep my com-mands,
3. "No great-er love is there than this: to

no long-er slaves, I call you friends."
lay down one's life, for a friend."

D.C.

Text: David Haas, b.1957
Tune: David Haas, b.1957; vocal arr. by David Haas, b.1957, Marty Haugen, b.1950
© 1983, GIA Publications, Inc.

Jesu Tawa Pano / Jesus, We Are Here   502

Je - su   ta-wa pa-no;   Je - su   ta - wa pa-no;
Je - sus,   we are here;   Je - sus,   we are here;

Je - su   ta-wa pa-no;   ta-wa pa-no, mu zi - ta re - nyu.
Je - sus,   we are here;   we are here   for   you.

Text: Zimbabwean; Patrick Matsikenyiri
Tune: Patrick Matsikenyiri
© 1990, Patrick Matsikenyiri

503 God It Was

1. God it was who said to A - bra - ham,
2. God it was who said to Mo - ses,
3. God it was who said to Jo - seph,
4. Christ it was who said to Mat - thew,
5. In this crowd of com - mon peo - ple,

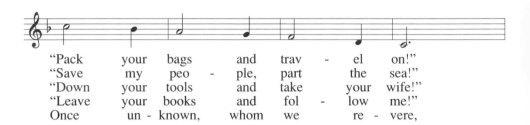

"Pack your bags and trav - el on!"
"Save my peo - ple, part the sea!"
"Down your tools and take your wife!"
"Leave your books and fol - low me!"
Once un - known, whom we re - vere,

God it was who said to Sar - ah,
God it was who said to Mir - i - am,
God it was who said to Mar - y,
Christ it was who said to Mar - tha,
God calls us to share his pur - pose

"Smile and soon you'll bear a son!"
"Sing and dance to show you're free!"
"In your womb I'll start my life!"
"Lis - ten first, then make the tea!"
Start - ing now and start - ing here.

Trav - 'ling folk and a - ged moth - ers
Shep - herd - saints and tam - bou - rin - ists
Car - pen - ter and coun - try maid - en
Civ - il ser - vants and house - keep - ers,
So we cel - e - brate his call - ing,

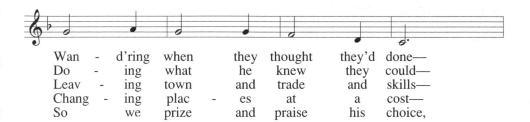

Wan	-	d'ring	when		they	thought		they'd	done—
Do	-	ing	what		he	knew		they	could—
Leav	-	ing	town		and	trade		and	skills—
Chang	-	ing	plac	- es	at		a	cost—
So		we	prize		and	praise		his	choice,

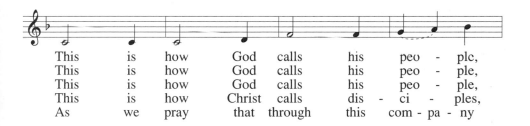

This	is	how	God	calls	his	peo	-	ple,
This	is	how	God	calls	his	peo	-	ple,
This	is	how	God	calls	his	peo	-	ple,
This	is	how	Christ	calls	dis	- ci	-	ples,
As	we	pray	that	through	this	com - pa	-	ny

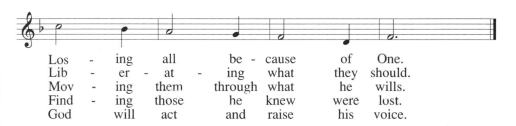

Los	-	ing	all		be - cause		of	One.
Lib	-	er	- at	- ing	what		they	should.
Mov	-	ing	them		through	what	he	wills.
Find	-	ing	those		he	knew	were	lost.
God		will	act		and	raise	his	voice.

Text: John L. Bell, b.1949
Tune: JESUS CALLS US, Irregular, adapt. from a Gaelic Air by John L. Bell, b.1949
© 1989, Iona Community, GIA Publications, Inc., agent

504 The Love of the Lord

1. All that I count - ed as gain
2. Rich - es and hon - ors will fade,
3. Sil - ver and gold have I none,
4. Faith is the wealth I pos - sess

now I con - sid - er as loss,
earth - ly de - light dis - ap - pear,
no land to count as my home, yet
Find - ing its source in my God:

emp - ty and worth - less to me in the
fade like the grass of the field in the
wealth be - yond meas - ure I own in the
faith in the prom - ise of Christ is my

1., 3.   *2., 4.*

light of the love of the Lord.
light of the love of the Lord.
light of the love of the Lord.
life and my love of the Lord.

What more could bring us hope than to know the pow'r of his

life? What more could bring us peace than to

share in his suf-f'ring and death? What more could be our

fi - nal wish than to live in the love of the Lord?

Text: Philippians 3:7-11; Michael Joncas, b.1951
Tune: Michael Joncas, b.1951
© 1988, GIA Publications, Inc.

Song of St. Patrick   505

Refrain

May the Spir - it of Christ be our hope through the day, be our guard through the night, our com - pan - ion on the way.

Verse 1

1. Christ be ev - er be - fore us, Christ be ev - er be - hind us, Christ be ev - er with - in.

D.C.

Verses 2-5

2. Christ up - on our left hand watch - ing, At our right hand guid - ing,
3. Christ be in each ho - ly si - lence, Christ be in our speak - ing,
4. Let us be God's light in the dark - ness, Let us be God's kind - ness;
5. God Cre - a - tor, bless and keep us, Christ, be ev - er near us;

Christ a - bove, be - neath us guard - ing, Near to us a - bid - ing.
Christ in ev - 'ry work we of - fer, Ev - er in our seek - ing.
Let us be God's jus - tice and mer - cy, Hands and feet of Christ.
Spir - it be the light be - fore us, Gen - tle be our path - way.

D.C.

Text: Based on *St. Patrick's Breastplate;* Marty Haugen, b.1950
Tune: Marty Haugen, b.1950
© 1986, GIA Publications, Inc.

506 I Am for You

1. There is a moun - tain there is a sea.
2. There was a wom - an small as a star,
3. There was a man who walked in the storm,
4. We are a - noint - ed, ser - vants of God;
5. There is a world that waits in the womb;

There is a wind with - in all breath - ing,
Full of the pa - tient dreams of her na - tion,
Caught in be - tween the waves and the light-ning,
We have been born a - gain of Spir - it.
There is a hope un - born God is bear - ing,

There is an arm to break ev - 'ry chain,
Wel - com - ing in an an - gel of God,
Shar - ing his bread with those cast a - side,
We are the word God speaks to the world,
Though the powers of death prowl the night,

There is a fire in all things
Wel - com - ing in God's bold in - vi -
Heal - ing by touch the lost and the
Free - dom and light to all who will
There is a day our God is pre -

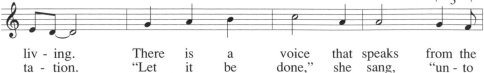

liv - ing. There is a voice that speaks from the
ta - tion. "Let it be done," she sang, "un - to
dy - ing. Send - ing us forth, he says to his
hear it. So let us be the word of the
par - ing. Sing 'round the fire to wa - ken the

flame:	"I am for you,	I am for
me.	I am for you,	I am for
friends:	"I am for you,	I am for
Lord:	I am for you,	I am for
dawn:	I am for you,	I am for

you,	I am for you is	my name."
you,	I am for you: let	it be."
you,	I am for you to	the end."
you,	I am for you ev -	er - more.
you,	I am for you: We	are one.

Text: Rory Cooney, b.1952
Tune: Rory Cooney, b.1952
© 1993, GIA Publications, Inc.

507 Never the Blade Shall Rise

Verse 1

1. Un-less a grain of wheat falls to the earth,

falls to the earth and dies, it re-mains on-ly a

grain of wheat and nev - er the blade shall rise.

Refrain 𝄋

For the grain of wheat pro - duc - es much fruit, but

on - ly if it dies. Un-less a grain of wheat

falls to the earth, nev - er the blade shall rise.

Verse 2

2. The one who loves the world - ly life

los - es the life so lived, while the one who hates the

D.S.

life in this world pre - serves it to life e - ter - nal.

Verse 3

3. If an - y - one would serve me, come and fol - low me; come and fol - low me; where I am, there will my ser - vant be.

Text: John 12; Kathy Powell, b. 1942
Tune: Kathy Powell, b. 1942
©1993, GIA Publications, Inc.

Guide My Feet 508

1., 6. Guide my feet while I run this race,
Guide my feet while I run this race,
Guide my feet while I run this race, for I
don't want to run this race in vain!

2. Hold my hand… 3. Stand by me... 4. I'm your child... 5. Search my heart...

Text: African-American spiritual
Tune: African-American spiritual; harm. by Diana Kodner, b. 1957, © 1994, GIA Publications, Inc.

509 Unless a Grain of Wheat

Refrain

Un - less a grain of wheat shall fall up - on the ground

and die, it re - mains but a sin - gle grain

|1.- 6. *To verses* |*Last time*

with no life.   2. If

Verses

1. If   we   have   died   with him   then   we   shall
2. an - y - one   serves   me   then   they must
3. ⟨ Make your   home   in   me   as   I   make
4. If   you   re - main   in   me   and   my   word
5. ⟨ Those who   love   me   are   loved by   my
6. ⟨ Peace I   leave with you,   my   peace I

live   with him;   if   we   hold   firm   we   shall
fol - low   me;   where - ev - er   I   am   my
mine in   you;   those who   re - main   in   me
lives in   you,   then   you   will   be   my   dis -
Fa - ther;   we   shall be   with   them and
give   to   you;   peace which the   world can - not

D.C.

reign with him.
ser - vants will   be.
bear   much fruit.
ci - ples.
dwell in   them.
give   is   my   gift.

Text: John 12:24; Bernadette Farrell, b.1957
Tune: Bernadette Farrell, b.1957

The Summons 510

1. Will you come and fol-low me If I but
2. Will you leave your-self be-hind If I but
3. Will you let the blind-ed see If I but
4. Will you love the 'you' you hide If I but
5. Lord, your sum-mons ech-oes true When you but

call your name? Will you go where you don't
call your name? Will you care for cruel and
call your name? Will you set the pris-'ners
call your name? Will you quell the fear in-
call my name. Let me turn and fol-low

know And nev-er be the same? Will you
kind And nev-er be the same? Will you
free And nev-er be the same? Will you
side And nev-er be the same? Will you
you And nev-er be the same. In your

let my love be shown, Will you let my
risk the hos-tile stare Should your life at-
kiss the lep-er clean, And do such as
use the faith you've found To re-shape the
com-pa-ny I'll go Where your love and

name be known, Will you let my life be
tract or scare? Will you let me an-swer
this un-seen, And ad-mit to what I
world a-round, Through my sight and touch and
foot-steps show. Thus I'll move and live and

grown In you and you in me?
pray'r In you and you in me?
mean In you and you in me?
sound In you and you in me?
grow In you and you in me.

Text: John L. Bell, b.1949, © 1987, Iona Community, GIA Publications, Inc., agent
Tune: KELVINGROVE, 7 6 7 6 777 6; Scottish traditional; arr. by John L. Bell, b.1949, © 1987, Iona Community, GIA Publications, Inc., agent

511 I Danced in the Morning

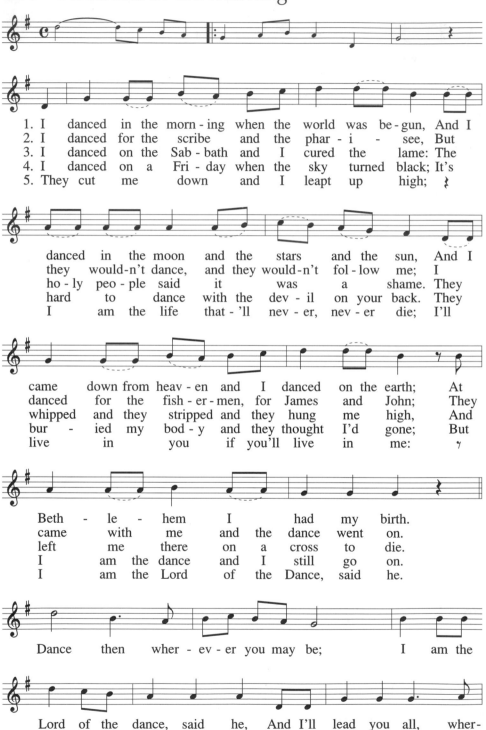

1. I danced in the morn-ing when the world was be-gun, And I
2. I danced for the scribe and the phar-i - see, But
3. I danced on the Sab-bath and I cured the lame: The
4. I danced on a Fri - day when the sky turned black; It's
5. They cut me down and I leapt up high;

danced in the moon and the stars and the sun, And I
they would-n't dance, and they would-n't fol - low me; I
ho - ly peo - ple said it was a shame. They
hard to dance with the dev - il on your back. They
I am the life that - 'll nev - er, nev - er die; I'll

came down from heav - en and I danced on the earth; At
danced for the fish - er - men, for James and John; They
whipped and they stripped and they hung me high, And
bur - ied my bod - y and they thought I'd gone; But
live in you if you'll live in me:

Beth - le - hem I had my birth.
came with me and the dance went on.
left me there on a cross to die.
I am the dance and I still go on.
I am the Lord of the Dance, said he.

Dance then wher - ev - er you may be; I am the

Lord of the dance, said he, And I'll lead you all, wher-

ev-er you may be, And I'll lead you all in the dance, said he.

Text: Sydney Carter, b.1915, © Stainer and Bell Ltd., London, England
Tune: SHAKER SONG, Irregular; American Shaker; harm. by Sydney Carter, b.1915, © Stainer and Bell Ltd., London, England

We Will Drink the Cup 512

Refrain

We will drink the cup, we will win the fight; we will

stand a-gainst the dark-ness of the night! We will

run the race, and see God's face, and

build the king - dom of love!

Verses

1. Do not fear, for I am with you, be
2. You will run, and not grow wea - ry, for
3. Re - joice and know you are my peo - ple; and
4. We are the Church, we are the bod - y;

D.C.

still and know that I am God!
I, your God, will be your strength!
know that I am your God!
we are God's great work of art!

Text: David Haas, b.1957
Tune: David Haas, b.1957
© 1991, GIA Publications, Inc.

513 The Harvest of Justice

(Refrain) May we find rich - ness in the har - vest of jus -
1. Gath-er with pa - tience for those who have noth -
2. For to have mer - cy on those for - got -
3. For to have lit - tle is to be in a - bun -

tice which Christ Je - sus has rip-ened for
ing. Leave them your rich - es, and you will re -
ten, this is my true law, this is my com -
dance. To give what re - mains, to give all we

us. Bread for the jour - ney,
ceive. Make room for the poor ones,
mand: Clothe the na - ked,
have, is to walk with the poor ones,

bread for the hun - gry, all for the
make way for the stran - ger; for I am the
be home for the or - phan, be hope for the
and be - come the stran - ger, one with the

glo - ry and praise of God.
Lord, the Lord your God.
wid - ow, and wel - come the lost.
Lord, the Lord our God.

Text: Philippians 1:11, Leviticus 19:9, 23:22, Deuteronomy 24:19; David Haas, b.1957
Tune: David Haas, b.1957
© 1985, GIA Publications, Inc.

On Holy Ground 514

Verses

1. The heav-ens em-brace the earth, then they sing of the new birth. The earth ech-oes and re-sounds that we are on ho-ly ground.
2. A-bran-se los cie-los, en el nom-bre de Cris-to Dios. Trans-for-men la tie-rra cau-ti-va a u-na tie-rra con li-ber-tad.
3. Let heav-en and earth sing praise to the one who from death was raised. Let hearts ut-ter words pro-found in pro-claim-ing this ho-ly ground.
4. Bless earth, wa-ter, fire, and wind. Bless your peo-ple with-out, with-in. Let beau-ty and birth sur-round in re-claim-ing this ho-ly ground.
5. La his-to-ria de los Pue-blos se-rá li-bre por la ver-dad. La cau-sa es ju-ti-fi-ca-da. San-ta tie-rra nues-tra se-rá.
6. U-nit-ed we join the light. We are born of the same right. We've come to re-lease what's bound, for we are on ho-ly ground.

Refrain

Assembly: Do you be-lieve in free-dom? Yes, we do Lord! Do you be-lieve in jus-tice? Jus-tice for all!

Assembly: ¿Y en la nue-va vi-da? ¡En su es-pí-ri-tu! ¿Quién es su li-be-ra-ción? ¡Tú, Se-ñor!

¡A-rri-ba! ¡Pro-cla-men! ¡San-ta Tie-rra!

We are on ho-ly ground!

Text: Donna Peña, b.1955
Tune: Donna Peña, b.1955; acc. by Diana Kodner, b.1957

515 Go Down, Moses

1. When Is - rael was in E - gypt's land:
2. The Lord told Mo - ses what to do,
3. As Is - rael stood by the wa - ter side,
4. When they had reached the oth - er shore,
5. Oh, let us all from bond - age flee,

Op - pressed so hard they
To lead the chil-dren of
Let my peo - ple go: At God's com - mand it
They sang the song of
And let us all in

could not stand,
Is - rael through,
did di - vide, Let my peo - ple go. Go down,
tri - umph o'er,
Christ be free,

Mo - ses, 'Way down in E - gypt land,

Tell ol' Phar - aoh, to let my peo - ple go.

Text: Exodus; African-American spiritual
Tune: African-American spiritual

Let Justice Roll Like a River 516

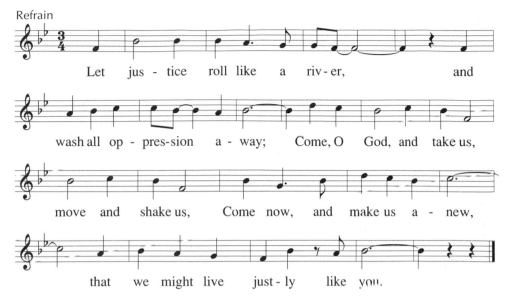

Refrain

Let jus-tice roll like a riv-er, and wash all op-pres-sion a-way; Come, O God, and take us, move and shake us, Come now, and make us a-new, that we might live just-ly like you.

Verses

1. Take from me your holy feasts, all your off'rings and your music;
   Let justice flow like waters, and integrity like an ever-flowing stream.

2. How long shall we wait, O God, for the day of your mercy to dawn,
   the day we beat our swords into ploughs, when your peace reigns over the earth?

3. Hear this, all of you who use the poor in your thirst of power and riches:
   the Lord will turn your laughter to tears, on the wondrous Day of our God.

4. Even now return to me, let your hearts be broken and humble,
   for I am gracious, gen'rous and kind; come and seek the mercies of God.

5. You have been told the way of life, the way of justice and peace;
   to act justly, to love gently, and walk humbly with God.

Text: Amos 5:21-24, 8:4, Micah 4:3-4, 6:8, Joel 2:12-14; Marty Haugen, b.1950
Tune: Marty Haugen, b.1950
© 1991, GIA Publications, Inc.

517 Free at Last

Free at last, free at last, I thank God I'm

free at last; Free at last, free at last,

1. I thank God I'm free at last. (O) **2.** free at last.

1. 'Way down yon - der in the grave - yard walk,
2. On a my knees when the light passed by,
3. Some of these morn - ings, bright and fair,

I thank God I'm free at last,
I thank God I'm free at last,
I thank God I'm free at last, Goin'

Me and my Je - sus goin' to meet and talk,
Thought my soul would rise and fly,
meet King Je - sus in the air,

D.C.

I thank God I'm free at last. (O)

Text: African-American spiritual
Tune: African-American spiritual

We Are Called 518

1. Come! Live in the light!
2. Come! O - pen your heart!
3. Sing! Sing a new song!

Shine with the joy and the love of the Lord! We are
Show your mer - cy to all those in fear! We are
Sing of that great day when all will be one! God will

called to be light for the king - dom, to
called to be hope for the hope - less so all
reign, and we'll walk with each oth - er as

live in the free - dom of the cit - y of God!
ha - tred and blind-ness will be no more!
sis - ters and broth-ers u - nit-ed in love!

We are called to act with jus-tice, we are called to

love ten - der - ly, we are called to serve one an - oth-er;

to walk hum - bly with God!

Text: Micah 6:8; David Haas, b.1957
Tune: David Haas, b.1957

519 Voices That Challenge

Refrain

Call us to hear the voic-es that chal-lenge, deep in the hearts of all

peo - ple! By serv-ing your world as lov - ers and dream-ers,

we be-come voic-es that chal-lenge, for we are the voice of God!

Verses 1, 2

All: *Cantor:*

1. Voic-es that chal-lenge: the   chil - dren who long to be
                          the   low - ly and bro-ken de-
                          the   old and the fear-ful who
2. Voic-es that chal-lenge: the   lives and the cries of the
                          the   young ones who dream of a
                          the   sick and the dy - ing who

1., 2., 4., 5.   *3., 6.*   **D.C.**

heard	and	re	spec-ted!
stroyed	by	op -	pres-sion!
hope	for	a	new day!
poor	and the	si -	lenced!
world	free of	ha -	tred!
cry	for com	-	pas-sion!

Verse 3

All: *Cantor:*

3. Voic-es that chal-lenge: the ones who seek peace by their
                          the wo - men who suf - fer the
                          the peo - ple with AIDS and those
                          the pro - phets and he - roes who
                          the hea - lers who teach us for -
                          the vic - tims of vio - lent a -
                          the Christ who gave his

521 Freedom Is Coming

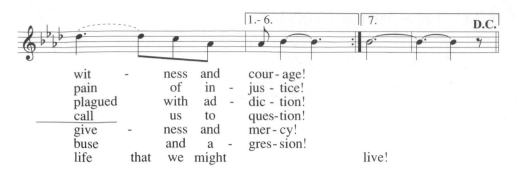

wit - ness and cour - age!
pain of in - jus - tice!
plagued with ad - dic - tion!
call us to ques - tion!
give - ness and mer - cy!
buse and a - gres - sion!
life that we might live!

Text: David Haas, b.1957
Tune: David Haas, b.1957
© 1990, GIA Publications, Inc.

If You Believe and I Believe 520

If you be-lieve and I be-lieve And we to-geth-er

pray, The Ho - ly Spir - it must come down And

set God's peo - ple free, And set God's peo - ple

free, And set God's peo - ple free; The

Ho - ly Spir - it must come down And set God's peo - ple free.

Text: Zimbabwean traditional
Tune: Zimbabwean traditional; adapt. of English traditional; as taught by Tarasai; arr. by John L. Bell, b.1949, © 1991, Iona Community,
    GIA Publications, agent

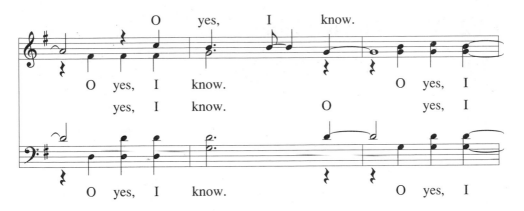

Text: South African
Tune: South African
© 1984, Utryck

522 We Shall Overcome

```
1. We   shall   o - ver - come,      we   shall   o - ver - come,
2. We'll walk  hand  in   hand,      we'll walk  hand  in   hand,
3. We   shall  live  in   peace,     we   shall  live  in   peace,
4. We   are   not   a - fraid,      we   are   not   a - fraid,
```

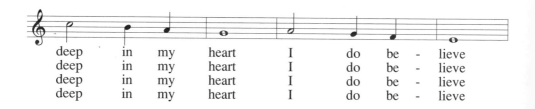

```
we   shall   o - ver - come some - day.         Oh,
we'll walk  hand  in   hand some - day.         Oh,
we   shall  live  in   peace some - day.        Oh,
we   are   not   a - fraid  to - day.           Oh,
```

```
deep   in   my   heart   I   do   be - lieve
deep   in   my   heart   I   do   be - lieve
deep   in   my   heart   I   do   be - lieve
deep   in   my   heart   I   do   be - lieve
```

```
we    shall   o - ver - come  some - day.
we'll  walk  hand  in   hand  some - day.
we    shall  live  in   peace some - day.
we    are   not   a - fraid  to - day.
```

5. We shall stand together...
6. The truth will make us free...
7. The Lord will see us through...
8. We shall be like him...
9. The whole wide world around...

Text: adapt. by Zilphia Horton, Frank Hamilton, Guy Carawan, and Pete Seeger, © 1960, 1963, Ludlow Music.
Tune: adapt. by Zilphia Horton, Frank Hamilton, Guy Carawan, and Pete Seeger, © 1960, 1963, Ludlow Music;
  harm. by J. Jefferson Cleveland, b.1937, from *Songs of Zion*, harm. © 1981, by Abingdon Press

World Peace Prayer 523

Refrain

Lead us from death to life, from false-hood to truth, from despair to hope, from fear to trust. Lead us from
hate to love, from war to peace; let peace fill our
hearts, let peace fill our world, let peace fill our u - ni - verse.

Verses

1. Still all the an - gry cries, still all the an - gry guns,
2. So man - y lone - ly hearts, so man - y bro - ken lives,
3. Let jus - tice ev - er roll, let mer - cy fill the earth,

still now your peo - ple die, earth's sons and daugh - ters.
long - ing for love to break in - to their dark - ness.
let us be - gin to grow in - to your peo - ple.

Let jus - tice roll, let mer - cy pour down,
Come, teach us love, come, teach us peace,
We can be love, we can bring peace,

D.C.

come and teach us your way of com - pas - sion.
come and teach us your way of com - pas - sion.
we can still be your way of com - pas - sion.

Text: Refrain, Upanishads, Satish Kumar; verses, Marty Haugen, b.1950, © 1985, GIA Publications, Inc.
Tune: Marty Haugen, b.1950, © 1985, GIA Publications, Inc.

524 Make Me a Channel of Your Peace

Verses 1, 2, 4

1. Make me a chan-nel of your peace. Where
2. Make me a chan-nel of your peace. Where
4. Make me a chan-nel of your peace. It

there is ha-tred, let me bring your love. Where
there's de-spair in life, let me bring hope. Where
is in par-don-ing that we are par-doned, in

there is in-ju-ry, your par-don, Lord, And
there is dark-ness, on-ly light, And
giv-ing of our-selves that we re-ceive, and in

1. where there's doubt, true faith in you.
where there's sad-ness, ev-er joy.
2., 4. dy-ing that we're born to e-ter-nal life.

Verse 3

3. Oh, Mas-ter, grant that I may nev-er seek So much to be con-

soled as to con-sole. To be un-der-stood as to un-der-

D.C.

stand. To be loved as to love with all my soul.

Text: *Prayer of St. Francis;* adapt. by Sebastian Temple, b. 1928, ©1967, 1975, 1980, Franciscan Communications
Tune: Sebastian Temple, b. 1928, © 1967, 1975, 1980, Franciscan Communications; acc. by Diana Kodner, b. 1957, © 1993, GIA Publications, Inc.
Dedicated to Mrs. Frances Tracy. Reprinted with permission.

How Good It Is 525

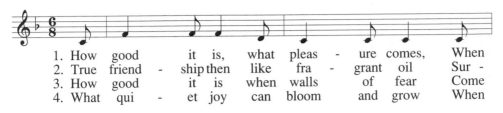

1. How good it is, what pleas - ure comes, When
2. True friend - ship then like fra - grant oil Sur -
3. How good it is when walls of fear Come
4. What qui - et joy can bloom and grow When

peo - ple live as one. When peace and jus - tice
rounds us with de - light; And bless - ings shine like
tum - bling to the ground. When arms are changed to
peo - ple work for peace, When hands and voic - es

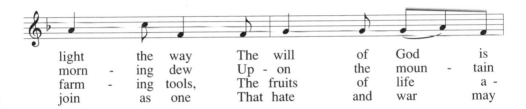

light the way The will of God is
morn - ing dew Up - on the moun - tain
farm - ing tools, The fruits of life a -
join as one That hate and war may

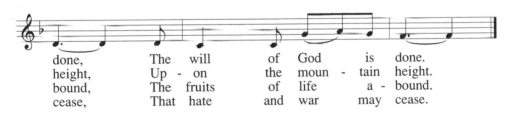

done, The will of God is done.
height, Up - on the moun - tain height.
bound, The fruits of life a - bound.
cease, That hate and war may cease.

Text: Psalm 133, Isaiah 2:1-4; Ruth Duck, b.1947, © 1992, GIA Publications, Inc.
Tune: DOVE OF PEACE, CM; American; harm. by Charles H. Webb, b.1933, © 1989, The United Methodist Publishing House

526 Peace Is Flowing Like a River

1. Peace   is flow-ing like a riv - er,
2. Joy   is flow-ing like a riv - er,   Flow - ing out through you and
3. Faith   is flow-ing like a riv - er,
4. Hope   is flow-ing like a riv - er,
5. Love   is flow-ing like a riv - er,

me;   Flow - ing out in - to the

des - ert,   Set - ting all the cap - tives free.

Text: Unknown
Tune: Unknown; acc. by Diana Kodner, b.1957, © 1993, GIA Publications, Inc.

527 Prayer of Peace

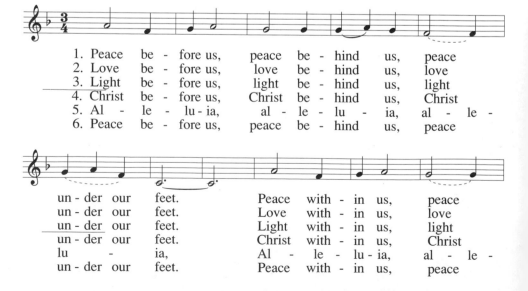

1. Peace be - fore us,   peace be - hind us,   peace
2. Love be - fore us,   love be - hind us,   love
3. Light be - fore us,   light be - hind us,   light
4. Christ be - fore us,   Christ be - hind us,   Christ
5. Al - le - lu - ia,   al - le - lu - ia,   al - le -
6. Peace be - fore us,   peace be - hind us,   peace

un - der our feet.   Peace with - in us,   peace
un - der our feet.   Love with - in us,   love
un - der our feet.   Light with - in us,   light
un - der our feet.   Christ with - in us,   Christ
lu - ia,   Al - le - lu - ia,   al - le -
un - der our feet.   Peace with - in us,   peace

o - ver us, let all a - round us be peace.
o - ver us, let all a - round us be love.
o - ver us, let all a - round us be light.
o - ver us, let all a - round us be Christ.
lu - ia, al - le - lu - ia.
o - ver us, let all a - round us be peace.

Text: Based on a Navajo prayer; David Haas, b.1957
Tune: David Haas, b.1957
© 1987, GIA Publications, Inc.

Dona Nobis Pacem   528

Canon

1. Do - na no - bis pa - cem, pa - cem.

Do - na no - bis pa - cem.

2. Do - na no - bis pa - cem.

Do - na no - bis pa - cem.

3. Do - na no - bis pa - cem.

Do - na no - bis pa - cem.

Text: *Grant us peace;* Unknown
Tune: Traditional; acc. by Diana Kodner, b.1957, © 1994, GIA Publications, Inc.

529 Let There Be Peace on Earth

Let there be peace on earth, and let it be - gin with me.

Let there be peace on earth, the peace that was meant to be. With

God as our Fa - ther, broth - ers / fam - 'ly all are we.

Let me / us walk with my broth-er / each oth - er in per-fect har-mo - ny.

Let peace be - gin with me; let this be the mo - ment now.

With ev - 'ry step I take, let this be my sol - emn vow; To

take each mo-ment, and live each mo-ment in peace e - ter-nal - ly!

Let there be peace on earth, and let it be - gin with me.

Text: Sy Miller, 1908-1941, Jill Jackson, © 1955, 1983, Jan-Lee Music
Tune: Sy Miller, 1908-1941, Jill Jackson © 1955, 1983, Jan-Lee Music; acc. by Diana Kodner, b.1957, © 1993 GIA Publications, Inc.
Used with permission

We Are Many Parts 530

Refrain

We are man-y parts, we are all one bod-y,

and the gifts we have we are giv-en to share.

May the Spir-it of love make us one in-deed;

one, the love that we share, one, our hope in de-spair,

one, the cross that we bear.

Verses

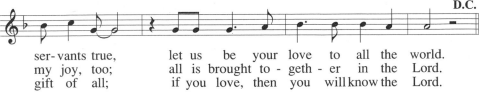

1. God of all, we look to you, we would be your
2. So my pain is pain for you, in your joy is
3. All you seek-ers, great and small, seek the great-est

D.C.

ser-vants true, let us be your love to all the world.
my joy, too; all is brought to-geth-er in the Lord.
gift of all; if you love, then you will know the Lord.

Text: 1 Corinthians 12, 13; Marty Haugen, b.1950
Tune: Marty Haugen, b.1950
© 1980, 1986, GIA Publications, Inc.

531 Song of Gathering

Refrain

Nei-ther Greek, nor Jew, nor slave, nor free, nei-ther wo-man, nor man, but chil-dren are we, of the same God, the one Lord, the Fa-ther of all, let it be.

Verses 1, 3

1. From the four winds, and the high seas, from the low-lands, and the val-leys we come to the ta-ble, to the Sav-ior, to the call.

3. From the one cup, from the one bread, at the one meal, we are all fed once more in the bod-y, in the Spir-it, in the dream.

D.C.

Verse 2

2. Your sons and your daugh-ters, young brides and old lov-ers, we come from the wa-ters that spring from your side.

D.C.

Text: Joe Wise
Tune: Joe Wise; acc. by David Barrickman, alt.
© 1982, GIA Publications, Inc.

No Longer Strangers 532

Verses

1. We once were lost; with-out
2. We once were cut off; but now
3. We who once were dead, now we

hope, with - out God; but now in Christ
we are brought near, for Christ is our
live in the light, we fol - low Christ

Je - sus, we have been found!
peace, we were bro - ken, now whole! One
Je - sus, a - bun - dant in grace! Who

Saved by the prom-ise of God!
spir - it, one Bod - y of Christ!
saved us, who raised us to life!

Refrain

No long - er stran-gers, no long-er lost and a - lone!

No long - er stran-gers, now we are saints! We are

one in the house of God!

Text: David Haas, b.1957
Tune: David Haas, b.1957, vocal arr. by Jeanne Cotter, b.1964

533 They'll Know We Are Christians

1. We are one in the Spir-it, we are one in the Lord, We are one in the Spir-it, we are one in the Lord, And we pray that all u-ni-ty may one day be re-stored:
2. We will walk with each oth-er, we will walk hand in hand, We will walk with each oth-er, we will walk hand in hand, And to-geth-er we'll spread the news that God is in our land:
3. We will work with each oth-er, we will work side by side, We will work with each oth-er, we will work side by side, And we'll guard hu-man's dig-ni-ty and save hu-man's pride:
4. All praise to the Fa-ther, from whom all things come, And all praise to Christ Je-sus, his on-ly Son, And all praise to the Spir-it, who makes us one:

And they'll know we are Chris-tians by our love, by our love, Yes, they'll know we are Chris-tians by our love.

Text: Peter Scholtes, b.1938
Tune: ST. BRENDAN'S, 7 6 7 6 8 6 with refrain; Peter Scholtes, b.1938

Many Are the Lightbeams   534

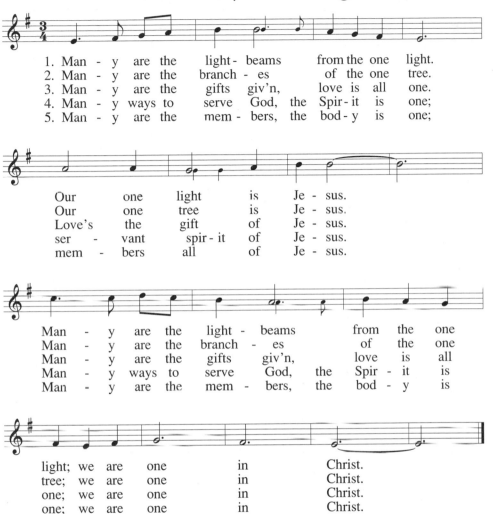

1. Man - y are the light- beams from the one light.
2. Man - y are the branch - es of the one tree.
3. Man - y are the gifts giv'n, love is all one.
4. Man - y ways to serve God, the Spir- it is one;
5. Man - y are the mem - bers, the bod - y is one;

Our one light is Je - sus.
Our one tree is Je - sus.
Love's the gift of Je - sus.
ser - vant spir- it of Je - sus.
mem - bers all of Je - sus.

Man - y are the light - beams from the one
Man - y are the branch - es of the one
Man - y are the gifts giv'n, love is all
Man - y ways to serve God, the Spir - it is
Man - y are the mem - bers, the bod - y is

light; we are one in Christ.
tree; we are one in Christ.
one; we are one in Christ.
one; we are one in Christ.
one; we are one in Christ.

Text: *De unitate ecclesiae*, Cyprian of Carthage, 252 A.D.; trans. by Anders Frostenson © Verbum Forlong AB
Tune: Olle Widestrand ©; acc. by Marty Haugen, b.1950, © 1987, GIA Publications, Inc.

535   The Broken Body

1. How can we live as Chris - tians here, Un -
2. Christ is the one who calls us one, Who
3. One is the wa - ter by which sign Our
4. But not in bread and wine as yet Are
5. If our still hands no bod - y take, Still
6. O Christ of vi - sion and of hope, With -

touched by one an - oth - er, Lip ser - vice pay - ing
leads us to each oth - er; His voice we hear, his
lives for God are cho - sen; One is the grace with
hearts and hands u - nit - ed, Though each can hear the
bind us in in - ten - tion: Com - mun - ion must come
out whose food we per - ish, Show us the way by

to the name Of sis - ter or of broth - er.
word we read And yet his will we smoth - er.
which our Lord From sin our - selves can loos - en;
ban - quet song To which all are in - vit - ed.
first through you And not by our in - ven - tion.
which, as one, We'll share the One we cher - ish.

Text: John L. Bell b.1949, © 1993, Iona Community, GIA Publications, Inc., agent
Tune: BARBARA ALLEN, 8 7 8 7; English folk song; acc. by John Bell, b.1949, © 1993, Iona Community, GIA Publications, Inc., agent

Diverse in Culture, Nation, Race   536

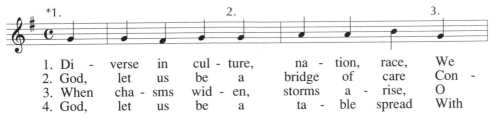

1. Di - verse in cul - ture, na - tion, race, We
2. God, let us be a bridge of care Con -
3. When cha - sms wid - en, storms a - rise, O
4. God, let us be a ta - ble spread With

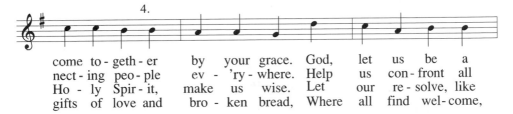

come to - geth - er by your grace. God, let us be a
nect - ing peo - ple ev - 'ry - where. Help us con - front all
Ho - ly Spir - it, make us wise. Let our re - solve, like
gifts of love and bro - ken bread, Where all find wel - come,

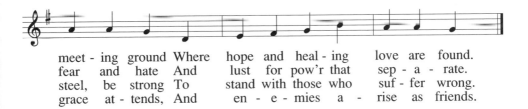

meet - ing ground Where hope and heal - ing love are found.
fear and hate And lust for pow'r that sep - a - rate.
steel, be strong To stand with those who suf - fer wrong.
grace at - tends, And en - e - mies a - rise as friends.

* May be sung as a two or four voice canon.

Text: Ruth Duck, b.1947, © 1992, GIA Publications, Inc.
Tune: TALLIS' CANON, LM; Thomas Tallis, c.1510-1583

537 Now the Feast and Celebration

Refrain

Now the feast and cel - e - bra-tion, all of cre - a-tion

sings for joy, to the God of life and love and free-dom;

praise and glo - ry for - ev - er - more!

Verse 1

1. Now is the feast of the Lamb once slain,

whose blood has freed and u - nit - ed us

D.C.

to be one great peo - ple of God.

Verse 2

2. Pow - er and rich-es, wis-dom and might, all hon - or and

D.C.

glo - ry to Christ for - ev - er.

Verse 3

3. For God has come to dwell with us, to make us

D.C.

peo-ple of God; to make all things new.

Text: Marty Haugen, b.1950
Tune: Marty Haugen, b.1950
© 1990, GIA Publications, Inc.

Come to Us   538

1. Come to me, come to us, you who are bur-dened.
2. Come to me, come to us, pil - grim or stran - ger,
3. Come to me, come to us, bro - ken or build-ing,

Come to the word, and come to the meal.
look - ing for change, or chal - lenge, or light.
Come with your chil-dren, your choic - es, your chains.

Come with-out ques - tion or pres - sure or price:
We are the peo - ple whose call - ing is care,
All are in - vit - ed to friend-ship or rest, to

Come, be em - braced by the bod - y of Christ.
bear - ers of mer - cy, nour-ished in prayer.
share in our strug-gle, our call and our quest.

Text: Rory Cooney, b.1952
Tune: Rory Cooney, b.1952
© 1986, North American Liturgy Resources

539 Gather Us In

1. Here in this place new light is stream-ing,
2. We are the young— our lives are a mys-t'ry,
3. Here we will take the wine and the wa-ter,
4. Not in the dark of build-ings con - fin - ing,

Now is the dark - ness van - ished a - way,
We are the old— who yearn for your face,
Here we will take the bread of new birth,
Not in some heav - en, light-years a - way, But

See in this space our fears and our dream-ings,
We have been sung through - out all of his - t'ry,
Here you shall call your sons and your daugh-ters,
here in this place the new light is shin - ing,

Brought here to you in the light of this
Called to be light to the whole hu - man
Call us a - new to be salt for the
Now is the King - dom, now is the

day.   Gath-er us in— the lost and for - sak - en,
race.   Gath-er us in— the rich and the haugh-ty,
earth.   Give us to drink the wine of com - pas - sion,
day.   Gath-er us in and hold us for ev - er,

Gath - er us in— the blind and the lame;
Gath - er us in— the proud and the strong;
Give us to eat the bread that is you;
Gath - er us in and make us your own;

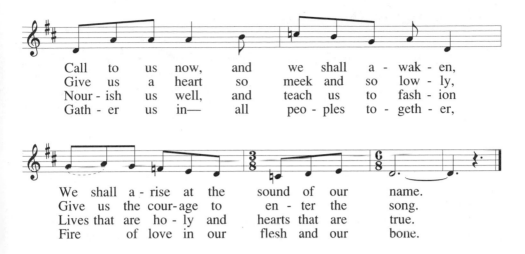

Call to us now, and we shall a - wak - en,
Give us a heart so meek and so low - ly,
Nour - ish us well, and teach us to fash - ion
Gath - er us in— all peo - ples to - geth - er,

We shall a - rise at the sound of our name.
Give us the cour - age to en - ter the song.
Lives that are ho - ly and hearts that are true.
Fire of love in our flesh and our bone.

Text: Marty Haugen, b.1950
Tune: GATHER US IN, Irregular; Marty Haugen, b.1950
© 1982, GIA Publications, Inc.

Jesus Christ, Yesterday, Today and Forever   540

Ostinato Refrain

Je - sus Christ, Je - sus Christ,

yes - ter - day, to - day and for - ev - er.

Text: Suzanne Toolan, SM, b.1927
Tune: Suzanne Toolan, SM, b.1927
© 1988, GIA Publications, Inc.

541 What Is This Place

1. What is this place where we are meet - ing?
2. Words from a - far, stars that are fall - ing,
3. And we ac - cept bread at his ta - ble,

On - ly a house, the earth its floor, Walls and a roof
Sparks that are sown in us like seed. Names for our God,
Bro - ken and shared, a liv - ing sign. Here in this world,

shel - ter - ing peo - ple, Win - dows for light, an o - pen door.
dreams, signs and won - ders Sent from the past are all we need.
dy - ing and liv - ing, We are each oth - er's bread and wine.

Yet it be - comes a bod - y that lives When we are
We in this place re - mem - ber and speak A - gain what
This is the place where we can re - ceive What we need

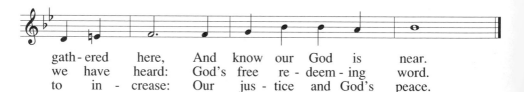

gath - ered here, And know our God is near.
we have heard: God's free re - deem - ing word.
to in - crease: Our jus - tice and God's peace.

Text: *Zomaar een dak boven wat hoofen;* Huub Oosterhuis, b.1933; trans. by David Smith, b.1933,
© 1967, Gooi en Sticht, bv., Baarn, The Netherlands. Exclusive English language agent: OCP Publications
Tune: KOMT NU MET ZANG, 9 8 9 8 9 66; Valerius' *Neder-landtsche gedenck-klanck;* acc. by Robert J. Batastini, b.1942,
© 1987, GIA Publications, Inc.

In Christ There Is a Table Set for All   542

1. Wel-come, all you no-ble saints of old,   As
2. El - ders, mar-tyrs, all are fall,ing down;   🎵
3. Beg - gars, lame, and har-lots al.so here;   Re -
4. Who is this who spreads the vic.t'ry feast?   🎵
5. Here he gives him-self to us as bread: 🎵
6. Wor - ship in the pres-ence of the Lord.   With
7. When at last this earth shall pass a - way.   When

now be - fore your ver - y eyes un - fold.   The
Pro - phets, pa - tri - archs are gath-'ring 'round.   What
pen - tant pub - li - cans are draw-ing near;   🎵
Who is this who makes our war - ring cease."   🎵
Here, as wine, we drink the blood he shed.   🎵
joy ful songs and hearts in one ac - cord.   And
Je - sus and his bride are one to stay.   The

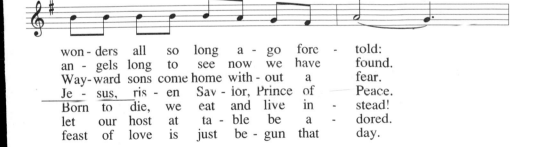

won - ders all so long a - go fore - told:
an - gels long to see now we have found.
Way-ward sons come home with - out a fear.
Je - sus, ris - en Sav - ior, Prince of Peace.
Born to die, we eat and live in - stead!
let our host at ta - ble be a - dored.
feast of love is just be - gun that day.

In Christ there is a ta - ble set for all.

Text: Robert J. Stamps
Tune: CENÉDIUS, Irregular, Robert J. Stamps
© 1972, Dawn Treader Music

543 We Gather in Worship

Verses

1. We gath-er in wor-ship, in prayer and in praise; The
2. We gath-er that jus-tice may roll like the streams, From
3. We gath-er to-geth-er, the Bod-y of Christ; No

bread here we break and the cup now we raise, For
all of our pris-ons, God's mer-cy re-deems; A
one is ex-clud-ed from Cal-va-ry's price. No

Je-sus lives in us and loves us and saves! We
home for the home-less, a strength for the weak, Good
class, sex, nor sta-tus, no creed, age nor race Is

trust in this prom-ise and are not a-fraid.
news for the poor and for all those who seek.
out-side as-sur-ance of God's end-less grace.

Refrain

Here in hope, here in peace, ev-'ry-one has a part. Here in faith, here in

grace, now we lift up our hearts. God's love is a riv-er that

Last time to coda ⊕

does not run dry; God's faith-ful-ness lifts like a full ris-ing tide.

⊕ Coda

tide. We gath-er in wor-ship, the Bod-y of Christ.

Text: Sylvia G. Dunstan, 1955-1993, © 1991, GIA Publications, Inc.
Tune: Bob Moore, b.1962, © 1993, GIA Publications, Inc.

545 Bless the Feast

1. Wel - come this mo - ment, this day of sweet
2. Here in this pres - ence, come to be
3. Free - dom to cap - tives, good news to the
4. Come to re - mem - ber who is the

grace, wel - come and en - ter this gath - er - ing
one, come to be gath - ered, eld - ers and
poor, light - ing the dark - ling, un - sight - ed, un -
one, come to re - mem - ber what has been

place. Wel - come these sym - bols, feast - ing and
young. Here in this pres - ence, gath - er - ing
sure. Tell - ing the sto - ry: love with - out
done. What name do we call you? From where is our

tell - ing; signs of thanks - giv - ing, signs of in -
force, pres - ent on pur - pose, life - giv - ing
end, breath of cre - a - tion, all life to de -
breath? Come to re - mem - ber life wrest - ed from

dwell - ing. Wel - come a priv - i - lege, sis - ter and
source. Now is this peo - ple, now to the
fend. Tell - ing the cov - e - nant sto - ry a -
death. Come to re - mem - ber in Euch - ar - ist

broth - er, shar - ing this in - break - ing light with each
last, fus - ing the fu - ture with pres - ent and
gain; ex - o - dus jour - ney for wom - en and
faith, this is the ban - quet, the cup we pro -

Come, Host of Heaven's High Dwelling Place 544

1. Come, Host of Heav'n's high dwell - ing place, Come,
2. Sur - round these walls with faith and love That
3. Bless and in - spire those gath - ered here With
4. Here may the los - er find his worth, The
5. Build, from the hu - man fab - ric, signs Of
6. So, to the Lord whose care en - folds The

earth's dis - put - ed guest; Find where we meet a
through the nights and days, When hu - man tongues from
pa - tience, hope, and peace, And all the joys that
stran - ger find a friend; Here may the hope - less
how your king - dom thrives, Of how the Ho - ly
world held in his hands, Be glo - ry, hon - or,

wel - come home, Stay here and take your rest.
speak - ing cease, These stones may ech - o praise.
know the depth In which all sor - rows cease.
find their faith And aim - less find an end.
Spir - it chang - es life By chang - ing lives.
pow'r and praise For which this com - p'ny stands.

Text: John L. Bell, b.1949, © 1989, Iona Community, GIA Publications, Inc., agent
Tune: ST. COLUMBA, 8 6 8 6; Irish traditional; arr. by John L. Bell, b.1949, © 1989, Iona Community, GIA Publications, Inc., agent

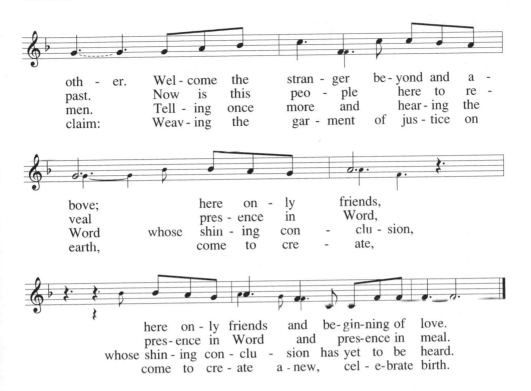

oth - er. Wel - come the stran - ger be - yond and a -
past. Now is this peo - ple here to re -
men. Tell - ing once more and hear - ing the
claim: Weav - ing the gar - ment of jus - tice on

bove; here on - ly friends,
veal pres - ence in Word,
Word whose shin - ing con - clu - sion,
earth, come to cre - ate,

here on - ly friends and be - gin - ning of love.
pres - ence in Word and pres - ence in meal.
whose shin - ing con - clu - sion has yet to be heard.
come to cre - ate a - new, cel - e - brate birth.

Text: James Hansen
Tune: James Hansen
© 1989, OCP Publications

546 Morning Has Broken

1. Morn-ing has bro-ken Like the first morn-ing, Black-bird has
2. Sweet the rain's new fall Sun-lit from heav-en, Like the first
3. Mine is the sun-light! Mine is the morn-ing Born of the

spo-ken Like the first bird. Praise for the sing-ing! Praise for the
dew-fall On the first grass. Praise for the sweet-ness Of the wet
one light E-den saw play! Praise with e - la-tion, Praise ev-'ry

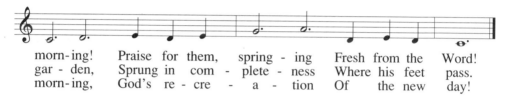

morn-ing! Praise for them, spring - ing Fresh from the Word!
gar-den, Sprung in com - plete-ness Where his feet pass.
morn-ing, God's re - cre - a - tion Of the new day!

Text: Eleanor Farjeon, 1881-1965, *The Children's Bells,* © David Higham Assoc., Ltd.
Tune: BUNESSAN, 5 5 5 4 D; Gaelic; acc. by Marty Haugen, b.1950, © 1987, GIA Publications, Inc.

This Day God Gives Me   547

1. This day God gives me Strength of high
2. This day God sends me Strength as my
3. God's way is my way, God's shield is
4. Ris - ing I thank you, Might - y and

heav - en, Sun and moon shin - ing,
guar - dian, Might to up - hold me,
'round me, God's host de - fends me,
strong One, King of cre - a - tion,

Flame in my hearth, Flash - ing of light - ning,
Wis - dom as guide. Your eyes are watch - ful,
Sav - ing from ill. An - gels of heav - en,
Giv - er of rest, Firm - ly con - fess - ing

Wind in its swift - ness, Depths of the
Your ears are lis - t'ning, Your lips are
Drive from me al - ways All that would
God in three Per - sons, One - ness of

o - cean, Firm - ness of earth.
speak - ing, Friend at my side.
harm me, Stand by me still.
God - head, Trin - i - ty blest.

Text: Ascribed to St. Patrick; James Quinn, SJ, b.1919, © 1969. Used by permission of Selah Publishing Co., Inc., Kingston, N.Y.
Tune: ANDREA, 5 5 5 4 D, David Haas, b.1957, © 1993, GIA Publications, Inc.

548 Today I Awake

1. To - day I a - wake and God is be - fore me. At
2. To - day I a - rise and Christ is be - side me. He
3. To - day I af - firm the Spir - it with - in me At
4. To - day I en - joy the Trin - i - ty round me, A -

night, as I dreamt, he sum-moned the day; For
walked through the dark to scat - ter new light. Yes,
wor - ship and work, in strug - gle and rest. The
bove and be - neath, be - fore and be - hind; The

God nev - er sleeps but pat - terns the morn - ing With
Christ is a - live, and beck - ons his peo - ple To
Spir - it in - spires all life which is chang - ing From
Mak - er, the Son, the Spir - it to - geth - er— They

slith - ers of gold or glo - ry in gray.
hope and to heal, re - sist and in - vite.
fear - ing to faith, from bro - ken to blest.
called me to life and call me their friend.

Text: John L. Bell, b.1949
Tune: SLITHERS OF GOLD, 11 10 11 10; John L. Bell, b.1949
© 1989, Iona Community, GIA Publications, Inc., agent

At Evening 549

1. Now it is eve - ning: Lights of the cit - y
2. Now it is eve - ning: Lit - tle ones sleep - ing
3. Now it is eve - ning: Food on the ta - ble
4. Now it is eve - ning: Here in our mect - ing

Bid us re - mem - ber Christ is our Light.
Bid us re - mem - ber Christ is our Peace.
Bids us re - mem - ber Christ is our Life.
May we re - mem - ber Christ is our Friend.

Man - y are lone - ly, Who will be neigh-bor?
Some are neg - lect - ed, Who will be neigh-bor?
Man - y are hun - gry, Who will be neigh-bor?
Some may be strang - ers, Who will be neigh-bor?

Where there is car - ing Christ is our Light.
Where there is car - ing Christ is our Peace.
Where there is shar - ing Christ is our Life.
Where there's a wel - come Christ is our Friend.

Text: Fred Pratt Green, b.1903, © 1974, Hope Publishing Co.
Tune: EVENING HYMN, 5 5 5 4 D; David Haas, b.1957, © 1985, GIA Publications, Inc.

550 Joyful Is the Dark

1. Joy-ful is the dark, ho - ly, hid - den God,
2. Joy-ful is the dark, Spir - it of the deep,
3. Joy-ful is the dark, shad - owed sta - ble floor;
4. Joy-ful is the dark, cool - ness of the tomb,
5. Joy-ful is the dark, depth of love di - vine,

Roll - ing cloud of night be - yond all nam - ing:
Wing-ing wild - ly o'er the world's cre - a - tion,
An - gels flick - er, God on earth con - fess - ing,
Wait - ing for the won - der of the morn-ing;
Roar-ing, loom-ing thun - der-cloud of glo - ry;

Maj - es - ty in dark-ness, En - er - gy of love,
Silk - en sheen of mid - night, plum - age black and bright,
As with ex - ul - ta - tion, Mar - y giv - ing birth,
Nev - er was that mid-night touched by dread and gloom:
Ho - ly, haunt-ing beau - ty, liv - ing, lov - ing God.

Word - in - Flesh, the mys - ter - y pro - claim-ing.
Swoop - ing with the beau - ty of a ra - ven.
Hails the in - fant cry of need and bless-ing.
Dark - ness was the cra - dle of the dawn-ing.
Hal - le - lu - jah! Sing and tell the sto - ry!

Text: Brian Wren, b.1936, © 1989, Hope Publishing Co.
Tune: JOYFUL DARKNESS, 10 10 11 10; Bob Moore, b.1962, © 1993, GIA Publications, Inc.

God of Day and God of Darkness   551

1. God of day and God of dark - ness, Now we
2. Still the na - tions curse the dark - ness, Still the
3. Show us Christ in one an - oth - er, Make us
4. You shall be the path that guides us, You the
5. Praise to you in day and dark - ness, You our

stand be - fore the night; As the shad - ows stretch and
rich op - press the poor; Still the earth is bruised and
ser - vants strong and true; Give us all your love of
light that in us burns; Shin - ing deep with - in all
source and you our end; Praise to you who love and

deep - en, Come and make our dark - ness bright. All cre -
bro - ken By the ones who still want more. Come and
jus - tice So we do what you would do. Let us
peo - ple, Yours the love that we must learn, For our
nur-ture us As a fa - ther, moth - er, friend. Grant us

a - tion still is groan - ing For the dawn - ing of your
wake us from our sleep - ing, So our hearts can - not ig -
call all peo - ple ho - ly, Let us pledge our lives a -
hearts shall wan - der rest - less 'Til they safe to you re -
all a peace-ful rest - ing, Let each mind and bod - y

might, When the Sun of peace and jus - tice
nore, All your peo - ple lost and bro - ken,
new, Make us one with all the low - ly,
turn; Find - ing you in one an - oth - er,
mend, So we rise re - freshed to - mor - row,

Fills the earth with ra - diant light.
All your chil - dren at our door.
Let us all be one in you.
We shall all your face dis - cern.
Hearts re - newed to King-dom tend.

Text: Marty Haugen, b.1950, © 1985, 1994, GIA Publications, Inc.
Tune: BEACH SPRING, 8 7 8 7 D; *The Sacred Harp,* 1844; harm. by Marty Haugen, b.1950, © 1985, GIA Publications, Inc.

552 Joyous Light of Heavenly Glory

1. Joy - ous light of heav - 'nly glo - ry, Lov - ing
2. In the stars that grace the dark - ness, In the
3. You who made the heav - en's splen - dor, Ev - 'ry

glow of God's own face, You who sing cre - a - tion's
blaz - ing sun of dawn, In the light of peace and
danc - ing star of night, Make us shine with gen - tle

sto - ry, Shine on ev - 'ry land and
wis - dom, We can hear your qui - et
jus - tice, Let us each re - flect your

race. Now as eve - ning falls a - round us, We shall
song. Love that fills the night with won - der, Love that
light. Might-y God of all cre - a - tion, Gen - tle

raise our songs to you, God of day - break, God of
warms the wea - ry soul, Love that bursts all chains a -
Christ who lights our way, Lov - ing Spir - it of sal -

shad - ows, Come and light our hearts a - new.
sun - der, Set us free and make us whole.
va - tion, Lead us on to end - less day.

Text: Marty Haugen, b.1950
Tune: JOYOUS LIGHT, 8 7 8 7 D; Marty Haugen, b.1950
© 1987, GIA Publications, Inc.

Our Darkness / La Ténèbre 553

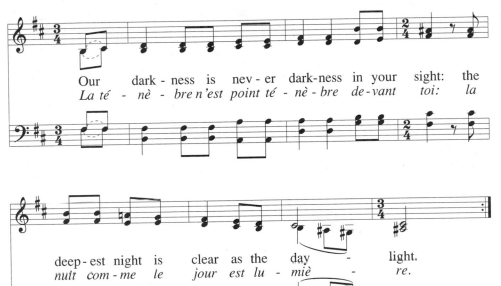

Our dark - ness is nev - er dark - ness in your sight: the
La té - nè - bre n'est point té - nè - bre de - vant toi: la

deep - est night is clear as the day - light.
nuit com - me le jour est lu - miè - re.

Text: Taizé Community
Tune: Jacques Berthier, 1923-1994
© 1991, Les Presses de Taizé, GIA Publications, Inc., agent

554 When the Lord in Glory Comes

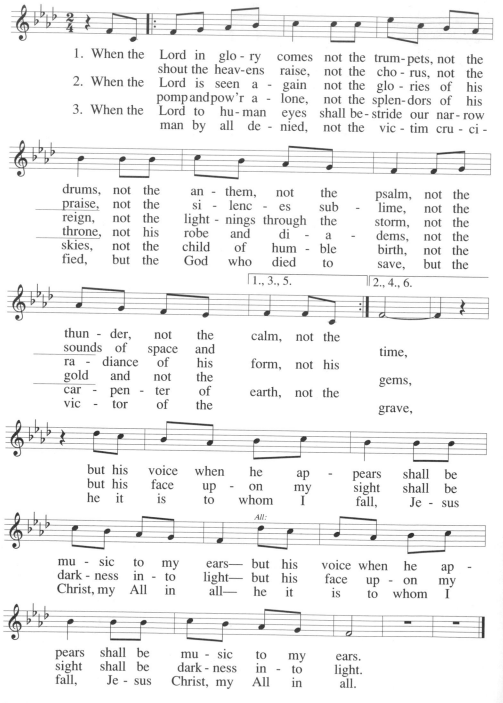

1. When the Lord in glo-ry comes not the trum-pets, not the
shout the heav-ens raise, not the cho-rus, not the
2. When the Lord is seen a-gain not the glo-ries of his
pomp and pow'r a-lone, not the splen-dors of his
3. When the Lord to hu-man eyes shall be-stride our nar-row
man by all de-nied, not the vic-tim cru-ci-

drums, not the an-them, not the psalm, not the
praise, not the si-lenc-es sub-lime, not the
reign, not the light-nings through the storm, not the
throne, not his robe and di-a-dems, not the
skies, not the child of hum-ble birth, not the
fied, but the God who died to save, but the

1., 3., 5.

thun-der, not the calm, not the
sounds of space and
ra-diance of his form, not his
gold and not the
car-pen-ter of earth, not the
vic-tor of the

2., 4., 6.

time,

gems,

grave,

but his voice when he ap-pears shall be
but his face up-on my sight shall be
he it is to whom I fall, Je-sus

All:

mu-sic to my ears— but his voice when he ap-
dark-ness in-to light— but his face up-on my
Christ, my All in all— he it is to whom I

pears shall be mu-sic to my ears.
sight shall be dark-ness in-to light.
fall, Je-sus Christ, my All in all.

Text: Timothy Dudley-Smith, b.1926, © 1967, Hope Publishing Co.
Tune: ST. JOHN'S, 77 77 77 D; Bob Moore, b.1962, © 1993, GIA Publications, Inc.

Soon and Very Soon 555

1. Soon and ver - y soon   we are goin' to see the King,
2. No   more cry - in' there   we are goin' to see the King,
3. No   more dy - in' there   we are goin' to see the King,
4. Soon and ver - y soon   we are goin' to see the King,

Soon and ver - y soon   we are goin' to see the King,
No more cry - in' there   we are goin' to see the King,
No more dy - in' there   we are goin' to see the King,
Soon and ver - y soon   we are goin' to see the King,

Soon and ver - y soon   we are goin' to see the King,
No more cry - in' there   we are goin' to see the King,   Hal-le -
No more dy - in' there   we are goin' to see the King,
Soon and ver - y soon   we are goin' to see the King,

1., 2.

lu - jah, Hal-le - lu - jah, we're goin' to see the King!

3., 4.

Hal - le - lu - jah, Hal - le - lu -

jah, Hal - le - lu - jah, Hal - le - lu - jah.

Text: Andraé Crouch
Tune: Andraé Crouch
© 1976, Bud John Songs, Inc./Crouch Music/ASCAP

556 The Day Is Near

1. For words and deeds en-shrined in gran-ite tombs, For
2. The word of God or-dains the day is near That
3. For all who dare re-ly on words and bread, A

all en-throned in re-gal splen-dor; For
all who weep should turn to laugh-ter; That
dwin-dling flame nev-er ex-tin-guished; Who

pow'r that lives on fear and clash of arms, Whose
home-less peo-ple find a dwell-ing place, That
cling to dreams and an-cient prom-is-es, How -

faith a-bides in steel and sil-ver. All things held in es-ti -
thirst and hun-ger should be end-ed. Then the bar-ren shall be
ev-er hard the task to do so. They may groan be-neath their

ma-tion: God's word leaves them all con -
fruit-ful; Or-phans shall them-selves be
bur-dens, And their strug-gle waged in

found-ed. In our weak-ness he may
fa-thers. Truth and mer-cy shall em -
se-cret. They may yet a-wake to

lend his strength And face the might-y with his jus-tice.
brace at last And peace will reign the whole world o-ver.
greet the dawn And not be-lieve what they are see-ing.

Text: Huub Oosterhuis, b.1933; trans. by Tony Barr, b.1945; rev. by Tom Conry
Tune: Bernard Huijbers, b.1922
© 1973, Gooi en Sticht, bv., Baarn, The Netherlands
Exclusive English-language agent: OCP Publications

My Lord Will Come Again 557

Refrain

My Lord will come a - gain, my Lord, my

Lord will come a - gain, My Lord will come a -

gain, my Lord will come a - gain! My Lord will come a -

gain, my Lord, and the king-dom will have no end! A -

men! A - men! My Lord will come a - gain!

Verses

1. I will bless the Lord at all times! I will praise God with all my life!
   For the Lord our God is risen, and death will be no more!
   Amen, Amen, My Lord will come again!

2. I will sing to God a new song: Make music to my God while I live!
   For the Lord our God is with us, and death will be no more!
   Amen, Amen, My Lord will come again!

3. I will see a new heaven and new earth! God will make a home within our hearts!
   And we will be God's people, and death will be no more!
   Amen, Amen, My Lord will come again!

4. God will wipe all tears from our eyes! The world of the past will be gone!
   Sadness, pain, and mourning: these will be no more!
   Amen, Amen, My Lord will come again!

Text: David Haas, b.1957
Tune: David Haas, b.1957
© 1991, GIA Publications, Inc.

558 We Shall Rise Again

1. Come to me, all you wea - ry, with your bur - dens and
2. Though we walk through the dark - ness, e - vil we do not
3. We de - pend on God's mer - cy, mer - cy which nev - er
4. Do not fear death's do - min - ion, look be - yond earth and
5. At the door there to greet us, mar - tyrs, an - gels, and

pain. Take my yoke on your shoul - ders and
fear. You are walk - ing be - side us with your
fades. We re - mem - ber our cov - e - nant and the
grave. See the bright - ness of Je - sus shin - ing
saints, And our fam - 'ly and loved ones, ev - 'ry -

learn from me: I am gen - tle and hum - ble,
rod and your staff. On - ly good - ness and kind - ness
prom - ise Je - sus made: If we die with Christ Je - sus,
out to light our way. Lov - ing Fa - ther and Spir - it,
one freed from their chains. We shall feel their ac - cep - tance,

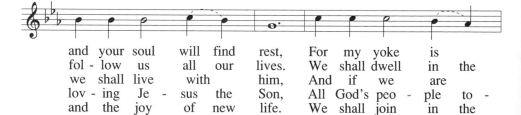

and your soul will find rest, For my yoke is
fol - low us all our lives. We shall dwell in the
we shall live with him, And if we are
lov - ing Je - sus the Son, All God's peo - ple to -
and the joy of new life. We shall join in the

eas - y and my bur - den is light.
Lord's house for so man - y years to come!
faith - ful, we shall reign with him!
geth - er, we shall live on as one!
gath - er - ing, re - u - nit - ed in God's love!

We shall rise a - gain on the last day with the faith - ful, rich and

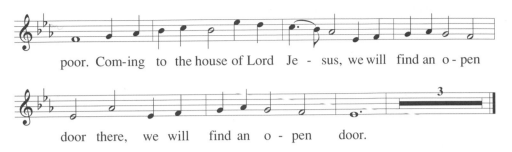

poor. Com-ing to the house of Lord Je - sus, we will find an o - pen

door there, we will find an o - pen door.

Text: Matthew 11:29-30, Psalm 23, John 11, 2 Timothy 2; Jeremy Young, b.1948
Tune: RESURRECTION; Irregular with refrain; Jeremy Young, b.1948
©1987, GIA Publications, Inc.

Steal Away to Jesus   559

Refrain

Steal a-way, steal a-way, steal a-way to Je - sus!

Steal a-way, steal a-way home, I ain't got long to stay here.

Verses

1. My Lord, he calls me, He calls me by the thun - der; The
2. Green trees are bend-ing, Poor sin - ners stand a trem-bling; The
3. My Lord, he calls me, He calls me by the light-ning; The

D.C.

trum-pet sounds with - in my soul; I ain't got long to stay here.

Text: African-American spiritual
Tune: African-American spiritual

560 Shall We Gather at the River

1. Shall we gath - er at the riv - er,
2. On the mar - gin of the riv - er,
3. Ere we reach the shin - ing riv - er,
4. Soon we'll reach the shin - ing riv - er,

Where bright an - gel feet have trod;
Wash - ing up its sil - ver spray,
Lay we ev - 'ry bur - den down;
Soon our pil - grim - age will cease,

With its crys - tal tide for ev - er Flow - ing
We will walk and wor - ship ev - er, All the
Grace our spir - its will de - liv - er, And pro -
Soon our hap - py hearts will quiv - er With the

by the throne of God?
hap - py gold - en day.
vide a robe and crown.
mel - o - dy of peace.

Yes, we'll gath - er at the riv - er, The

beau - ti - ful, the beau - ti - ful riv - er; Gath - er with the saints at the

riv - er That flows by the throne of God.

Text: Robert Lowry, 1826-1899
Tune: Robert Lowry, 1826-1899

God   of   Is - ra - el,   Who
- ing   the   cov - e - nant,   God
- er   mer - cy,   God   will   send   The

love   and   pow'r,   Who   rais - es   from   the
cues   us   from   fear,   That   we   might   serve   in
- spring   from   on   high,   Our   ris - ing   sun,   the

roy - al   house   De - liv - 'rance   in   this   hour.   Through
ho - li - ness   And   peace   from   year   to   year;   And
light   of   life   For   those   who   sit   and   sigh.   God

ho - ly   proph - ets   God   has   sworn   To
you,   my   child,   shall   go   be - fore   To
comes   to   guide   our   way   to   peace,   That

free   us   from   a - larm,   To   save   us   from   the
preach,   to   proph - e - sy,   That   all   may   know   the
death   shall   reign   no   more.   Sing   prais - es   to   the

heav - y   hand   Of   all   who   wish   us   harm.
ten - der   love,   The   grace   of   God   most   high.
Ho - ly   One!   O   wor - ship   and   a - dore!

Text: *Benedictus*, Luke 1:68-79; Ruth Duck, b.1947, © 1992, GIA Publications, Inc.
Tune: FOREST GREEN, CMD; English; harm. by Michael Joncas, b.1951, © 1987, GIA Publications, Inc.

PRESENTATION OF THE LORD

1. Now   let   your   ser - vant
2. Be - fore   the   peo - ples   you
3. Child,   you   are   cho - sen   as
4. Now   let   us   sing   our   Sav - io

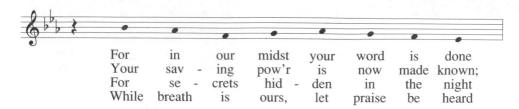

Let   praise   and   bless - ing   here   in - crease;
Your   way   of   life   which   all   may   share.
To   test   the   hu - man   heart   and   mind;
And   tell   God's   good - ness   all   our   days.

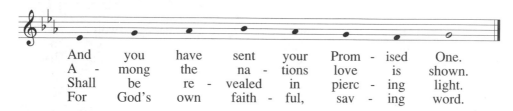

For   in   our   midst   your   word   is   done
Your   sav - ing   pow'r   is   now   made   known;
For   se - crets   hid - den   in   the   night
While   breath   is   ours,   let   praise   be   heard

And   you   have   sent   your   Prom - ised   One.
A - mong   the   na - tions   love   is   shown.
Shall   be   re - vealed   in   pierc - ing   light.
For   God's   own   faith - ful,   sav - ing   word.

Text: *Nunc dimittis,* Luke 2:29-35; Ruth Duck, b. 1947, © 1992 GIA Publications, Inc.
Tune: CONDITOR ALME SIDERUM, LM; Mode IV; acc. by Gerard Farrell, OSB, b. 1919, © 1986, GIA Publications, Inc.

569 Give Thanks to God on High

1. Give thanks to God on high For saints of
2. Their vi - sion long ful - filled, Our prayer is
3. New tasks to - day are ours Who serve a
4. Give thanks to God on high For all the

oth - er days, Whose hope it was to
still the same; Up - on their work of
world of pain, New calls to chal - lenge
fu - ture sends, In praise of Christ to

live and die In love's con - sum - ing blaze,
faith to build, Their word of truth pro - claim,
all our pow'rs Of heart and hand and brain,
live and die Who calls his ser - vants friends,

For Christ and his king-dom, His glo - ry and his praise.
For Christ and his king-dom, And for his ho - ly name.
For Christ and his king-dom, While life and breath re - main.
For Christ and his king-dom, Whose glo - ry nev - er ends.

Text: Timothy Dudley-Smith, b.1926, © 1985, Hope Publishing Co.
Tune: BALDWIN, 6 6 8 6 6 6; James J. Chepponis, b.1956, © 1987, GIA Publications, Inc.

Magnificat 568

Refrain

All that I am sings of the God who brings new life to birth in me. My spir-it soars on the wings of my Lord.

Verses

1. My soul gives glory to the Lord, rejoicing in my saving God,
   Who looks upon me in my state, and all the world will call me blest;
   For God works marvels in my sight, and holy, holy is God's name!

2. God's mercy is from age to age, on those who follow in fear;
   Whose arm is power and strength, and scatters all the proud of heart;
   Who casts the mighty from their thrones and raises up the lowly ones!

3. God fills the starving with good things, the rich are left with empty hands;
   Protecting all the faithful ones, rememb'ring Israel with mercy,
   The promise known to those before and to their children for ever!

Text: Luke 1:46-55; David Haas, b.1957
Tune: David Haas, b.1957
© 1990, GIA Publications, Inc.

567 All Who Claim the Faith of Jesus

1. All who claim the faith of Je - sus Sing the
2. Bless - ed were the cho - sen peo - ple Out of
3. There-fore let all faith - ful peo - ple Sing the
4. "Mag - ni - fy, my soul, God's great - ness; In my

won - ders that were done When the love of God the
whom the Lord did come; Bless - ed was the land of
hon - or of her name; Let the Church, in her fore -
Sav - ior I re - joice; All the ag - es call me

Fa - ther O'er our sins the vic - t'ry
prom - ise Fash - ioned for his earth - ly
shad - owed, Part in her thanks - giv - ing
bless - ed, In his praise I lift my

won, When God made the Vir - gin
home; But more bless - ed far the
claim; What Christ's moth - er sang in
voice; God has cast down all the

Mar - y Moth - er of the on - ly Son.
moth - er, She who bore him in her womb.
glad - ness Let Christ's peo - ple sing the same;
might - y, And the low - ly are his choice."

Text: Vincent Stuckey Stratton Coles, 1845-1929, alt.; St. 4, F. Bland Tucker, 1895-1984
Tune: TILLFLYKT, 8 7 8 7 8 7; *Sionstoner,* 1889; harm. by Marty Haugen, b.1950, © 1987, GIA Publications, Inc.

There Is Nothing Told 566

Verses

1.-6. There is noth - ing   told a-bout this wom - an,   But that

she   had   once be-come en - gaged,   And an
she   had   brought in - to the   world,   In the
she   had   searched for three long   days   For her
she   at   Ca - na was a   guest,   And that
she   was   stand - ing by the   cross   When her
she   was   one   in prayer with   those   Up - on

an - gel   ad - dressed her and   said: "You   are
land   of   Ju - de - a, her   son;   For some
child   who   was   bus - y else - where,   And her
Je - sus changed wa - ter to   wine,   So   that
son   stretched his   arms   out on   high,   And met
whom   tongues of   fire   did de - scend,   And the

bless - ed   a - mong   all   your   kind."
shep - herds have passed   on   this   tale.
heart   then   did   not   un - der - stand.
all   might   be - lieve   who   he   was.
death   with   a   thief   on   each   side.
Spir - it   bap - tized   them   with   flame.

Refrain

On this   day   all   earth and all   par - a - dise   join in

nam - ing you hap - py and   blessed;   Vir - gin

Mar - y,   bless - ed   are   you.

Text: Didier Rimaud
Tune: BENEDICTA ES, 10 9 9 9 with refrain; Christopher Willcock
© 1988, Christopher Willcock

565 Ave Maria

Verses

1. Hail Mar - y full of grace, the
2. Ho - ly Mar - y moth-er of God, the

Lord is with you.
Lord is with you.

Bless - ed are you a - mong all wo - men,
Pray for us sin - ners, pray for us sin - ners,

Blest is the fruit of your womb.
Now and at the hour of our death.

Refrain

Je - sus, formed in your faith, A - ve Ma - ri - a al - le - lu -

ia. Je - sus, born in your love, A - ve Ma -

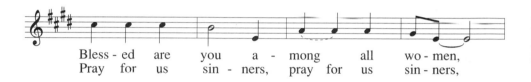

ri - a al - le - lu - ia.

Text: Hail Mary; additional text by Dan Kantor, b.1960
Tune: Dan Kantor, b.1960; arr. by Rob Glover
© 1993, GIA Publications, Inc.

Verse 1

1. You were cho - sen by the Fa - ther;

you were cho - sen for the Son.

You were cho - sen from all wom - en and for

D.S.

wom - an, shin - ing one.

Verse 2

2. Bless - ed are you a - mong wom - en,

blest in turn all wom - en, too. Bless - ed

they with peace - ful spir - its.

D.S.

Bless - ed they with gen - tle hearts.

Text: *Hail Mary,* alt; Carey Landry
Tune: Carey Landry; arr. by Martha Lesinski, alt.
© 1975, Carey Landry and North American Liturgy Resources

564 Hail Mary: Gentle Woman

Hail Mar - y, full of grace, the
Lord is with you. Bless-ed are you a - mong
wo - men, and blest is the fruit of your womb, Je - sus.
Ho-ly Mar - y, Moth-er of God,
pray for us sin - ners now and at the hour of
death. A - men.

Refrain
Gen - tle wom-an, qui-et light, morn-ing
star, so strong and bright, gen - tle
Moth - er, peace - ful dove, teach us
wis - dom; teach us love.

I Sing a Maid 563

1. I sing a maid of ten - der years To whom an an - gel came, And knelt, as to a might - y queen, And bowed bright wings of flame: A na - tion's hope in her re - ply, This maid of match - less grace; For God's own son be - came her child, And she his rest - ing place.

2. She watched him grow to man - hood's strength To meet his des - tin - y, And when the dan - ger of his truth Brought him to Cal - va - ry, She stood by him all pow - er - less To ease his dy - ing pain, 'Til in the dark - est hour of all, She held her son a - gain.

3. And if the song had end - ed then, Our eyes would fill with tears, But ah! the song had just be - gun To ech - o down the years! Now lift your voic - es, hearts and souls, To sing with one ac - cord To hon - or Mar - y, Moth - er of The Christ, the Ris - en Lord!

Text: M. D. Ridge, b.1938, © 1987, GIA Publications, Inc.
Tune: THE FLIGHT OF THE EARLS; 14 14 14 14; trad. Celtic melody; harm. by Michael Joncas, b.1951, © 1987, GIA Publications, Inc.

Litany of the Saints 570

Repeat each invocation immediately after the priest or cantor:

Lord, have mer-cy. Christ, have

mer-cy. Lord, have mer-cy.

(Saint Invocation) 1.- 4. Pray for us, Pray for us.
("Lord, be merciful.") 5. Save your peo-ple. Save your peo-ple.
("Lord, give new life.") 6. Hear our prayer. Hear our prayer.

Pray for us. Pray for us Pray for
Save your peo-ple. Save your peo-ple. Save your
Hear our prayer. Hear our prayer. Hear our

us. Pray for us. Pray for us.
peo-ple. Save your peo-ple. Save your peo-ple.
prayer. Hear our prayer. Hear our prayer.

Pray for us. 1.- 4. All you ho-ly
Save your peo-ple. 5.- 6. Christ, hear us;
Hear our prayer.

men and wo-men, pray for us.
Lord Je-sus, hear our prayer.

Text: Litany of the Saints
Tune: John D. Becker, © 1987, published by OCP Publications

571 Covenant Hymn

1. Wher - ev - er you go, I will fol - low, Wher -
2. What - ev - er you dream, I am with you, When
3. And though you should fall, you will find me, When
4. Wher - ev - er you die, I will be there To
5. Wher - ev - er you go, I will fol - low, Be -

ev - er you live is my home. Though
stars call your name in the night. Though
no oth - er friend can you claim, When
sing you to sleep with a psalm, To
hold! The ho - ri - zon shines clear. The

days be of bless - ing or sor - row, Though
shad - ows and mist cloud the fu - ture, To -
foes beat you down or be - tray you And
soothe you with tales of our jour - ney, Your
pos - si - ble gleams like a cit - y: To -

house be of can - vas or stone, Though
geth - er we bear there a light. Like
oth - ers de - sert you in shame. When
fears and your doubts I will calm. We'll
geth - er we've noth - ing to fear. So

E - den be lost to the past, Though
A - bram and Sar - ah we stand, With
home and dreams aren't e - nough, And
live when jour - neys are done For -
speak with words bold and true The

moun - tains be - fore us be vast, Wher -
on - ly a prom - ise in hand. But
you run a - way from my love, I'll
ev - er in mem - 'ry as one. And
mes - sage my heart speaks to you. You

ev - er	you	go,	I	am	with you,	I
lead where	you	dream:	I	will	fol - low.	To
raise	you	from where	you	have	fall - en.	
we will	be	bur - ied	to -	geth - er,	And
won't	be	a - lone,	I	have	prom - ised.	Wher -

nev - er	will	leave	you	a -	lone.
dream	with	you	is	my	de - light.
Faith - ful	to	you	is	my	name.
wak - en	to	greet	a	new	dawn.
ev - er	you	go,	I	am	here.

Text: Ruth 1:16; Rory Cooney, b 1952
Tune: Gary Daigle, b.1957
© 1993, GIA Publications, Inc.

Baptized in Water 572

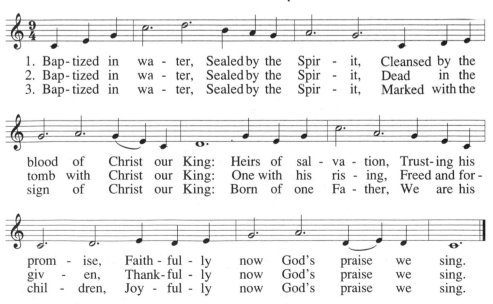

1. Bap-tized in	wa - ter,	Sealed by the	Spir - it,	Cleansed by the
2. Bap-tized in	wa - ter,	Sealed by the	Spir - it,	Dead in the
3. Bap-tized in	wa - ter,	Sealed by the	Spir - it,	Marked with the

blood of	Christ our King:	Heirs of	sal - va - tion,	Trust-ing his
tomb with	Christ our King:	One with his	ris - ing,	Freed and for -
sign of	Christ our King:	Born of one	Fa - ther,	We are his

prom - ise,	Faith - ful - ly	now	God's	praise	we	sing.
giv - en,	Thank-ful - ly	now	God's	praise	we	sing.
chil - dren,	Joy - ful - ly	now	God's	praise	we	sing.

Text: Michael Saward, b.1932, © 1982, Hope Publishing Co.
Tune: BUNESSAN, 5 5 8 D; Gaelic melody; acc. by Marty Haugen, b.1950, © 1987, GIA Publications, Inc.

573 Alive in Christ Jesus

Refrain

A - live! A - live in Christ Je - sus! A - live!

New life from the dead! A - live! For death has no

pow - er! We are a - live with God!

Verse 1

All:

1. Are you not a - ware?

Cantor:

We who were
We were

born in Christ Je - sus were born in - to his death.
bur - ied with Je - sus that we too might live?

All:

Are you not a - ware?

Cantor:

We are u - nit - ed with

him, so that we will rise now with him.

D.C.

Verse 2

All:

2. This we know:

Cantor:

That our
If we have
The

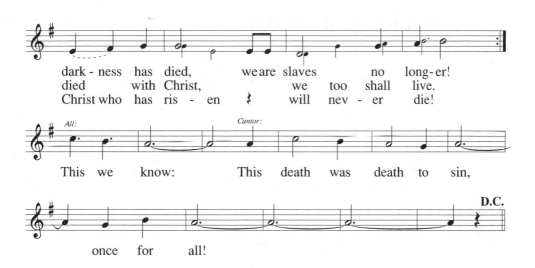

dark - ness has died, we are slaves no long-er!
died with Christ, we too shall live.
Christ who has ris - en will nev - er die!

All: This we know: *Cantor:* This death was death to sin,

D.C.

once for all!

Text: Romans 8; David Haas, b.1957
Tune: David Haas, b.1957
© 1991, GIA Publications, Inc.

Christ Will Be Your Strength 574

Christ will be your strength! Learn to know and fol-low him!

Text: David Haas, b.1957
Tune: David Haas, b.1957
© 1988, GIA Publications, Inc.

575 For the Life of the World

Refrain

For the life of the world, we will stand to - geth - er, we will serve the

Lord. For the life of the world, we will cry for jus - tice, and

ev - 'ry heart will sing that Je - sus Christ is Lord!

Verses

1. We walk to - geth - er to be chil - dren of light,
2. We are em - pow - ered by the love of Christ,
3. We are the cho - sen peo - ple God has called,
4. The lost and bro - ken will be healed from their shame,
1. *Nos da la fuer - za el a - mor de Dios.*
2. *Hoy lu - char - e - mos por jus - ti - cia, Se - ñor.*
3. *Glo - ri - fi - que - mos al Se - ñor, Je - sus.*

our God calls each of us by name!
whose life has con - quered sin and death!
the life we live is not our own!
the poor will see the face of God!
Su vi - da qui - ta nues - tro mal.
Te ser - vir - e - mos y por fin.
Can - tan - do le - van - té - mos - nos,

Christ moves with - in us, we are God's work of art!
There is no oth - er name but Je - sus the Lord!
If we will die with Christ, then we will be free!
Sent by the Spir - it, we are called to serve!
No que - da na - die me - nos el Se - ñor.
Ten - dre - mos paz sin ham - bre ni do - lor.
Por - que él vie - ne ¡a - le - gré - mo - nos!

D.C.

1.-4. We live no long - er for our - selves!
1.-3. ¡So - mos el pueb - lo de Dios!

Text: David Haas, b.1957; Spanish verses by Jeffrey Judge
Tune: David Haas, b.1957; acc. by Jeanne Cotter, b.1964
© 1993, GIA Publications, Inc.

I've Just Come from the Fountain 576

I've just come from the foun-tain, I've just come from the

foun - tain, Lord, I've just come from the foun - tain, His

O broth-ers, I love Je - sus, O
name's so sweet. O sis - ters, I love Je - sus, O
Been drink-ing from the foun-tain, Been

broth-ers, I love Je - sus, O broth-ers, I love
sis - ters, I love Je - sus, O sis - ters, I love
drink-ing from the foun-tain, Been drink-ing from the

Je - sus,
Je - sus, His name's so sweet.
foun-tain,

Text: African-American spiritual
Tune: African-American spiritual

577 Awake, O Sleeper

Refrain

A - wake, O sleep-er, a - rise from death, a - ban-don the shad-ows of night; the wind of the spir-it shall be your breath, and Christ will fill you with light.

Verses 1, 2

1. Once you were dark-ness, once you were lost in the shad-ows. Once you were dark-ness, now you are chil-dren of light.

2. Live as God's peo-ple, live as God's jus-tice and mer-cy, filled with com - pas-sion, filled with the pow-er of love.

Verse 3

3. Shine out with the splen-dor of love, shine with jus-tice and right-eous-ness. Sing the mu-sic your spir-it has heard, the songs of glo-ry and light.

Text: Ephesians 5; Marty Haugen, b.1950
Tune: Marty Haugen, b.1950
© 1987, GIA Publications, Inc.

Little Heart of Ages 578

1. Lit - tle heart of a - ges, spir - it child;
2. Ev - 'ry lamb is yours, Lord, ev - 'ry one,
3. Wel-come to the chil - dren on their way,

Heav - en - ly our dream - er, here you lie;
Leap-ing out of time now, to the sun;
Bless-ings to all pil - grims on this day;

Light is all a - bout you, Pet - al now e - ter -
Nev - er was a soul born that was not a treas -
Glo - ry to the light that leads us to the king -

nal; Lit - tle heart of a - ges,
ure; Ev - 'ry lamb is yours, Lord,
dom; Wel - come to the chil - dren

spir - it child.
ev - 'ry one.
on their way.

Text: Michael Dennis Browne
Tune: John Foley, SJ, b. 1939
© 1993, GIA Publications, Inc.

579 Sign Me Up

Refrain

Sign me up, Sign me up for the Chris-tian ju-bi-lee,

Write my name, Write my name on the roll

For, I've been changed, I've been changed since the

Lord has lift-ed me, I want to be

read-y when Je-sus comes.

Verse 1

1. When Je-sus comes, oh, the trum-pet will sound

loud, When my Sav-ior comes, all the

saints in Christ shall rise, Oh, I'm glad I've been

changed since he lift-ed me, I

want to be read-y when Je-sus comes.

Verse 2

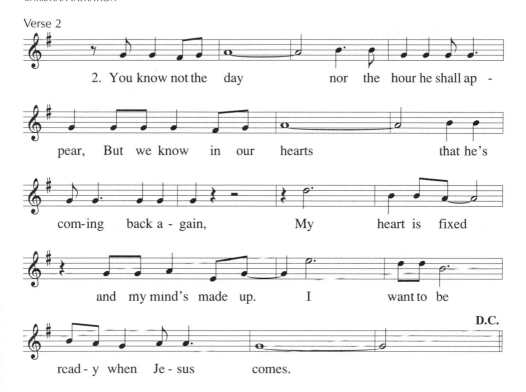

2. You know not the day nor the hour he shall ap -

pear, But we know in our hearts that he's

com-ing back a - gain, My heart is fixed

and my mind's made up. I want to be

D.C.

read - y when Je - sus comes.

580 We Are God's Work of Art /
Somos la Creación de Dios

Refrain

We are God's work of art, fash-ioned in
So-mos la crea - ción de Dios, co - mo en

Christ, fash-ioned to shine with good-ness and light.
Cris - to, el nos hi - zo bri - llar con su luz.

As it was from the start— formed by this
A - sí fue al co - men - zar, con gran a -

great, great love, we are God's
mor, el nos for - mó, so - mos gran - des

great, won - drous work of art.
o - bras del ar - te del Se - ñor.

Verses

1. When we were dead in sin, you brought us to life in Christ,
   and raised us up, up to the heavens.

1. *Cuando en pecado morimos,*
   nos trajo la vida en Cristo y nos llevó a las alturas.

2. How rich is the grace of God, how strong is the love of God,
   to send us Christ for our salvation.

2. *Qué rica_es la gracia de Dios qué fuerte es su amor,*
   envió a Cristo para nuestra salvacion.

3. We are strangers no longer, outcasts no longer,
   we are saints in the house of God.

3. *No somos extranjeros, no mas desterrados,*
   somos santos en la casa del Señor.

4. We are the temple that our God has fashioned,
   in Christ we are the dwelling place of love.

4. *Somos el templo que_el Señor hizo,*
   en Cristo somos morada de su_amor.

5. From the foundation of the world you have chosen us,
   destined in love to be your sons and daughters,
   You have revealed to us the myst'ry of grace, to unite all things in Christ.

5. *Desde_el principio del mundo nos escogiste el destino de ser tus hijos y tus hijas.*
   Nos reveló el misterio de gracia, para unir todas las cosas en Cristo.

Text: Ephesians 2:1, 4-7, 10, 19, 21-22; Marty Haugen, b.1950; Spanish trans. by Donna Peña, b.1955
Tune: Marty Haugen, b.1950
© 1991, GIA Publications, Inc.

There Is One Lord 581

Ostinato Refrain

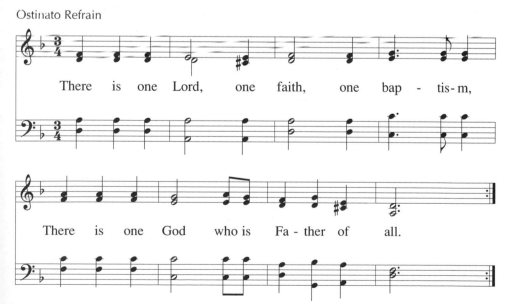

Text: Ephesians 4. Taizé Community, 1984
Tune: Jacques Berthier, b.1923
© 1984, Les Presses de Taizé, GIA Publications, Inc., agent

582 You Are God's Work of Art

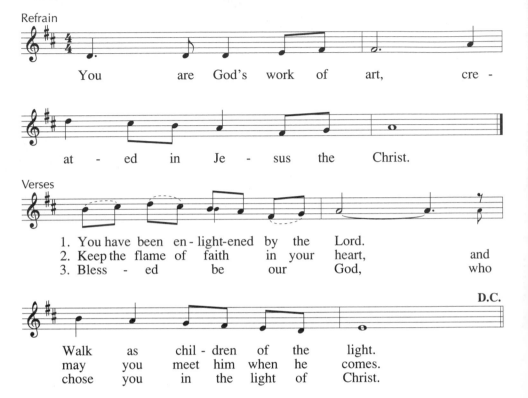

Refrain

You are God's work of art, cre -
at - ed in Je - sus the Christ.

Verses

1. You have been en - light-ened by the Lord.
2. Keep the flame of faith in your heart, and
3. Bless - ed be our God, who

D.C.

Walk as chil - dren of the light.
may you meet him when he comes.
chose you in the light of Christ.

Text: Ephesians 1:4, 2:10, *Rite of Baptism,* David Haas, b.1957
Tune: David Haas, b.1957
© 1988, GIA Publications, Inc.

Wade in the Water 583

Refrain

Wade in the wa-ter, wade in the wa-ter, chil-dren, wade in the wa-ter,
God's a gon - na trou - ble the wa - ter.

Verses

Cantor:

1. See that host all dressed in white,
2. See that band all dressed in red,
3. Look o - ver yon - der, what do I see?
4. If you don't be - lieve I've been re - deemed,

All: *Cantor:*

God's a gon - na trou - ble the wa - ter; The
God's a gon - na trou - ble the wa - ter; Looks
God's a gon - na trou - ble the wa - ter; The
God's a gon - na trou - ble the wa - ter; Just

lead - er looks like the Is - ra - el - ite,
like the band that Mo - ses led,
Ho - ly Ghost a com - in' on me,
fol - low me down to Jor - dan's stream,

All: **D.C.**

God's a gon - na trou - ble the wa - ter.
God's a gon - na trou - ble the wa - ter.
God's a gon - na trou - ble the wa - ter.
God's a gon - na trou - ble the wa - ter.

Text: African-American spiritual
Tune: African-American spiritual; harm. by Diana Kodner, b.1957, © 1994, GIA Publications, Inc.

584   Song of the Chosen

Refrain

We are God's cho-sen peo-ple, we are the

saints.   We   are   God's work of art

signed and   set   a - part.   Let us   sing!

Verses 1, 3, 5

1. Re - joice, you saints, in God, for praise from you is
3. God speaks and it is done, whose Word ex - ist - ence
5. No king is safe from death, though ar - mies guard him

right!   Mu - sic mak - ers, sing by day, and
gives.   So   let the world its   God re - vere, and
well.   No   war - rior, armed and   mount - ed strong can

play with all your might!   Sing God a
hear the One who lives.   Your won - drous
long es - cape from hell.   But see! the

new song; play well up - on your strings, for right and jus - tice
plan, O God, is known to you a - lone, and hap - py is the
eyes of God gaze earth-ward, west and east, to snatch the poor from

D.C.

our God loves; whose word does won-drous   things.
peo - ple you have cho - sen for your   own!
fam - ine's thrall, and call them to the   feast.

Verses 2, 4, 6

2. God's kind-ness fills our world, whose word the
4. From heav-en, our God sees the ways of
6. So wait up-on the One who is our

heav-ens forms, Whose sing-ing mouth, to
hu-man-kind. God knows the dwell-ers
help and shield. Re-joice, you saints, in

north and south, has spo-ken stars and storms, Whose
of our globe, and probes the heart and mind. No,
that great name, pro-claim God's might re-vealed.

might for-bids the waves to tres-pass on the land
none es-capes the glance of God who reigns on high,
May your kind-ness, God, be on us all our days,

And gath-ers all the o-ceans up to
No se-cret can cre-a-tion keep on
We hope in you, we trust in you, to

cup them in a hand, Who
earth or sea or sky, No
you be end-less praise, We

gath-ers all the o-ceans up to
se-cret can cre-a-tion keep on
hope in you, we trust in you, to

D.C.

cup them in a hand.
earth or sea or sky.
you be end-less praise.

Text: Psalm 33; Rory Cooney, b.1952
Tune: Rory Cooney, b.1952
© 1986, North American Liturgy Resources

585 Let Us Be Bread

Refrain

Let us be bread, blessed by the Lord, bro-ken and shared,

life for the world. Let us be wine, love free-ly poured.

Let us be one in the Lord.

Verse 1

1. I am the bread of life, bro - ken for all.

D.C.

Eat now and hun - ger no more.

Verse 2

2. You are my friends if you keep my com - mands,

D.C.

no long - er ser - vants but friends.

Verse 3

3. See how my peo - ple have noth - ing to eat.

D.C.

Give them the bread that is you.

Verse 4

4. As God has loved me so I have loved you.

D.C.

Go and live on in my love.

Jesus, Wine of Peace   586

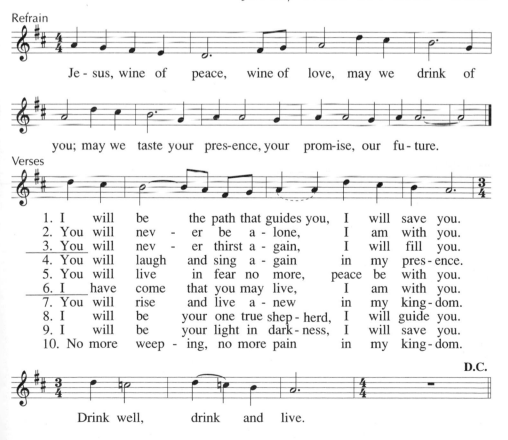

Refrain

Je - sus, wine of peace, wine of love, may we drink of

you; may we taste your pres-ence, your prom-ise, our fu-ture.

Verses

1. I will be the path that guides you, I will save you.
2. You will nev - er be a - lone, I am with you.
3. You will nev - er thirst a - gain, I will fill you.
4. You will laugh and sing a - gain in my pres - ence.
5. You will live in fear no more, peace be with you.
6. I have come that you may live, I am with you.
7. You will rise and live a - new in my king - dom.
8. I will be your one true shep - herd, I will guide you.
9. I will be your light in dark - ness, I will save you.
10. No more weep - ing, no more pain in my king - dom.

D.C.

Drink well, drink and live.

587 As We Remember

Refrain

As we re-mem-ber, we are be-com-ing; what we see

bro-ken, we hope to be. Show us your mer-cy, show us your

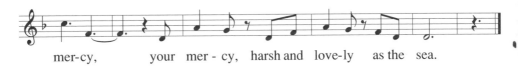

mer-cy, your mer-cy, harsh and love-ly as the sea.

Verses 1, 2, 4, 5, 7, 8

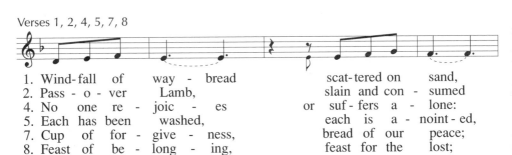

1. Wind-fall of way - bread scat-tered on sand,
2. Pass - o - ver Lamb, slain and con - sumed
4. No one re - joic - es or suf - fers a - lone:
5. Each has been washed, each is a - noint - ed,
7. Cup of for - give - ness, bread of our peace;
8. Feast of be - long - ing, feast for the lost;

D.C.

lav - ished by love we can - not un - der - stand.
that we be slaves not to tempt-er nor tomb.
meal of the spir - it brings man - y to one.
ser - vant and heal - er and proph-et ap - point-ed.
chil - dren come home to a Fa - ther's em - brace.
ban - quet e - ter - nal where Christ is the host.

Verses 3, 6, 9, 10

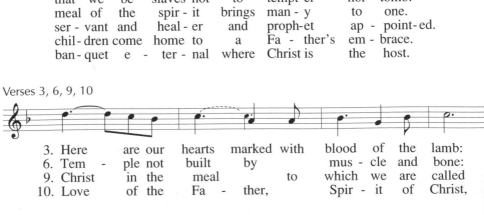

3. Here are our hearts marked with blood of the lamb:
6. Tem - ple not built by mus - cle and bone:
9. Christ in the meal to which we are called
10. Love of the Fa - ther, Spir - it of Christ,

589 All Who Hunger

Verses

1. All who hun-ger, gath-er glad-ly; ho - ly man-na
2. All who hun-ger, nev-er stran-gers, seek-er, be a
3. All who hun-ger, sing to - geth-er; Je - sus Christ is

is our bread. Come from wil - der - ness and wan-d'ring.
wel-come guest. Come from rest - less - ness and roam - ing.
liv - ing bread. Come from lone - li - ness and long - ing.

Here, in truth, we will be fed. You that yearn for
Here, in joy, we keep the feast. We that once were
Here, in peace, we have been led. Blest are those who

days of full-ness, all a - round us is our food.
lost and scat-tered in com - mun-ion's love have stood.
from this ta - ble live their lives in grat - i - tude.

Refrain

Taste and see the grace e - ter-nal. Taste and see that God is good.

Text: Sylvia G. Dunstan, 1955-1993, © 1991, GIA Publications, Inc.
Tune: Bob Moore, b. 1962, © 1993, GIA Publications, Inc.

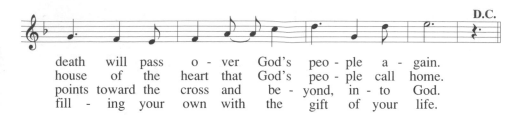

death will pass o - ver God's peo - ple a - gain.
house of the heart that God's peo - ple call home.
points toward the cross and be - yond, in - to God.
fill - ing your own with the gift of your life.

Text: Rory Cooney, b.1952
Tune: Rory Cooney, b.1952, acc. alt.
© 1987, North American Liturgy Resources

Eat This Bread   588

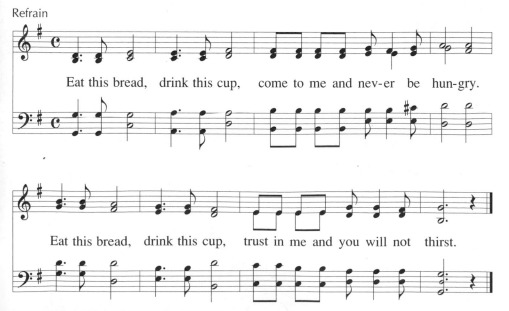

Eat this bread, drink this cup, come to me and nev-er be hun-gry.

Eat this bread, drink this cup, trust in me and you will not thirst.

Text: John 6; adapt. by Robert J. Batastini, b.1942, and the Taizé Community
Tune: Jacques Berthier, b.1923
© 1984, Les Presses de Taizé, GIA Publications, Inc., agent

Bread of Life, Hope of the World   590

Refrain

Bread of life,   hope of the world,   Je-sus Christ, our   broth-er:

feed us now,   give us life,   lead us   to   one an-oth-er.

Verses

1. As   we   pro-claim your death,   as   we   re-call your life,
2. The bread we break and   share   was scat-tered once as   grain:
3. We   eat   this   liv-ing   bread,   we drink this   sav-ing cup:
4. Hold   us   in   u-ni-ty,   in   love   for   all   to   see;
5. You   are   the bread of   peace,   you   are   the   wine of   joy,

D.C.

we re-mem-ber your   prom-ise   to   re-turn   a-gain.
just   as   now   it   is   gath-ered,   make your peo-ple   one.
sign of hope in   our   bro-ken world,   source   of   last-ing   love.
that the world may be-lieve in   you,   God   of   all   who live.
bro-ken now for your   peo-ple,   poured   in   end-less love.

Text: Bernadette Farrell, b.1957
Tune: Bernadette Farrell, b.1957
© 1982, 1987, Bernadette Farrell, published by OCP Publications

591 Life-Giving Bread, Saving Cup

Refrain

Life-giv-ing bread, sav-ing cup, we of-fer in thanks-giv-ing, O God.

Life-giv-ing bread sav-ing cup, we of-fer as a sign of our love.

Verses

1. For bread that is bro - ken, we give thanks. For
2. We thank you, O Fa - ther, for your name which
3. Cre - a - tor of all, we of - fer thanks. You
4. Re - mem - ber your Church which sings your praise. Per -

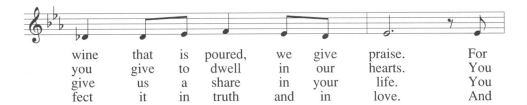

wine that is poured, we give praise. For
you give to dwell in our hearts. You
give us a share in your life. You
fect it in truth and in love. And

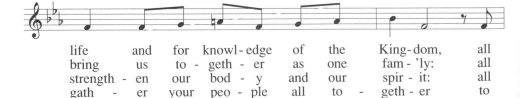

life and for knowl-edge of the King-dom, all
bring us to - geth - er as one fam - 'ly: all
strength - en our bod - y and our spir - it: all
gath - er your peo - ple all to - geth - er to

D.C.

praise to you un - til the end of time!
praise to you un - til the end of time!
praise to you un - til the end of time!
praise you un - til the end of time!

Text: Adapted from the *Didache,* 2nd C.; James J. Chepponis, b.1956
Tune: James J. Chepponis, b.1956
© 1987, GIA Publications, Inc.

Behold the Lamb   592

Verses

1. Those who were in the dark are thank-ful for the
2. Peace-ful now, those whose hearts are blessed with un - der -
3. Gen - tle one, Child of God, join with us at this
4. Lord of all, give us light. De - liv - er us from

sun - light; We who live, we who die are
stand-ing Of the wheat, of the wine u -
ta - ble. Bless our lives; nour-ish all who
e - vil. Make us one; be our shield. Make

grate - ful for this gift, thank-ful for God's love.
nit - ed with God's word and the love we share.
hung - er for this feast; shel-ter them with peace.
still the winds that blow; cra-dle us with love.

Refrain

Be - hold, be - hold the Lamb of God. All who eat,

all who drink shall live; and all, all who dwell in

God, shall come to know God's glo-ry!

Text: Martin Willett, alt.
Tune: Martin Willett; acc. by Craig S. Kingsbury, b.1952
© 1984, OCP Publications

593 I Myself Am the Bread of Life

Refrain

I my-self am the bread of life.

You and I are the bread of life,

tak - en and blessed, bro - ken and shared by Christ

that the world might live.

Verses

1. This bread is spir - it, gift of the Mak - er's
2. Here is God's king-dom giv - en to us as
3. Lives bro - ken o - pen, sto - ries shared a -

love, and we who share it know that we can be
food. This is our bod - y, this is our
loud, be - come a ban - quet, a shel - ter for the

D.C.

one:
blood: a liv-ing sign of God in Christ.
world:

Text: Rory Cooney, b.1952
Tune: Rory Cooney, b.1952
© 1987, North American Liturgy Resources

As the Grains of Wheat 594

Text: Marty Haugen, b.1950
Tune: Marty Haugen, b.1950
© 1990, GIA Publications, Inc.

Refrain

As the grains of wheat once scat-tered on the hill were

gath-ered in - to one to be - come our bread;

so may all your peo-ple from all the ends of earth be

gath - ered in - to one in you.

Verses

1. As this cup of bless-ing is shared with-in our midst,
2. Let this be a fore-taste of all that is to come when

D.C.

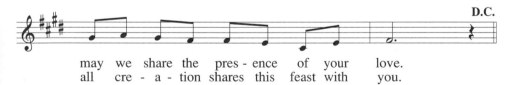

may we share the pres-ence of your love.
all cre - a - tion shares this feast with you.

595 Here in This Place

Refrain

Are not our hearts burn-ing with-in us? Are not our

lives shared as one bread? Here in our hands,

here in this place: Je-sus, our hope, life from the dead.

Verses

1. In the breaking of the bread, may we know the Lord.
   We were lost, and now are found, home again with God!

2. You are food for all our hunger, you are all we need.
   You are our promise and our hope, life for the world.

3. As grain, once scattered on the hill, was gathered all as one,
   may we be one in this bread: Behold the Lamb of God!

4. As this bread is broken, as this cup is shared, we give our lives,
   broken and outpoured. We will serve the Lord!

Text: Luke 24:13-35; David Haas, b.1957
Tune: David Haas, b.1957
© 1992, GIA Publications, Inc.

Bread for the World   596

Refrain

Bread for the world: a world of hun - ger.

Wine for all peo - ples: peo - ple who thirst. May we who eat

be bread for oth-ers. May we who drink pour out our love.

Verses

1. Lord Je - sus Christ, you are the bread of life, bro - ken to
2. Lord Je - sus Christ, you are the wine of peace, poured in - to
3. Lord Je - sus Christ, you call us to your feast, at which the

reach and heal the wounds of hu - man pain. Where we di -
hearts once bro - ken and where dry - ness sleeps. Where we are
rich and pow'r - ful have be - come the least. Where we sur -

vide your peo - ple you are wait - ing there on bend - ed
tired and wea - ry you are wait - ing there to be the
vive on oth - ers in our hu - man greed you walk a -

D.C.

knee to wash our feet with end - less care.
way which beck - ons us be - yond des - pair.
mong us beg - ging for your ev - 'ry need.

Text: Bernadette Farrell, b.1957
Tune: Bernadette Farrell, b.1957
© 1990, Bernadette Farrell, published by OCP Publications

597 I Am the Bread of Life / Yo Soy el Pan de Vida

Verses

1. I am the Bread of life. You who
2. The bread that I will give is my
3. Un - less you eat of the
4. I am the Res - ur - rec - tion,
5. Yes, Lord, I be - lieve that

1. Yo soy el pan de vi - da. El que
2. El pan que yo da - ré es mi
3. Mien - tras no co - mas el
4. Yo soy la re - su - rrec - ción.
5. Sí, Se - ñor, yo cre - o que

come to me shall not hun - ger; and who be -
flesh for the life of the world, and if you
flesh of the Son of Man and
I am the life. If you be -
you are the Christ, the

vie - ne a mí no ten - drá ham - bre. El que
cuer - po vi - da del mun - do, y el que
cuer - po del hi - jo del hom - bre, y
Yo soy la vi - da. El que
tú e - res el Cris - to, El

lieve in me shall not thirst. No one can come to
eat of this bread, you shall live for
drink of his blood, and drink of his
lieve in me, e - ven though you
Son of God, Who has

cree en mí no ten - drá sed. Na - die vie - ne a
co - ma de mi car - ne ten - drá vi - da e -
be - bas de su san - gre, y be - bas de su
cree en mí, aun - que mu - rie -
Hi - jo de Dios, que vi - no al

me   un - less   the___   Fa - ther___   beck-ons.
ev - er,_____   you   shall___   live   for___   ev - er.
blood,   you   shall   not have life   with -   in   you.
die,_____   you   shall___   live   for___   ev - er.
come   in - to_____   the_____   world.___
mí_____   mien - tras el   Pa - dre nos   lla - me.
ter - na,_____   ten - drá___   vi - da e - ter - na.
san - gre,   no   ten - drá___   vi - da___   en   ti.
ra,_____   ten - drá vi - da   e - ter - na.
mun - do_____   pa - ra   sal - var - nos.

Refrain

And I will   raise   you   up,   and I will   raise   you
Yo le re - su - ci - ta - ré,   Yo le re - su - ci - ta -

up,   and I will   raise   you up   on the   last   day.
ré,   Yo le re - su - ci - ta - ré   el   di - a   de Fl.

Text: John 6; Suzanne Toolan, SM, b.1927; translator unknown
Tune: BREAD OF LIFE, Irregular with refrain; Suzanne Toolan, SM, b.1927; acc. by Diana Kodner, b.1957

598 Shepherd of Our Hearts

Refrain

Shep-herd of our hearts, re - ceive our song of praise. Lead us to the King-dom, and guide us all our days.

Verses

1. Shep-herd of souls, re-fresh and bless your
2. We would not live by bread a - lone, but
3. Be known to us in break-ing bread, but
4. Lord, sup with us in love di - vine; your

cho - sen pil - grim flock with
by your word of grace, in
do not then de - part; O
Bod - y and your Blood, that

man - na in the wil - der - ness, with
strength of which we trav - el on to
Lord, a - bide with us, and spread your
liv - ing bread, that heav'n - ly wine be

D.C.

wa - ter from the rock.
our a - bid - ing place.
ta - ble in our heart.
our im - mor - tal food.

Text: Verses by James Montgomery, 1771-1854, alt; refrain by James J. Chepponis, b.1956
Tune: James J. Chepponis, b.1956
© 1988, GIA Publications, Inc.

One Bread, One Body   599

Refrain

One bread, one bod-y, one Lord of all, one cup of bless - ing which we bless. And we, though man-y, through-out the earth, we are one bod - y in this one Lord.

Verses

1. Gen - tile   or   Jew,   ser - vant   or   free,
2. Man - y   the   gifts,   man - y   the   works,
3. Grain for   the   fields,   scat-tered and   grown,

D.C.

wom - an   or   man   no   more.
one   in   the   Lord   of   all.
gath-ered   to   one   for   all.

Text: I Corinthians 10:16; 17, 12:4, Galatians 3:28; the *Didache* 9; John Foley, SJ, b.1939
Tune: John Foley, SJ, b.1939
©1978, John B. Foley, SJ, and New Dawn Music

600 Now in This Banquet

Refrain

Now in this ban - quet, Christ is our bread;
Advent: God of our jour - neys, day - break to night;
Lent: Lord, you can o - pen hearts that are stone;

Here shall all hun - gers be fed.
Lead us to jus - tice and light.
Live in our flesh and our bone;

Bread that is bro - ken, wine that is poured,
Grant us com - pas - sion, strength for the day,
Lead us to won - der, mys - t'ry and grace,

Love is the sign of our Lord.
Wis - dom to walk in your way.
One in your lov - ing em - brace.

Verses 1, 2

1. You who have touched us and graced us with love,
2. Let our hearts burn with the fire of your love;

D.C.

make us your peo - ple of good - ness and light.
o - pen our eyes to the glo - ry of God.

Verse 3

3. God who makes the blind to see, God who makes the lame to walk,

May be sung in canon.

bring us danc-ing in-to day, lead your peo-ple in your way.

Verse 4

4. Hope for the hope-less, light for the blind,

"Strong" is your name, Lord, "Gen-tle" and "Kind."

Verse 5

5. Call us to be your light, call us to be your love,

make us your peo - ple a - gain.

Verse 6

6. Come, O Spir - it! re - new our hearts!

We shall a - rise to be chil-dren of light.

Text: Marty Haugen, b.1950
Tune: Marty Haugen, b.1950
© 1986, GIA Publications, Inc.

601 Seed, Scattered and Sown

Refrain

Seed, scat-tered and sown, wheat, gath-ered and grown,

bread, bro-ken and shared as one, the Liv-ing Bread of God.

Vine, fruit of the land, wine, work of our hands, one cup that is

shared by all; the Liv-ing Cup, the Liv-ing Bread of God.

Verses

1. Is not the bread we break a
2. The seed which falls on rock will
3. As wheat up - on the hills was

shar - ing in our Lord? Is not the
with - er and will die. The seed with -
gath - ered and was grown, So may the

D.C.

cup we bless the blood of Christ out - poured?
in good ground will flow - er and have life.
church of God be gath - ered in - to one.

Text: *Didache* 9, 1 Corinthians 10:16-17, Mark 4:3-6; Dan Feiten
Tune: Dan Feiten; keyboard arr. by Eric Gunnison, R.J. Miller
© 1987, Ekklesia Music, Inc.

O Taste and See   602

Refrain

O taste, taste and see the good-ness of God, the bless-ings of God.

Verses

1. I will sing God's praises all the days that I shall live.
   My soul will glory in my God, the lowly will hear and be glad.
   O glorify God's name with me, together let us rejoice.

2. For God has heard my anguished cries, and delivered me from all my foes.
   O look to God that you might shine, your faces be radiant with joy.

3. When the poor cry out, God hears and saves them,
   rescues them from their distress.
   God's angel watches near to those who look to their God to save them.

4. O taste and see that God is good, how happy the ones who find refuge.
   The mighty shall grow weak and hungry, those who seek God lack nothing.

5. Come, my children, hear me, I will teach you the fear of God.
   Come, all of you who thirst for life and seek joy in all of your days.

6. For God is close to the brokenhearted, near to those crushed in spirit.
   The hand of God redeems your life, a refuge for all those who seek.

Text: Psalm 34:2-4, 5-6, 7-8, 9, 11, 12-13, 19; Marty Haugen, b.1950
Tune: Marty Haugen, b.1950
© 1993, GIA Publications, Inc.

603 We Know and Believe

Refrain

We know and be - lieve in God's love for us.

Make us one in love and peace.

Verses

1. Nourish us well with this bread of the kingdom,
   the gift of yourself so freely given.
   To make us all one you call us to the table,
   to eat and drink of your flesh and blood.

2. Happy are we who eat at your table.
   Happy are we who drink of this cup.
   Your blood once shed, your body once broken,
   now call us to rise again daily with you.

3. God's love we embrace in each brother and sister.
   The signs of your presence are constantly new.
   Though many we are we become one in Jesus,
   one body, one bread, we are sign of you.

4. Neither Jew nor Greek, male nor female,
   We are all one in your presence, O Lord.
   All fighting and discord will melt in your mercy.
   We are one in your Spirit and one in your peace.

Text: Rob Glover, b.1950
Tune: Rob Glover, b.1950
© 1992, GIA Publications, Inc.

Taste and See 604

Refrain

Taste and see, taste and see the good-ness of the Lord.

Taste and see, taste and see the good-ness of the Lord.

Verses

1. I will nev - er stop thank - ing my God
2. Join the sing - ing in praise of our God;
3. Look to God and be ra - diant with joy;
4. God of jus - tice, rain down on the poor,

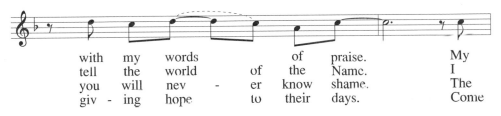

with my words of praise. My
tell the world of the Name. I
you will nev - er know shame. The
giv - ing hope to their days. Come

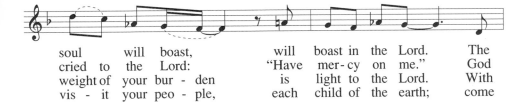

soul will boast, will boast in the Lord. The
cried to the Lord: "Have mer-cy on me." God
weight of your bur - den is light to the Lord. With
vis - it your peo - ple, each child of the earth; come

D.C.

low - ly will hear me and be lift - ed in praise.
calmed all my fears and then set me free.
ten - der com - pas - sion God will call you by name.
vis - it us now and bring us to a new birth.

Text: Psalm 34:1-3; Francis Patrick O'Brien, b.1958
Tune: Francis Patrick O'Brien, b.1958
© 1992, GIA Publications, Inc.

605 In the Breaking of the Bread / Cuando Partimos el Pan del Señor

Refrain

In the break - ing of the bread
Cuan-do par - ti - mos el pan del Se - ñor,

We have known him; we have been fed.
lo co - no - ce - mos, nos da de co - mer. Je -

Je - sus the stran - ger, Je - sus the Lord,
sús des-co - no - ci - do, Je - sús, Se - ñor,

Be our com - pan - ion, be our hope.
nues-tro com - pa - ñe - ro, y fuen-te de fe.

Verses

1. Bread for the jour - ney, strength for our years,
1. *Pan pa - ra el via - je, Pan de la vi - da,*
2. Bread of the prom - ise, peo - ple of hope,
2. *Pan del pro - me - sa, Pan de es - pe - ran - za,*

Man - na of ag - es, of strug - gle and tears.
Pan de los si - glos de lu - cha y do - lor,
Wine of com - pas - sion, life for the world
Vi - no de vi - da, de su com - pa - sión,

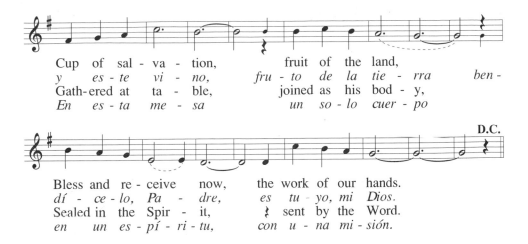

Cup of sal - va - tion,   fruit of the land,
y es - te vi - no,   fru - to de la tie - rra ben -
Gath-ered at ta - ble,   joined as his bod - y,
En es - ta me - sa   un so - lo cuer - po

Bless and re - ceive now,   the work of our hands.
dí - ce - lo, Pa - dre,   es tu - yo, mi Dios.
Sealed in the Spir - it,   sent by the Word.
en un es - pí - ri - tu,   con u - na mi - sión.

Original Verses:

1. Once I was helpless, sad and confused; darkness surrounded me, courage removed.
And then I saw him by my side. Carry my burden, open my eyes.

2. There is no sorrow, pain or woe; there is no suffering he did not know.
He did not waver; he did not bend. He is the victor. He is my friend.

Text: Bob Hurd, b.1950, and Michael Downey, © 1984, 1987; Spanish text by Stephen Dean and Kathleen Orozco, © 1989, OCP Publications
Tune: Bob Hurd, b.1950, © 1984; acc. by Dominic MacAller, b.1959, © 1984, OCP Publications
Published by OCP Publications

606 Take and Eat This Bread

Refrain

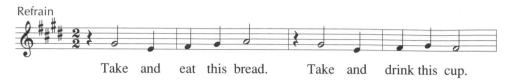

Take and eat this bread. Take and drink this cup.

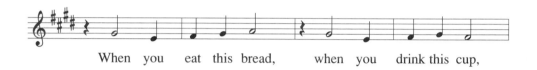

This is my bod - y and my blood.

When you eat this bread, when you drink this cup,

you live in me and I in you.

Verses

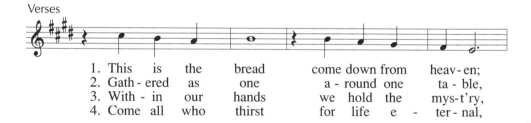

1. This is the bread come down from heav - en;
2. Gath - ered as one a - round one ta - ble,
3. With - in our hands we hold the mys-t'ry,
4. Come all who thirst for life e - ter - nal,

D.C.

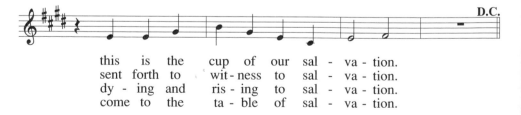

this is the cup of our sal - va - tion.
sent forth to wit - ness to sal - va - tion.
dy - ing and ris - ing to sal - va - tion.
come to the ta - ble of sal - va - tion.

Look Beyond 607

Refrain

Look be-yond the bread you eat; See your Sav-ior and your Lord.

Look be-yond the cup you drink; See his love poured out as

To verses | Final ending   poured out as blood.

1. Give us a sign that we
2. I am the bread which
3. The bread I give you will
4. This man speaks harsh - ly; who can
5. You, my dis - ci - ples, will

might be-lieve in you. Mos - es had
from the heav-ens came; Those who eat this
be my ver - y flesh; My blood will
lis - ten to his word? We shall no
you al - so leave? Lord to

D.C.

man - na from the sky.
bread will nev - er die.
tru - ly be your drink.
long - er fol - low him.
whom can we go?

Text: Darryl Ducote, b.1945
Tune: Darryl Ducote, b.1945
© 1969, 1979, Damean Music. Distributed by GIA Publications, Inc.

608 You Are Our Living Bread

Refrain

You are our liv-ing bread;
you are our
ho-ly wine, Lord Je-sus Christ!

Verses

1. I feed my peo-ple on the fin-est of bread, on my
2. I feed my peo-ple on the fin-est of wine, on my
3. Where two or three have gath-ered in my name, there am

D.C.

bod - y bro - ken for them.
blood of suf - f'ring and shame.
I in the midst of them.

Text: Michael Joncas, b.1955
Tune: Michael Joncas, b.1955
© 1979, New Dawn Music

Taste and See

Refrain

Taste and see, taste and see the good-ness of the Lord. O taste and see, taste and see the good-ness of the Lord, of the Lord.

Verses

1. I will bless the Lord at all times.
2. Glo-ri-fy the Lord with me.
3. Wor-ship the Lord, all you peo-ple.

Praise shall al-ways be on my lips;
To-geth-er let us all praise God's name.
You'll want for noth-ing if you ask.

my soul shall glo-ry in the Lord
I called the Lord who an-swered me;
Taste and see that the Lord is good;

for God has been so good to me.
from all my troub-les I was set free.
in God we need put all our trust.

D.C.

Text: Psalm 34; James E. Moore, Jr., b.1951
Tune: James E. Moore, Jr., b.1951
© 1983, GIA Publications, Inc.

,thout Seeing You

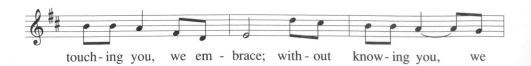

With-out   see - ing you,   we love   you; with - out

touch-ing you,   we em - brace; with - out   know-ing you,   we

fol - low; with - out   see-ing you,   we be - lieve.

Verses

1. We re - turn to   you   deep with - in,   leave the
2. The   spar - row will   find   a   home,   near to
3. For   ev - er we   sing   to   you   of   your
4. For   you are our   shep - herd,   there is

past   to   the   dust; turn to   you with tears and
you,   O   God; how   hap - py, we who
good - ness, O   God; pro - claim-ing to
noth - ing that we   need; in   green pas - tures we will

D.C.

fast - ing;   you are read - y to for - give.
dwell with you,   for - ev - er in your house.
all   the world of your faith-ful-ness and love.
find our rest, near the wa - ters of   peace.

Text: Inspired by 1 Peter 1:8; David Haas, b. 1957
Tune: David Haas, b. 1957
© 1993, GIA Publications, Inc.

The Song of the Supper

Verses

1. The time was ear - ly eve - ning, The
2. The com - pa - ny of Je - sus Had
3. "The bread and bod - y bro - ken The
4. On both sides of the ta - ble, On
5. Lord, Je - sus, now a - mong us, Con -

place a room up - stairs; The guests were the dis -
met to share a meal, But he, who made them
wine and blood out - poured, The cross and kitch - en
both sides of the grave, The Lord joins those who
firm our faith's in - tent, As, with your words and

ci - ples, Few in num - ber and few in prayers.
wel - come, Had much more to re - veal.
ta - ble Are one by my sign and word."
love him To serve them and to save.
ac - tions, We u - nite in this sac - ra - ment.

Refrain

Oh, the food comes from the bak - er, the

drink comes from the vine, the words come from the

sav - ior, "I will meet you in bread and wine."

Text: John L. Bell, b.1949, © 1988, Iona Community, GIA Publications, Inc., agent
Tune: AFTON WATERS, Irregular; Scottish folk song; acc. by John L. Bell, b.1949, © 1993, Iona Community, GIA Publications, Inc., agent

One Is the Body

One is the bod-y, one is the bread, one are the

liv-ing, the un-born, the dead. One is the cup, one

blood in us flows, one is the breath of the star and the rose.

One is the Spir-it with Mak-er and Son, just as the

source and the riv-er are one; one are the stran-ger, my

foe and my friend. To this I will say, "A - men."

Verses

1. Gath - er, dis - ci - ples, your mas - ter to meet.
2. Now split the tim - ber, now turn the stone;
3. I am the hun - gry, you are the poor;

Learn to for - give from the bread that you eat;
look where you will, you are nev - er a - lone.
God is the stran - ger who waits at the door.

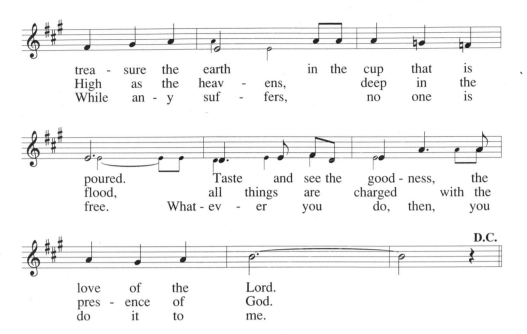

trea - sure the earth in the cup that is
High as the heav - ens, deep in the
While an - y suf - fers, no one is

poured.   Taste   and   see the   good - ness,   the
flood,   all   things   are   charged   with the
free.   What - ev - er   you   do,   then,   you

D.C.

love   of   the   Lord.
pres - ence   of   God.
do   it   to   me.

Text: Rory Cooney, b.1952
Tune: Rory Cooney, b.1952
© 1993, GIA Publications, Inc.

613 Song of the Body of Christ /
Canción del Cuerpo de Cristo

Refrain

We come to share our sto - ry, we
Ve - ni-mos a de - cir del mis - te - rio, *y par -*

come to break the bread, We come to know our
tir el pan de vi - da. Ve - ni - mos a sa - ber de

ris - ing from the dead.
nues - tra e - ter - ni - dad.

Verses

1. We come as your peo - ple, we
2. We are called to heal the bro - ken, to be
3. Bread of life and cup of prom - ise, in this
4. You will lead and we shall fol - low, you will
5. We will live and sing: "A - lo - ha," "Al - le -
   (live and sing your prais - es,)

come as your own, u - nit - ed with each
hope for the poor, we are called to feed the
meal we all are one. In our dy - ing and our
be the breath of life; liv - ing wa - ter, we are
lu - ia" is our song. May we live in love and

D.C.

oth - er, love finds a home.
hun - gry at our door.
ris - ing, may your king - dom come.
thirst - ing for your light.
peace our whole life long.

Verses

1. Ve - ni - mos, co - mo su pueb - lo en es -
2. Nos lla - ma pa - ra cu - rar y
3. Pan de vi - da y co - pa de pro - me - sa, so - mos
4. Nos guia - rás y te se - gui - re - mos, por - que
5. Vi - vi - re - mos can - tan - do "A - lo - ha." "A - le -

pí - ri - tu de ver - dad. U - ni - dos en su a -
ser su es - per - an - za. So - mos su - yos pa - ra_a - li - men -
u - no en es - ta co - mi - da. Ven - drá su rei - no_en
e - res la luz que bus - ca - mos. En el di - a o en la
lu - ya" es nues - tra can - ción. Por siem - pre vi - vi -

D.C.

mor, so - mos un cor - a - zón.
tar a los po - bres.
nues - tra trans - for - ma - ción.
no - che, bri - lla - rás.
re - mos en su paz.

Text: David Haas, b.1957, Spanish translation by Donna Peña, b. 1955
Tune: NO KE ANO' AHI AHI, Irregular, Hawaiian traditional, arr. by David Haas, b.1957
© 1989, GIA Publications, Inc.

614 Take and Eat

Refrain

Take and eat; take and eat: this is my bod - y
giv-en up for you. Take and drink; take and drink:
this is my blood giv - en up for you.

Verses

1. I am the Word that spoke and light was made;
2. I am the way that leads the ex - ile home;
3. I am the Lamb that takes a - way your sin;
4. I am the cor - ner - stone that God has laid;
5. I am the light that came in - to the world;
6. I am the first and last, the Liv - ing One;

I am the seed that died to be re - born;
I am the truth that sets the cap - tive free;
I am the gate that guards you night and day;
A cho-sen stone and pre - cious in his eyes;
I am the light that dark - ness can - not hide;
I am the Lord who died that you might live;

I am the bread that comes from heav'n a - bove;
I am the life that rais - es up the dead;
You are my flock: you know the shep-herd's voice;
You are God's dwell - ing place, on me you rest;
I am the morn - ing star that nev - er sets;
I am the bride-groom, this my wed - ding song;

D.C.

I	am	the	vine	that	fills your	cup	with	joy.
I	am	your peace,		true	peace my	gift	to	you.
You	are	my	own:	your	ran - som	is	my	blood.
Like	liv - ing	stones,		a	tem - ple	for	God's	praise.
Lift	up	your	face,	in	you my	light	will	shine.
You	are	my	bride,	come	to	the	mar - riage	feast.

Text: Verse text, James Quinn, SJ, b.1919, © 1989. Used by permission of Selah Publishing., Inc., Kingston, N.Y.; refrain text,
     Michael Joncas, b.1951, © 1989, GIA Publications, Inc.
Tune: Michael Joncas, b.1951, © 1989, GIA Publications, Inc.

615 Pan de Vida

Refrain

* Pan de Vi - da, cuer-po del Se - ñor,

cup of bless - ing, blood of Christ the Lord.

At this ta - ble the last shall be first, ** po -

der es ser - vir, por-que Dios es a - mor.

Verses

1. We are the dwell-ing of God,
*** 2. Us - te - des me lla - man "Se - ñor," me in -
3. There is no Jew or Greek,

fra - gile and wound-ed and weak. We are the
cli - no_a la - var - les los pies: Ha - gan lo
there is no slave or free: there is no

bod - y of Christ, called to be the com -
mis - mo, hu - mil - des, sir - vién - do - se
wom-an or man; on - ly heirs of the

D.C.

pas - sion of God.
u - nos a o - tros.
prom - ise of God.

Bread of Life, body of the Lord,   **power is for service, because God is Love.*
****You call me "Lord," and I bow to wash your feet:*
you must do the same, humbly serving each other.

Text: John 13:1-15, Galatians 3:28-29; Bob Hurd, b.1950, and Pia Moriarty, © 1988, Bob Hurd
Tune: Bob Hurd, b.1950, © 1988; acc. by Craig Kingsbury, b.1952, © 1988, OCP Publications; arr. © 1988, OCP Publications
Published by OCP Publications

Table Song   616

Refrain

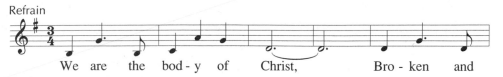

We are the bod-y of Christ, Bro - ken and

poured out, prom - ise of life from death,

we are the bod-y of Christ.

Verses

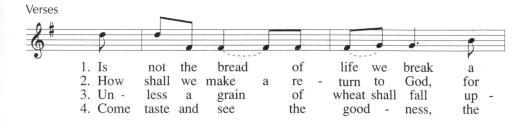

1. Is not the bread of life we break a
2. How shall we make a re - turn to God, for
3. Un - less a grain of wheat shall fall up -
4. Come taste and see the good - ness, the

shar - ing in the life of God? Is not the cup of
good-ness un - sur - pass - ing? This sav - ing cup we
on the earth, it shall re - main a sin - gle grain; but
won - ders of the ris - en one! Come bless our God, in

peace out - poured the blood of Christ?
shall hold high, and call out God's name!
if it dies, it will come to life!
all things, let praise be our song!

Text: David Haas, b. 1957
Tune: David Haas, b. 1957
© 1991, GIA Publications, Inc.

617 We Come to Your Feast

Verses
Cantor or choir:

1. We place up - on your ta - ble
2. We place up - on your ta - ble
3. We place up - on your ta - ble
4. We ga - ther 'round your ta - ble,

a gleam-ing cloth of white: the weav-ing of our
a hum - ble loaf of bread: the gift of field and
a sim - ple cup of wine: the fruit of hu - man
we pause with - in our quest, we stand be-side our

sto - ries, the fab - ric of our lives;
hill - side, the grain by which we're fed;
la - bor, the gift of sun and vine;
neigh-bors, we name the stran - ger "guest."

the dreams of those be - fore us, the an-cient hope-ful
we come to taste the pres-ence of him on whom we
we come to taste the pres-ence of him we claim as
The feast is spread be - fore us; you bid us come and

cries, the prom - ise of our
feed, to strength - en and con -
Lord, his dy - ing and his
dine: in bless - ing we'll un -

fu - ture: our need-ing and our nur-ture lie here be - fore our eyes.
nect us, to chal-lenge and cor - rect us, to love in word and deed.
liv - ing, his lead-ing and his giv-ing, his love in cup out-poured.
cov- er, in shar-ing we'll dis - cov - er your sub-stance and your sign.

Refrain

We come to your feast, we come to your feast: the young and the old, the fright-ened, the bold, the great-est and the least. We come to your feast, we come to your feast with the fruit of our lands and the work of our hands, we come to your feast.

Text: Michael Joncas, b.1951
Tune: Michael Joncas, b.1951

618 The Living Bread of God

Refrain

Je - sus, the liv - ing Bread of God,

Je - sus, the sav - ing cup of Christ.

Ev- 'ry time we eat this bread, ev - 'ry time we drink this cup,

we pro - claim your glo - ry un - til you come a - gain.

Verses

1. You are the bread of life.
   If we come to you, we will never be in need.
   If we believe in you, we will never thirst, and we will live for ever.

2. You are the life of the world.
   If we come to you, we will never know death.
   If we eat of this bread, we will be renewed, and and we will live for ever.

3. You are the living bread,
   our bread from heaven, our food from above.
   If we eat and drink, we will be like you, and we will live for ever.

4. You are the living Christ.
   If we follow you, we will see the face of God.
   If we die with you, we will rise again, and we will live for ever.

Text: 1 Corinthians 11:26; David Haas, b.1957
Tune: Kate Cuddy
© 1992, GIA Publications, Inc.

I Know That My Redeemer Lives   619

Refrain

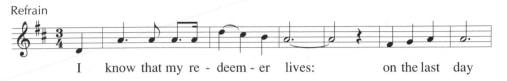

I know that my re - deem - er lives: on the last day

I shall rise a - gain, and in my flesh I shall see

God.   On the last day I shall rise a - gain!

Verses

Cantor:

1. I shall see my Sav - ior's face; and my own
2. With - in my heart this hope I hold; that in my

All:

eyes shall be - hold my God.   On the last day
flesh I shall see my God.   On the last day

D.C.

I shall rise a - gain!
I shall rise a - gain!

Text: Job 19:25-27; David Haas, b.1957
Tune: David Haas, b.1957

620 How Lovely Is Your Dwelling

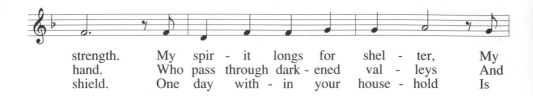

1. How love-ly is your dwell-ing, O God, my hope and
2. How blest are those whose trav-els Are strength-ened by your
3. Look on me, God of good-ness, You are my sun and

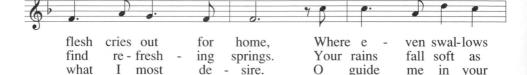

strength. My spir - it longs for shel - ter, My
hand. Who pass through dark - ened val - leys And
shield. One day with - in your house - hold Is

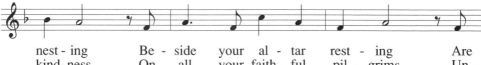

flesh cries out for home, Where e - ven swal-lows
find re - fresh - ing springs. Your rains fall soft as
what I most de - sire. O guide me in your

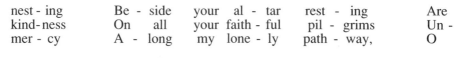

nest - ing Be - side your al - tar rest - ing Are
kind-ness On all your faith - ful pil - grims Un -
mer - cy A - long my lone - ly path - way, O

ev - er prais-ing you, Are ev - er prais - ing you.
til they come to you, Un - til they come to you.
bring me safe - ly home. O bring me safe - ly home.

Text: Psalm 84; Jean Janzen, © 1991
Tune: GILMAN, 7 6 7 6 77 6; John Foley, SJ, b.1939, © 1993, GIA Publications, Inc.

I Shall See My God 621

Text: Kevin Keil, b.1965
Tune: Kevin Keil, b.1965
© 1993, GIA Publications, Inc.

622 The Hand of God Shall Hold You

Refrain

The hand of God shall hold you, the peace of God en -

fold you, the love that dreamed and formed you still sur -

rounds you here to - day; The light of God be - side you, a -

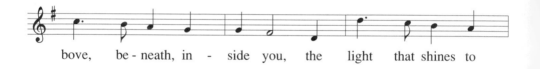

bove, be - neath, in - side you, the light that shines to

guide you home to the lov - ing hand of God.

Verses

1. May God's light shine ever upon you, may you rest in the arms of God;
   may you dwell for evermore in communion with all the blessed.

2. May the angels lead you into paradise; may the martyrs come to welcome you
   and take you to the holy city, the new and eternal Jerusalem.

Text: Marty Haugen, b.1950, © 1994, GIA Publications, Inc.; verse 2 from *In paradisum; Rite of Funerals,* © 1970, ICEL
Tune: Marty Haugen, b.1950, © 1994, GIA Publications, Inc.

I, the Lord   623

I,   the Lord   am   with you,   al - ways   by your   side.

Come and take my   hand,   for I   will lead you   home. Fol - low

me,   fol - low me.

Verse 1

1. I   am   the res - ur - rec - tion,   and I   am the   life.   If

D.C.

you be - lieve in   me   you shall live for - ev - er.

Verse 2

2. You   shall have   new   life   and live it to the   full.

D.C.

Turn   your sor - row   in - to joy, for life has just be - gun.

Text: John 6:35-38, 11:25-26
Tune: Tom Kendzia, acc. alt.
© 1983, North American Liturgy Resources

624 Song of the Exile

Refrain

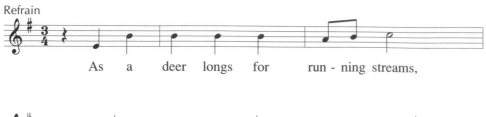

As a deer longs for run - ning streams,

so my soul longs for you, and my

heart thirsts for the God of my life.

When shall I go to see the

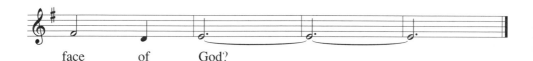

face of God?

Verses

1. I remember, and my soul melts within me:
   I am on my way to your wonderful tent,
   to the house of God, singing my songs of joy and thanksgiving.

2. I am broken, so I call to my Savior;
   as the waves roar down, sweeping over my head,
   and I call to you, be with me now, O God of my life.

3. In the daytime may the Lord's love be with me;
   in the night your song will be still on my lips.
   I will sing to you, sing prayers to you, the God of my life.

Text: Psalm 42:2-3, 5, 7-9; para. by Marty Haugen, b.1950
Tune: Marty Haugen, b.1950
© 1980, GIA Publications, Inc.

Saints of God   625

Refrain

Re - ceive his/her soul, re - ceive his/her soul,

and pre - sent him/her to God the Most High,

and pre - sent him/her to God the Most High.

Verses

1. Saints of God, come to his/her aid!
   Hasten to meet him/her, angels of the Lord!

2. May Christ, who called you, take you to himself;
   may angels lead you to the bosom of Abraham.

3. Eternal rest grant unto him/her, O Lord, and let
   perpetual light shine upon him/her.

Text: *Order of Christian Funerals,* © 1985, ICEL
Tune: Steven R. Janco, b. 1961, © 1990, GIA Publications, Inc.

626   Song of Farewell

Refrain

Dy-ing you de - stroyed our death! Ris-ing you re - stored our life!

Lord Je - sus,   Lord Je - sus,   come in glo - ry!

Verses

1. May Christ who died for you lead you into his kingdom;
   may Christ who died for you lead you this day into paradise.

2. May Christ, the Good Shepherd, lead you home today
   and give you a place within his flock.

Alternate children's verse:
2. May Christ, the Good Shepherd, take you on his shoulders
   and bring you home, bring you home today.

3. May the angels lead you into paradise;
   may the martyrs come to welcome you
   and take you to the Holy City, the new and eternal Jerusalem.

4. May the choirs of angels come to meet you,
   may the choirs of angels come to meet you;
   where Lazarus is poor no longer may you have eternal life in Christ.

Alternate children's verse:
4. May the choirs of angels come to meet you,
   may the choirs of angels come to meet you;
   and with all God's children may you have eternal life in Christ.

Text: Memorial Acclamation © 1973, ICEL; *In paradisum;* Michael Marchal, © 1988, GIA Publications, Inc.
Tune: Michael Joncas, b.1951, © 1988, GIA Publications, Inc.

In Love We Choose to Live   627

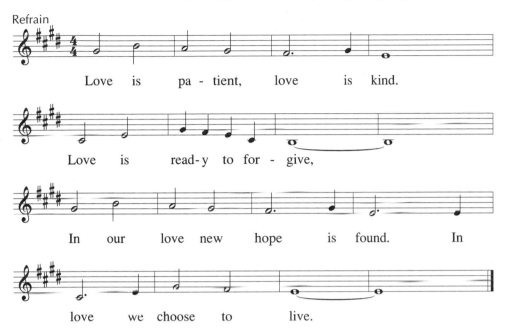

Refrain

Love is pa - tient, love is kind.

Love is read-y to for - give,

In our love new hope is found. In

love we choose to live.

Verses

1. May love be our home; rest to soothe tired bones.
   May love be healing for our wounds.
   May love speak the truth; free us from our fear.
   May love be the heart of our anger!
   For...

2. May love be the sun shining in our darkness.
   May love fill the lives of our children.
   May love be our strength, to live a life of justice.
   May love be our call to live the Kingdom!
   For...

Text: 1 Corinthians 13; Jeanne Cotter, b.1964
Tune: Jeanne Cotter, b.1964
© 1993, GIA Publications, Inc.

628 When Love Is Found

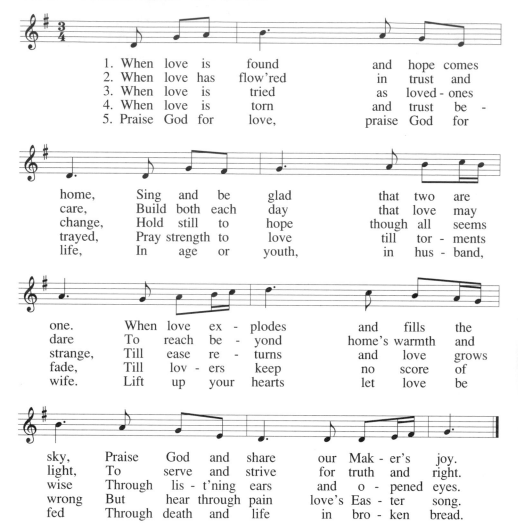

1. When love is found and hope comes home, Sing and be glad that two are one. When love ex - plodes and fills the sky, Praise God and share our Mak - er's joy.
2. When love has flow'red in trust and care, Build both each day that love may dare To reach be - yond home's warmth and light, To serve and strive for truth and right.
3. When love is tried as loved - ones change, Hold still to hope though all seems strange, Till ease re - turns and love grows wise Through lis - t'ning ears and o - pened eyes.
4. When love is torn and trust be - trayed, Pray strength to love till tor - ments fade, Till lov - ers keep no score of wrong But hear through pain love's Eas - ter song.
5. Praise God for love, praise God for life, In age or youth, in hus - band, wife. Lift up your hearts let love be fed Through death and life in bro - ken bread.

Text: Brian Wren, b.1936
Tune: O WALY WALY, LM; English; harm. by Martin West, b.1929
© 1983, Hope Publishing Co.

Love Is the Sunlight   629

1. Love is the sun - light Shaped of your splen - dor,
2. Love is the spa - cious Qui - et of shad - ows,
3. May we in glad - ness Grow in your sun - shine,

Love is the star bright Born of your hand,
Love is the gra - cious Shade of re - lease,
May we in sad - ness Rest in your shade,

Bless - ing of heav - en Gra - cious - ly giv - en,
Mist of the morn - ing, Mid - day a - dorn - ing,
Giv - ing and gain - ing, Ev - er re - main - ing,

Ra - diant with glo - ry From your com -
Cool with the twi - light Breath of your
One in the mar - riage Your love has

mand.
peace.
made.

Text: Borghild Jacobson, © 1981, Concordia Publishing House
Tune: SHADE, 5 5 5 4 D; David Haas, b.1957, © 1993, GIA Publications, Inc.

630 Wherever You Go

Refrain

Wher-ev-er you go, I will go; wher-ev-er you live, I'll be with you. Wher-ev-er you lie, I'll be there be-side you. Wher-ev-er you go, I'll be there.

Verses

1. Come, set me like a seal upon your heart; a seal protecting your arm.
   Deep waters cannot quench this love; the ocean will not sweep it away.

2. Arise my beloved, come to me; the rains are gone, the winter is past.
   The flowers appear, the vines are pruned, and the dove's song is heard in our land.

3. Wherever you stay, I will stay; your people will be my people.
   Wherever you die, so will I die with you in the arms of God!

Text: Ruth 1:16-17; Song of Songs 2:10-12, 7:6-7; David Haas, b.1957
Tune: David Haas, b.1957

God, in the Planning 631

1. God, in the plan - ning and pur-pose of life,
2. Je - sus was found, at a sim - i - lar feast,
3. There-fore we pray that his spir - it pre - side
4. Praise then the Mak - er, the Spir - it, the Son,

Hal - lowed the un - ion of hus - band and wife:
Tak - ing the roles of both wait - er and priest,
O - ver the wed - ding of bride - groom and bride,
Source of the love through which two are made one.

This we em - bod - y where love is dis - played,
Turn - ing the world - ly to - wards the di - vine,
Ful - fill - ing all that they've hoped will come true,
God's is the glo - ry, the good-ness, and grace

Rings are pre - sent - ed and prom - is - es made.
Tears in - to laugh - ter and wa - ter to wine.
Light - ing with love all they dream of and do.
Seen in this mar - riage and known in this place.

Text: John L. Bell, b.1949, © 1989, Iona Community, GIA Publication, Inc., agent
Tune: SLANE, 10 10 10 10; Irish traditional; harm. by Erik Routley, 1917-1982, © 1985, Hope Publishing Co.

632 We Will Serve the Lord

Refrain

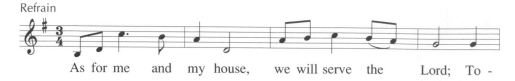

As for me and my house, we will serve the Lord; To -

geth-er on our jour-ney, we'll walk with our God.

As for me and my house, we will serve the Lord.

May our lives to-geth-er be a bless-ing to God.

Verses

1. Hands quick to wel-come, hearts to em-brace the
2. Rest for the wea-ry, home for the lost. May
3. Man-na from heav-en, food for the earth.

D.C.

lone - ly and all those in need!
Christ be the love that we share!
May we be bread for the world!

Text: David Haas, b.1957
Tune: David Haas, b.1957
© 1993, GIA Publications, Inc.

A Nuptial Blessing 633

Refrain

May God bless you, hold and keep you;

may God's mer - cy shine on you,

guide your work and guard your rest - ing,

keep your love for ev - er new.

Verses

1. May God satisfy your longing, be refreshment at your table,
and provide your daily bread,
guard your going and your coming, be the solace in your silence:
life within the lives you wed.

2. May God join your hopeful spirits, fill your hearts with truth and courage,
trust to share both joy and tears,
teach love to your children's children; may your household learn to witness
living faith through all your years.

3. May God make your home a refuge where you warmly welcome strangers
and the lowly find a place;
make you caring, kind companions, help you meet the needs of neighbors,
finding Christ in ev'ry face.

Text: Vicki Klima; adapt. by Michael Joncas, b.1951, and George Szews
Tune: Michael Joncas, b.1951
© 1989, GIA Publications, Inc.

634 Blessing the Marriage

1. That hu - man life might rich - er be, That
2. As two we love are wed this day And
3. Par - ents and fam - i - lies they leave, Their
4. This is as God meant it to be, That
5. Then, bless the bride - groom, bless the bride, The

chil - dren may be named and known, That love finds its own
we stand wit - ness to their vow, We call on God, the
own new fam - i - ly to make; And, shar - ing what their
man and wom - an should be one And live in love and
dreams they dream, the hopes they share; And thank the Lord whose

sanc - tua - ry, That those in love stay not a - lone.
Trin - i - ty, To sanc - ti - fy their pledg - es now.
pasts have taught, They shape it for the fu - ture's sake.
love through life, As Christ on earth has taught and done.
love in - spires The joy their lips and ours de - clare.

Praise, praise the Mak - er, Spir - it, Son,

bless - ing this mar - riage now be - gun.

Text: John L. Bell, b.1949, © 1989, Iona Community, GIA Publications, Inc., agent
Tune: SUSSEX CAROL, 8 8 8 8 88; harm. by Ralph Vaughan Williams, 1872-1958

Wherever You Go   635

1. Wher-ev-er you go   I shall go.
Wher-ev-er you live   so shall I live. Your peo-ple will be my peo-ple, and your God will be my God too.

2. Wher-ev-er you die   I shall die and there shall I be bur-ied be-side you. We will be to-geth-er for ev-er, and our love will be the gift of our life.

Text: Ruth 1:16, 17; Gregory Norbet, b.1940
Tune: Gregory Norbet, b.1940; arr. by Mary David Callahan, b.1923
© 1972, 1980, The Benedictine Foundation of the State of Vermont, Inc.

636 Out of the Depths

1. Out of the depths, O God, we call to you.
2. Out of the depths of fear, O God, we speak.
3. God of the lov - ing heart, we praise your name.

Wounds of the past re-main, af - fect-ing all we do.
Break - ing the si - len - ces, the sear - ing truth we seek.
Dance through our lives and loves; a - noint with Spir - it flame.

Fac - ing our lives, we need your love so much.
Safe a - mong friends, our grief and rage we share.
Your light il - lu - mines each fam - il - iar face.

Here in this com - mun - i - ty, heal us by your touch.
Here in this com - mun - i - ty, hold us in your care.
Here in this com - mun - i - ty, meet us with your grace.

Text: Psalm 130:1; Ruth Duck, b.1947, © 1992, GIA Publications, Inc.
Tune: FENNVILLE, 10 12 10 12; Robert J. Batastini, b.1942, © 1994, GIA Publications, Inc.

Precious Lord, Take My Hand   637

1. Pre-cious Lord, take my hand, Lead me on, let me stand, I am tired, I am weak, I am worn. Through the storm, through the night, Lead me on to the light, Take my hand, pre-cious Lord, lead me home.

2. When my way grows drear, Pre-cious Lord, lin-ger near, When my life is al-most gone, Hear my cry, hear my call, Hold my hand lest I fall. Take my hand, pre-cious Lord, lead me home.

3. When the dark-ness ap-pears And the night draws near, And the day is past and gone, At the riv-er I stand, Guide my feet, hold my hand. Take my hand, pre-cious Lord, lead me home.

Text: Thomas A. Dorsey, 1899-1993, © 1938, Unichappell Music, Inc.
Tune: PRECIOUS LORD 66 9 D; George N. Allen, © 1938, Unichappell Music, Inc.; arr. by Kelly Dobbs Mickus, b. 1966,
© 1994, GIA Publications, Inc.

638 Jesus, Heal Us

Refrain

Je - sus, heal us; Je - sus.

Je - sus, hear us now.

Verse 1

1. All who fear the Lord: Wait for God's mer - cy.

D.C.

All who love the Lord: Come, he will fill you.

Verse 2

2. All who fear the Lord: Fol - low the way.

D.C.

All who love the Lord: Hope in God's good - ness.

Verse 3

3. All who fear the Lord: Keep your hearts pre - pared.

D.C.

All who love the Lord: Be hum - bled in God's pres - ence.

Verse 4

4. All who trust the Lord: God will up-

hold you. Let us cling to our God; let us

D.C.

fall in the arms of the Lord!

Text: David Haas, b.1957
Tune: David Haas, b.1957
© 1988, GIA Publications, Inc.

639 He Healed the Darkness of My Mind

1. He healed the dark - ness of my mind the
2. Let oth - ers call my faith a lie, or
3. Ask me not how! But I know who has

day he gave my sight to me: It was not sin that
try to stir up doubt in me: Look at me now! None
o - pened up new worlds to me: This Je - sus does what

made me blind; It was no sin - ner made me see.
can de - ny I once was blind, and now I see.
none can do I once was blind, and now I see!

Text: John 9; Fred Pratt Green, b.1903, © 1982, Hope Publishing Co.
Tune: ARLINGTON, LM; David Haas, b.1957, © 1988, GIA Publications, Inc.

Deep Down in My Soul 640

Refrain

The Lord is kind and mer-ci-ful, and all my be-ing, bless God's name! The Lord is kind and mer-ci-ful! Bless the Lord, deep down in my soul!

Verses

1. O my soul; bless the Lord, and now with all my being, bless God's holy name!
   O my soul: I will bless the Lord,
   forgetting not the benefits, rememb'ring God's faithfulness!

2. O my soul: bless the Lord, forgiving our offenses, healing all our ills!
   O my soul: I will bless the Lord,
   who redeems us from destruction, and crowns us with compassion!

3. Merciful, and gracious; Our God is slow to anger, abounding in love!
   Our tender God will not haunt us with our sins;
   no longer abandoned! Our God is here to save us!

4. As the east is from the west, God will come and cast away all guilt and shame!
   With tenderness, as parents to their children
   healing and compassion, for those who fear the Lord!

Text: Psalm 103; David Haas, b.1957
Tune: David Haas, b.1957; arr. by David Haas and Rob Glover, b.1950

641 Remember Your Love

Refrain

Re - mem - ber your love and your faith - ful - ness, O

Lord. Re - mem - ber your peo-ple and have mer-cy on us, Lord.

Verses

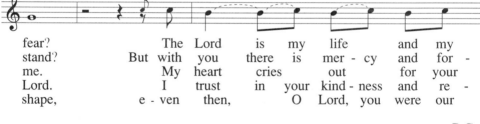

1. The Lord is my light and my sal - va - tion, whom should I
2. If you dwelt, O Lord, up - on our sin - ful - ness, then who could
3. O Lord, hear the sound of my call and an - swer
4. As watch-man who waits up - on the day - light, wait for the
5. Be - fore all the moun - tains were be - got - ten and earth took

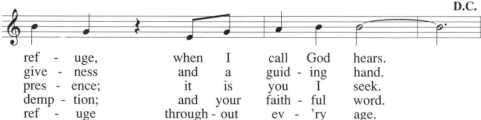

fear? The Lord is my life and my
stand? But with you there is mer - cy and for -
me. My heart cries out for your
Lord. I trust in your kind - ness and re -
shape, e - ven then, O Lord, you were our

D.C.

ref - uge, when I call God hears.
give - ness and a guid - ing hand.
pres - ence; it is you I seek.
demp - tion; and your faith - ful word.
ref - uge through - out ev - 'ry age.

Text: Psalm 27; Mike Balhoff, b.1946
Tune: Darryl Ducote, b.1945, and Gary Daigle, b.1957
© 1978, Damean Music. Distributed by GIA Publications, Inc.

Healer of Our Every Ill   642

Refrain

Heal-er of our ev-'ry ill, light of each to - mor-row,

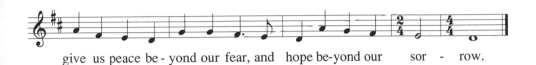

give us peace be - yond our fear, and hope be-yond our sor - row.

Verses

1. You who know our fears and sad - ness,
2. In the pain and joy be - hold - ing,
3. Give us strength to love each oth - er,
4. You who know each thought and feel - ing,

Grace us with your peace and glad - ness,
How your grace is still un - fold - ing,
Ev - 'ry sis - ter, ev - 'ry broth - er,
Teach us all your way of heal - ing,

D.C.

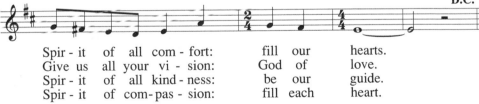

Spir - it of all com - fort: fill our hearts.
Give us all your vi - sion: God of love.
Spir - it of all kind - ness: be our guide.
Spir - it of com-pas - sion: fill each heart.

Text: Marty Haugen, b.1950
Tune: Marty Haugen, b.1950
© 1987, GIA Publications, Inc.

643   Ashes

1. We rise a-gain from ash-es, from the good we've failed to do. We rise a-gain from ash-es, to cre-ate our-selves a-new. If all our world is ash-es, then must our lives be true, An of-fer-ing of ash-es, an of-fer-ing to you.

2. We of-fer you our fail-ures, we of-fer you at-tempts, The gifts not ful-ly giv-en, the dreams not ful-ly dreamt. Give our stum-bl-ings di-rec-tion, give our vi-sions wid-er view, An of-fer-ing of ash-es, an of-fer-ing to you.

3. Then rise a-gain from ash-es, let heal-ing come to pain, Though spring has turned to win-ter, and sun-shine turned to rain. The rain we'll use for grow-ing, and cre-ate the world a-new From an of-fer-ing of ash-es, an of-fer-ing to you.

4. Thanks be to the Fa-ther, who made us like him-self. Thanks be to the Son, who saved us by his death. Thanks be to the Spir-it, who cre-ates the world a-new From an of-fer-ing of ash-es, an of-fer-ing to you.

Text: Tom Conry, b.1951
Tune: Tom Conry, b.1951; acc. by Michael Joncas, b.1951
© 1978, New Dawn Music

I Want to Call You   644

Refrain

I want to call you by your name while I live.

I will call you: "My God." I will

thank you, I will sing my praise to you.

Verses

1. God calls to me: "Come forth from your grave." Like an
2. God will for-give, God is ten - der-ness and love. Love is
3. God knows us well, to our God we be - long. God is

D.C.

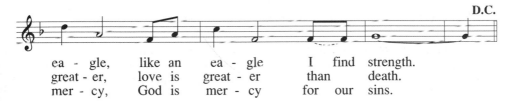

ea - gle, like an ea - gle I find strength.
great - er, love is great - er than death.
mer - cy, God is mer - cy for our sins.

Text: David Haas, b.1957
Tune: David Haas, b.1957
© 1989, GIA Publications, Inc.

645 Remember Your Mercy, Lord

Refrain

Re - mem-ber, re - mem-ber your mer - cy, Lord. Re -

mem - ber, re - mem - ber your mer - cy, Lord.

Hear your peo - ple's prayer as they call to you: re -

mem - ber, re - mem - ber your mer - cy, Lord.

Verses

1. Lord, make me know your ways. Lord, teach me your paths.
   Make me walk in your truth, and teach me: for you are God my Savior.

2. Remember your mercy, Lord, and the love you have shown from of old.
   Do not remember the sins of my youth. In your love, remember me,
   in your love, remember me, because of your goodness, O Lord.

3. The Lord is good and upright. He shows the path to all who stray,
   he guides the humble in the right path; he teaches his way to the poor.

Text: Psalm 25:4-9; © 1963, The Grail, GIA Publications, Inc., agent; refrain, Paul Inwood, b.1947, © 1987
Tune: Paul Inwood, b.1947, © 1987
Published by OCP Publications

God of Eve and God of Mary 646

Refrain

God of Eve and God of Mar - y,

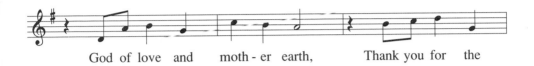

God of love and moth - er earth, Thank you for the

ones who with us Shared their life and gave us birth.

Verses

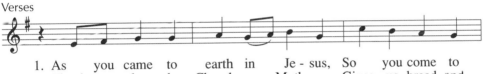

1. As you came to earth in Je - sus, So you come to
2. Thank you, that the Church, our Moth - er, Gives us bread and
3. Thank you for be - long - ing, shel - ter, Bonds of friend-ship,
4. God of Eve and God of Mar - y, Christ our broth - er,

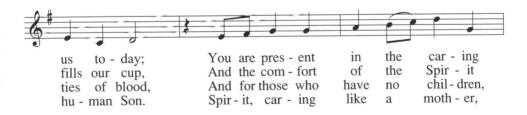

us to - day; You are pres - ent in the car - ing
fills our cup, And the com - fort of the Spir - it
ties of blood, And for those who have no chil - dren,
hu - man Son. Spir - it, car - ing like a moth - er,

D.C.

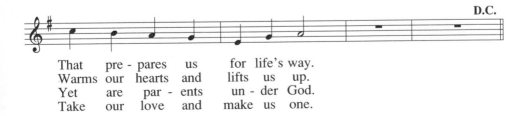

That pre - pares us for life's way.
Warms our hearts and lifts us up.
Yet are par - ents un - der God.
Take our love and make us one.

Text: Fred Kaan, b.1929, © 1989, Hope Publishing Co.
Tune: FARRELL, 8 7 8 7 with refrain; Thomas J. Porter, b.1958, © 1994, GIA Publications, Inc.

647 God of Adam, God of Joseph

Refrain

God of A - dam, God of Jo - seph,
God of sow - ing, soil and seed, Thank you for your
world of prom - ise: Milk and hon - ey, wine and bread.

Verses

1. God, you make us your com-pan-ions, Shar-ers of your
2. May your pas - sion for cre - a - tion Be re - flect - ed
3. Thank you for all men en - trust-ed With the charge of
4. Ab - ba (Fa - ther), God of Jo-seph, Hu - man Christ whose

lov - ing cup; Thank you for the gen - er - a - tions,
in our own; For our role in birth and nur - ture
fa - ther-hood, And for those who have no chil-dren,
name we bear, Spir - it, womb of life and wis-dom:

Weave of names and threads of hope.
Make through us your pres - ence known.
Yet are par - ents un - der God.
Thank you, God, for who we are!

Text: Fred Kaan, b.1929, © 1989, Hope Publishing Co.
Tune: FARRELL, 8 7 8 7 with refrain; Thomas J. Porter, b.1958, © 1994, GIA Publications, Inc.

The God of All Eternity 648

1. The God of all e - ter - ni - ty, Un - bound by
2. What shall we of - fer God to - day— Our dreams of
3. God does not share our doubts and fears, Nor shrinks from
4. Let faith or for - tune rise or fall, Let dreams and
5. God grant that we, in this new year, May show the

space yet al - ways near, Is pres - ent
what we can - not see, Or, with eyes
the un - known or strange: The one who
dread both have their day; Those whom God
world the King - dom's face, And let our

where his peo - ple meet To cel - e -
fas - tened to the past, Our dread of
fash - ioned heav'n and earth Makes all things
loves walk un - a - fraid With Christ their
work and wor - ship thrive As signs of

brate the com - ing year.
what is yet to be?
new and ush - ers change.
guide and Christ their way.
hope and means of grace.

Text: John L. Bell, b.1949, © 1989, Iona Community, GIA Publications, Inc., agent
Tune: O WALY WALY 8 8 8 8; English traditional; arr. by John L. Bell, b.1949, © 1989, Iona Community, GIA Publications, Inc., agent

649 Greet Now the Swiftly Changing Year

1. Greet now the swift - ly chang - ing year With
2. This Je - sus came to wage sin's war; The
3. His love a - bun - dant far ex - ceeds The
4. With such a Lord to lead our way In
5. "All glo - ry be to God on high And

joy and pen - i - tence sin - cere; Re - joice, re-joice, with
Name of names for us he bore; Re - joice, re-joice, with
vol - ume of a whole year's needs; Re - joice, re-joice, with
want and in pros - per - i - ty, What need we fear in
peace on earth," the an - gels cry; Re - joice, re-joice, with

thanks em - brace An - oth - er year of grace.
thanks em - brace An - oth - er year of grace.
thanks em - brace An - oth - er year of grace.
earth or space In this new year of grace?
thanks em - brace An - oth - er year of grace.

Text: Slovak, 17th C.; tr. Jaroslav J. Vajda, b.1919, alt. © 1969, Concordia Publishing House
Tune: SIXTH NIGHT, 88 86; Alfred V. Fedak, © 1989, Selah Publishing Co.

SERVICE MUSIC

Acknowledgements/*continued*

Box 13248, Portland, OR 97213-0248. All rights reserved. Used with permission.

199 Music: © 1979, 1988, Les Presses de Taizé, GIA Publications, Inc., agent.

203 Music: © 1984, Les Presses de Taizé, GIA Publications, Inc., agent.

204 © 1985, Fintan O'Carroll and Christopher Walker. Published by OCP Publications. All rights reserved.

205 Arrangement: © 1990, Iona Community, GIA Publications, Inc., agent.

209 Text and Tune: © 1984 by Bob Hurd. Accompaniment: © 1984, OCP Publications. Published by OCP Publications. All rights reserved.

211 Music: © 1980, Les Presses de Taizé, GIA Publications, Inc., agent.

212 Arrangement: © 1990, Iona Community, GIA Publications, Inc., agent.

213 Tune: © 1987, Dinah Reindorf. Arrangement: © 1990, Iona Community, GIA Publications, Inc., agent.

236 Music: © 1973, Robert J. Dufford, SJ and Daniel L. Schutte. Administered by New Dawn Music, P.O. Box 13248, Portland, OR 97213-0248. All rights reserved. Used with permission.

237 Music: © 1977, 1979, Robert J. Dufford, SJ and Daniel L. Schutte. Administered by New Dawn Music, P.O. Box 13248, Portland, OR 97213-0248. All rights reserved. Used with permission.

238 Music: © 1973, Robert J. Dufford, SJ and Daniel L. Schutte. Administered by New Dawn Music, P.O. Box 13248, Portland, OR 97213-0248. All rights reserved. Used with permission.

239 Adaptation: © 1980, Church Pension Fund.

245 Music: © 1993, Tony Way. Published and distributed in North America by GIA Publications, Inc.

248 Arr. © 1994, GIA Publications, Inc.

249 © 1990, GIA Publications, Inc.

250 © 1993, GIA Publications, Inc.

251 Text and Music: © 1976, Robert J. Dufford, SJ, and New Dawn Music, P.O. Box 13248, Portland, OR 97213-0248. All rights reserved. Used with permission.

252 © 1982, GIA Publications, Inc.

253 © 1994, GIA Publications, Inc.

254 © 1993, GIA Publications, Inc.

255 © 1988, GIA Publications, Inc.

256 © 1984, Les Presses de Taizé, GIA Publications, Inc., agent.

257 Text and Music: © 1982, Bernadette Farrell. Administered in England by the St. Thomas More Group. Published by OCP Publications. All rights reserved.

258 Text and Tune: © 1971, The United Church Press. Reprinted from *A New Song 3*. Accompaniment: © 1987, GIA Publications, Inc.

259 © 1983, GIA Publications, Inc.

260 © 1974, 1975 CELEBRATION. (Administered by MARANATHA! MUSIC c/o THE COPYRIGHT COMPANY, NASHVILLE, TN) All Rights Reserved. International Copyright Secured. Used By Permission.

261 © 1984, GIA Publications, Inc.

263 © 1990, Pablo Sosa

264 © Text and Tune: © 1945, Boosey and Co., Ltd.; Copyright Renewed. Reprinted by permission of Boosey & Hawkes, Inc. Accompaniment: © 1993, GIA Publications, Inc.

265 © 1983, GIA Publications, Inc.

266 © 1992, GIA Publications, Inc.

267 © 1987, Iona Community, GIA Publications, Inc., agent.

268 © 1992, GIA Publications, Inc.

269 © Text: "A Christmas Hymn" from *Advice to a Prophet and Other Poems* ©1961, Richard Wilbur. Reprinted by permission of Harcourt Brace and Company. Music: © 1992, GIA Publications, Inc.

270 © 1991, GIA Publications, Inc.

272 Text: English Text by J. E. Middleton: © The Frederick Harris Music Co., Limited, Oakville, Ontario, Canada. All rights reserved. Arrangement: © 1992, GIA Publications, Inc.

273 Text: © 1980 by Hope Publishing Co., Carol Stream, IL 60188. All rights reserved. Used by permission. Music: © 1985, GIA Publications, Inc.

274 © 1992, GIA Publications, Inc

275 © 1987, GIA Publications, Inc.

276 Arrangement: © 1990, Iona Community, GIA Publications, Inc., agent.

277 © 1987, Iona Community, GIA Publications, Inc., agent.

278 Harmonization: © 1987, GIA Publications, Inc.

279 © 1978, Damean Music. Distributed by GIA Publications, Inc.

280 Text: © 1989 by Hope Publishing Co., Carol Stream, IL 60188. All rights reserved. Used by permission. Music: © 1991, GIA Publications, Inc.

281 Text: © 1982, Thomas H. Cain. Music: © 1988, GIA Publications, Inc.

282 © 1972, 1980, The Benedictine Foundation of the State of Vermont, Inc., Weston Priory, Weston, Vermont.

283 © 1990, 1991, GIA Publications, Inc.

284 © 1990, GIA Publications, Inc.

285 Copyright © 1984, North American Liturgy Resources, 11036 N. 23rd Ave., Phoenix, AZ 85029. All rights reserved.

286 © 1990, Bernadette Farrell. Administered in England by the St. Thomas More Group. Published by OCP Publications. All rights reserved.

287 Music: © 1984, GIA Publications, Inc.

288 © 1984, GIA Publications, Inc.

289 © 1993, GIA Publications, Inc.

290 © 1987, GIA Publications, Inc.

291 © 1990, GIA Publications, Inc.

292 © 1988, GIA Publications, Inc.

293 © 1981, Les Presses de Taizé, GIA Publications, Inc., agent.

294 Text: Verses 3-9 © 1991, GIA Publications, Inc. Harmonization: © 1987, GIA Publications, Inc.

295 Text: (except first verse for Holy Thursday and Good Friday, and final two verses for Easter Vigil) © 1987, GIA Publications, Inc. Accompaniment: © 1987, GIA Publications, Inc.

296 © 1982 by Hope Publishing Co., Carol Stream, IL 60188. All rights reserved. Used by permission.

297 © 1992, GIA Publications, Inc.

298 © 1984, Les Presses de Taizé, GIA Publications, Inc., agent.

299 © 1988, GIA Publications, Inc.

300 Copyright © 1986, North American Liturgy Resources, 11036 N. 23rd Ave., Phoenix, AZ 85029. All rights reserved.

301 © 1979, Les Presses de Taizé, GIA Publications, Inc., agent.

302 Harmonization: © 1987, GIA Publications, Inc.

303 © 1991, Les Presses de Taizé, GIA Publications, Inc., agent.

304 Text and Music: © 1981, Robert F. O'Connor, SJ, and New Dawn Music, P.O. Box 13248, Portland, OR 97213-0248. All rights reserved. Used with permission.

306 Text and Music: © 1976, Daniel L. Schutte and New Dawn Music, P.O. Box 13248, Portland, OR 97213-0248. All rights reserved. Used with permission.

307 © 1986, GIA Publications, Inc.

Acknowledgements/*continued*

308 © 1988, Iona Community, GIA Publications, Inc., agent.

309 © 1993, GIA Publications, Inc.

10 © 1978, Les Presses de Taizé, GIA Publications, Inc.

311 Text: © 1986, by Hope Publishing Co., Carol Stream, IL 60188. All rights reserved. Used by permission. Music: © 1991, GIA Publications, Inc.

312 Text and Tune: © 1972, Francisco Gómez Argüello y Ediciones Musical PAX. All rights reserved. Sole U.S. Agent: OCP Publications. English text: © 1988, OCP Publications. All rights reserved. Accompaniment: © 1993, GIA Publications, Inc.

313 Text and Music: © 1975, Robert J. Dufford, SJ, and New Dawn Music, P.O. Box 13248, Portland, OR 97213-0248. All rights reserved. Used with permission.

314 © 1984, Les Presses de Taizé, GIA Publications, Inc., agent.

315 © 1969 by Hope Publishing Co., Carol Stream, IL 60188. All rights reserved. Used by permission.

316 Harmonization: © 1984, Jack W. Burnam.

317 Text and Tune: © 1973, The Word of God. All rights reserved. P.O. Box 8617, Ann Arbor, MI 48107, U.S.A. Descant harmonization: © 1979 CELEBRATION (Administered by MARANATHA! MUSIC c/o THE COPYRIGHT COMPANY, NASHVILLE, TN) All Rights Reserved. International Copyright Secured. Used By Permission.

318 Text: From *Oxford Book of Carols,* © Oxford University Press. Accompaniment: © 1987, GIA Publications, Inc.

319 © 1988, Iona Community, GIA Publications, Inc., agent.

320 © 1980, GIA Publications, Inc.

321 Copyright © 1987, North American Liturgy Resources, 11036 N. 23rd Ave., Phoenix, AZ 85029. All rights reserved.

322 © 1983, GIA Publications, Inc.

323 © 1981 by Word Music (a div. of WORD, INC.). All Rights Reserved. Used by Permission.

324 Text and music: © 1988, Bob Hurd. Accompaniment and arrangement: © 1988, OCP Publications. Published by OCP Publications. All rights reserved.

325 © 1987, GIA Publications, Inc.

326 © 1979, Les Presses de Taizé, GIA Publications, Inc., agent.

327 © 1989, GIA Publications, Inc.

328 © 1969 and this arrangement © 1987 by Hope Publishing Co., Carol Stream, IL 60188. All rights reserved. Used by permission.

329 © 1981, 1982, 1987, GIA Publications, Inc.

330 Transcription and paraphrase © 1990, I-to-Loh.

331 Text: © 1989 by Hope Publishing Co., Carol Stream, IL 60188. All rights reserved. Used by permission. Arrangement: © 1991, GIA Publications, Inc.

332 © 1988, GIA Publications, Inc.

333 Text: © 1983 by Hope Publishing Co., Carol Stream, IL 60188. All rights reserved. Used by permission. Music: © 1994, GIA Publications, Inc.

334 © 1988, GIA Publications, Inc.

335 Text: © 1986 by Hope Publishing Co., Carol Stream, IL 60188. All rights reserved. Used by permission. Music: © 1993, GIA Publications, Inc.

336 © 1993, GIA Publications, Inc.

337 © 1985, GIA Publications, Inc.

338 Text: © 1916, Walton Music Corp. Music: © 1993, Iona Community, GIA Publications, Inc., agent.

339 © 1990, Bernadette Farrell. Administered in England by the St. Thomas More Group. Published by OCP Publications. All rights reserved.

340 © 1989, GIA Publications, Inc.

341 Text: © 1991, Ramon and Sario Oliano. Music: © 1991, Iona Community, GIA Publications, Inc., agent.

342 © 1980, GIA Publications, Inc.

343 © 1987, GIA Publications, Inc.

344 Text: © 1981 by Hope Publishing Co., Carol Stream, IL 60188. All rights reserved. Used by permission. Music: © 1986, GIA Publications, Inc.

345 © 1993, GIA Publications, Inc.

346 © 1992, GIA Publications, Inc.

347 Text and Music: © 1984, TEAM publications. Published by OCP Publicatons. All rights reserved.

348 © 1982, 1988, GIA Publications, Inc.

349 Text and Music: © 1978, John B. Foley, SJ, and New Dawn Music, P.O. Box 13248, Portland, OR 97213-0248. All rights reserved. Used with permission.

350 © 1991, GIA Publications, Inc.

351 Text and Music: © 1979, New Dawn Music, P.O. Box 13248, Portland, OR 97213-0248. All rights reserved. Used with permission.

352 Text and Tune: © 1970, CELEBRATION (Administered by MARANATHA! MUSIC c/o THE COPYRIGHT COMPANY, NASHVILLE, TN) All Rights Reserved. International Copyright Secured. Used By Permission. Accompaniment: © 1987, GIA Publications, Inc.

353 © 1966, Vernacular Hymns Publishing Co.

354 © 1985, GIA Publications, Inc.

355 Text and Tune: © 1978, 1979, Greg Hayakawa. Accompaniment: © 1985, OCP Publications. Published by OCP Publications. All rights reserved.

356 © 1987, GIA Publications, Inc.

357 © 1984, Utryck, Walton Music Corporation, agent.

359 © 1987, Iona Community, GIA Publications, Inc., agent.

360 © 1986, Bernadette Farrell. Administered in England by the St. Thomas More Group. Published by OCP Publications. All rights reserved.

361 © 1986, GIA Publications, Inc.

362 © 1983, GIA Publications, Inc.

363 © 1993, GIA Publications, Inc.

364 © 1980, Les Presses de Taizé, GIA Publications, Inc., agent.

365 Tune: © Editora Sinodal, Sao Leopoldo. Arrangement: © 1991, Iona Community, GIA Publications, Inc., agent.

366 © 1987, Iona Community, GIA Publications, Inc., agent.

367 © 1983, GIA Publications, Inc.

368 Text: © 1969, James Quinn, Published by Geoffrey Chapman, a division of Cassell Publications. Used by permission of Selah Publishing Co., Inc., Kingston, NY. Music: © 1979, GIA Publications, Inc.

369 © 1990, Iona Community, GIA Publications, Inc., agent.

370 © 1978, Damean Music. Distributed by GIA Publications, Inc.

371 Text and Tune: © 1979, Manuel José Alonso, José Pagán y Ediciones Musical PAX. All rights reserved. Sole U.S. Agent: OCP Publications. Accompaniment: © 1994, GIA Publications, Inc.

372 © 1992, GIA Publications, Inc.

373 Text and Tune: © 1981, Ernest Sands. Accompaniment: © 1986, Paul Inwood. Administered in England by the St. Thomas More Group. Published by OCP Publications. All rights reserved.

374 © 1992, GIA Publications, Inc.

375 Text and Tune: © 1976, Resource Publications, Inc. 160 E. Virginia St., #290, San Jose, CA 95112. Accompaniment: © 1993, GIA Publications, Inc.

376 © 1990, GIA Publications, Inc.

377 © 1979, Les Presses de Taizé, GIA Publications, Inc., agent.

Acknowledgements/*continued*

378 © 1981, Robert J. Dufford, SJ, and New Dawn Music, P.O. Box 13248, Portland, OR 97213-0248. All rights reserved. Used with permission.

379 Text and Music: © 1973 by Hope Publishing Co., Carol Stream, IL 60188. All rights reserved. Used by permission.

380 Text and Music: © 1976, Daniel L. Schutte and New Dawn Music, P.O. Box 13248, Portland, OR 97213-0248. All rights reserved. Used with permission.

381 © 1993, GIA Publications, Inc.

382 Text and Tune: © 1984, Bob Hurd. Accompaniment: © 1984, OCP Publications. Published by OCP Publications. All rights reserved.

383 Text: © 1987, Iona Community, GIA Publications, Inc., agent. Accompaniment: © 1993, Iona Community, GIA Publications, Inc., agent.

384 Text and Music: © 1972, Daniel L. Schutte. Administered by New Dawn Muisc, P.O. Box 13248, Portland, OR 97213-0428. All rights reserved. Used with permission.

385 Text: © 1991, Iona Community, GIA Publications, Inc., agent. Tune: © 1989, Salvador T. Martinez. Arrangement: © 1991, Iona Community, GIA Publications, Inc., agent.

386 © 1974, CELEBRATION (Administered by MARANATHA! MUSIC c/o THE COPYRIGHT COMPANY, NASHVILLE, TN) All Rights Reserved. International Copyright Secured. Used By Permission.

387 Text and Tune: © 1981, Robert F. O'Connor, SJ, and New Dawn Music, P.O. Box 13248, Portland, OR 97213-0248. All rights reserved. Used with permission. Accompaniment: ©1994, GIA Publications, Inc.

388 Text: Stanzas 1-4 © 1982 by Hope Publishing Co., Carol Stream, IL 60188. All rights reserved. Used by permission. Stanzas 5-6 © 1993, GIA Publications, Inc. Harmonization: © 1992, GIA Publications, Inc.

389 © 1985, Damean Music. Distributed by GIA Publications, Inc.

390 © 1983, 1987, GIA Publications, Inc.

391 Text: © 1972 by Hope Publishing Co., Carol Stream, IL 60188. All rights reserved. Used by permission. Music: © 1989, GIA Publications, Inc.

392 © 1981, John B. Foley, SJ, and New Dawn Music, P.O. Box 13248, Portland, OR 97213-0248. All rights reserved. Used with permission.

393 © 1981, GIA Publications, Inc.

394 © 1984, Utryck, Walton Music Corporation, agent.

395 Text and Tune: © 1986, Guillermo Cuellar. Accompaniment: © 1993, GIA Publications, Inc.

396 © 1986, 1991, Les presses de Taizé, GIA Publications, Inc., agent.

397 © 1990, GIA Publications, Inc.

398 © 1982, 1991, Les Presses de Taizé, GIA Publications, Inc., agent.

399 © 1985, Damean Music. Distributed by GIA Publications, Inc.

400 © 1953, Doris Akers. All rights administered by Unichappell Music, Inc. International Copyright Secured. All Rights Reserved.

401 © 1989, Iona Community, GIA Publications, Inc., agent.

402 Text: © 1979, Stainer and Bell, Ltd., London, England. Music: © 1987, GIA Publications, Inc.

404 Text: © 1979 by The Hymn Society, Texas Christian University, Fort Worth, TX 76129. All rights reserved. Used by permission. Music: © 1989, GIA Publications, Inc.

405 Music: © 1991, Iona Community, GIA Publications, Inc., agent.

406 Text: © 1983, The Pastoral Press. Music: © 1991, GIA Publications, Inc.

407 © 1989, Iona Community, GIA Publications, Inc., agent.

408 Text and Tune: © Copyright 1964 (Renewed) by Appleseed Music, Inc., 200 West 57th St., New York, NY 10019. Arrangement: ©1982, GIA Publications, Inc.

409 © 1987, GIA Publications, Inc.

410 © 1982, Les Presses de Taizé, GIA Publications, Inc., agent.

412 © 1993, GIA Publications, Inc.

413 Tune: Adapt. © 1983 by Abingdon Press. Used from *Hymns from the Four Winds*. Accompaniment: © 1993, GIA Publications, Inc.

414 Music: © 1984, GIA Publications, Inc.

415 Text: © 1986 by Hope Publishing Co., Carol Stream, IL 60188. All rights reserved. Used by permission. Music: © 1990, GIA Publications, Inc.

416 Music: © 1990, Iona Community, GIA Publications, Inc., agent.

417 © 1980, GIA Publications, Inc.

418 © 1976, John B. Foley, SJ, and New Dawn Music, P.O. Box 13248, Portland, OR 97213-0248. All rights reserved. Used with permission.

419 © 1988, GIA Publications, Inc.

420 Copyright © 1986, North American Liturgy Resources, 11036 N. 23rd Ave., Phoenix, AZ 85029. All rights reserved.

421 © 1989, GIA Publications, Inc.

422 Music and refrain text: © 1985, Paul Inwood. Administered in England by the St. Thomas More Group. Published by OCP Publications. All rights reserved. Verse text: © 1963, 1993, The Grail, GIA Publications, Inc., agent.

423 © 1967, Gooi en Sticht, bv., Baarn, The Netherlands. All rights reserved. Exclusive English-language agent: OCP Publications.

424 © 1976, John B. Foley, SJ, and New Dawn Music, P.O. Box 13248, Portland, OR 97213-0248. All rights reserved. Used with permission.

425 © 1969, 1979, Damean Music. Distributed by GIA Publications, Inc.

426 © 1975, Daniel L. Schutte and New Dawn Music, P.O. Box 13248, Portland, OR 97213-0248. All rights reserved. Used with permission.

427 Text: © 1957, 1964, Sanga Music, Inc., 250 W. 57th St., Ste. 710, New York, NY 10107. Harmonization: © 1987, GIA Publications, Inc.

428 © 1971, Daniel L. Schutte. Administered by New Dawn Music, P.O. Box 13248, Portland, OR 97213-0248. All rights reserved. Used with permission.

429 © 1980, Savgos Music, Inc.

430 © 1975, Robert J. Dufford, SJ, and New Dawn Music, P.O. Box 13248, Portland, OR 07213-0248. All rights reserved. Used with permission.

431 © 1978, Damean Music. Distributed by GIA Publications, Inc.

432 © 1982, Dennis Vessels.

433 © 1979, New Dawn Music, P.O. Box 13248, Portland, OR 07213-0248. All rights reserved. Used with permission.

434 Accompaniment: © 1993, GIA Publications, Inc.

435 Text and Tune: © 1989, M. D. Ridge. Accompaniment: © 1990, OCP Publications. Published by OCP Publications. All rights reserved.

Acknowledgements/*continued*

Acknowledgements/*continued*

Acknowledgements/*continued*

589 Text: © 1991, GIA Publications, Inc. Music: © 1993, GIA Publications, Inc.

590 © 1982, 1987, Bernadette Farrell. Administered in England by the St. Thomas More Group. Published by OCP Publications. All rights reserved.

591 © 1987, GIA Publications, Inc.

592 Text and Music: © 1984, OCP Publications. All rights reserved.

593 Copyright © 1987 by North American Liturgy Resources, 11036 N. 23rd Ave., Phoenix, AZ 95029. All rights reserved.

594 © 1990, GIA Publications, Inc.

595 © 1992, GIA Publications, Inc.

596 © 1990, Bernadette Farrell. Administered in England by the St. Thomas More Group. Published by OCP Publications. All rights reserved.

597 © 1966, 1970, 1986, 1993, GIA Publications, Inc.

598 © 1988, GIA Publications, Inc.

599 Text and Music: © 1978, John B. Foley, SJ, and New Dawn Music, P.O. Box 13248, Portland, OR 97213-0248. All rights reserved. Used with permission.

600 © 1986, GIA Publications, Inc.

601 © 1987, EKKLESIA Music, Inc., P.O. Box 22967, Denver, CO 80222.

602 © 1993, GIA Publications, Inc.

603 © 1992, GIA Publications, Inc.

604 © 1992, GIA Publications, Inc.

605 English text and Tune: © 1984, Bob Hurd. Revised English Text: © 1987, Bob Hurd and Michael Downey. Spanish text: © 1989, OCP Publications. Accompaniment: © 1984, OCP Publications. All rights reserved. Published and distributed by OCP Publications.

606 © 1992, GIA Publications, Inc.

607 © 1969, 1979, Damean Music. Distributed by GIA Publications, Inc.

608 © 1979, New Dawn Music, P.O. Box 13248, Portland, OR 97213-0248. All rights reserved. Used with permission.

609 © 1983, GIA Publications, Inc.

610 © 1993, GIA Publications, Inc.

611 Text: © 1988, Iona Community, GIA Publications, Inc., agent. Accompaniment: © 1993, Iona Community, GIA Publications, Inc., agent.

612 © 1993, GIA Publications, Inc.

613 © 1989, GIA Publications, Inc.

614 Verse text: © 1969, James Quinn, SJ. Used by permission of Selah Publishing Co., Inc., Kingston, N.Y. Refrain text and Tune: © 1989, GIA Publications, Inc.

615 Text and Tune: © 1988, Bob Hurd. Accompaniment and arrangement: © 1988, OCP Publications. All rights reserved. Published by OCP Publications.

616 © 1991, GIA Publications, Inc.

617 © 1994, GIA Publications, Inc.

618 © 1992, GIA Publications, Inc.

619 © 1990, GIA Publications, Inc.

620 Text: © 1991, Jean Janzen. Music: © 1993, GIA Publications, Inc.

621 © 1993, GIA Publications, Inc.

622 Refrain and verse 1 text and Music: © 1994, GIA Publications, Inc. Verse 2 text from *In paradisum; Rite of Funerals*, © 1970, International Commission on English in the Liturgy.

623 Copyright © 1983 by North American Liturgy Resources, 11036 N. 23rd Ave., Phoenix, AZ 95029. All rights reserved.

624 © 1980, GIA Publications, Inc.

625 Text: *Order of Christian Funerals*, © 1985, International Commission on English in the Liturgy. Music: © 1990, GIA Publications, Inc.

626 Refrain text: © 1973, International Commission on English in the Liturgy. Verse text and Music: © 1988, GIA Publications, Inc.

627 © 1993, GIA Publications, Inc.

628 © 1983 by Hope Publishing Co., Carol Stream, IL 60188. All rights reserved. Used by permission.

629 Text: © 1981, Concordia Publishing House. Music: © 1993, GIA Publications, Inc.

630 © 1993, GIA Publications, Inc.

631 Text: © 1989, Iona Community, GIA Publications, Inc., agent. Harmonization: © 1985 by Hope Publishing Co., Carol Stream, IL 60188. All rights reserved. Used by permission.

632 © 1993, GIA Publications, Inc.

633 © 1989, GIA Publications, Inc.

634 Text: © 1989, Iona Community, GIA Publications, Inc., agent.

635 © 1972, 1980, The Benedictine Foundation of the State of Vermont, Inc., Weston Priory, Weston, Vermont.

636 Text: © 1992, GIA Publications, Inc. Music: © 1994, GIA Publications, Inc.

637 Text and Tune: © 1938 by Unichappell Music, Inc. Copyright Renewed. International Copyright Secured. All Rights Reserved. Arrangement: © 1994, GIA Publications, Inc.

638 © 1988, GIA Publications, Inc.

639 Text: © 1982 by Hope Publishing Co., Carol Stream, IL 60188. All rights reserved. Used by permission. Music: © 1988, GIA Publications, Inc.

640 © 1993, GIA Publications, Inc.

641 © 1978, Damean Music. Distributed by GIA Publications, Inc.

642 © 1987, GIA Publications, Inc.

643 © 1978, New Dawn Music, P.O. Box 13248, Portland, OR 97213-0248. All rights reserved. Used with permission.

644 © 1989, GIA Publications, Inc.

645 Verse text: © 1963, 1993, The Grail, GIA Publications, Inc., agent. Refrain text and Music: © 1987, Paul Inwood. Published by OCP Publications. All rights reserved.

646 Text: © 1989 by Hope Publishing Co., Carol Stream, IL 60188. All rights reserved. Used by permission. Music: © 1994, GIA Publications, Inc.

647 Text: © 1989 by Hope Publishing Co., Carol Stream, IL 60188. All rights reserved. Used by permission. Music: © 1994, GIA Publications, Inc.

648 Text and Arrangement: © 1989, Iona Community, GIA Publications, Inc., agent.

649 Text: © 1969, Concordia Publishing House. Music: © 1989, Selah Publishing Co., Inc., Kingston, NY.

GENESIS

1:	Joyful Is the Dark	550
1:	Many and Great	338
1:	Song Over the Waters	409
1:	The Earth Is the Lord's	341
1:	This Day God Gives Me	547
1:2-3	Psalm 107 Give Thanks to the Lord	91
1:14-19	All Things New	309
1:26-27	God, beyond All Names	339
1:26-28	Psalm 112 A Light Rises in the Darkness	93
1:27-30	God of Adam, God of Joseph	647
2:15	God of Adam, God of Joseph	647
2:18-23	Blessing the Marriage	634
2:18-23	God, in the Planning	631
12:1-4	God It Was	503
12:1-5	God of Abraham	286
18:	This Is the Day	320
18:9-15	God It Was	503
18:9-15	God of Abraham	286
28:10-15	We Are Climbing Jacob's Ladder	497
28:12-13	Calvary	305

EXODUS

3:	Go Down, Moses	515
3:9-10	God It Was	503
3:13-15	I Am for You	506
4:1-17	God of Abraham	286
12:1-14	As We Remember	587
13:3-16	Bless the Feast	545
13:21	Eternal Lord of Love	281
14:	All Things New	309
14:	Go Down, Moses	515
15:	Go Down, Moses	515
15:1-6	Song at the Sea: Exodus 15	126
15:17-18	Song at the Sea: Exodus 15	126
15:20-21	God It Was	503
16:	Shepherd of Our Hearts	598
16:4	All Things New	309
16:13-15	Change Our Hearts	285
16:21	Psalm 78 The Lord Gave Them Bread	68
17:	Shepherd of Our Hearts	598
17:5-7	Change Our Hearts	285
34:	I Will Not Die	467

LEVITICUS

19:9	The Harvest of Justice	513
23:22	The Harvest of Justice	513
25:8-12	Sign Me Up	579
25:42	Psalm 81 Sing with Joy to God	71

NUMBERS

6:22-27	Bwana Awabariki / May God Grant You a Blessing	411
6:24	A Nuptial Blessing	633
6:24-26	May the Lord, Mighty God	413
14:33	May We Be One	247

DEUTERONOMY

8:3	Not by Bread Alone	362
8:3	Shepherd of Our Hearts	598
24:19	The Harvest of Justice	513

JOSHUA

24:14-24	We Will Serve the Lord	473
24:15	We Will Serve the Lord	632

RUTH

1:16-17	Wherever You Go	630
1:16	Wherever You Go	635
1:	God of Abraham	286

Scripture Passages Related to Hymns/*continued*

86:9-10	Psalm 86 Lord, You Are Good and Forgiving	75
86:15-16	Psalm 86 Lord, You Are Good and Forgiving	75
89:	Psalm 89 For Ever I Will Sing	76
89:1-16	Let Heaven Your Wonders Proclaim	385
90:	The Lord Is My Hope	435
90:2	Remember Your Love	641
90:3-6	Psalm 90 In Ev'ry Age	77
90:12-14	Psalm 90 In Ev'ry Age	77
90:12-17	Psalm 90 Fill Us with Your Love, O Lord	78
90:17	Psalm 90 In Ev'ry Age	77
91:	Blessed Be the Lord	437
91:	On Eagle's Wings	433
91:	Psalm 91 Be with Me	79
91:11-12	Saints of God / Song of Farewell	625
92:2-3	Psalm 92 Lord, It Is Good	80
92:13-16	Psalm 92 Lord, It Is Good	80
93:1-2	Psalm 93 The Lord Is King	81
93:5	Psalm 93 The Lord Is King	81
95:	My Soul in Stillness Waits	252
95:	Psalm 95 Psalm 95 If Today You Hear God's Voice	82 82
95:	This Is the Day	320
95:	To God with Gladness Sing	368
96:	This Is the Day	320
96:1	A New Song	367
96:1-3	Psalm 96 Proclaim to All the Nations	83
96:1-3	Psalm 96 Today Is Born Our Savior	84
96:1	Sing Our God Together	381
96:7-10	Psalm 96 Proclaim to All the Nations	83
96:11-13	Psalm 96 Today Is Born Our Savior	84
97:1	Lord, Today	279
97:1-2	Psalm 97 The Lord Is King	85
97:6-7	Psalm 97 The Lord Is King	85
97:9	Psalm 97 The Lord Is King	85
98:	All the ends of the earth	378
98:	Cantai ao Senhor	365
98:	Psalm 98 All the Ends of the Earth	86
98:	Sing a New Song	384
98:	Sing a New Song to the Lord	379
100:	All the Earth, Proclaim God's Glory	374
100:	Joyfully Singing	389
100:	Jubilate, Servite	377
100:	Lift Up Your Hearts	387
100:	Psalm 100 We Are His People	87
100:	Sing of the Lord's Goodness	373
100:	To God with Gladness Sing	368
100:3	Be Still	438
102:2	O Lord, Hear My Prayer	410
102:2	Standin' in the Need of Prayer	403
103:	Blessed Be God	334
103:	Deep Down in My Soul	640
103:	Jesus, Heal Us	638
103:	Our God Is Rich in Love	464
103:	Praise the Lord, My Soul	393
103:	Psalm 103 The Lord Is Kind and Merciful	89
103:1-2	Psalm 103 The Lord Is Kind and Merciful	88
103:3-6	Psalm 146 Happy the Poor in Spirit	123
103:6	Psalm 103 The Lord Is Kind and Merciful	88
103:8	Psalm 103 The Lord Is Kind and Merciful	88
103:17-18	Psalm 103 The Lord Is Kind and Merciful	88
104:	Blessed Be God	334
104:	God of All Creation	343
104:	Psalm 104 Lord, Send Out Your Spirit	90
104:	Spirit Blowing through Creation	325
104:	This Day God Gives Me	547
104:	World without End	383
104:	You Are the Voice	390
104:24	We Praise You	370
104:30	Envía Tu Espíritu / Send Our Your Spirit	324
104:30	Send Down the Fire	327
104:30	Send Us Your Spirit	329

137:1-6	Psalm 137 Let My Tongue Be Silent 116
138:1-3	Psalm 138 Lord, Your Love Is Eternal 117
138:1-5	Psalm 138 The Fragrance of Christ 118
138:6-7	Psalm 138 Lord, Your Love Is Eternal 117
139:	Lover of Us All 448
139:	You Are Near 428
139:1-3	Psalm 139 Filling Me with Joy 119
139:9-10	The Hand of God Shall Hold You 622
139:13-15	Psalm 139 Filling Me with Joy 119
141:	Psalm 141/Incense Psalm 12
141:1-5	Psalm 141 Evening Offering 120
141:8-9	Psalm 141 Evening Offering 120
145:	Psalm 145 I Will Praise Your Name 121
145:8-10	Psalm 145 Our God Is Compassion 122
145:13-20	Psalm 146 Happy the Poor in Spirit 123
145:15	Psalm 145 Our God Is Compassion 122
145:17-18	Psalm 145 Our God Is Compassion 122
145:18	The Lord Is Near 431
145:18	The Lord Is Near 439
145:18	You Are All We Have 346
146:	Psalm 146 Lord, Come and Save Us 124
146:2	A New Song 367
146:7-10	Psalm 146 Happy the Poor in Spirit 123
147:	How Shall I Sing to God? 415
147:	Psalm 147 Bless the Lord, My Soul 125
147:14	You Are Our Living Bread 608
148:	All You Works of God 340
148:	Creating God 404
148:	I Want to Praise Your Name 382
149:	I Want to Praise Your Name 382
150:	I Want to Praise Your Name 382
150:	Sing of the Lord's Goodness 373

SONG OF SONGS

| 2:10-12 | Wherever You Go 630 |
| 7:6-7 | Wherever You Go 630 |

WISDOM

| 9:4 | O God of Matchless Glory 372 |

ISAIAH

2:1-4	How Good It Is 525
5:1-7	Psalm 80 The Vineyard of the Lord 69
6:3	Santo, Santo, Santo/Holy, Holy, Holy 395
6:3	Sing to the Mountains 313
6:8	Here I Am, Lord 492
9:1-2	City of God 485
9:1-5	Lord, Today 279
9:2-11	Child of Mercy 270
11:1-5	Lord, Today 279
11:6	Walk in the Reign 249
12:1-2	Isaiah 12 129
12:3	In the Lord I'll Be Ever Thankful 396
12:3	You Will Draw Water 440
12:5-6	Isaiah 12 129
27:2-6	Psalm 80 The Vineyard of the Lord 69
35:1-6	Walk in the Reign 249
40:1	Walk in the Reign 249
40:9	Like a Shepherd 251
40:31-34	Though the Mountains May Fall 426
40:31	We Will Drink the Cup 512
41:10	We Will Rise Again 462
43:2-3	Be Not Afraid 430
49:15	Though the Mountains May Fall 426
49:16	You Are Mine 461
52:7	Great Is the Lord 490
53:1-5	Wherever You Go 635
53:4	Behold the Wood 306
54:6-10	Though the Mountains May Fall 426
55:	Come to the Feast 350

55:1-2	All You Who Are Thirsty 348
55:1-3	Come to Us 538
55:1-2	Come to the Water 349
55:1	Take and Eat this Bread 606
55:1-3	We Come to Your Feast 617
55:10-11	Sow the Word 361
55:10	Thy Kingdom Come 466
57:15	Psalm 138 Lord, Your Love Is Eternal 117
58:9-14	Return to God 283
61:1	Advent Gathering 250
61:1-2	Bless the Feast 545
61:1-4	God Has Chosen Me 488
61:1-4	Good News 486
61:1-4	Great Is the Lord 490
61:1	Penitential Litany - Penitential Litany 289
61:1	Song of the Body of Christ / Canción del Cuerpo 613
61:1-2	The Carpenter 336
61:1-2	You Have Anointed Me 483
67:7	Easter Alleluia 307

JEREMIAH

8:22	Balm in Gilead 460
31:3	I Have Loved You 351
31:33	Deep Within 290

EZEKIEL

11:19	Here I Am, Lord 492
34:11	Like a Shepherd 251
36:26-28	Deep Within 290
37:23	I Will Be with You 322
47:1-12	Healing River 408

DANIEL

3:	Surrexit Christus 314
3:52-90	All You Works of God 340
3:52-56	Daniel 3 130

HOSEA

2:16	Hosea 282
3:3	Hosea 282
6:1	Hosea 282
14:2	Deep Within 290
21:	Hosea 282

JOEL

2:12	Deep Within 290
2:12	Hosea 282
2:12	Return to God 283
3:1	Song Over the Waters 409
12:12-14	Let Justice Roll Like a River 516

AMOS

1:2	Psalm 146 Happy the Poor in Spirit 123
9:2	Psalm 139 Filling Me with Joy 119
5:21-24	Let Justice Roll Like a River 516
8:4	Let Justice Roll Like a River 516

MICAH

4:3-4	Let Justice Roll Like a River 516
6:8	Let Justice Roll Like a River 516
6:8	Lord, Today 279
6:8	Servant Song 489
6:8	We Are Called 518

MATTHEW

1:18-24	God of Adam, God of Joseph 647
1:20-21	God It Was 503
2:	Brightest and Best 278
2:	Night of Silence 261
2:1-11	The Virgin Mary Had a Baby Boy 264

2:11	'Twas in the Moon of Wintertime	272
2:11	God's Surprise	267
2:13-23	God of Adam, God of Joseph	647
3:3	On Jordan's Bank	260
4:1-11	Tree of Life	288
4:4	Not by Bread Alone	362
4:4	Shepherd of Our Hearts	598
4:16	Child of Mercy	270
4:18-19	Gifts That Last	407
4:18-22	Lord, When You Came / Pescador de Hombres	500
4:18-22	Sing Hey for the Carpenter	496
5:1-6	Jerusalem, My Destiny	284
5:3-12	Blest Are They	469
5:3-12	The People of God	465
5:3-11	We Are the Light of the World	353
5:4	Sing Hey for the Carpenter	496
5:13-16	Bring Forth the Kingdom	468
5:13	Gather Us In	539
5:14	I Am the Light of the World	355
5:14-16	This Little Light of Mine	358
5:14-16	We Are the Light of the World	353
6:9-13	Mayenziwe / Your Will Be Done	416
6:9-10	Thy Kingdom Come	466
6:25-34	Today I Awake	548
6:26	Come to Me	462
6:28	Come to Me	462
6:30-31	Come to Me	462
6:33-34	Come to Me	462
7:7-8	Come to Me	462
9:21-22	I Danced in the Morning	511
10:28	Now Go Forward	495
11:2-6	Hold Me in Life	423
11:28-30	Come to Me	459
11:28-30	Come to Me, O Weary Traveler	454
11:28	Come to Us	538
11:28-30	Come to the Water	349
11:28	Like a Shepherd	251
11:29-30	O God of Matchless Glory	372
11:29-30	We Shall Rise Again	558
13:4-30	Anthem	494
13:4-23	Bring Forth the Kingdom	468
18:20	The God of All Eternity	648
18:20	You Are Our Living Bread	608
21:9	Hosanna	292
25:3-12	Whatsoever You Do	477
25:13	Sign Me Up	579
25:31-46	Bread for the World	596
25:31-46	One Is the Body	612
25:35-44	A Nuptial Blessing	633
25:39-40	God of Day and God of Darkness	551
25:40	A Touching Place	452
26:26	Take and Eat	614
26:26	Take and Eat this Bread	606
26:30	When, in Our Music, God Is Glorified	391
26:36-46	Stay Here and Keep Watch	298
26:38	Nada Te Turbe / Nothing Can Trouble	451
27:35	Were You There	302
27:50	Calvary	305
28:1-10	Christ Has Risen	308
28:5-6	Now the Green Blade Rises	318
28:5-6	Surrexit Christus	314
28:5-6	Surrexit Dominus Vere II	310
28:16-20	Go	323
28:18-20	Halleluya! We Sing Your Praises	394
28:18	I Will Be with You	322
28:18-20	Now Go Forward	495
28:19-20	I Am for You	506
28:20	We Gather in Worship	543

Scripture Passages Related to Hymns/*continued*

MARK

1:3	On Jordan's Bank 260
1:14-20	Anthem 494
1:16-20	Lord, When You Came / Pescador de Hombres 500
1:16-20	Sing Hey for the Carpenter 496
1:19-20	I Danced in the Morning 511
1:32-34	The Carpenter 336
2:1-12	Now in This Banquet 600
2:21	You Are Mine 461
4:3-6	Seed, Scattered and Sown 601
4:35-41	Psalm 107 Give Thanks to the Lord 91
4:39	Be Still 438
6:41-44	The Word of Life 359
6:45-52	I Am for You 506
8:34-38	Gifts That Last 407
9:2-8	Tree of Life 288
9:49	Shake Up the Morning 366
10:31	Walk in the Reign 249
10:38-39	We Will Drink the Cup 512
11:9-10	Hosanna 292
11:9	Ride On, Jesus, Ride 294
14:22	Take and Eat this Bread 606
14:32-42	Stay Here and Keep Watch 298
14:32-36	The Word of Life 359
14:35	Nada Te Turbe / Nothing Can Trouble 451
15:25-33	Were You There 302
15:39	Calvary 305
15:46-47	Joyful Is the Dark 550
16:1-8	Christ Has Risen 308
16:3	Were You There 302
16:5-6	Now the Green Blade Rises 318
16:5-6	Surrexit Christus 314
16:5-6	Surrexit Dominus Vere II 310

LUKE

1:26-32	Ave Maria 565
1:26-38	Hail Mary: Gentle Woman 564
1:26-38	I Am for You 506
1:26-38	I Say "Yes," Lord / Digo "Sí," Señor 421
1:26-38	I Sing a Maid 563
1:28	There Is Nothing Told 566
1:46-55	All Who Claim the Faith of Jesus 567
1:46-58	Canticle of the Turning 376
1:46-55	Gospel Canticle 14
1:46-55	Magnificat / Luke 1:46-55; 127
1:46-55	Magnificat 568
1:46-55	Holy Is Your Name / Luke 1:46-55 128
1:46-55	Ps. 80/85/Lk.1 Lord, Make Us Turn to You 70
1:46-55	Thanks Be to You 397
1:68-79	Canticle of Zachary 561
1:68-79	Now Bless the God of Israel 5
2:	Awake, Awake and Greet the New Morn 265
2:	Carol at the Manger 275
2:	Night of Silence 261
2:1-8	Joyful Is the Dark 550
2:6-19	Song of the Stable 273
2:7	A Stable Lamb Is Lighted 269
2:7-14	The Aye Carol 277
2:7	The Tiny Child to Bethlehem Came 268
2:7-21	The Virgin Mary Had a Baby Boy 264
2:7	The Word of Life 359
2:7-52	There Is Nothing Told 566
2:11-14	'Twas in the Moon of Wintertime 272
2:11-14	Child of Mercy 270
2:11-14	God's Surprise 267
2:11-14	Nativity Carol 274
2:11-14	Rise Up, Shepherd, and Follow 271
2:11-14	The Age of Expectation 266
2:14	Gloria 263
2:14	Gloria, Gloria 199

2:14	Greet Now the Swiftly Changing Year	649
2:29-35	Now Let Your Servant Go	562
3:4	On Jordan's Bank	260
4:18-19	God Has Chosen Me	488
4:18-19	Good News	486
4:18-19	Great Is the Lord	490
4:18	Hold Us in Your Mercy: Penitential Litany	289
4:18	Song of the Body of Christ / Canción del Cuerpo	613
4:18-19	The Carpenter	336
4:18-19	You Have Anointed Me	483
5:1-11	Lord, When You Came / Pescador de Hombres	500
5:1-11	Sing Hey for the Carpenter	496
6:20	Be Not Afraid	430
6:21	The Day Is Near	556
9:25	The Love of the Lord	504
9:59-60	Christ Will Be Your Strength	574
10:1-9	Now Go Forward	495
11:1-4	Mayenziwe / Your Will Be Done	416
11:2	Song of the Body of Christ / Canción del Cuerpo	613
11:2-4	Thy Kingdom Come	466
11:9-13	If You Believe and I Believe	520
12:37	Serving You	297
12:49	Shake Up the Morning	366
13:29	As the Grains of Wheat	594
13:34	Shelter Me, O God	449
19:36-38	A Stable Lamb Is Lighted	269
19:38	Hosanna	292
22:19	Bless the Feast	545
22:40-46	Stay Here and Keep Watch	298
23:33-34	The Word of Life	359
23:33-44	Were You There	302
23:42	Jesus, Remember Me	293
23:44	A Stable Lamb Is Lighted	269
23:47	Calvary	305
24:1-2	Gifts That Last	407
24:5-6	Now the Green Blade Rises	318
24:5-6	Surrexit Christus	314
24:5-6	Surrexit Dominus Vere II	310
24:13-29	Christ Has Risen	308
24:13-35	Here in This Place	595
24:13-15	In the Breaking of Bread	605
24:28-35	Shepherd of Our Hearts	598
24:29	Many and Great	338

JOHN

1:5	God Is Love	445
1:14	He Came Down	276
1:23	On Jordan's Bank	260
1:29	Lamb of God	245
1:35-42	Lord, When You Came / Pescador de Hombres	500
1:35-42	Sing Hey for the Carpenter	496
1:41-42	The Summons	510
2:1-11	God, in the Planning	631
2:1-12	May We Be One	247
2:1-11	There Is Nothing Told	566
3:16	Love One Another	446
4:4-42	Tree of Life	288
4:10-15	Dust and Ashes	280
4:10	Song of the Body of Christ / Canción del Cuerpo	613
4:14	Jerusalem, My Destiny	284
5:1-9	Healing River	408
5:1-5	Wade in the Water	583
6:	Behold the Lamb	592
6:	Eat This Bread	588
6:	I Am the Bread of Life	597
6:	Look Beyond	607
6:35-38	I, the Lord	623
6:48	Bread for the World	596
6:48	I Myself Am the Bread of Life	593
6:50	Take and Eat this Bread	606

Scripture Passages Related to Hymns/*continued*

EPHESIANS

1:2	Dwelling Place 418	
1:4	You Are God's Work of Art 582	
2:1	We Are God's Work of Art/Somos la Creación de Dios	580
2:4-7	We Are God's Work of Art/Somos la Creación de Dios	580
2:7-10	Lover of Us All 448	
2:10	We Are God's Work of Art/Somos la Creación de Dios	580
2:10	You Are God's Work of Art 582	
2:12-22	We Are God's Work of Art/Somos la Creación de Dios	580
2:19-20	No Longer Strangers 532	
2:19	We Are God's Work of Art/Somos la Creación de Dios	580
3:14-17	Dwelling Place 418	
3:14	You Are Called to Tell the Story 487	
3:16-19	The Word Is in Your Heart 363	
4:	There Is One Lord 581	
4:4-6	Let Us Be Bread 585	
4:4-6	The Broken Body 535	
5:8-9	Church of God 472	
5:8-10	I Want to Walk as a Child of the Light 352	
5:8	Morning Hymn 2	
5:8-9	Out of Darkness 493	
5:8	We Are Marching 357	
5:8	You Are God's Work of Art 582	
5:14	Awake, O Sleeper 577	
5:14	I Am the Light of the World 355	
5:14	Light of Christ/Exsultet 356	
5:19-20	Lover of Us All 448	

PHILIPPIANS

1:11	The Harvest of Justice 513
2:5-7	Stand Up, Friends 335
2:10-11	I Will Sing, I Will Sing 386
2:11	For the Life of the World 575
3:7-14	Do Not Fear to Hope 420
3:7-11	Only This I Want 499
3:7-11	The Love of the Lord 504
3:12-15	Guide My Feet 508
4:6-8	We Will Drink the Cup 512
4:13	Christ Will Be Your Strength 574

COLOSSIANS

1:13	Spirit Friend 328
1:26-27	We Live a Mystery 419

1 THESSALONIANS

3:13	Saints of God / Song of Farewell 625
4:13-18	Free at Last 517
5:5	For the Life of the World 575
13:18	When the Lord in Glory Comes 554
16:18	Sign Me Up 579

2 TIMOTHY

2:	Now We Remain 498
1:7	Song at the Center 345
2:	We Shall Rise Again 558

TITUS

3:5	Song at the Center 345

HEBREWS

5:8	We Live a Mystery 419
10:7	Psalm 40 Here I Am 47
12:1	I Want to Walk as a Child of the Light 352
13:8	Jesus Christ, Yesterday, Today and Forever 540

JAMES

3:11	I've Just Come from the Fountain 576

1 PETER

1:3-5	Praise the Lord, My Soul 393
1:8	Without Seeing You 610
2:5	Take and Eat 614
2:9	Light of Christ/Exsultet 356
2:9-10	Out of Darkness 493

2 PETER

1:19	People of the Night 259
1:19	Take and Eat 614
1:19	Up from the Earth 321
3:8-13	Wash Me, Cleanse Me 291

1 JOHN

1:	Now We Remain 498
1:5	Evening Hymn 10
1:5	God Is Love 445
1:5	I Want to Walk as a Child of the Light 352
1:5	Our Darkness / La Tenebre 553
1:7	Morning Hymn 2
2:10	I Am the Light of the World 355
3:2	God Is Love 445
4:	God Is Love 445
4:	Ubi Caritas 301
4:	Where Charity and Love Prevail 443
4:1-16	Shout for Joy 388
4:7	Faith, Hope and Love 442
4:7-21	Faithful Family 300
4:7	Love One Another 446
4:12	Love One Another 446
9:12-16	Easter Alleluia 307

REVELATION

5:11-12	Alabaré 371
5:11-13	Now the Feast and Celebration 537
5:12	Come Away to the Skies 316
6:2	Ride On, Jesus, Ride 294
18:23	Evening Hymn 10
19:7	Come Away to the Skies 316
19:11-16	The King Shall Come When Morning Dawns 248
19:16	Christ the Lord Is Risen 315
21:1-4	My Lord Will Come Again 557
21:5	All Things New 309
21:5-6	Christ Is Risen! Shout Hosanna! 311
21:5	The Earth Is the Lord's 341
21:6	God of All Creation 343
21:6	Jesus Christ, Yesterday, Today and Forever 540
21:22-24	I Want to Walk as a Child of the Light 352
21:23	Evening Hymn 10
22:1	Shall We Gather at the River 560
22:1-5	Triduum Hymn: Wondrous Love 295
22:5	Light of Christ/Exsultet 356
22:16	Come to Set us Free 257
22:17	In Christ There Is a Table Set for All 542
22:20	Each Winter As the Year Grows Older 258
22:20	God of All People 255
22:20	Soon and Very Soon 555

ADVENT
Seasonal Psalms
Psalm 25: To You, O Lord 34
Psalm 25: Levanto Mi Alma 35
Psalm 85: Lord, Let Us See Your Kindness 73
Psalm 85: Come, O Lord, and Set Us Free 74

ADVENT I
A - Psalm 122: Let Us Go Rejoicing 107
  Psalm 122: I Was Glad 108
B - Psalm 80/85/Luke 1: Lord, Make Us Turn to You 70
C - Psalm 25: To You, O Lord 34
  Psalm 25: Levanto Mi Alma 35

ADVENT II
A - Psalm 72: Every Nation on Earth 67
B - Psalm 85: Lord, Let Us See Your Kindness 73
  Psalm 85: Come, O Lord, and Set Us Free 74
C - Psalm126: God Has Done Great Things for Us 110

ADVENT III
A - Psalm 146: Happy the Poor in Spirit 123
  Psalm 146: Lord, Come and Save Us 124
B - Magnificat / Luke 1:46-55 127
  Holy Is Your Name / Luke 1:46-55 128
C - Isaiah 12:2-3, 4, 6 129

ADVENT IV
A - Psalm 24: We Long to See Your Face 32
B - Psalm 89: For Ever I Will Sing 76
C - Psalm 80/85/Luke 1: Lord, Make Us Turn to You 70

CHRISTMAS
Seasonal Psalm
Psalm 98: All the Ends of the Earth 86

CHRISTMAS/VIGIL
Psalm 89: For Ever I Will Sing 76

CHRISTMAS/MASS AT MIDNIGHT
Psalm 96: Today Is Born Our Savior 84

CHRISTMAS/MASS AT DAWN
Psalm 97: The Lord Is King 85

CHRISTMAS/MASS DURING THE DAY
Psalm 98: All the Ends of the Earth 86

HOLY FAMILY
Psalm 128: Blest Are Those Who Love You 111

MARY, MOTHER OF GOD
Psalm 67: May God Bless Us in His Mercy 62

EPIPHANY
Psalm 72: Every Nation on Earth 67

BAPTISM OF THE LORD
Psalm 29: The Lord Will Bless His People 38

LENT
Seasonal Psalms
Psalm 51: Be Merciful, O Lord 53
Psalm 91: Be with Me 79
Psalm 130: With the Lord There Is Mercy 113

ASH WEDNESDAY
Psalm 51: Be Merciful, O Lord 53

LENT I
A - Psalm 51: Be Merciful, O Lord 53
B - Psalm 25: Remember Your Mercies 33
C - Psalm 91: Be with Me 79

LENT II
A - Psalm 33: Let Your Mercy Be on Us 43
B - Psalm 116: I Will Walk in the Presence of God 97
C - Psalm 27: The Lord Is My Light 37

LENT III
A - Psalm 95: If Today You Hear God's Voice 82
B - Psalm19: Lord, You Have the Words 26
C - Psalm 103: The Lord Is Kind and Merciful 88

LENT IV
A - Psalm 23: Shepherd Me, O God 29
  Psalm 23: The Lord Is My Shepherd 30
  Psalm 23: Nada Me Falta 31
B - Psalm 137: Let My Tongue Be Silent 116
C - Psalm 34: Taste and See 45

LENT V
A - Psalm 130: With the Lord There Is Mercy 113
B - Psalm 51: Create in Me 54
C - Psalm 126: God Has Done Great Things for Us 110

HOLY WEEK
Seasonal Psalm
Psalm 22: My God, My God 28

PASSION SUNDAY
Psalm 22: My God, My God 28

HOLY THURSDAY
Psalm 116: Our Blessing-Cup 96
Psalm 116: The Name of God 98

GOOD FRIDAY
Psalm 31: I Put My Life in Your Hands / Pongo Mi
  Vida 40
Psalm 31: I Put My Life in Your Hands 41

EASTER VIGIL
Seasonal Psalm
Psalm 136: Love Is Never Ending 115

EASTER VIGIL
1 - Psalm 104: Lord, Send Out Your Spirit 90
  Psalm 33: Let Your Mercy Be On Us 43
2 - Psalm 16: Keep Me Safe, O God 22
  Psalm 16: You Will Show Me the Path of Life 23
3 - Song at the Sea / Exodus 15 126
4 - Psalm 30: I Will Praise You, Lord 39
5 - Isaiah 12:2-3, 4, 6 129
6 - Psalm 19: Lord, You Have the Words 26
7 - Psalm 41-42: Song of Longing 49
  Psalm 51: Create in Me 54

EASTER
Seasonal Psalms
Psalm 118: Alleluia, Alleluia 101
Psalm 118: Let Us Rejoice 102
Psalm 66: Let All the Earth 61

EASTER SUNDAY
Psalm 118: Alleluia, Alleluia 101
Psalm 118: Let Us Rejoice 102

EASTER II
Psalm 118: Alleluia, Alleluia 101
Psalm 118: Let Us Rejoice 102

EASTER III
A - Psalm 16: You Will Show Me the Path of Life 23
B - Psalm 4: Let Your Face Shine upon Us 19
C - Psalm 30: I Will Praise You, Lord 39

EASTER IV
A - Psalm 23: Shepherd Me, O God 29
    Psalm 23: The Lord Is My Shepherd 30
    Psalm 23: Nada Me Falta 31
B - Psalm 118: Alleluia, Alleluia 101
    Psalm 118: Let Us Rejoice 102
C - Psalm 100: We Are God's People 87

EASTER V
A - Psalm 33: Let Your Mercy Be on Us 43
B - Psalm 22: I Will Praise You, Lord 27
C - Psalm 145: I Will Praise Your Name 121

EASTER VI
A - Psalm 66: Let All the Earth 61
B - Psalm 98: All the Ends of the Earth 86
C - Psalm 67: May God Bless Us in His Mercy 62

ASCENSION
Psalm 47: God Mounts His Throne 51

EASTER VII
A - Psalm 27: In the Land of the Living 36
B - Psalm 103: The Lord Is Kind and Merciful 88
    Psalm 103: The Lord Is Kind and Merciful 89
C - Psalm 97: The Lord Is King 85

PENTECOST
Psalm 104: Lord, Send Out Your Spirit 90

TRINITY SUNDAY
A - Song of the Three Children / Daniel 3:52-56 130
B - Psalm 33: Let Your Mercy Be on Us 43
C - Psalm 8: How Glorious Is Your Name 20

BODY AND BLOOD OF CHRIST
A - Psalm 147: Bless the Lord, My Soul 125
B - Psalm 116: The Name of God 98
C - Psalm 110: You Are a Priest for Ever 92

SACRED HEART
A - Psalm 103: The Lord Is Kind and Merciful 88
    Psalm 103: The Lord Is Kind and Merciful 89
B - Isaiah 12:2-3, 4, 6 129
C - Psalm 23: Shepherd Me, O God 29
    Psalm 23: The Lord Is My Shepherd 30
    Psalm 23: Nada Me Falta 31

ORDINARY TIME
Seasonal Psalms
Psalm 19: Lord, You Have the Words 27
Psalm 27: The Lord Is My Light 37
Psalm 34: I Will Bless the Lord 44
Psalm 34: Taste and See 45
Psalm 63: My Soul Is Thirsting 57
Psalm 63: Your Love Is Finer Than Life 58
Psalm 95: If Today You Hear God's Voice 82
Psalm 100: We Are God's People 87
Psalm 103: The Lord Is Kind and Merciful 88
Psalm 103: The Lord Is Kind and Merciful 89
Psalm 145: I Will Praise Your Name 121

LAST WEEKS IN ORDINARY TIME
Seasonal Psalms
Psalm 122: Let Us Go Rejoicing 107
Psalm 122: I Was Glad 108

ORDINARY TIME
SECOND SUNDAY
A - Psalm 40: Here I Am 47
B - Psalm 40: Here I Am 47
C - Psalm 96: Proclaim to All the Nations 83

THIRD SUNDAY
A - Psalm 27: The Lord Is My Light 37
B - Psalm 25: Remember Your Mercies 33
C - Psalm 19: Lord, You Have the Words 26

FOURTH SUNDAY
A - Psalm 146: Happy the Poor in Spirit 123
B - Psalm 95: If Today You Hear God's Voice 82
C - Psalm 71: I Will Sing 66

FIFTH SUNDAY
A - Psalm 112: A Light Rises in the Darkness 93
B - Psalm 147: Bless the Lord, My Soul 125
C - Psalm 138: The Fragrance of Christ 118

SIXTH SUNDAY
A - Psalm 119: Happy Are Those Who Follow 103
B - Psalm 32: I Turn to You 42
C - Psalm 1: Happy Are They 18

SEVENTH SUNDAY
A - Psalm 103: The Lord Is Kind and Merciful 88
    Psalm 103: The Lord Is Kind and Merciful 89
B - Psalm 41: Lord, Heal My Soul 48
C - Psalm 103: The Lord Is Kind and Merciful 88
    Psalm 103: The Lord Is Kind and Merciful 89

EIGHTH SUNDAY
A - Psalm 62: In God Alone 56
B - Psalm 103: The Lord Is Kind and Merciful 88
    Psalm 103: The Lord Is Kind and Merciful 89
C - Psalm 92: Lord, It Is Good 80

NINTH SUNDAY
A - Psalm 31: I Put My Life in Your Hands 41
B - Psalm 81: Sing with Joy to God 71
C - Psalm 117: Go Out to All the World 100

TENTH SUNDAY
A - Psalm 50: To the Upright 52
B - Psalm 130: With the Lord There Is Mercy 113
C - Psalm 30: I Will Praise You, Lord 39

ELEVENTH SUNDAY
A - Psalm 100: We Are God's People 87
B - Psalm 92: Lord, It Is Good 80
C - Psalm 32: I Turn to You 42

TWELFTH SUNDAY
A - Psalm 69: Lord, in Your Great Love 64
B - Psalm 107: Give Thanks to the Lord 91
C - Psalm 63: My Soul Is Thirsting 57
    Psalm 63: Your Love Is Finer Than Life 58

THIRTEENTH SUNDAY
A - Psalm 89: For Ever I Will Sing 76
B - Psalm 30: I Will Praise You, Lord 39
C - Psalm 16: You Will Show Me the Path of Life 23

FOURTEENTH SUNDAY
- A - Psalm 145: I Will Praise Your Name 121
- B - Psalm 123: Our Eyes Are Fixed on the Lord 109
- C - Psalm 66: Let All the Earth 61

FIFTEENTH SUNDAY
- A - Psalm 65: The Seed That Falls on Good Ground 60
- B - Psalm 85: Lord, Let Us See Your Kindness 73
  - Psalm 85: Come, O Lord, and Set Us Free 74
- C - Psalm 69: Turn to the Lord in Your Need 65

SIXTEENTH SUNDAY
- A - Psalm 86: Lord, You Are Good and Forgiving 75
- B - Psalm 23: Shepherd Me, O God 29
  - Psalm 23: The Lord Is My Shepherd 30
  - Psalm 23: Nada Me Falta 31
- C - Psalm 15: They Who Do Justice 21

SEVENTEENTH SUNDAY
- A - Psalm 119: Lord, I Love Your Commands 104
- B - Psalm 145: I Will Praise Your Name 121
  - Psalm 145: Our God Is Compassion 122
- C - Psalm 138: The Fragrance of Christ 118

EIGHTEENTH SUNDAY
- A - Psalm 145: I Will Praise Your Name 121
  - Psalm 145: Our God Is Compassion 122
- B - Psalm 78: The Lord Gave Them Bread 68
- C - Psalm 95: If Today You Hear God's Voice 82

NINETEENTH SUNDAY
- A - Psalm 85: Lord, Let Us See Your Kindness 73
  - Psalm 85: Come, O Lord, and Set Us Free 74
- B - Psalm 34: Taste and See 45
  - Psalm 34: I Will Bless the Lord 44
- C - Psalm 33: Let Your Mercy Be on Us 43

TWENTIETH SUNDAY
- A - Psalm 67: May God Bless Us in His Mercy 62
- B - Psalm 34: Taste and See 45
  - Psalm 34: I Will Bless the Lord 44
- C - Psalm 40: Here I Am 47

TWENTY-FIRST SUNDAY
- A - Psalm 138: Lord, Your Love Is Eternal 117
- B - Psalm 34: Taste and See 45
  - Psalm 34: I Will Bless the Lord 44
- C - Psalm 117: Go Out to All the World 100

TWENTY-SECOND SUNDAY
- A - Psalm 63: My Soul Is Thirsting 57
  - Psalm 63: Your Love Is Finer Than Life 58
- B - Psalm 15: They Who Do Justice 21
- C - Psalm 68: You Have Made a Home for the Poor 63

TWENTY-THIRD SUNDAY
- A - Psalm 95: If Today You Hear God's Voice 82
- B - Psalm 146: Happy the Poor in Spirit 123
- C - Psalm 90: In Ev'ry Age 77

TWENTY-FOURTH SUNDAY
- A - Psalm 103: The Lord Is Kind and Merciful 88
  - Psalm 103: The Lord Is Kind and Merciful 89
- B - Psalm 116: I Will Walk in the Presence of God 97
- C - Psalm 51: Create in Me 54

TWENTY-FIFTH SUNDAY
- A - Psalm 145: I Will Praise Your Name 121
- B - Psalm 54: The Lord Upholds My Life 55
- C - Psalm 113: Praise His Name 94

Psalm 113: Praise the Lord 95

TWENTY-SIXTH SUNDAY
- A - Psalm 25: Remember Your Mercies 33
- B - Psalm 19: Lord, You Have the Words 26
- C - Psalm 146: Happy the Poor in Spirit 123
  - Psalm 146: Lord, Come and Save Us 124

TWENTY-SEVENTH SUNDAY
- A - Psalm 80: The Vineyard of the Lord 69
- B - Psalm 128: Blest Are Those Who Love You 111
- C - Psalm 95: If Today You Hear God's Voice 82

TWENTY-EIGHTH SUNDAY
- A - Psalm 23: Shepherd Me, O God 29
  - Psalm 23: The Lord Is My Shepherd 30
  - Psalm 23: Nada Me Falta 31
- B - Psalm 90: Fill Us with Your Love, O Lord 78
- C - Psalm 98: All the Ends of the Earth 86

TWENTY-NINTH SUNDAY
- A - Psalm 96: Proclaim to All the Nations 83
- B - Psalm 33: Let Your Mercy Be on Us 43
- C - Psalm 121: Our Help Comes from the Lord 106

THIRTIETH SUNDAY
- A - Psalm 18: I Love You Lord, My Strength 25
- B - Psalm 126: God Has Done Great Things for Us 110
- C - Psalm 34: The Lord Hears the Cry of the Poor 46

THIRTY-FIRST SUNDAY
- A - Psalm 131: My Soul Is Still 114
- B - Psalm 18: I Love You Lord, My Strength 25
- C - Psalm 145: I Will Praise Your Name 121

THIRTY-SECOND SUNDAY
- A - Psalm 63: My Soul Is Thirsting 57
  - Psalm 63: Your Love Is Finer Than Life 58
- B - Psalm 146: Happy the Poor in Spirit 123
  - Psalm 146: Lord, Come and Save Us 124
- C - Psalm 17: Lord, When Your Glory Appears 24

THIRTY-THIRD SUNDAY
- A - Psalm 128: Blest Are Those Who Love You 111
- B - Psalm 16: Keep Me Safe, O God 22
  - Psalm 16: You Will Show Me the Path of Life 23
- C - Psalm 98: All the Ends of the Earth 86

CHRIST THE KING
- A - Psalm 23: Shepherd Me, O God 29
  - Psalm 23: The Lord Is My Shepherd 30
  - Psalm 23: Nada Me Falta 31
- B - Psalm 93: The Lord Is King 81
- C - Psalm 122: Let Us Go Rejoicing 107
  - Psalm 122: I Was Glad 108

ASSUMPTION
Psalm 45: The Queen Stands at Your Right Hand 50

ALL SAINTS
Psalm 24: We Long to See Your Face 32

IMMACULATE CONCEPTION
Psalm 98: All the Ends of the Earth 86

Liturgical Index/*continued*

Topical Index/*continued*

Topical Index/*continued*

Topical Index/*continued*

Topical Index/*continued*

Topical Index/*continued*

Topical Index/*continued*

Topical Index/*continued*

490 Great Is the Lord
623 I, the Lord
550 Joyful Is the Dark
385 Let Heaven Your Wonders Proclaim
127 Magnificat / Luke 1:46-55
338 Many and Great
372 O God of Matchless Glory
91 Psalm 107 Give Thanks to the Lord
92 Psalm 110 You Are a Priest for Ever
95 Psalm 113 Praise the Lord
101 Psalm 118 Alleluia, Alleluia
102 Psalm 118 Let Us Rejoice
110 Psalm 126 God Has Done Great Things for Us
38 Psalm 29 The Lord Will Bless His People
51 Psalm 47 God Mounts His Throne
52 Psalm 50 To the Upright
60 Psalm 65 The Seed That Falls on Good Ground
68 Psalm 78 The Lord Gave Them Bread
81 Psalm 93 The Lord Is King
85 Psalm 97 The Lord Is King
379 Sing a New Song to the Lord
126 Song at the Sea: Exodus 15
341 The Earth Is the Lord's
435 The Lord Is My Hope
344 The Stars Declare His Glory
547 This Day God Gives Me
368 To God with Gladness Sing

MARY (*see Liturgical Index*)

MERCY

633 A Nuptial Blessing
250 Advent Gathering
309 All Things New
332 Alleluia, Sing!
587 As We Remember
437 Blessed Be the Lord
468 Bring Forth the Kingdom
305 Calvary
561 Canticle of Zachary
376 Canticle of the Turning
538 Come to Us
640 Deep Down in My Soul
14 Gospel Canticle
423 Hold Me in Life
620 How Lovely Is Your Dwelling
644 I Want to Call You
638 Jesus, Heal Us
389 Joyfully Singing
405 Kyrie Guarany
245 Lamb of God
387 Lift Up Your Hearts
251 Like a Shepherd
127 Magnificat / Luke 1:46-55
568 Magnificat
128 Holy Is Your Name / Luke 1:46-55
464 Our God Is Rich in Love
289 Hold Us in Your Mercy: Penitential Litany
88 Psalm 103 The Lord Is Kind and Merciful
89 Psalm 103 The Lord Is Kind and Merciful
93 Psalm 112 A Light Rises in the Darkness
104 Psalm 119 Lord, I Love Your Commands
109 Psalm 123 Our Eyes Are Fixed on the Lord
113 Psalm 130 With the Lord There Is Mercy
122 Psalm 145 Our God Is Compassion

30 Psalm 23 The Lord Is My Shepherd
31 Psalm 23 Nada Me Falta
33 Psalm 25 Remember Your Mercies
34 Psalm 25 To You, O Lord
36 Psalm 27 In the Land of the Living
39 Psalm 30 I Will Praise You, Lord
42 Psalm 32 I Turn to You
43 Psalm 33 Let Your Mercy Be on Us
48 Psalm 41 Lord, Heal My Soul
53 Psalm 51 Be Merciful, O Lord
54 Psalm 51 Create in Me
63 Psalm 68 You Have Made a Home for the Poor
75 Psalm 86 Lord, You Are Good and Forgiving
77 Psalm 90 In Ev'ry Age
78 Psalm 90 Fill Us with Your Love, O Lord
84 Psalm 96 Today Is Born Our Savior
641 Remember Your Love
645 Remember Your Mercy, O Lord
283 Return to God
294 Ride On, Jesus, Ride
193 Rite of Sprinkling
327 Send Down the Fire
489 Servant Song
379 Sing a New Song to the Lord
373 Sing of the Lord's Goodness
126 Song at the Sea: Exodus 15
584 Song of the Chosen
604 Taste and See
397 Thanks Be to You
439 The Lord Is Near
465 The People of God
426 Though the Mountains May Fall
519 Voices That Challenge
353 We Are the Light of the World
543 We Gather in Worship
603 We Know and Believe
558 We Shall Rise Again
473 We Will Serve the Lord
523 World Peace Prayer
254 Your Mercy Like Rain

MESSIANIC

250 Advent Gathering
270 Child of Mercy
257 Come to Set us Free
267 God's Surprise
467 I Will Not Die
129 Isaiah 12
516 Let Justice Roll Like a River
279 Lord, Today
252 My Soul in Stillness Waits
260 On Jordan's Bank
470 Onward to the Kingdom
360 Praise to You, O Christ, Our Savior
70 Ps. 80/85/Lk.1 Lord, Make Us Turn to You
92 Psalm 110 You Are a Priest for Ever
27 Psalm 22 I Will Praise You, Lord
28 Psalm 22 My God, My God
67 Psalm 72 Every Nation on Earth
74 Psalm 85 Come, O Lord, and Set Us Free
73 Psalm 85 Lord, Let Us See Your Kindness
76 Psalm 89 For Ever I Will Sing
83 Psalm 96 Proclaim to All the Nations
84 Psalm 96 Today Is Born Our Savior

85 Psalm 97 The Lord Is King
266 The Age of Expectation
556 The Day Is Near
248 The King Shall Come When Morning Dawns
256 Wait for the Lord
249 Walk in the Reign
253 Within Our Hearts Be Born
254 Your Mercy Like Rain
(*also Second Coming*)

MINISTRY

452 A Touching Place
485 City of God
402 Come to Us, Creative Spirit
539 Gather Us In
488 God Has Chosen Me
503 God It Was
486 Good News
490 Great Is the Lord
492 Here I Am, Lord
511 I Danced in the Morning
322 I Will Be with You
296 Jesu, Jesu
500 Lord, When You Came / Pescador de Hombres
491 Moved by the Gospel, Let Us Move
600 Now in This Banquet
289 Hold Us in Your Mercy: Penitential Litany
123 Psalm 146 Happy the Poor in Spirit
474 Pues Si Vivimos / If We Are Living
329 Send Us Your Spirit
489 Servant Song
384 Sing a New Song
373 Sing of the Lord's Goodness
409 Song over the Waters
299 Song of the Lord's Supper
361 Sow the Word
325 Spirit Blowing through Creation
328 Spirit Friend
482 The God Who Sends Us Forth
465 The People of God
363 The Word Is in Your Heart
288 Tree of Life
301 Ubi Caritas
326 Veni Sancte Spiritus
518 We Are Called
512 We Will Drink the Cup
391 When, in Our Music, God Is Glorified
443 Where Charity and Love Prevail
487 You Are Called to Tell the Story
483 You Have Anointed Me
(*also Commitment, Discipleship, Mission, Service*)

MISSION

367 A New Song
471 As a Fire Is Meant for Burning
354 Be Light For Our Eyes
430 Be Not Afraid
437 Blessed Be the Lord
468 Bring Forth the Kingdom
574 Christ Will Be Your Strength
485 City of God
571 Covenant Hymn
575 For the Life of the World
407 Gifts That Last
323 Go
488 God Has Chosen Me
503 God It Was
286 God of Abraham
486 Good News
490 Great Is the Lord
394 Halleluya! We Sing Your Praises
492 Here I Am, Lord

Topical Index/*continued*

PRESENCE OF GOD

Topical Index/*continued*

Topical Index/*continued*

Topical Index/*continued*

Index of First Lines and Common Titles/*continued*

Index of First Lines and Common Titles/*continued*

Index of First Lines and Common Titles/*continued*

Index of First Lines and Common Titles/*continued*

Index of First Lines and Common Titles/*continued*